SCHIZOPHRENIA

SCHIZOPHRENIA
Treatment, Management, and Rehabilitation

Edited by

ALAN S. BELLACK, PH.D.
Professor of Psychiatry
The Medical College of Pennsylvania
at Eastern Pennsylvania Psychiatric Institute
Philadelphia, Pennsylvania

G&S
GRUNE & STRATTON, INC.
(Harcourt Brace Jovanovich, Publishers)
Orlando San Diego San Francisco New York London
Toronto Montreal Sydney Tokyo São Paulo

Library of Congress Cataloging in Publication Data

Main entry under title:
Schizophrenia: treatment, management, and rehabilitation.

Includes bibliographies and index.
1. Schizophrenia. I. Bellack, Alan S. II. Title.
[DNLM: 1. Schizophrenia. 2. Schizophrenia—Therapy.
WM 203 S3397]
RC514.S33648 1984 616.89'82 84-3830
ISBN 0-8089-1640-8

Grune & Stratton, Inc.
Orlando, FL 32887

Distributed in the United Kingdom by
Grune & Stratton, Ltd.
24/28 Oval Road, London NW 1

Library of Congress Catalog Number 84-3830
International Standard Book Number 0-8089-1640-8
Printed in the United States of America
84 85 86 87 10 9 8 7 6 5 4 3 2 1

To Barbara, Jonathan, and Adam

CONTENTS

PREFACE

Schizophrenia is one of the most significant health problems confronting our society, having a tremendous cost in dollars and human suffering. The cost of providing inpatient and outpatient care for schizophrenic patients coupled with the wages and tax revenues lost from their (frequent) inability to work is staggering. The pain and dislocation experienced by patients and their families is incalculable. Many thousands of mental health professionals and social service workers are involved in the treatment, care, and rehabilitation of schizophrenic patients. Yet, these vast efforts are only moderately successful. The majority of patients are on a treadmill: breakdown and hospitalization, partial recovery and discharge, marginal community adjustment, followed by breakdown and rehospitalization.

This sorry situation is by no means the result of lack of effort by the scientific and clinical communities to solve the puzzle of schizophrenia. It has long been the subject of theorizing, research, and debate. Conceptualizations and definitions of the disorder have gone through frequent changes, as old ideas have failed to provide lasting solutions, and promising new "breakthroughs" have been promoted. Numerous treatment strategies have been proposed, many of which provide some help. But, none have proven to be uniformly effective or sufficient.

While there continues to be much disagreement and controversy, there appears to be a growing consensus about two general factors. First, "schizophrenia" is probably not a homogeneous disease entity with a single cause. Rather, it is a heterogeneous phenomenon resulting from a variable combination of genetic predisposition, biochemical dysfunction, and psychosocial stress. Second, there is not now and probably never will be a single treatment that cures the disorder. Rather, effective treatment requires a comprehensive, multidisciplinary effort, including pharmacotherapy, living skills and social skills training, rehabilitation, family therapy, and extensive social support. Given the multifaceted nature of this intervention package, it has been most difficult for professionals from any one discipline to be fully aware of the current issues and practices employed by other disciplines. In fact, treatment in many settings can be likened to the six blind men feeling an elephant. Each discipline focuses only on its own perspective or techniques, with little integration or coordination of modalities.

This volume is designed to help alleviate this problem by serving as a sourcebook that presents an up-to-date picture of the diverse approaches and issues that should be considered in the treatment and care of schizophrenics. The term "care" represents our conviction that most patients will require long term support in the community, as well as specific time-limited "treatment." The contributors are leading authorities on their particular areas of expertise. Despite their diverse backgrounds and orientations, there is a remarkable degree of consistency in their overall recommendation. It is hoped that this volume will serve as a catalyst for improved clinical services in the short term, and multidisciplinary research that, in the long term, will lead to meaningful and lasting changes in the quality of life of schizophrenic patients.

CONTRIBUTORS

WILLIAM A. ANTHONY, PH.D., *Professor and Director, Center for Rehabilitation Research and Training in Mental Health, Boston University, Boston, Massachusetts*

ALAN S. BELLACK PH.D., *Professor of Psychiatry, The Medical College of Pennsylvania at Eastern Pennsylvania Psychiatric Institute, Philadelphia, Pennsylvania*

JOHN M. DAVIS, M.D., *Director of Research, Illinois State Psychiatric Institute, Chicago, Illinois*

MICHAEL E. DAWSON, PH.D., *Camarillo State Hospital, Department of Psychiatry, University of California in Los Angeles; West Los Angeles VA Medical Center, Los Angeles, California*

JERI A. DOANE, PH.D., *Camarillo State Hospital, Department of Psychology, University of California in Los Angeles; West Los Angeles VA Medical Center, Los Angeles, California*

RICHARD B. FERRELL, M.D., *Associate Professor of Clinical Psychiatry, Department of Psychiatry, Dartmouth Medical School, Hanover, New Hampshire*

BEN GIERL, M.D., *I.S.P.I. Head of Inpatient Geriatric Service, Illinois State Psychiatric Institute, Chicago, Illinois*

IRA GLICK, M.D., *Professor of Psychiatry, Cornell University Medical College, New York, New York*

MICHAEL J. GOLDSTEIN, PH.D., *Professor of Psychology, Department of Psychology, University of California, Los Angeles, California*

BEVERLY GOMES-SCHWARTZ, PH.D., *Assistant Professor, Department of Psychiatry, Family Crisis Program, Tufts University School of Medicine, Boston, Massachusetts*

JESSE G. HARRIS, JR., PH.D., *Professor and Chairman, Department of Psychology, University of Kentucky, Lexington, Kentucky*

SAMUEL J. KEITH, M.D., *Chief, Center for Studies of Schizophrenia, Clinical Research Branch, Division of Extramural Research Programs, National Institute of Mental Health, Rockville, Maryland*

ROBERT P. LIBERMAN, M.D., *Camarillo State Hospital, Department of Psychiatry, University of California in Los Angeles; West Los Angeles VA Medical Center, Los Angeles, California*

RAYMOND F. LUBER, *M. Div., President, American Association for Partial Hospitalization, Pittsburgh, Pennsylvania*

PETER A. MAGARO, PH.D., *Director of Clinical Training, Department of Psychology, The Ohio State University, Columbus, Ohio*

STEPHEN R. MARDER, M.D., *Camarillo State Hospital, Department of Psychiatry, University of California in Los Angeles; West Los Angeles VA Medical Center, Los Angeles, California*

BARRINGER D. MARSHALL, JR., M.D., *Clinical Research Unit, Camarillo State Hospital, University of California in Los Angeles; West Los Angeles VA Medical Center, Los Angeles, California*

SUSAN MATTHEWS, B.A., *Research Analyst, Center for Studies of Schizophrenia, Clinical Research Branch, Division of Extramural Research Programs, National Institute of Mental Health, Rockville, Maryland*

JUAN E. MEZZICH, M.D., PH.D., *Associate Professor of Psychiatry, Director, Diagnostic and Evaluation Center & the Clinical Information System, Western Psychiatric Institute and Clinic, University of Pittsburgh School of Medicine, Pittsburgh, Pennsylvania*

RANDALL L. MORRISON, PH.D., *Assistant Professor, The Medical College of Pennsylvania at Eastern Pennsylvania Psychiatric Institute, Philadelphia, Pennsylvania*

PATRICIA B. NEMEC, B.A., *Training Assistant, Center for Rehabilitation Research and Training in Mental Health, Boston University, Boston, Massachusetts*

KEITH H. NUECHTERLEIN, PH.D., *Camarillo State Hospital, Department of Psychiatry, University of California in Los Angeles; West Los Angeles VA Medical Center, Los Angeles, California*

TREVOR R. P. PRICE, M.D., *Associate Professor of Psychiatry and Medicine, Dartmouth Medical School, Hanover, New Hampshire*

STEVEN S. SHARFSTEIN, M.D., M.P.H., *Deputy Medical Director, American Psychiatric Association, Washington, D.C.*

ROBERT I. SLAYTON, M.D., M.P.H., *Assistant Professor of Psychiatry, Western Psychiatric Institute and Clinic, University of Pittsburgh School of Medicine, Pittsburgh, Pennsylvania*

JOHN A. TALBOTT, M.D., *Professor of Psychiatry, Cornell University Medical College, New York, New York*

MARY ANN TEST, PH.D., *Associate Professor, School of Social Work, University of Wisconsin, Madison, Wisconsin*

GARY J. TUCKER, M.D., *Professor and Chairman, Department of Psychiatry, Dartmouth Medical School, Hanover, New Hampshire*

multi-determined outcomes of organismic + enviro conditions

vicious circle
interaction.

Robert Paul Liberman, Barringer D. Marshall, Jr.
Stephen R. Marder, Michael E. Dawson
Keith H. Nuechterlein, Jeri A. Doane

1

The Nature and Problem of Schizophrenia

Current conceptualizations regarding schizophrenia are converging toward operational descriptions of its symptom states and associated behavioral impairments that are viewed as multi-determined outcomes of organismic and environmental conditions. Despite considerable advances in the neuro-sciences schizophrenia remains a clinical entity, which is recognized and diagnosed by observing and eliciting characteristic subjective experiences and overt behavioral functioning of the patient. The phenomenology of schizophrenia is fluid and dynamic, changing and in flux both within an individual over time and across individuals. The onset, continuance, exacerbation, relapse, remission, and adaptation of schizophrenic symptoms and behaviors are presumed to be in some form of homeostatic balance with biological and socio-environmental events. This conceptualization of schizophrenia is the currently popular *stress-diathesis* model (Marsella & Snyder, 1981; Zubin & Spring, 1977). The signs and symptoms that are identified as pathognomonic of schizophrenia are but flimsy and changing barometers of the interacting determinants from underlying biological and external social processes.

Schizophrenia can first and foremost be delineated as a group of characteristic symptoms in the areas of thought (delusions, passivity experiences, incoherence), perception (hallucinations), affect (anhedonia, flat or inappropriate), and motor activity (catatonia). Beyond symptoms, schizophrenia pervades almost all areas of an individual's

SCHIZOPHRENIA
ISBN 0-8089-1640-8

personal and social functioning. There are impairments in social relationships (withdrawal, avoidance), work (distractibility, apathy), cognitive processing (poor vigilance, sensory overload), and self-care (poor grooming, sleep disturbances). Schizophrenia can be viewed as a major mental illness because it produces major impairments and disruptions in so many domains of human experience. These multi-modal deficits and problems in living, as well as the characteristic symptoms, are what will be referred to during this chapter as schizophrenia.

Multidimensional Interactive Model of Schizophrenia

An interactive model of schizophrenia that can serve as a guide for understanding the nature of this ubiquitous disorder that afflicts one percent of the world's population is used heuristically at the Camarillo-UCLA Clinical Research Center. If we indeed view the symptoms and impairments that comprise the schizophrenic experience and syndrome as being in equilibrium with biological and environmental determinants, then what processes mediate the impact of the biological and environmental events on the person?

The appearance or increase in characteristic schizophrenic symptoms may occur in a susceptible individual when:

1. The underlying biological diathesis or vulnerability increases.
2. Stressful life events intervene that overwhelm the individual's coping in social and instrumental roles.
3. The individual's social support network weakens or diminishes.
4. Social problem-solving skills, which the individual previously had in his or her repertoire, wither or atrophy as a result of disuse, reinforcement of the sick role, loss of motivation as in depressive states, or an individual moving to a locale that is socially isolated and possesses few opportunities for active participation in life.

Neuroleptic medication reduces a schizophrenic's vulnerability to relapse and protects the person from the stressful impact of life events and pathological family relationships (Leff, Hirsch, Gaird, Rohde, & Stevens, 1973; Vaughn & Leff, 1976); however, the modulation of biological vulnerability by drugs cannot fully remediate an individual's susceptibility to relapse through stressors, loss of social support, or diminution in problem-solving skills. This helps to explain why, even with reliable ingestion of neuroleptics, upwards of 30 percent of schizophrenics relapse within a year.

From this vantage point, an increase or reappearance of symptoms in a person vulnerable to schizophrenia is an outcome of the balance or interaction between the amount and threat of life stressors and the problem-solving capacities of the individual and his or her support network (Liberman, Wallace, Vaughn, Snyder & Rust, 1980). Either too much environmental change or stressors or too little coping skills and social support can lead to symptomatic flare-ups. The significance of this bi-directional model of symptom formation lies in the emphasis given to the active role of the patient's coping skills and support network in reducing vulnerability to relapse.

A somewhat simplified interactive model of schizophrenic symptom formation is presented in Figure 1-1. The model has three domains of variables; those in the external environment, in the individual's behavior, and in the biological substrate, which are characterized by three time dimensions including enduring vulnerability characteristics, transient intermediate states, and outcome indicators.

Social stressors and non-supportive social networks can increase the probability of relapse. Social stressors include life events as well as exposure to critical and emotionally over-involved family members. Loss or estrangement of friends, relatives, neighbors, co-workers, and help-givers all reduce the supportiveness of the social network. The effects of social stressors and social network variables are assumed to interact. For example, the death of a loved one may be compounded by the lack of other social support or may be minimized by the presence of other supportive figures.

The enduring, trait-like characteristics of the individual reflect biological diathesis, environmental deprivation (especially during critical periods of psychosocial development), and resulting behavioral incompetence. Presumed central nervous system deficiencies present as information processing dysfunctions and arousal dysfunctions. There is some evidence that first degree relatives of schizophrenics also show these anomalies (Dawson, Nuechterlein, & Liberman, 1982). These biobehavioral dysfunctions may be relatively permanent but latent, and become detectable only when the individual is unduly stressed. In other cases, the enduring vulnerability, genetic loading, and psychological dysfunctions may be so great that even minor life events or small losses of social support may tip the balance into psychosis. In either case, the pre-existing vulnerability factors make the individual susceptible to symptom formation.

Transient intermediate states are induced by environmental stressors and are characterized by sensory overload, hyperarousal, and deficient processing of social stimuli. Hyperarousal occurs when the vulnerable individual is stressed beyond a certain threshold that taxes his or her problem-solving capacities. The activation of these intermediate states can produce a chain reaction eventuating in dam-

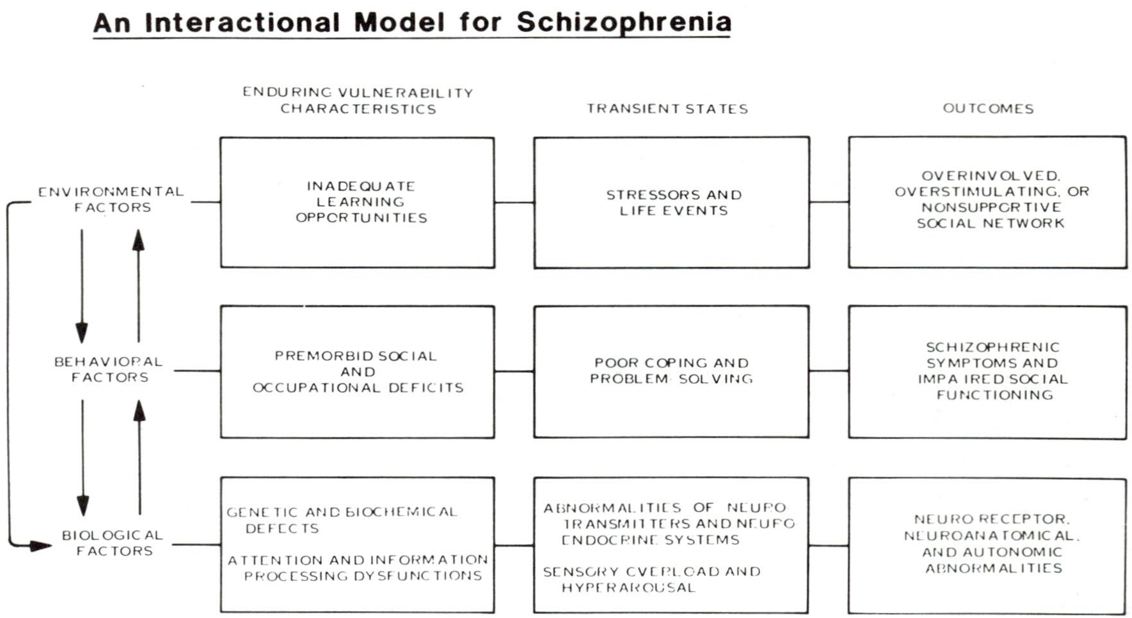

Fig. 1-1. Interactive model of schizophrenic symptom formation

age to the individual's family and social support systems. For example, an individual showing cognitive disorganization and irritability is likely to elicit more criticism or emotional overinvolvement from family members and rejection by members of his social network. Hence a vicious cycle is created, the person feels overwhelmed and unable to cope and then experiences schizophrenic symptoms.

The appearance of schizophrenic symptoms, impaired social and occupational functioning, and perhaps rehospitalization are the outcome indicators in this interactive model of schizophrenia. Some schizophrenic individuals with good interpersonal problem-solving skills might be able to actively cope to reduce the environmental stressors and recruit greater social support. The schizophrenic with good premorbid social and vocational adjustment, for example, would have resources to mitigate the negative impacts of social stressors, sensory overload, and hyperarousal thereby breaking the vicious cycle and minimizing or alleviating symptomatology.

In summary, a diathesis-stress interactive model for the formation of schizophrenic symptoms consists of noxious social events combining with preexisting vulnerability to produce intermediate states of sensory overload, hyperarousal, and impaired processing of social stimuli. These intermediate states and their behavioral concomitants generate even more stressors leading to the appearance of schizophrenic symptoms and impaired functioning.

DIAGNOSIS OF SCHIZOPHRENIA

At present schizophrenia may be defined by one or more diagnostic systems. There are no absolute pathognomonic findings or universally accepted standards for diagnosis. The clinical laboratory and medical sciences offer little or no help. The recently published *Diagnostic and Statistical Manual—Third Edition* (DSM-III) of the American Psychiatric Association provides explicit diagnostic criteria, derived in part from Schneider's first rank symptoms (Schneider, 1959; Wing, 1978). Characteristic symptoms include bizarre delusions and thought disturbances (feelings that the patient's will, emotions, or behavior are taken over and controlled by external agents or forces, thought broadcasting, thought insertion, and thought withdrawal), specific hallucinations (voices commenting on the patient's thoughts or actions, voices talking to each other), as well as incoherence of speech (i.e., thought disorder) that is accompanied by flattened affect, delusions, hallucinations, or grossly disorganized behavior. Other criteria include a deteriorating social course of at least six months duration, age of onset before 45, and exclusion of those patients with major affective syndromes or symptoms caused by toxic agents (alcohol, drugs), organic mental disorder, or mental retardation.

The determination to append the label of schizophrenia to a given patient is usually dependent upon one interview or at most a few interviews with the examining clinician. Clearly the patient's verbal productivity and articulateness will be major factors in the final decision. Some are facile with words while others are tangential, verbally impoverished, or otherwise have great difficulty expressing themselves. Some fabricate and some forget. Is the mute or catatonic patient depressed, brain damaged, or schizophrenic? Patients acutely ill may not be able to respond to an interview, and in such cases a wise diagnostician will return later to the quest for information and experiences.

The examiner's skills in eliciting and interpreting information plays a role but also important is the examiner's bias or expectational set. Certainly we are all subject to hearing what we expect to hear. Even objective interpretation of plentiful, reliable information fails to assure consistent diagnosis because of the variability and number of diagnostic systems in use. There is no single disease entity that can be termed schizophrenia. More accurately, the variability that is subsumed as schizophrenic disorders or syndromes may eventually be determined to be a heterogeneous group of disorders marked by many different underlying biological influences.

The quantity and quality of information provided by the patient may be augmented by increasing the number of interviews, querying relatives and other acquaintances, reviewing available records, and careful observations. The dilemma presented by mutism or catatonia may, to some extent at least, be clarified by thorough neurologic, laboratory, and x-ray examinations to search for organic brain disease, by audiometry if deafness is a consideration, by measurement of the effects of the administration of dexamethasone and thyrotropin releasing hormone to aid in the diagnosis of depression (Pranse, Wilson, & Lara, 1972; Klerman, 1983), and, if the patient has been receiving neuroleptics, by addition of an antiparkinson agent or reduction of antipsychotic medication to rule out akinesia or drug-induced catatonia.

The assurance of a rigorously comprehensive and accurate mental status examination may best be accomplished through the use of structured interviews employing such instruments as the Present State Examination (Wing, Cooper, & Sartorious, 1974) or the Schedule for Affective Disorders and Schizophrenia (Spitzer & Endicott, 1977). Perhaps it is not reasonable to expect the busy clinician and diagnostician to be trained in the use of these procedures and to apply them to each patient, but shortcuts and the tendency to ask only those questions that tend to conform preexisting bias must be avoided. At the very least an interview format should be established and adhered to. This might consist of a series of screening questions that if answered in the affirmative should lead to more detailed exploration. It is essential that the patient and the interviewer not be permitted to "take the easy way out" by offering only cursory yes or no type answers. Any suspicion that schizophrenic psychopathology may be present requires thorough investigation for corroboration. The topic may be approached from different vantage points on several occasions during the interview and "open-ended" questions should be employed to document verbatim elaborations and examples of the characteristic symptoms.

The unreliability of schizophrenic diagnosis in earlier eras was caused by vague theoretical constructs that could not be clearly defined nor easily agreed upon. Reliability between diagnosticians has been considerably improved upon in the past decade by the development and implementation of structured interviews and diagnostic schemata employing specified criteria (Wims, Birley, Cooper, Graham, & Isaacs, 1967). These newer diagnostic systems, developed largely in response to research needs, only recently gained general application in American psychiatry and ultimately led to the *DSM-III*. In 1972 Feighner and his colleagues (Feighner, Robins, Guze, Woodruff, Winoker, & Munoz, 1972) published *Diagnostic Criteria for Psychiatric Research. The New Haven Schizophrenia Index* (Astrachan, Harrow, Adler, Brauer, Schwartz, Schwartz, Tucker, 1972) appeared at approximately the same time as the Feighner criteria and these have been followed by *Flexible System for the Diagnosis of Schizophrenia* (Carpenter, Strauss, & Bartko, 1973), the *Research Diagnostic Criteria for Schizophrenia* or RDC (Spitzer, Endicott, & Robins, 1975), and the Texas Actuarial Criteria (Overall & Hollister, 1979). It is beyond the scope of this chapter to review these systems in detail, but differences include the relative weight given to various signs, symptoms, or historical features; exclusionary criteria such as the presence of an affective syndrome; and requirements for specific duration of illness.

The reliability and predictive validity of the various systems has been investigated (Overall, Cobb, & Click, 1982; Endicott, Nee, Fleiss, Cohen, Williams, & Simon, 1982) and reveals widely divergent findings, especially with regard to the relative rates of defining cohorts of patients as "schizophrenic."

The various systems each have their adherents but it is the *DSM-III* that, in the USA, offers the most widespread clinical usage. In the absence of external criteria for validating the construct of schizophrenia, it is not possible to point to any one set of criteria as "better" than any other. The populations defined by different diagnostic criteria are somewhat different but overlapping. The more restrictive criteria may define more homogeneous cohorts for research purposes but the results of such studies may be of less relevance to the practicing clinician. From this standpoint more widespread use of the *DSM-III* criteria seems justified along with continuing efforts to refine these criteria for both research and clinical use (Guze, Strauss, Katz, & Kendall, 1982). Because of the potent therapeutic and prophylactic effects of neuroleptic drugs on schizophrenia symptoms and the hazardous side effects associated with long-term neuroleptic usage, it is very important to make the diagnosis of schizophrenia as carefully as possible. The *DSM-III* and available structured interviews and rating instruments are guideposts for the clinician. The clinician should also become knowledgeable and competent in using a variety of assessment instruments for rating the severity of psychotic signs and symptoms periodically over the course of a hospitalization or episode of treatment. Rating scales (such as the Brief Psychiatric Rating Scale, the Psychiatric Status Schedule, the Psychiatric Assessment Scale, or the "change" version of the Schedule of Affective Disorders and Schizophrenic) provide operationalized and reliable means of charting the progress of patients and thereby elucidating clinical decision-making regarding treatment interventions (Taylor, Liberman, & Agras, 1982; Wallace, 1981).

Multimodal Behavioral Assessment of Schizophrenia

Schizophrenia is a disorder tht pervades almost all of the patient's human potentialities. In developing treatment plans, it is essential that a multimodal approach to assessment that taps the patient's premorbid and current functioning in such areas as socialization, self-care, work, family life, leisure and recreation, affect, and other instrumental roles be employed. While it is the accurate characterization of typical positive symptoms of delusions, hallucinations, thought interference, and thought disorder that determines the use of neuroleptic drugs, other treatment decisions must be built upon assessment of the individual's behavioral level of functioning. Occasionally, behavioral functioning returns nearly to premorbid levels once the acute and florid psychiatric symptoms subside; thus, it is advisable to postpone active treatment planning for rectifying wider scale behavioral deficits and excesses until the picture of positive symptoms clears. Another reason to approach the assessment and treatment of behavioral disorders in a deliberate and gradual fashion is the tendency for still-symptomatic patients to be overstimulated by premature psychosocial interventions and, as a consequence, to suffer exacerbations of their illness (Liberman, 1982b).

When the patient's favorable response to neuroleptics and to the therapeutic "asylum" features of inpatient hospitalization becomes clearer, however, it is important to move ahead with multimodal behavioral assessment. This is also advisable for the approximately 20 percent of patients who show little or no symptomatic improvement during hospitalization. The importance of assessing the family system and its emotional climate is emphasized in a succeeding section of this chapter; thus, this section will focus primarily on the assessment of social skills, since they are important in designing treatment interventions and in predicting treatment outcome and subsequent quality of life. It should be noted, however, that assessment of work, self-care, and other instrumental role skills and deficits are important for the clinician interested in a comprehensive evaluation and grasp of the patient's disorder.

Social Skills in Schizophrenia

Social skills refer to the everyday conversations, encounters, and transactions that people have with each other. Social skills that are deficient in schizophrenia include the ability to give and obtain information and to express and exchange attitudes, opinions, and feelings. Social skills can be divided into those that mediate *instrumental* vs. *social-emotional* functions. Instrumental interactions enable an individual to meet survival needs such as shelter, food, job, finances, and transportation. Social-emotional interactions provide support, warmth, friendship, and intimacy. Individuals suffering from schizophrenic disorders usually show major deficits in both spheres of social interactions (Liberman, 1982a).

Deficits in social skills can be measured in a variety of ways. Topographically, the verbal content and nonverbal elements in conversation can be assessed. For example, schizophrenics have been found deficient in duration of verbal response, eye contact, intonation, hand gestures, and facial expression. An alternative mode of assessing social skills is to view them as subserving problem-solving and information processing functions. Schizophrenic individuals tend to have limitations in generating alternatives for solving problems and to have difficulty initiating social behavior. The person with schizophrenia has impairments in accurately perceiving social situations and understanding social expectations. Finally, a *functional* approach to assessing social skills assumes that attainment of instrumental and social-emotional goals reflects competence and adaptation. Individuals with schizophrenia are defined by their experiencing a decrement in their social adjustment and level of functioning, partly because of the interference of symptoms in social interaction. The schizophrenic's likelihood of achieving his or her goals, however, is also markedly impaired by failure to grasp generally accepted social norms, never having learned effective verbal and non-verbal skills, loss of interest and spontaneity in social relations, or by long years of institutionalism and lack of social practice. As a common denominator that cuts across almost all domains of human experience, social skills are important markers of the spectrum of schizophrenic disorders and vital targets for intervention aimed at restoration of function and community survival.

Biological Vulnerability

Certain properties of schizophrenia have convinced researchers over the years that abnormal biological mechanisms are associated with the disorder. Particularly convincing is the observation that, with the exception of extraordinary and prolonged environmental stressors, normal individuals only experience schizophrenic symptoms, such as delusions and hallucinations, under circumstances when normal biology is perturbed by certain drugs or by organic disease processes such as tumors or epilepsy. These observations have led to numerous, albeit unsuccessful, attempts to locate a discrete biological abnormality that is present in schizophrenic patients but not in normals. Although there is no identified biological abnormality that is both necessary and sufficient for the development of schizophrenia, much has been learned about the biological factors that appear to make individuals more prone to develop this illness.

Genetic Evidence for Vulnerability

A compelling body of evidence indicates that individuals may inherit a vulnerability to develop schizophrenia. This is supported by the observation that relatives of schizophrenic patients have a much greater probability of developing the illness than the general population. Whereas the lifetime risk for developing schizophrenia is about one percent in most population studies, the sibling or offspring of an identified patient has about a 10 percent risk of developing schizophrenia (Gottesman, 1978). The risk decreases in more distant relatives who have less genetic overlap.

The evidence that vulnerability to develop schizophrenia can be inherited does not exclude or even minimize the importance of environmental factors. The weight of the evidence supports an interaction between genetic and environmental factors just as it does for nearly every other medical illness. For example, the higher concordance for schizophrenia in monozygotic as opposed to dizygotic twins (Gottesman & Shields, 1976) is important additional evidence supporting genetic gransmission. If only impaired genes were both necessary and sufficient for the development of schizophrenia, however, concordance rates would approach 100 percent. The reported rates of 35–58 percent indicate that other factors (i.e., environmental) play a role in the development of the illness.

It also appears that there is no environment that is necessary and sufficient to cause a person to become schizophrenic. This is important to acknowledge since earlier theories of the etiology of schizophrenia that focused on disturbed family environments (Gottesman, 1978) pointed out that one of the important contributions of the adoption studies of Kety and his co-workers (1975) has been to demonstrate that adoptees with a biological schizophrenic parent are not protected from schizophrenia when they are adopted out. Furthermore, being raised by a schizophrenic parent does not appear to increase the likelihood that the adoptee will develop schizophrenia if the child does not have a genetic vulnerability. In a similar vein, no one has as yet described a series of events or an environment that will invariably result in a schizophrenic illness. These results were recently summarized by Cancro (1982) who concluded that people inherit through their genes a particular potential to manifest schizophrenic symptoms given sufficient social stress.

It needs to be emphasized that the finding that a vulnerability to develop schizophrenia can be inherited should not discourage attempts to understand the environmental factors that influence the development and course of the illness. It is likely, perhaps even inevitable, that experiences during childhood and adolescence will influence which vulnerable individuals develop the illness and what form the illness takes. Recent research, which is reviewed in a later section of this chapter, indicates that after the illness has developed, its course and outcome are likely to be profoundly influenced by one's social environment.

Biology of Schizophrenia

The discovery of drugs with clearly demonstrable anti-psychotic effects has resulted in a shift away from the search for endogenous psychotogens and towards attempts to understand the neurochemical effects of these drugs on the behavior of schizophrenic patients; and, instead of a search for a particular psychosis-inducing substance, biologists have derived biochemical hypotheses based upon the neuropharmacological effects of drugs that either exacerbate or ameliorate psychosis.

The most important hypothesis for a biochemical mechanism underlying schizophrenia is the dopamine (DA) hypothesis. In its simplest form, the DA hypothesis contends that schizophrenia is related to an overactivity of central nervous system DA. The major support for this theory comes from converging and related observations that drugs that increase DA activity tend to make schizophrenic patients worse and can cause schizophrenic-like symptoms in normals, and drugs that decrease DA activity improve schizophrenic symptoms.

This form of the DA hypothesis has inspired a considerable amount of research, that has consisted largely of searching every available body fluid for evidence of impaired DA metabolism. These studies have yet to reveal differences between schizophrenic and non-schizophrenic individuals. In recent studies using postmortem human brains, however, MacKay and his colleagues (1980) compared brains of dying patients with a hospital diagnosis of schizophrenia to those of non-schizophrenic patients. In the schizophrenic patients, DA concentrations were elevated in the nucleus accumbens and anterior perforated substance. Using radio-receptor techniques, these investigators also found that the schizophrenic brains had a greater number of DA receptors in the nucleus accumbens and caudate. All of these neural areas have been implicated in schizophrenia (MacKay, Bird, Iverson, Spokes, Creek, & Snyder, 1980). These findings are controversial, since they may be merely artifacts related to prior neuroleptic treatment.

Although there is only limited evidence for an impaired DA system leading to schizophrenia, there is considerable evidence to support the view that antipsychotic or neuroleptic drugs improve schizophrenia by blocking DA receptors. New techniques now permit direct studies of the properties of DA receptors. Homogenates are prepared from areas of animal brains, such as the caudate nucleus, that are rich in DA receptors. Antipsychotic drugs, such as haloperidol are radio-labeled and added to the homogenate. Specialized techniques permit the separation of specific binding of the radio-labeled drug with the receptor from nonspecific binding. Using this technique, investigators have found that there is an impressive correlation between the clinical dose potency of commonly prescribed neuroleptic drugs and their affinity for DA receptors.

Acknowledging the lack of evidence for an impaired DA system in schizophrenia, Davis (1978) proposed a two-factor theory to explain the convincing evidence that neuroleptics work by blocking DA receptors and the lack of evidence of abnormal DA mechanisms in the etiology of schizophrenia. Rather than the DA system being the single mechanism accounting for vulnerability to schizophrenia, neural malfunctioning may be modulated by drugs through the DA system. Thus, whatever the biological determinants of schizophrenia, they may exert their influence through regulating the DA system such as a control knob modulates the volume on a radio. A two-factor theory of biological influences on schizophrenia can be compared to hypertension, in which some drugs regulate blood pressure by mechanisms totally unrelated to the cause of the disorder.

Anatomical Abnormalities in Schizophrenia

Early studies using pneumoencephalography pointed to enlarged cerebral ventricles as being common in schizophrenia. The present availability of computerized tomography (CT) scans has permitted the study of ventricular morphology using a method that is both safe and reliable. Weinberger and his co-workers (1979) found a significant difference in ventricular size between chronic schizophrenic patients and controls, with 53 percent of those with chronic schizophrenia having ventricular sizes more than two standard deviations larger than the mean of the controls. This very interesting finding has been confirmed by some but not all investigators.

Additional studies (Weinberger, Bigelow, Kleinman, Klein, Rosenblatt, & Wyatt, 1980) have suggested that chronic schizophrenic patients with enlarged ventricles may form a biologically homogeneous subgroup of neurologically impaired individuals. Such patients respond poorly to antipsychotic drug treatment relative to a matched group of chronic schizophrenic patients with normal-sized ventricles. Enlarged ventricles appear to be more common in those patients who perform poorly on cognitive and neuropsychological tests. On CT scans, some schizophrenic patients also showed evidence of cortical abnormalities and some had reverses in cortical asymmetry. Taken together, these studies suggest that structural brain abnormalities may be useful in forming clinical subtypes of schizophrenic patients.

Biological Heterogeneity of Schizophrenia

It is apparent that there is little evidence for any single biological marker that is associated only with schizophrenia. The relentless search for a unitary biological explanation and the failure to find it have convinced many investigators that the most useful strategy is to acknowledge the heterogeneity of schizophrenia. Crow (1980), adopted such an approach in proposing two different disease processes in schizophrenia. The Type I syndrome is characterized by a relatively acute course and positive symptoms of schizophrenia such as hallucinations, delusions, and thought disorder. The Type II syndrome consists of a chronic course and negative symptoms such as flattened affect and impoverished speech. Patients with the Type I syndrome respond well to neuroleptics and are postulated to have increased numbers of brain DA receptors. On the other hand, patients with the Type II syndrome respond poorly to neuroleptics and are more likely to show intellectual impairment as well as structural brain abnormalities on CT scan. Some patients may have characteristics of both syndromes. Crow's theory explains a considerable amount of the data and is more consistent with the view of most clinicians that multiple biological and socio-psychological processes interact to determine the onset and course of schizophrenic disorders.

Psychophysiological Abnormalities in Schizophrenia

Psychophysiology is a scientific discipline that studies the interrelationships between psychological states and processes, on the one hand, and noninvasively measured physiological responses on the other hand. Certain peripheral physiological measures change reliably with behavioral, psychological, and emotional events (Grings & Dawson, 1978; Hasset, 1978; Stern, Ray, & Davis, 1980). For example, it is common to experience sweaty palms and heart palpitations when one is afraid. Psychophysiological measures may provide an easily accessible "window" through which to detect the biological vulnerability of certain individuals to schizophrenia.

Psychophysiology and Electrodermal Activity

Psychophysiologists typically measure physiological responses noninvasively by placing recording devices on the surface of the skin. For example, one of the most widely studied physiological measures is electrodermal activity. In measuring electrodermal activity, electrodes are placed on the fingertips or palms of the hand and a small electrical current (too small to feel) is passed through the skin. One can then measure the tonic electrical conductivity of the skin (skin conductance level, SCL) as well as phasic increases in skin conductance (skin conductance responses, SCRs). The SCRs may be stimulus-elicited (specific SCRs) or may occur "spontaneously", without identifiable eliciting stimuli (nonspecific SCRs). These vario ermal phenomena primarily reflect activity of the eccrine s which are neurally controlled by the sympathetic division nomic nervous system (Fowles, 1974; Venables & Christie, 1

Electrodermal activity is closely associated with imp psychological processes such as emotional arousal and attention. In general, increases in arousal and attention are associated with increases in SCL and frequency of nonspecific SCRs as well as specific SCRs. Thus, the skin becomes a better conductor of electricity during emotional arousal and effortful attention.

Other physiological measures are also commonly employed by psychophysiologists; for example, heart rate, blood pressure, skin temperature, pupillary dilation, and event-related brain potentials. Electrodermal activity, however, has been the most widely used measure in psychophysiological studies of schizophrenia.

Electrodermal Activity and Schizophrenia

Psychophysiological studies have identified two electrodermal abnormalities in different subgroups of schizophrenic patients. First, typically between 40 and 50 percent of schizophrenic patients fail to exhibit specific SCRs to innocuous environmental stimuli (e.g., mild tones). This response, a component of the orienting response, fails to occur usually in only 5–10 percent of normal subjects. The lack of specific SCRs suggests that this subgroup of patients fails to adequately attend to, and cognitively process, novel environmental stimuli. Consistent with this interpretation, the subgroup of SCR nonresponders tends to be the more conceptually disorganized and withdrawn patients.

The second electrodermal abnormality is found principally among those schizophrenia patients who exhibit specific SCRs to innocuous environmental stimuli. These patients, at least when unmedicated, display abnormally high psychophysiological arousal. That is, SCLs and frequency of nonspecific SCRs are higher than normal. Other indices of psychophysiological arousal, such as heart rate and systolic blood pressure, also are high in this subgroup of patients. Symptomatically, these patients tend to be more active, excited, anxious, and belligerant. The subgroup of hyperaroused patients appears to have some of the primary characteristics of Crow's Type I syndrome mentioned earlier, whereas the subgroup of SCR nonresponders has some of the principal characteristics of Crow's Type II syndrome. Thus, electrodermal measures may prove to be helpful in identifying meaningful subgroups in the heterogenous group of schizophrenics.

Recent studies have suggested that the electrodermal abnormalities may have prognostic significance. Among recently hospitalized, unmedicated, acute schizophrenic patients, high electrodermal arousal is associated with poor short-term prognosis (Frith, Stevens, Johnstone, & Crow, 1979; Zahn, Carpenter, & McGlashan, 1981). Good short-term prognosis is associated with more normal levels of arousal. More research is needed in this theoretically and clinically important area, including tests of whether the electrodermal abnormalities can serve a useful role in determining the proper type and dosage of medication and whether they are related to the long-term likelihood of relapse.

Electrodermal Activity and Vulnerability to Schizophrenia

The evidence reviewed thus far indicates that most patients with a schizophrenic disorder exhibit either an abnormal absence of specific SCRs or abnormally high psychophysiological arousal levels (Bernstein, Frith, Gruzelier, Patterson, Straube, Venables, & Zahn, 1982; Dawson & Nuechterlein, in press; Öhman, 1981). More recent research has focused on the issue of whether these abnormalities are state-like indicators of current symptomatology or are trait-like indicators of an enduring vulnerability to schizophrenic episodes.

One method of shedding light on the state versus trait issue is to determine whether the psychophysiological abnormalities are present in remitted schizophrenic patients. One recent study (Iacono, 1982) found that remitted schizophrenic patients, compared to nonpsychiatric patients exhibited a heightened incidence of SCR nonresponsiveness to innocuous environmental stimuli (46 percent vs. 18 percent). The remainder of the schizophrenic patients showed abnormally high electrodermal arousal levels. The finding that nearly half of the remitted schizophrenic patients were SCR nonresponders, while the remainder exhibited higher than normal electrodermal arousal, is strikingly similar to findings obtained with symptomatic schizophrenics. Hence, the results suggest that psychophysiological abnormalities may be enduring trait-like qualities that persist after the psychotic symptoms disappear and that may be related to biological vulnerability to schizophrenia.

Another method of investigating the state versus trait issue involves studying individuals, such as children of schizophrenic parent(s), who have never experienced schizophrenic symptoms but are at heightened risk for future episodes of schizophrenia. Three studies have found SCR hyperresponsivity to aversive loud noises in the offspring of schizophrenic parents (Mednick & Schulsinger, 1968; Prentky, Salzman, & Klein, 1981; Van Dyke, Rosenthal, & Rasmussen, 1974). Electrodermal hyperresponsivity was found even among offspring of schizophrenic parents who were raised by nonschizophrenic foster parents, thus eliminating possible effects of a disturbed childhood environment on the results (Van Dyke, et al., 1974). Unlike symptomatic patients, however, the offspring of schizophrenic patients do not show tonic hyperarousal. Thus, the results suggest that sympathetic hyperresponsivity to aversive stimulation may be a long-standing trait associated with the vulnerability to schizophrenia, whereas tonic hyperarousal may develop later, perhaps when life events become too stressful.

One of the most common electrodermal abnormalities in symptomatic schizophrenic patients, SCR nonresponsiveness to innocuous stimuli, has not been observed among the offspring of schizophrenic patients. One possible interpretation is that SCR nonresponsiveness is not related to the vulnerability to schizophrenia, but rather represents the erecting of biobehavioral barriers as a secondary strategy for coping with stressful life events and emerging psychotic symptoms.

INFORMATION PROCESSING IN SCHIZOPHRENIA

Eugen Bleuler, who coined the term *schizophrenia,* described the lack of cognitive control displayed by patients with schizophrenia when he noted that they were "incapable of holding the train of thought in the proper channel" (Bleuler, 1951). This inadequate control over continuity of thought seemed to Emil Kraepelin, another pioneer in the conceptualization of schizophrenic disorders, to be associated with deficits in attentional processes: "This behavior is without doubt related to the disorder of attention which we frequently find conspicuously developed in our patients. It is quite common for them to lose both inclination and ability on their own initiative to keep their attention fixed for any length of time" (Kraepelin, 1919). Kraepelin distinguished between *Auffasung,* or spontaneous registration of information which he felt was generally intact, and *Aufmerksamkeit,* or active, sustained, and directed attention, which he felt was almost always deficient in schizophrenic disorder.

Roughly paralleling the distinction made by Kraepelin, contemporary theorists within cognitive psychology have proposed a distinction between cognitive processes that are automatic and those that are conscious (Posner, 1978), effortful (Hasher & Zacks, 1979), or controlled (Shiffrin & Schneider, 1977). This distinction has been a central one for several contemporary theories of the information-processing deficit in schizophrenia and serves as a useful framework for viewing attentional abnormalities as markers for biological disturbances in the central nervous system. Although the distinction between these two polar types of processes differs somewhat across theorists, automatic processes are generally viewed as occurring without intention, without necessarily leading to awareness, and without interfering with other information processing. On the other hand, conscious, effortful, or controlled processes demand resources from a limited-capacity, central processing system. Controlled, directed attentional processes are assumed to be serial in nature and somewhat slower than automatic processes. Due to the demands on limited capacity, consciously directing attention to one task will interfere with performance on other tasks. The initial registration and encoding of the physical features of stimuli are typically viewed as automatic, while serial comparisons, rehearsal, subjective organization, and elaborative memory are seen as active, limited-capacity processes. With sufficient practice in situations in which stimulus-response connections are consistent, however, fairly complex processing sequences can become automatized.

Contemporary theorists have argued that schizophrenia is characterized by deficits in controlled, serial processing; on the other hand, automatic processing of information is seen as either not as markedly affected (Neale & Oltmanns, 1980) or actually normal or supernormal (Callaway & Naghdi, 1982). These current views roughly parallel that of Kraepelin in his distinction between the relatively intact processes of stimulus registration and the impaired processes of active, sustained, and directed attention in schizophrenia.

Deficits in Automatic and Effortful Cognitive Processes

One productive task for the examination of deficits in relatively automatic processing versus controlled or effortful processing in schizophrenic disorder has been serial recall with and without distraction (Oltmanns, 1978). Subjects are asked to recall short, random sequences of words or digits shortly after their auditory presentation. Recall of items that are presented near the end of a sequence (the recency effect) is considered to reflect mainly passive, automatic processes of sensory storage, whereas recall of the items at the beginning of a sequence (the primacy effect) demands effortful, controlled processes such as rote rehearsal. Oltmanns (1978) found that auditory distraction interfered with schizophrenic short-term recall primarily by reducing recall for items early in each word string. Thus, effortful, controlled processes appear to be especially susceptible to interference in schizophrenia.

The possible relevance of this disruption of effortful, controlled processing beyond periods of schizophrenic episodes is suggested in two additional studies. The differential impairment of recall for the early, as compared to late, serial-position items during auditory serial recall was found by Frame and Oltmanns (1982) to be present among schizophrenic patients both shortly after hospitalization and just prior to discharge after symptomatic improvement. Using a digit-span auditory serial recall task, Harvey, Winters, Weintraub, and Neale (1981) found that children of schizophrenic parents were more impaired than children of unipolar affective disorder, bipolar affective disorder, or normal parents in their recall of early serial-position items presented with auditory distraction. These findings are consistent with the hypothesis that susceptability of effortful, controlled processes to disruption may be an index of biological vulnerability to schizophrenic disorder.

An alternative viewpoint has been expressed, however, that places greater emphasis on deficits in the components of information processing that apparently demand little or no processing capacity among normal individuals. Frith (1979) has argued that the mental operations that are normally completed automatically and are not limited in capacity require conscious attention in schizophrenia. Frith describes possible means by which such a dysfunction in automatic parallel processing could underlie schizophrenic hallucinations, delusions, and thought disorder. For example, he posits that the schizophrenic patient does not automatically select the appropriate meaning from long-term memory during the normally parallel process of encoding very familiar stimuli. Instead, alternative meanings intrude into consciousness as information is processed.

Such disruptions in normally automatic processes have been evident in subjective reports of schizophrenic patients. Chapman (1966) reported a patient's statements that "None of my movements come automatically to me now" and "I've been thinking too much about them, even walking properly, talking properly, and smoking—doing anything." Similarly, a young schizophrenic patient reported to McGhie and Chapman (1961) that, "Everything seems to grip my attention although I am not particularly interested in anything. I am speaking to you now but I can hear noises going on next door and in the corridor—often the silliest things going on seem to interest me. That's not even true; they don't interest me but I find myself attending to them and wasting a lot of time this way."

A dysfunction in parallel, automatic processing would be expected to force many normally automatic cognitive operations to be completed by conscious, effortful, controlled processing. Nuechterlein (1982) has noted that this deflection of processing capacity to normally automatic processes, such as stimulus feature encoding, might allow adequate, although slower, completion of these cognitive operations but would leave less processing capacity available for higher-level controlled processes. Such a reallocation of processing capacity to stimulus recognition processes could account for the disruption of active rehearsal in the serial recall tasks used by Oltmanns (1978), Frame and Oltmanns (1982), and Harvey et al. (1981). Because schizophrenic patients and children of schizophrenic patients would devote more processing capacity than normal individuals to recognizing the relevant stimuli as they were registered by the senses, especially when distracting stimuli were interpolated between relevant stimuli, they would tend to have less processing capacity available for the active rehearsal that is necessary to recall items early in each stimulus sequence.

Deficits in Stimulus Recognition

This newer interpretation of serial recall deficits in schizophrenic disorder helps to account for recent results indicating that stimulus recognition in schizophrenia is inefficient, at least among poor prognosis patients. Tachistoscopic studies have indicated that single letter stimuli in a forced-choice task must be presented for longer durations for poor prognosis schizophrenic patients to obtain the same level of detectability shown by normal, depressed, manic, or good prognosis schizophrenic patients (Braff & Saccuzzo, 1981; Saccuzzo & Braff, 1981). In addition, recognition of single letters requires a longer interval between the presentation of the letter and a subsequent visual mask among poor prognosis schizophrenic patients and schizotypal personality disorder patients than among non-schizophrenic psychiatric patients and normal subjects (Braff, 1981; Saccuzzo & Braff, 1981; Saccuzzo & Schubert, 1981).

Deficits among children born to schizophrenic mothers have also recently been demonstrated on a vigilance task that involved immediate recognition and response to tachistoscopic presentation of single degraded numeral stimuli (Nuechterlein, 1983; Neuchterlein, Phipps-Yonas, Driscoll, & Garmezy, 1982). These deficits were not present among children of mothers with psychiatric disorders falling outside the schizophrenia spectrum. The children of schizophrenic mothers showed an overall lower level of perceptual sensitivity to the target/

nontarget discrimination throughout the vigilance task, which suggests that difficulties in rapid extraction of relevant stimulus features in each trial may be involved. Stimulus recognition inefficiency has been demonstrated among patients with schizophrenia and schizotypal personality disorder and among children of parents with schizophrenic disorder.

In summary, several recent accounts of schizophrenic information processing have employed a distinction between automatic processing and conscious, controlled, or effortful processing that is derived from cognitive psychology. Many schizophrenic patients and some of their children show deficits in controlled, effortful processing. At the present time, it seems possible that this deficit may represent a primary dysfunction in controlled processing or may be secondary to a primary dysfunction in automatic, parallel processing. In either case, the information-processing deficit appears to extend beyond the period of active psychosis and may index vulnerability to schizophrenic episodes.

FAMILY DEVIANCE IN COMMUNICATION: ATTITUDES AND AFFECT

The biological and psychological processes operating in schizophrenia that have been described above are in constant interaction with environmental factors. The social environment is the major source of inadequate learning of behavioral competencies and hence can be seen as making a contribution to the enduring vulnerability of individuals to a major mental disorder. The social environment is also a major source of stressful life events that can contribute to the onset and course of schizophrenic disorders. Families constitute an important portion of the social environment.

During the mid-1950s clinical and conceptual studies of schizophrenia began to emphasize the role of intrafamilial attributes in the development of schizophrenia. As this trend progressed, several theories emerged that implicated the whole family in the etiology of the illness. Gradually throughout the 1960s and into the 1970s, investigators began to study the link between schizophrenic psychopathology and disordered family interaction patterns. Much attention was given to concepts such as Bateson's double-bind hypothesis (Bateson, Jackson, Haley, & Weakland, 1956). Wynne and Singer's communication deviance theory (Singer & Wynne, 1963), and Lidz's skewed and schismatic families (Lidz, Cornelison, Carlson, & Fleck, 1958). Much of the efforts in this area have been cross-sectional; they have examined whether certain characteristic ways of behaving by key family members co-exist with the presence of an already diagnosed psychiatrically ill family member.

Although efforts to study the family's role in the etiology of schizophrenia continue, a shift has occurred over the past decade in the kinds of research being carried out with families of schizophrenics. Increasingly, interest is shifting away from the search for attributes of the family that cause the onset of schizophrenia (onset) to efforts aimed at studying to what extent the family environment serves as a positive influence or as a negative stressor on the course and outcome of schizophrenia in the vulnerable family member.

This shift in emphasis has occurred for a number of reasons. First, the current pattern of community-based care for schizophrenic patients, has evolved into a relatively brief inpatient period followed by extended aftercare in the community. Because adequate transitional living environments are rare, these patients often return to a family environment in states of partial remission. Examinations of these family environments and the problems provoked by the homecoming of a disturbed and disturbing relative have revealed that families sometimes cope well and at other times experience considerable difficulty coping with the newly assigned care-giver role. Thus, concern with the nature of the family environment and the reciprocal impacts of the schizophrenic patient on his or her relatives and vice-versa has revived interest in developing ways to help reduce family burden and strengthen families as a resource to the patient. Thus, a shift has occurred away from seeing the family as "the villain."

In the past several years, several research projects in the United States and Western Europe have been studying the communicational patterns of key relatives (parents or spouse) of schizophrenics. The underlying assumption of thse studies is that enduring patterns of attitudes, communication styles, and characteristic ways of behaving, sampled in tests, interviews, or direct interaction tasks, are reflective of the relatives' behavior when they are with the patient on a day-to-day basis. Recently, much of this work has focused on two constructs: *communication deviance,* previously studied as a parental characteristic of parents of diagnosed schizophrenics, and *expressed emotion,* studied as a parent or spouse predictor of subsequent relapse of schizophrenia. The working hypothesis of investigators studying these variables in families of diagnosed schizophrenics is that deviance in the family environment can operate as non-specific stressors for the vulnerable family member and therefore may exert a significant influence on the course of the disorder once it has emerged. A more specific goal of many of these investigators is to identify discrete components of the family environment that have a crucial impact on the course of the disorder in the schizophrenic family member.

Communication Deviance

Communication deviance is a measure that reflects an inability of the parent to establish and maintain a shared focus of attention during transactions with another person (Singer & Wynne, 1963). Repeated parent-offspring exchanges, characterized by high levels of parental communication deviance, may contribute to disturbed thinking and communication in vulnerable offspring. Projective test materials (e.g., the TAT, Rorschach) are often used to elicit a standardized sample of speech from which communication deviance is measured. Previous studies have found communication deviance to be characteristic of parents of schizophrenics, and in one study, to be predictive of onset of schizophrenic spectrum disorders (Doane, West, Goldstein, Rodnick, & Jones, 1981). Currently, studies are underway to determine whether different types or amounts of deviance in the parents of schizophrenics are related to the course of schizophrenia, and whether they influence the degree to which the family can effectively utilize psychosocial interventions.

Deviant Emotional Attitudes

The work by Brown and colleagues (Brown, Birley, & Wing, 1972) and Vaughn and Leff (1976a) in Great Britain provided empirical evidence that family environments may have a crucial influence on the course of schizophrenia once it has developed in a family member. Criticism, hostility, and emotional overinvolvement are assessed through a structured interview (Vaughn & Leff, 1976b). Families are then rated as high or low on *expressed emotion* (EE) depending on the level of criticism, hostility, or emotional overinvolvement they express toward the patient during the interview. Patients released to high EE family environments have been found in several replication studies (Vaughn, Snyder, Freeman, Jones, Falloon, & Liberman, 1982) to have approximately a 55 percent chance of relapse during the first 9 months after discharge, while those returning to low EE families have only a 15 percent chance.

Currently, investigators on a number of different projects are carrying out replication studies of this EE/relapse relationship in an attempt to determine whether the relationship is valid for different patient populations such as recent-onset cases and families of other cultural or ethnic groups. In one of the rare instances in clinical psychiatry in which research on social and behavioral factors is used to development of treatment strategies, attempts to modify the emotional climate of the family through psychosocial family education and therapy are showing promising results. Treatment studies have suggested that a combination of maintenance neuroleptic medication and family-based psychosocial intervention are effective in preventing relapses in the vulnerable family member (Falloon, Boyd, McGill, Moss, Razani, & Guilderman, 1982; Goldstein, 1981).

Deviant Family Interaction

Another major trend in research with families of schizophrenics involves the observation of family members while they are in direct communication with one another, rather than during an interview or tests with an examiner. These conjoint family interaction procedures allow for assessment of patterns or styles of relating between family members. Patterns of leadership coalitions, problem-solving efficiency, and ability to stay with the task can be measured from procedures such as revealed differences methods (Strodtbeck, 1951). In addition, the inclusion of direct interaction procedures in the assessment of families allows the researcher to examine the validity of measures obtained from other data sources such as self reports, tests, or interviews. An example of the value of sampling behavior at multiple levels will perhaps illustrate the advantages of this approach for research on intrafamilial attributes. As mentioned previously, schizophrenic patients returning to homes where relatives hold high EE attitudes have a much greater likelihood of relapsing than those who return to low EE households. Recently Doane (Doane, West, Goldstein, Rodnick, & Jones, 1981) has developed a system for assessing the emotional climate of the family as expressed in direct interaction with the patient. This measure, called *affective style,* assesses the amount of criticism, guilt-inducement, and intrusive remarks made by family members during an emotionally charged family discussion. Findings from a project being carried out in Los Angeles suggest that the measure of affective style adds to the EE variable in predicting both relapse and subsequent social functioning of the vulnerable schizophrenic patient nine months later (Doane, Falloon, Goldstein, & Mintz, 1984).

The strategies of family assessment outlined here are not intended to be exhaustive of ongoing research with schizophrenics and their families. However, these variables do appear to indicate a number of promising leads for unraveling the role of the family with regard to the onset, course, and treatment of schizophrenia. In summary, there appears to be a trend developing in which the family is increasingly recognized as a potentially positive factor in the aftercare period of a schizophrenic illness. Attempts to identify, measure, and then to perhaps modify certain key family characteristics are beginning to replace previous ideas that resulted in mental health professionals' rejection or isolation of the patient's family. Currently, there is growing recognition that with proper assessment, education, support systems, and intervention the family of the schizophrenic patient can be a positive factor in aftercare.

SOCIAL AND COMMUNITY FACTORS

While in many cases, the family provides the most proximal and emotionally arousing of social stimuli to schizophrenic patients, there are other life events that influence the onset and course of this illness. Aside from family factors, much theoretical and experimental evidence has pointed toward other interpersonal and socioeconomic features of the environment that serve as antecedents or precipitants of acute schizophrenic reactions.

Life Events and Relapse

The best work in the field has been carried out in England where investigators ascertained the frequency of life events in schizophrenics during a three month period preceding a psychotic breakdown that required hospitalization (Birley & Brown, 1970; Brown & Birley, 1968). Life events were determined by having the patient and significant others describe disappointments, losses, damages, and fulfillments that could be specifically dated. Life events were both agreeable (e.g., getting married, finding a new job, moving to a better residence) and noxious (e.g., losing a friend, suffering a drop in income, experiencing a theft) and included events that were outside the control of the patient as well as those linked with the patient's behavior. Comparisons were made for the same three month interval with a sample of normal people. During the three month reporting period, the proportion of normals having life events remained constant; however, the proportion of schizophrenics experiencing a life event increased markedly in the three weeks before the onset of their symptoms. Sixty percent of the schizophrenic sample had an abrupt change in their social environment during this 3 week pre-breakdown period, compared to only 14 percent of the normal controls. Birley and Brown (1970) found that this concentration of life events occurred just prior to the first psychotic episode in young schizophrenics as well as prior to exacerbations and repeated relapses in more chronic schizophrenics.

While most of the inventories used in recording life events focus on major changes, it is very possible that schizophrenics, because of their perceptual and cognitive impairments and increased psychological vulnerability, are stressed by mundane, small-scale, and everyday life events that would not be upsetting to normals. The accumulation of minor but unexpected or confusing changes in a schizophrenic's life space could conceivably tip the balance toward decompensation. A clinical anecdote attributed to Werner Mendel (personal communication) regarding a schizophrenic breakdown illustrates this phenomenon. A middle-aged schizophrenic man had lived continuously, albeit marginally, in the community for many years. He held a regular job to which he commuted every day by bus from his apartment in the city. His social life was constricted to brief conversations with the check-out clerks in the local supermarket and a friendly nod and "Good day" exchanged with the genial woman manager of his apartment house twice daily upon leaving for and returning from work. One day he noted that the manager's door was uncharacteristically shut and on his return from work discovered a new manager who happened to be a large, burly man. Within hours the patient's delusions and hallucinations had returned. He ran naked through the streets, and required hospitalization.

In a further investigation of the relationship of stressful events with relapse, psychiatrists at London's Social Psychiatry Research Unit found that patients who relapsed while taking neuroleptic medication were more likely to have experienced major life events in the period immediately preceding the flare-up of symptoms than other relapsing schizophrenics who were not taking medication (Leff & Wing, 1971; Leff, Hirsch, Gaind, Rohde, Stevens, & Wing, 1973). These investigators concluded that medication may protect vulnerable schizophrenic patients from the demands of daily living but not from stressful, large changes in their environments.

At a more macroeconomic level of analyzing social antecedents to schizophrenic psychopathology, Brenner (1973) studied the relationship between unemployment rate and admissions to New York State public and private mental hospitals from 1914 to 1967. There was a substantial correlation between poor economic conditions and hospital admissions, many of whom were schizophrenic. There are several explanations for this correlation, one of which is that poor economic conditions precipitate the onset or exacerbation of symptoms by increasing the number of noxious life events (e.g., loss of job, reduced income, changing jobs, losing employment or welfare benefits) to which an individual must adapt.

Social Networks

The social environment and the support it offers determines to a large extent the final common pathway and impact of life stressors and economic problems on the individual vulnerable to schizophrenia. It was found that patients experiencing close social relationships were more likely to remain in the community irrespective of the type of their living environment. Others have reported that the quality of hospital and post-hospital environments were significantly related to outcome (Kayton, Beck, & Koh, 1976; Wing, 1978; Zubin et al., 1961). In particular, socially isolated, unstimulating, deprived, and custodial living environments tend regularly to produce the social breakdown syndrome or institutionalism—apathy, social withdrawal, loss of self-care skills, and other "negative" symptoms of schizophrenia. The nature of the schizophrenic person's "social network" will modulate the impact of over- or under-stimulating environments on psychiatric symptoms and behavioral functioning.

The concept of social network encapsulates the reciprocal relationship between a patient and his or her interpersonal resources. The quality of this reciprocity can determine whether the social network has a salutary or damaging effect on the patient. In one of the rare empirical studies of social networks and their effects on psychiatric outcome, Tolsdorf (1976) intensively interviewed ten percent hospitalized schizophrenic patients and ten patients hospitalized for medical reasons. The two groups of patients were hospitalized in a VA Hospital and were matched on the basis of age, marital status, education, and socioeconomic level. Quantitative and qualitative information about the social network was gathered during a lengthy interview and validated by telephone calls to two members of each patient's designated network. Results indicated that while both groups had similar numbers of social contacts, the psychiatric patients reported fewer intimate relationships, fewer more powerful figures in the network, and fewer relationships with individuals other than family members. Qualitatively, the schizophrenic patients had a much more pessimistic and negative view of the ability and interest of their social networks to assist them in times of need, a view that reportedly developed long before the onset of the schizophrenic symptoms. A corollary of the negative attitudes held by the patients toward their social networks was the greater number of life stressors perceived by the patients as stemming from an excessively high set of expectations and demands for instrumental role functioning coming from the figures in the network.

Life events and stressors can thus be mitigated or amplified by the patient's social environment and, in addition, often vary greatly from patient to patient. For a patient living in a quiet and unstimulating board-and-care home, a major life event might be loss of the TV set for two weeks or the arrival of a new, energetic staff member; on the other hand, a patient living independently in the middle of New York City would more likely suffer a life event if someone broke into his or her apartment or if a stranger offered a seat on the subway. Changes in a patient's interpersonal life space will be experienced as stressful if it is relevant to the individuals' level of functioning; that is, if it places an adaptational demand or challenge on the person.

A major weakness of most stress research has been its limitation to a two-step process—a life event occurs and then symptoms of schizophrenia are observed. While such simplistic and retrospective studies have highlighted the impact of stressors on the schizophrenic process, they are not taking enough of the stress-response phenomenon into account to lead us to higher levels of understanding. Psychopathological end-states are not solely a function of the type and magnitude of environmental stressors, but are also affected by the responses of the individual to the stressors. Responses to stressors include perceptual filtering, cognitive labeling and processing, defensive reactions, coping style, and problem-solving efforts. At the interpersonal level, the adaptive capacity of the individual is strengthened by the supportiveness, encouragement, and reinforcement provided by primary relationships and figures in one's social network. A comprehensive view of the schizophrenic process requires us to evaluate the many levels on which human life proceeds. Interactions of schizophrenics with their environments have biological, intrapersonal, interpersonal, and sociocultural implications. The specific variables in this multi-modal scheme of adaptation to stressors interact in complex ways to determine onset, exacerbation, and remission of schizophrenic symptoms.

SUMMARY

Some persons experience delusions, hallucinations, incoherence, and associated social and behavioral impairments, but a person is generally not schizophrenic 24 hours a day. Some, more than others, must cope with varying degrees of cognitive distortions, psychophysiological arousal, information overload, and thought disorder. But the vulnerability to and symptoms of schizophrenia are marked more by variability than by constancy over time and across individuals.

Some level of vulnerability to developing schizophrenic symptoms appears to reside in most people, given sufficient environmental stressors. When "normals" are asked to free associate without reference to the content of their speech, something similar to schizophrenic incoherence occurs. Soldiers with good premorbid adjustments have schizophrenic-like episodes if exposed to intense and prolonged combat. Furthermore, attempts to demonstrate discontinuities in prognoses of patients diagnosed as suffering from schizophrenic vs. affective disorders have revealed not bimodal distributions, but rather outcomes on a continuum.

The biologic bases for schizophrenia also show continuity between this disorder and other psychiatric disturbances. Genetic studies, for example, suggest that probands suffering with schizophrenic symptoms also have a disproportionate number of relatives with certain psychiatric disorders other than schizophrenia. The neuroleptic drugs are not specific to schizophrenic symptoms, but rather appear to possess broad, antipsychotic properties. Many of the presumptive biochemical markers for schizophrenia are, in fact, found in a wide range of psychotic disorders.

Although promising cognitive and psychophysiologic markers for the underlying biologic vulnerability to schizophrenic symptoms are being investigated, there is no evidence that such potential markers are discontinuous or dichotomous in their manifestations. In summary, intraindividual and interindividual variability are such visible features of the disorder that they should govern our conceptualization of the nature of schizophrenia.

Variability and continuity in the manifestation of the disorder suggest that the nature of schizophrenia is to be found in the multiple interactions among behavior, environment, and genes. The causes, remissions, relapses, and idiosyncratic manifestations of symptoms and impairments in schizophrenia might best be discovered by methods that reveal the many faceted relationships among the individual's multimodal behavior, the biological matrix, and the environment. The multiplicity of environmental stressors, reinforcers, and supports; the probablistic and plastic events within the central nervous system; and the ephemeral and dynamic modes of experience and behavior all promote the heterogeneity that emerges as the fundamental fact of schizophrenia.

ACKNOWLEDGMENT

This chapter was co-authored by investigators working within the Mental Health Clinical Research Center for the Study of Schizophrenia, co-sponsored by UCLA, West Los Angeles VA Medical Center and Camarillo State Hospital. Liberman authored the Introduction, the section on Social and Community Factors, and The Summary. Marshall wrote the section on Diagnosis, Marder the section on Biological Vulnerability, Dawson the section on Psychophysiological Abnormalities, Nuechterlein the section on Information Processing Abnormalities, and Doane the section on Family Deviance. The conceptualization of Schizophrenia in a multidimensional stress-vulnerability framework was developed by Nuechterlein, Dawson, and Liberman. The writing of this chapter was supported in part by NIMH Research Grant MH 30911 and NIHR Rehabilitation Research and Training Center Grant G008006802.

REFERENCES

Alevizos PN, & Callahan EJ. Assessment of psychotic behavior. In AR Ciminero, H Adams, & K Calhoun (Eds.), *Handbook of behavioral assessment.* New York: Wiley, 1977, pp. 683–721

American Psychiatric Association Committee on nomenclature and statistics. *Diagnostic and statistical manual of mental disorders,* (Ed. 3). New York: American Psychiatric Association, 1982

Astrachan BM, Harrow M, Adler D, Brauer L, Schwartz A, Schwartz C, & Tucker G. A checklist for the diagnosis of schizophrenia. *British Journal of Psychiatry,* 1972, *121,* 529–569

Bateson G, Jackson D, Haley J, & Weakland J. Toward a theory of schizophrenia. *Behavioral Science,* 1956, *1,* 251–264

Bernstein AS, Frith CD, Gruzelier JH, Patterson T, Straube E, Venables PH, & Zahn TP. An analysis of the skin conductance orienting response in samples of American, British, and German schizophrenics. *Biological Psychology,* 1982, *14,* 155–211

Birley JLT, & Brown GW. Crises and life changes preceding the onset or relapse of acute schizophrenia. *British Journal of Psychiatry,* 1970, *116,* 327–333

Blashfield RK, Feighner J. Invisible colleges and the Matthew effect. *Schizophrenia Bulletin,* 1982, *8,* 1–6

Bleuler EP. *Textbook of psychiatry.* (Translated by A.A. Brill) New York: Dover, 1951 (originally 1924)

Braff DL. Impaired speed of information processing in nonmedicated schizotypal patients. *Schizophrenia Bulletin,* 1981, *7,* 499–508

Braff DL, & Saccuzzo DP. Information processing dysfunction in paranoid schizophrenia: A two-factor deficit. *American Journal of Psychiatry,* 1981, *138,* 1051–1056

Brenner MH. *Mental Illness and the Economy.* Cambridge: Harvard University Press, 1973

Brown GW, & Birley JLT. Crises and life changes and the onset of schizophrenia. *Journal of Health and Social Behavior,* 1968, *9,* 203–214

Brown GW, Birley JLT, & Wing JF. Influence of family life on the course of schizophrenic disorders: A replication. *British Journal of Psychiatry*, 1972, *121*, 241–258

Callaway E, & Naghdi S. An information processing model for schizophrenia. *Archives of General Psychiatry*, 1982, *39*, 399–347

Cancro R. The role of genetic factors in the etiology of schizophrenic disorders. In L Grinspoon (Ed.), *Psychiatry 1982: Annual Review*. Washington D.C.: American Psychiatric Press, 1982

Carpenter WT, Strauss JS, & Bartko JJ. Flexible system for the diagnosis of schizophrenia: Report from the WHO international pilot study of schizophrenia. *Science*, 1973, *182*, 1275–1278

Carrol BJ, Curtis GC, & Mendels J. Neuroendocrine regulation in depression I: Limbic system—adrenocortical dysfunction. *Archives of General Psychiatry*, 1976, *33*, 1039–1044

Carrol BJ, Curtis GC, & Mendels J. Neuroendocrine regulation in depression II: Discrimination of depressed from nondepressed patients. *Archives of General Psychiatry*, 1976, *33*, 1051–1058

Chapman J. The early symptoms of schizophrenia. *British Journal of Psychiatry*, 1966, *112*, 225–251

Crow TJ. Molecular pathology of schizophrenia: More than one disease process? *British Medical Journal*, 1980, *280*, 166–168

Davis JM. Dopamine theory of schizophrenia: A two-factor theory. In LC Wynne, RL Cromwell, & S Matthysse (Eds.), *The nature of schizophrenia: New approaches to research and treatment*. New York: Wiley, 1978, pp. 105–115

Dawson ME, & Nuechterlein KH. Electrodermal and other psychophysiological anomalies in the developmental course of schizophrenic disorders. *Schizophrenia Bulletin*, in press

Doane JA, Falloon IRH, Goldstein MJ, & Mintz J. Parental affective style and the treatment of schizophrenic: Predicting course of schizophrenia and social functioning. *Archives of General Psychiatry*, in press, 1984

Doane JA, West KL, Goldstein MJ, Rodnick EH, & Jones JE. Parental communication deviance and affective style: Predictors of subsequent schizophrenia spectrum disorders in vulnerable adolescents. *Archives of General Psychiatry*, 1981, *38*, 679–685

Endicott J, Nee J, Fleiss J, Cohen J, Williams J, Simon R. Diagnostic criteria for schizophrenia: Reliabilities and agreement between systems. *Archives of General Psychiatry*, 1982, *39*, 884–889

Falloon IRH, Boyd JL, McGill CW, Razani J, Mess HB, & Guilderman AM. Family management in the prevention of exacerbations of schizophrenia. *New England Journal of Medicine*, 1982, *306*, 1437–1440

Feighner JP, Robins E, Guze SB, Woodruff R, Winoker G, Munoz R. Diagnostic criteria for use in psychiatric research. *Archives of General Psychiatry*, 1972, *26*, 57–63

Fowles DC. Mechanisms of electrodermal activity. In RI Thompson & MM Patterson (Eds.), *Methods in physiological psychology: Part C. Receptor and effector processes*. New York: Academic Press, 1974, pp. 231–271

Frame CL, & Oltmanns TF. Serial recall by schizophrenic and affective patients during and after psychotic episodes. *Journal of Abnormal Psychology*, 1982, *91*, 311–318

Frith CD. Consciousness, information processing and schizophrenia. *British Journal of Psychiatry*, 1979, *134*, 225–235

Frith CD, Stevens M, Johnstone EC, & Crow TJ. Skin conductance responsivity during acute episodes of schizophrenia as a predictor of symptomatic improvement. *Psychological Medicine*, 1979, *9*, 101–106

Goldstein MJ (Ed.). *New developments in interventions with families of schizophrenics.* San Francisco: Jossey-Bass, 1981

Gottesman II. Schizophrenia and genetics: Where are we? Are you sure? In LC Wynne, RL Cromwell, & S Matthysse, (Eds.), *The nature of schizophrenia: New approaches to research and treatment.* New York: John Wiley, 1978

Gottesman II, & Shields J. A critical review of recent adoption, twin, and family studies of schizophrenia: Behavioral genetics perspectives. *Schizophrenia Bulletin,* 1976, *2,* 360

Grings WW, & Dawson ME. *Emotions and bodily responses.* New York: Academic Press, 1978

Guze SB, Strauss JS, Katz MM, & Kendall RE. Comments on the Blashfield article. *Schizophrenia Bulletin,* 1982, *8,* 6–12

Harvey P, Winters K, Weintraub S, & Neale JM. Distractability in children vulnerable to psychopathology. *Journal of Abnormal Psychology,* 1981, *90,* 298–304

Hasher L, & Zacks RT. Automatic and effortful processses in memory. *Journal of Experimental Psychology: General,* 1979, *108,* 356–388

Hasset J. *A primer of psycophysiology.* San Francisco: Freeman, 1978

Holzman PS, Levy DL, & Proctor LR. The several qualities of attention in schizophrenia. *Journal of Psychiatric Research,* 1978, *14,* 99–110

Iacono WG. Bilateral electrodermal habituation-dishabituation and resting EEG in remitted schizophrenics. *Journal of Nervous and Mental Disorders,* 1982, *170,* 91–101

Kety SS, Rosenthal D, Wender PM, Schulsinger F, & Jacobsen B. Mental illness in the biological and adoptive families of adopted individuals who have become schizophrenic: A preliminary report based upon psychiatric interviews. In A Fieve, D Rosenthal, & M Brill (Eds.), *Genetic research in psychiatry.* Baltimore: Johns Hopkins University Press, 1975

Klerman G. Depressible disorders. In L Grinsporn (ed.) *Psychiatry 1983: Annual Review.* Washington D.C.: American Psychiatric Press, 1983

Kraepelin E, Demertia praecox and paraphrerig (translated by RM Barclay from the 8th edition of *Psychiatrie*—Barth—Leipzig) Edinburgh: Livingstone, 1919

Leff JP, Hirsch SR, Gaind R, Rohde PD, & Stevens BS. Life events and maintenance therapy in schizophrenic relapse, *British Journal of Psychiatry,* 1973 *123,* 659–660

Leff JP, & Wing JK. Trial of maintenance therapy in schizophrenia, *British Medical Journal* 1971, *3,* 599–604

Liberman RP. Assessment of social skills. *Schizophrenia Bulletin.* 1982, *8,* 62–84(a)

Liberman RP. Social factors in schizophrenia. In L. Grinspoon (Ed.), *Psychiatry 1982 Annual Review.* Washington, D.C.: American Psychiatric Press, 1982, pp. 97–111(b)

Liberman RP, Wallace CJ, Vaughn CE, Snyder KS, & Rust C. Social and family factors in the course of schizophrenia. In J Strauss, M Bowers (eds.) *Psychotherapy of Schizophrenia: Current Status and New Directions.* New York: Plenum, 1980

Lidz T, Cornelison A, Carlson D, & Fleck S. Intrafamilial environment of the schizophrenic patient: The transmission of irrationality. *Archives of Neurological Psychiatry,* 1958, *79,* 305–316

Mackay AVP, Bird ED, Iverson LL, Spokes EG, Creese I, & Snyder SM. Dopaminergic abnormalities in postmortem schizophrenic brain. In F Cattabeni, G Racoghi, PF Spare, & E Costa (Eds.), *Long-term effects of neuroleptics.* New York: Raven Press, 1980

Marsella AJ, & Snyder KS. Stress, social supports, and schizophrenic disorders: Toward an interactional model. *Schizophrenia Bulletin,* 1981, *7,* 152–163

McGhie A, & Chapman J. Disorders of attention and perception in early schizophrenia. *British Journal of Medical Psychology*, 1961, *34*, 103–116

Mednick SA, & Schulsinger F. Some premorbid characteristics related to breakdown in children with schizophrenic mothers. In D Rosenthal & S Katy (Eds.), *Transmission of schizophrenia*. New York: Pergamon Press, 1968

Neale JM, & Oltmanns TF *Schizophrenia*. New York: Wiley, 1980.

Nuechterlein KH, Phipps-Yonas S, Driscoll R, & Garmezy N. The role of different components of attention in children vulnerable to schizophrenia. In M.J. Goldstein (Ed.), *Preventive intervention in schizophrenia: Are we ready?* (DHHS Pub. No. [ADM] 82-1111). Washington, D.C.: U.S. Government Printing Office, 1982

Nuechterlein KH. Schizophrenic information-processing deficit: What type or level of processing is disordered? *The Behavioral and Brain Sciences*, 1982, *5*, 609–610

Nuechterlein KH. Signal detection in vigilance tasks and behavioral attributes among offspring of schizophrenic mothers and among hyperactive children. *Journal of Abnormal Psychology*, 1983, *92*, 4–28

Öhman A. Electrodermal activity in schizophrenia: A review. *Biological Psychology*, 1981, *12*, 87–145

Oltmanns TF. Selective attention in schizophrenic and manic psychoses: The effect of distraction on information processing. *Journal of Abnormal Psychology*, 1978, *87*, 212–225

Overall JE, Cobb JC, & Click Jr, MA. The reliability of psychiatric diagnosis based on alternative research criteria. *Journal of Psychiatric Treatment and Evaluation*, 1982, *4*, 209–220

Overall JE, & Hollister LE. Comparative evaluation of research diagnostic criteria for schizophrenia. *Archives of General Psychiatry*, 1979, *36*, 1198–1205

Posner MI. *Chronometric explorations of mind*. Hillsdale, N.J.: Lawrence Erlbaum, 1978

Prange AJ Jr, Wilson IC, Lara PP. Effects of thyrotropin-releasing hormone in depression. *Lancet*, 1972, *2*, 999–1002

Prentky RA, Salzman LF, & Klein RH. Habituation and conditioning of skin conductance responses in children at risk. *Schizophrenia Bulletin*, 1981, *7*, 281–291

Saccuzzo DP, & Braff DL. Early information processing deficit in schizophrenia: New findings using schizophrenic subgroups and manic control subjects. *Archives of General Psychiatry*, 1981, *38*, 175–179

Saccuzzo DP, & Schubert DL. Backward masking as a measure of slow processing in schizophrenia spectrum disorders. *Journal of Abnormal Psychology*, 1981, *90*, 305–312

Schneider K. *Clinical psychopathology*. Translated by MW Hamilton. New York: Grune & Stratton, 1959

Shiffrin RM, & Schneider W. Controlled and automatic human information processing: II. Perceptual learning, automatic attending, and a general theory. *Psychological Review*, 1977, *84*, 127–190

Singer M, & Wynne L. Differentiating characteristics of parents of childhood schizophrenics, childhood neurotics, and young adult schizophrenics. *American Journal of Psychiatry*, 1963, *120*, 234–243

Spitzer RL, Endicott J, & Robins E. Research and Diagnostic Criteria (RDC). *Psychopharmacology Bulletin*, 1975, *11*, 22–24

Spitzer RL, & Endicott J. *Schedule of Affective Disorders and Schizophrenia (SADS)*. New York: Biometrics Research—New York Psychiatric Institute, 1977

Stern RM, Ray WJ, & Davis CM. *Psychophysiological recording*. New York: Oxford University Press, 1980

Strodtbeck F. Husband-wife interaction over revealed differences. *American Sociological Review,* 1951, *16,* 468–473

Taylor CB, Liberman RP, & Agras WS. Treatment evaluation and behavior therapy. In J Lewis & G Usdin (Eds.), *Treatment planning in psychiatry.* Washington, D.C.: American Psychiatric Press, 1982, pp. 151–224

Van Dyke JL, Rosenthal D, & Rasmussen PV. Electrodermal functioning in adopted-away offspring of schizophrenics. *Journal of Psychiatric Research,* 1974, *10,* 199–215

Vaughn CE, & Leff JP. The influence of family and social factors on the course of psychiatric illness: A comparison of schizophrenic and depressed neurotic patients. *British Journal of Psychiatry,* 1976, *129,* 125–137(a)

Vaughn CE, & Leff JP. The measurement of expressed emotion in the families of psychiatric patients. *British Journal of Social Clinical Psychology,* 1976, *15,* 157–165(b)

Vaughn C, Snyder KS, Jones J, Freeman W, Fallom IRH, & Liberman, RP. Family factors in schizophrenic relapse: A replication. *Schizophrenia Bulletin,* 1982, 425–426

Venables PH, & Christie MJ. Electrodermal activity. In I. Martin & P.H. Venables (Eds.), *Technicques in psychophysiology.* New York: Wiley and Sons, 1980, pp. 3–67

Venables PH, & Christie MJ. Mechanisms, instrumentation, recording techniques, and quantification of responses. In WF Prokasy & DC Raskin (Eds.), *Electrodermal activity in psychological research.* New York: Academic Press, 1973, pp. 1–124

Wallace CJ. The assessment of psychotic behavior. In M Hersen & AS Bellack (Eds.), *Behavioral assessment: A practical handbook* (Revised) New York: Pergamon, 1981, pp. 261–305.

Weinberger DR, Bigelow LB, Kleinman JE, Klein ST, Rosenblutt JE, & Wyatt RJ. Cerebral ventricular enlargement in chronic schizophrenia: An association with poor response to treatment. *Archives of General Psychiatry,* 1980, *37,* 11–13

Weinberger DR, Torrey EF, Neophytides AN, & Wyatt RJ. Lateral cerebral ventricular enlargement in chronic schizophrenia. *Archives of General Psychiatry,* 1979, *36,* 735–739

Wing JK. Clinical concepts of schizophrenia. In JK Wing (Ed.), *Schizophrenia: Towards a new synthesis.* London: Academic Press, 1978, pp. 1–30

Wing JK, Birley JLT, Cooper JE, Graham P and Isaacs, A. Reliability of a procedure for measuring and classifying 'Present Psychiatric State'. *British Journal of Psychiatry,* 1967, *113,* 499–515

Wing JK, Cooper JE, & Sartorius N. *Measurement and classification of psychiatric symptoms.* London: Cambridge Univ Press, 1974

Zahn TP, Carpenter WT, & McGlashan TH. Autonomic nervous system activity in acute schizophrenia II. Relationships to short-term prognosis and clinical state. *Archives of General Psychiatry,* 1981, *38,* 260–266

Zubin J, & Spring B. Vulnerability: A new view of schizophrenia. *Journal of Abnormal Psychology,* 1977, *86,* 103–126

Juan E. Mezzich
Robert I. Slayton

2

Assessment and Diagnosis

The complexity of schizophrenia imposes special demands on the assessment and diagnosis of patients experiencing this condition. A proper consideration of this topic must be framed, however, by a review of assessment and diagnosis in general psychopathology.

GENERAL CONCEPTS AND PROCEDURES

Two main themes appear to underlie modern efforts to advance the quality of psychopathological assessment and diagnosis. One is to improve the accuracy of the evaluation in such a way as to optimize the identification and differentiation of mental disorders, and the other is to enhance the comprehensiveness of the diagnostic formulation to accord greater justice to the complexity of the clinical condition.

Improving Evaluation Accuracy

The process of psychopathological evaluation typically includes interviewing the subject as well as available relatives and associates, reviewing documents that contain information obtained into appropriate historical and examination formats, and formulating a diag-

SCHIZOPHRENIA
ISBN 0-8089-1640-8

nostic summary. This is a complex process, which in some cases includes additional elements such as the conduction of formal testing.

In the interest of obtaining reproducible or reliable evaluative judgments (i.e., judgments on which there is agreement among clinicians actually or potentially involved), analyses have been carried out to elucidate the main sources of undesirable variability in the evaluation process (e.g., Ward, Beck, Mendelson, Mock, & Erbaugh, 1962). Two of the major sources of diagnostic unreliability are variability in the process of obtaining clinical information and variability in the process of diagnostic formulation.

Two primary methodological developments have taken place in the past decade, specifically addressed to minimizing undesirable variability in the two sources listed above. These developments are structured clinical interviews and explicit diagnostic criteria.

Generically, structured clinical interviews attempt to decrease variability in the process of obtaining clinical information. They do this by controlling one or more of the following aspects of this process: specifying the items to be investigated, providing definitions or prompts for these items, specifying questions to explore the items of interest, and providing instructions for rating the presence and severity of the items involved.

One of the earliest and most widely known structured clinical interviews is the Present State Examination developed by John Wing and associates at the Institute of Psychiatry in London. It has been used in several international studies on psychodiagnosis, including the U.S.-U.K. Diagnostic Project (Cooper, Kendell, Gurland, Sharpe, Copeland, & Simon, 1972) and the International Pilot Study of Schizophrenia (World Health Organization, 1973). The Present State Examination, in its Ninth Edition (Wing, Cooper, & Sartorius, 1974), has 140 items that attempt to cover current (past month) psychopathological manifestations. The procedure guides the interviewer in the exploration of these items through branching and cut-off points and by providing obligatory and optional probing questions as well as instructions for rating each item on a three-point scale (absent, mild, severe) plus special codes for "not known" and "not applicable." Definitional statements for the items are separately furnished in a glossary.

Another well-known structured clinical interview is the Schedule for Affective Disorders and Schizophrenia (SADS), developed by Endicott and Spitzer (1978) within the framework of the NIMH Collaborative Program on the Psychobiology of Depression. The SADS has two parts, one dealing with the current episode and the other with past psychiatric disturbance. Part 1 deals with the symptomatology

Table 2-1
Suggested Questions and Provided Rating Instructions for an Item from the Manic Syndrome

Unusually energetic, more active than his usual level without expected fatigue
Have you had more energy than usual to do things?
(More than just a return to normal or usual level?)
(Did it seem like too much energy?)
0 No information
1 No different than usual or less energetic
2 Slightly more energetic but of questionable significance
3 Little change in activity level but less fatigued than usual
4 Somewhat more active than usual with little or no fatigue
5 Much more active than usual with little or no fatigue
6 Unusually active all day long with little or no fatigue

of the subject both at its more severe level during the current episode and during the week preceding the evaluation. The items are rated on scales having various numbers of points ranging from three to nine, and many are judgmentally clustered into eight summary scales. Part 1 also assesses the presence or absence of serious impairment in functioning or hospitalization during the week prior to the interview. Part 2 of the SADS explores past psychiatric disturbance in terms of both symptoms and presence or absence of serious impairment in functioning during the most severe period.

The SADS has three versions: (1) a regular one, (2) a lifetime version (which is similar to the regular part 2 except that the time period is not limited to the past and includes any current disturbance), and (3) a version for measuring change (which has a similar symptom set as the regular part 1 and can be used for subsequent evaluations). The schedule provides for a progression of questions, items, and criteria that rule in and rule out specific diagnoses from the Research Diagnostic Criteria, which will be described later. The SADS instructs the interviewer to use all sources of information available and as many general or specific questions as necessary, and provides defined levels of severity for each item. Table 2-1 presents the questions suggested and the rating instructions provided for an item from the manic syndrome.

Rigidly structured interview procedures are exemplified by the National Institute of Mental Health (NIMH) Diagnostic Interview Schedule (DIS) developed by Robins, Helzer, Croughan, and Ratcliff (1981) for use in situations in which it is not feasible to have interviewers with professional training in psychopathology. Its main intended application was the Epidemiological Catchment Area Project sponsored by NIMH to survey for psychiatric disorders in the general population using lay interviewers. The information collected is then processed through computerized algorithms that make diagnostic decisions covering all diagnoses in Feighner and Associates' (1972) diagnostic system and the Research Diagnostic Criteria (Spitzer, Endicott, & Robins, 1978), as well as a group of DSM-III diagnoses (selected from Axes I and II). All diagnoses are first made on a lifetime basis and then their current status is determined. To allow diagnoses to be made by computer, the interview covers each criterion in the form of one or more pre-coded, close-ended questions.

Actual use of the DIS in certain community and primary medical care settings (Ganguli & Saul, 1982) suggests that for several areas of the interview the standard probing provided for laymen is inadequate and that clinical judgment is required in order to probe and code with validity.

A more fundamental limitation of the DIS and, in general, of rigidly structured clinical interviews is that their application does not appear to be feasible in most regular clinical settings, particularly those that involve management of crises and making dispositions of patients. There appears to be, thus, a need for procedures that are clinically feasible and acceptable and at the same time increase rigor in the collection of data. This need has motivated interest in the so-called semi-structured interview procedures. An example of this type of evaluation procedure is the Initial Evaluation Form (Mezzich, Dow, Rich, Costello, & Himmelhoch, 1981), which will be described in more detail later.

The second major methodological development aimed at reducing undesirable variability or unreliability in the diagnostic evaluation process is the development and use of explicit or specific diagnostic criteria. Generically, this procedure involves setting clear, denotative, and objective rules for assigning diagnostic categories to individuals under examination. The clinical information used for making these assignments may have been obtained through unstructured, semi-structured, or rigidly structured interview procedures.

Some of the best known sets of explicit psychiatric diagnostic criteria are those developed by Feighner et al., (1972), the so-called Research Diagnostic Criteria (Spitzer et al., 1978), and those included in Axes I and II of DSM-III (American Psychiatric Association, 1980). These three criteria sets were developed in a sequential line, each building heavily upon the previous one. They will be reviewed later in this article, with a focus on their definitions of schizophrenia.

Enhancing Diagnostic Thoroughness

The second primary theme underlying current diagnostic work involves the attempt to make more comprehensive and thorough descriptions of the clinical condition, which is reflected most clearly in the multiaxial diagnostic model. This model consists of the systematic formulation of the patient's condition and its etiological and associated factors in terms of several variables, aspects, or axes that are thought to have high clinical information value and are conceptualized and rated as quasi-independent of each other. The word multiaxial has become the prevalent characterizing term, although it is somewhat confusing given its multidimensional connotation. Individual axes may be either categorical or dimensional (quantitative), and, in fact, most of the proposals reported in the literature have a mixed categorical and dimensional structure (Mezzich, 1979, 1980).

To better understand the possibilities and problems encompassed by the multiaxial model, it seems appropriate to review next its historical roots, specific multiaxial systems proposed in the literature, and some important trends and issues.

Historical Context of Multiaxial Diagnosis

Although the impact of multiaxial diagnosis is relatively recent, its origins are not. The contrast between the multiaxial and the conventional uniaxial diagnostic system may perhaps be traced to the old nosological controversy reviewed by Kendell (1975, p. 60) between, on the one hand, the idealized and abstract Platonic disease entity and, on the other, the more clinical, and therefore closer-to-the-patient, Hippocratic approach.

This contrast was revived early in this century by the argument between Kraepelin, who thoroughly endorsed the disease entity model, and Hoche, who proposed the separation of syndrome and etiology in the diagnostic formulation. Kraepelin's position prevailed and nothing much was heard about this issue until 1947 when Essen-Möller and Wohlfahrt suggested the amendment of the official Swedish classification of mental disorders separating syndrome and etiology.

Increased interest in multiaxial models for psychiatric diagnosis was then prompted by various symposia on the classification of mental disorders sponsored by the World Health Organization and by the American Psychopathological Association. These symposia reviewed a number of fundamental methodological issues in diagnosis and also some germinal multiaxial ideas (e.g., Rutter, Lebovici, Eisenberg, Sneznevskij, Sadoun, Brooke, & Lin, 1969; Stengel, 1959; Zubin, 1961). More recently, in some way building upon the diagnostic separation of syndrome and etiology put forward by Essen-Möller and Wohlfahrt (1947) and Essen-Möller (1961, 1971), a number of multiaxial models have been proposed in various parts of the world, including England (Rutter, Shaffer, & Shepherd, 1975; Wing, 1970), Germany (Helmchen, 1975; von Cranach, 1977), Japan (Kato, 1977), Sweden (Ottosson & Perris, 1973), and the United States of America (American Psychiatric Association, 1980; Strauss, 1975). Additionally attesting to the significance of the multiaxial model is the incorporation of a transitional form of it in the new U.S. *Diagnostic and Statistical Manual of Mental Disorders (DSM-III),* as well as its serious consideration for possible implementation in the future Tenth Revision of the International Classification of Diseases.

A Synopsis of Proposed Multiaxial Diagnostic Systems

An examination of the international psychiatric literature and reports presented at major professional meetings yields nine representative proposals for multiaxial psychiatric diagnostic systems. These systems are outlined in Table 2-2 in order to highlight conceptual and structural trends and issues, which will be discussed in the following subsection of this article. The axes and subaxes included in these systems are listed with the actual order numbers and wordings used by the respective authors. The years appearing after the authors' names indicate the representative publications or reports containing the various versions (if several) of the proposed system. In each case, the system outlined corresponds to the most recent publication.

The first formal model for multiaxial psychiatric diagnosis was proposed by Essen-Möller and Wohlfahrt (1947) as a suggestion for the amendment of the official Swedish classification of mental disorders. Later, Essen-Möller (1961, 1971) elaborated on the original separation of syndrome and etiology by subdividing the former into specified syndrome and gross syndrome.

Wing (1970), from the Institute of Psychiatry in London, reported on a tetraxial diagnostic system that included cause (organic or psychological), psychiatric condition, mental subnormality (severity level coded in addition to "intelligence quotient"), and additional physical illness or handicap. This system has been implemented in the Camberwell psychiatric case register.

Ottosson and Perris (1973), from the psychiatry departments of the Universities of Göteborg and Umeå, respectively, proposed a tetraxial system. This system appears to be a significant elaboration on Essen-Möller's proposal. It separated "severity" as an independent axis and added an axis on "course." A number of papers have appeared more recently reporting experience with a slightly modified version of this multiaxial system (e.g., von Knorring, Perris, & Jacobsson, 1978).

Helmchen (1975), from the Frei Universtät in Berlin, building on experience gained by using Essen-Möller's (1961) proposal and Zeh's (1962) suggestions, has developed a pentaxial diagnostic system that includes symptomatology, etiology, time frame, intensity, and certainty of ratings on axes. It is noteworthy that etiological factors are classified according to the timing of their psychopathological impact. Also interesting is that the first two axes are further coded according to "intensity," and all of the first three axes according to "certainty," which constitutes an unusual inter-axial arrangement.

Child psychiatrists, probably because of the particular complexity of their field, have long been important contributors to the development of multiaxial diagnostic systems. Rutter, Lebovici, Eisenberg, Sneznevskij, Sadoun, Brooke, and Lin (1969), as participants in the fifth WHO seminar on psychiatric diagnosis, proposed a triaxial classification of childhood mental disorders, which included clinical psychiatric syndrome, intellectual level, and medical condition. Later, the reliability of a tetraxial system developed by adding an axis on abnormal psychosocial situations was evaluated by Rutter, Shaffer, and Shepherd (1975). The most recent version of this classification has five axes, obtained by removing "specific delays in development" from "clinical psychiatric syndrome" in order to constitute a separate second axis (Rutter, Shaffer, & Sturge, 1975).

There were some relatively early American suggestions for a multiaxial conceptualization of psychiatric nosology (e.g., Ziskind, 1965) More recently, Strauss (1975) proposed the first systematic and comprehensive multiaxial model generated in the U.S.A. It includes axes dealing with symptoms, duration and course of symptoms, associated factors, personal relationships, and work functioning. The last two axes, which cover the area of social functioning, represent a distinct innovation in the history of multiaxial systems.

The American Psychiatric Association (1980) recently published the third edition of the *Diagnostic and Statistical Manual of Mental Disorders.* Major characteristics of DSM-III are the use of operational or explicit criteria for assigning patients to diagnostic categories and the implementation of a multiaxial framework. The latter includes the following five axes: clinical psychiatric syndrome, which is not a purely symptomatological axis as it has some categories rated according to either severity, periodicity, or chronicity; personality disorders for adults and specific developmental delays for children and adolescents; non-mental medical or physical disorders; severity of psycho-

Table 2-2
A Synopsis of Multiaxial Psychiatric Diagnostic Systems

Type of Axes	Essen-Möller and Wohlfahrt (1947) Essen-Möller (1961, 1971)	Wing (1970)	Ottosson & Perris (1973) von Knorring et al (1977)
Phenomenology	Syndrome Specific syndrome Gross syndrome Psychosis Neurosis Habitual abnormality (personality disorder, mental retardation)	Psychiatric condition Mental subnormality (I.Q. also coded)	Symptomatology
Etiological or Associated Factors	Etiology Classic somatic diseases Additional items Hereditary taint Situational stress Postpsychotic Cryptogenic	Cause (organic or psychological) Additional physical illness or handicap	Etiopathogenesis Somatogenic Histogenic Chemogenic Hereditary Psychogenic Sociogenic Characterological Multifactorial Cryptogenic
Time Frame			Course Episodic Periodic, same disorder

			Periodic, different disorder Chronic stable Chronic progressive
Social Functioning			
Other			Severity Healthy Nonpsychotic Psychotic Occasionally psychotic
Type of Axes	Helmchen (1975)	Rutter et al. (1975b)	Strauss (1975)
Phenomenology	Symptomatology	Psychiatric syndrome Specific delays in development Intellectual level	Symptoms
Etiological or Associated Factors	Etiology Disposition Precipitation Fixation	Medical conditions Abnormal psychosocial situations	Associated factors Physical illness Drug-alcohol abuse Environment stresses
Time Frame	Time Onset age Onset speed Duration Course		Duration and course of symptoms Duration Long term Moderate duration Recent onset

(continued)

Table 2-2 (continued)

			Course Remittent Fluctuating Continuous
Social Functioning			Personal relations (5-point scale) Work functioning (5-point scale)
Other	Intensity (of Axes I and II) Certainty (of Axes I, II, and III)		
Type of Axes	DSM-III, APA (1980)	Kato (1977)	von Cranach (1977)
Phenomenology	Clinical psychiatric syndrome (some categories sub-classified according to duration, course, and severity) Personality disorder (adults) or specific		Symptomatology Personality disorder

	developmental disorder (children)		
Etiological or Associated Factors	Physical disorder Psychosocial stressors severity (7-point scale)		Etiology Biological Psychosocial
Time Frame			Acuity of episodes Course of illness Episodic Intermittent First episode Chronic
Social Functioning	Highest level of functioning in past year (7-point scale)		
Other		Illness (medically evaluated) Illness (culturally evaluated)	

Modified from Mezzich, JE Patterns and issues in multiaxial psychiatric diagnosis. *Psychol Med, 9:*128–129, 1979 With permission.

social stressors; and highest level of adaptive functioning in the past year.

Kato (1977), from the Japanese National Institute of Mental Health, proposed an interesting system based mainly on two axes, "illness" (medically evaluated) and "caseness" (culturally evaluated). Additionally, he endorsed the appropriateness of considering axes on symptomatology, etiology, intelligence level, and personality, but did not elaborate on them.

Von Cranach (1977) has reported on a multiaxial model developed and used in the psychiatry department of Universität München, West Germany. This model includes five axes including symptomatology, acuity of episode, course of illness, etiology (divided into biological and psychosocial), and personality disorder.

Trends and Issues in the Conceptualization of Axial Content

As indicated in Table 2-2, the axes considered in the various systems proposed in several parts of the world and briefly described in the above section could be grouped according to their content into the following major types or themes:

1. Phenomenology, which includes symptomatology, personality disorder, and intellectual functioning.
2. Etiological or associated factors, which include axes on biological and psychosocial factors conceptualized and organized in various ways. Causation may include predisposing, precipitating, and maintaining factors.
3. Time frame, which includes axes dealing with onset, duration, and course of psychopathology.
4. Social functioning, which includes axes dealing with work performance, interpersonal relations, and other aspects of adaptive functioning.
5. Other, including psychopathological severity and certainty, and the "illness" versus "caseness" contrast. It should be noted that some axes, such as "certainty," have a "moderator" meaning, rather than being conceptually independent axes.

In regard to the frequency with which specific axes are included in the various proposals, almost universal consensus (Kato's 1977 special system being the exception) can be noted on the inclusion of symptomatology or syndrome and etiological or associated factors. The latter always included biological and psychosocial factors (as separate axes in Rutter et al., 1975; and DSM-III).

Four multiaxial systems (Helmchen, 1975; Ottosson & Perris, 1973; Strauss, 1975; von Cranach, 1977) deal with "time frame of psychopathology" through axes such as "duration" and "course." A fifth system (DSM-III) uses within its Axis I (Clinical psychiatric syndrome) "duration," for additionally rating schizophrenic disorders, and "course," for alcohol and other drug use disorders.

"Personality disorder" is included as a pure axis in two systems (DSM-III; von Cranach, 1977) and as a subdivision of the symptomatology axis in the original Ottosson and Perris (1973) proposal. It is additionally combined with psychopathological severity in Essen-Möller's (1961) proposal.

"Intellectual level" or "mental subnormality" are included in two multiaxial systems (Rutter et al., 1975; Wing, 1970).

"Social or adaptive functioning" is considered in two proposals. This concept is implemented as a single axis in DSM-III, and is divided into two axes (personal relationships and work functioning) in Strauss' (1975) system.

"Severity" is considered in two systems (Helmchen, 1975; Ottosson & Perris, 1973). It is a clearly separated axis and specifically refers to psychopathology (more particularly, to degree of psychoticism) in the Ottosson and Perris system, and is used to further rate both axes I (symptomatology) and II (etiology) in Helmchen's model. Additionally, psychopathological "severity" is combined with "habitual condition" in Essen-Möller's (1961) "gross syndrome," and is used in DSM-III to further characterize affective disorders and child conduct disorders contained in Axis I (Clinical psychiatric syndrome).

Axes included in just one multiaxial proposal are Helmchen's (1975) "certainty" (used to further rate axes I, symptomatology, II, etiology, and III, time frame), and Kato's (1977) "illness" and "caseness."

The innovation in the structure of psychiatric diagnosis represented by the multiaxial model has opened the door to the proposal of new clinical aspects or axes as additions to or modifications of those formulated above. Examples of such other axes are "family relationships" (Strauss, 1975) and "interaction with other individuals and groups," which, together with "work functioning" and "functioning in family," attempt to cover the social functioning area (Mezzich, Keener, Kraemer, & Worthington, 1978). The advantages of these proposals have to be assessed in light of the issues of manageability or the number of axes and the need for axial evaluation.

The fulfillment of the potential of the multiaxial approach to improve reliability and validity might be facilitated if new axes were to be formulated in a way that is clear and explicit, as well as conceptually distinct and differentiable from others. The following specific problems can be identified in regard to the conceptualization of axial content.

Unclear axial definition. This may be caused by difficulties in neatly conceptualizing a given axis ("psychosocial stressors" is a good example of such a difficult axis), and/or in operationally and explicitly defining it, using denotative rather than connotative terms.

Inter-axis overlap. This refers to some mixture of the nature or definitions of two or more axes. Two axes that are particularly vulnerable to such an overlap are "social functioning" and "environmental stressors." For example, "experiencing difficulties at work" may, on the one hand, reflect poor social functioning and, on the other, represent an environmental stressor.

Variable axial role of a given condition. For example, alcoholism may be conceptualized both as an overt psychiatric syndrome and as an etiological factor (Wing, 1970). Another example is personality disturbance, which may be considered under symptomatology, characterogenic etiology, and course (Ottosson & Perris, 1973).

DSM-III

The first edition of the *Diagnostic and Statistical Manual of Mental Disorders* (DSM-I) appeared in 1952, and was prepared by the United States Public Health Service and the American Psychiatric Association, in response to widespread dissatisfaction with the Sixth Edition of the *International Classification of Diseases* (ICD-6). DSM-I replaced the very limited mental illness section of the American Medical Association's *Standard Classified Nomenclature of Disease* and the systems previously devised by the military and the Veterans Administration. Its pervasive use of the term "reaction" to refer to the various diagnostic categories expressed the impact of Adolph Meyer's environmental orientation, and its frequent connotative reference to defense mechanisms reflected the predominance of psychoanalytic ideas at that time.

The second edition of the *Diagnostic and Statistical Manual of Mental Disorders* (DSM-II) was published in 1968 by the American Psychiatric Association. The preparation of DSM-II was guided by an interest in observing its compatibility with the ICD-8 catalog of mental disorders, while defining each disorder for U.S. use. DSM-II attempted to be more descriptive or objective in its designation of mental disorders, as reflected in the elimination of the term "reaction" from its diagnostic labels.

In 1980 the third edition of the *Diagnostic and Statistical Manual of Mental Disorders* (DSM-III), the current U.S. psychiatric diagnostic system, was published by the American Psychiatric Association. The mandate given to the development committee was to prepare a diagnostic system that was more concerned with being consonant with current clinical research and experience than with the contemporary version of the *International Classification of Diseases* (ICD-9). Since its publication, it has attracted considerable interest and, along with a recognition of its limitations, it is being widely judged in this country and abroad as a significant step forward towards a more accurate and thorough characterization of psychiatric patients. Its most important features are the use of explicit or operational criteria for the definition of diagnostic categories and the use of a multiaxial framework. These two features, which represent some of the most important methodological developments in diagnosis in recent years, were discussed earlier in this article.

The multiaxial system in DSM-III includes three typological axes (I. Clinical psychiatric syndromes, II. Personality and specific developmental disorders, and III. Physical disorders) and two dimensional ones (IV. Severity of psychosocial stressors and V. Highest level of adaptive functioning in the past year). A patient is diagnosed in a typological axis through the use of qualitatively distinct categories; while in a dimensional axis the patient is described by the indication of his or her standing on an interval or rank scale.

Axis I: Clinical Psychiatric Syndromes

Axis I of DSM-III comprises the catalog of mental disorders (other than personality and specific developmental disorders) and related conditions. Most of the these disorders have explicit diagnostic criteria, one of the landmarks of DSM-III.

Organic mental disorders are divided into two parts. One part includes two broad categories with specified etiology or pathophysiology; that is, dementias arising in the senium and presenium and substance-induced organic mental disorders. The second part corresponds to organic mental disorders described in terms of behavioral syndromes, the etiology or pathophysiology of which is either noted under Axis III (Physical disorders) or is unknown.

Substance use disorders cover both alcohol and other drugs. They are essentially classified as either abuse or dependence (the latter differentially characterized by manifestations of tolerance or withdrawal, or both). Drug use syndromes newly considered in DSM-III (in contrast with DSM-II) are phencyclidine (PCP) abuse and tobacco dependence.

The schizophrenic disorders have a tightened description in comparison to that in DSM-II, including the requirement of a six-month chronicity. The "simple" subtype of DSM-II was deleted and schizoaffective disorders are placed outside the schizophrenic category.

"Psychotic disorders not elsewhere classified" is a new, broad, and interesting category. It includes schizophreniform disorder, which has all the cross-sectional features of schizophrenia, but a chronicity of more than two weeks and less than six months; brief reactive psychosis, which appears immediately following a recognizable psychosocial stressor; schizoaffective disorder, which does not have explicit diagnostic criteria and is used whenever a differentiation between affective disorder and either schizophrenic or schizophreniform disorder is not possible; and atypical psychosis, which encompasses two main meanings: a psychosis not fitting the definitions of the psychotic disorders specified elsewhere, or a psychosis left unspecified because of inadequate information at the time of the evaluation.

The section on affective disorders constitutes one of the most significant innovations in DSM-III. First, major affective disorders are divided principally into bipolar disorder (manic, depressed with a history of mania, or mixed) and major depression (which has a very encompassing definition and prevails over concomitant neurotic syndromes of various kinds). Other specific affective disorders (cyclothymic and dysthymic disorders) represent milder and chronic affective conditions. Atypical bipolar and depressive disorders represent unspecified or residual categories.

Axis II: Personality and Specific Developmental Disorders

This axis tends to represent stable behavioral handicaps. It seems, however, that to do justice to this conceptualization it should also include mental retardation.

Personality disorders in DSM-III covers most of the characteriologic conditions of DSM-II. Exceptions are the additions of schizotypal, avoidant, narcissistic, and borderline personality disorders, and the transfer of cyclothymic and explosive personality disorders to Axis I.

Specific development disorders represent an innovation in DSM-III, reflecting the axis on developmental delays from the multiaxial system for child psychopathology developed by Rutter et al. (1975) under the sponsorship of the World Health Organization.

Axis III: Physical Disorders

Axis III includes any current physical disorders or conditions relevant to the understanding or management of the individual. Such conditions are catalogued in the non-mental disorder sections of the International Classification of Diseases (ICD-9-CM) (United States National Center for Health Statistics, 1978).

Axis IV: Psychosocial Stressors

Axis IV assesses psychosocial stressors judged to have been significant contributors to the development or exacerbation of the current disorder. First, specific psychosocial stressors (e.g., death of sister) are to be identified and listed in order of importance. Then, the overall stressor severity is rated on a 7-point scale from 1 = none to 7 = Catastrophic.

Axis V: Highest Level of Adaptive Functioning in the Past Year

Axis V assesses an individual's highest level of adaptive functioning (for at least a few months) during the past year. Adaptive functioning is conceptualized mainly as a composite of social relations (breadth and quality of interpersonal relations with family, friends, and other people) and occupational functioning (consistency and quality of performance as a worker, student, or homemaker). Use of leisure time is considered supplementally. Axis V is rated on a 7-point scale from 1 = superior to 7 = grossly impaired.

A format to facilitate the formulation of DSM-III diagnoses and a description of its use with a large psychiatric population was recently published (Mezzich, Coffman, & Goodpastor, 1982).

THE INITIAL EVALUATION FORM: A SEMI-STRUCTURED EVALUATION APPROACH

Competent clinical evaluation has several competing requirements including adequate data collection and sensitivity to the patient's feelings and needs. Data collection adequacy in turn requires an organized and methodic procedure to ensure coverage of important information and generalizability of ratings, as well as skillful probing to ensure meaningfulness in the data obtained. The various structured interview procedures mentioned earlier (i.e., the Present State Examination, the Schedule for Affective Disorders and Schizophrenia, and the Diagnostic Interview Schedule) are quite pertinent to ensuring rigor in data collection. However, as Spitzer, Skodol, Williams, Gibbon, and Kass (1982) indicate after reviewing their experience in supervising intake evaluations, these instruments are "all too highly structured and limited in their coverage of personality disturbance and other areas of psychopathology to be used in an initial clinical contact with a patient. There is clearly a need for a flexible and comprehensive interview guide that will help clinicians doing intake evaluations to make accurate DSM-III diagnoses without interfering with developing therapeutic relationships."

The Initial Evaluation Form (IEF) is a semi-structured evaluation procedure that is to be used by well-educated clinicians and is addressed to obtaining a diagnostic formulation covering all disorders and axes of DSM-III. Its first version was completed in 1980 (Mezzich, Dow, Rich, Costello, & Himmelhoch, 1981). Since then it has been implemented as the first component of the clinical information system (Mezzich, Dow, & Coffman, 1981) of the Western Psychiatric Institute and Clinic (WPIC), a comprehensive university psychiatric facility providing care to child, adolescent, adult, and geriatric patients. On the basis of two years of experience using the IEF with all new patients presenting for care at WPIC, the form was revised in 1982. This version will be highlighted later in this section.

Approach

The IEF represents a semi-structured evaluation approach that increases rigor in data collection and yet is feasible and manageable in regular clinical settings. As such, this approach differs from traditional free-format interviews in that most aspects of the information to be obtained (e.g., item set, time frame, severity scale, etc.) are specified. It differs from rigidly structured interviews in that it makes use of the skills of well-trained clinicians to decide and articulate the sequence of the interview, depth of probing, attention to the patient's feelings and needs, etc.

This procedure recognized the importance of the phenomenological attitude for the elucidation of psychopathology—not the expedient and superficial phenomenology of some contemporary trends in descriptive psychiatry, but the phenomenology of "being with the patient." In the words of Jaspers (1963), psychopathological description requires intimate awareness of the inner world of patients; that is, becoming familiar with the patient's subjective experience through both language-oriented cognitive processes and empathetic communication. Carpenter, Strauss, and Bartko (1981) point out that the scientific foundation of psychiatry rests on clinical observation, and that the failure of clinical research methods to achieve phenomenological soundness not only leaves the field inadequately informed but is misleading as to the complex nature of disease and treatment. In line with the above, the IEF procedure considers the patient-clinician relationship to be every bit as important as the gathering of data necessary to formulate diagnoses. Indeed, if the patient feels that the clinician is more interested in completing a data form than in listening to his or her individual problems, the data base is likely to be inaccurate.

Another important feature of the IEF approach is its use of all available sources of information, i.e., not only the patient himself, but also relatives and associates, past clinical records, educational and legal reports, etc. If the patient has been referred by another professional, that person should be contacted and the reason for referral and the patient's previous history should be obtained. The clinician is then expected to exercise professional judgment in weighting conflicting information obtained from the various sources and the examination of the patient, and to then make clinical ratings on the basis of their comparative clarity, consistency, and credibility.

Format

The basic format of the IEF involves narrative and standardized components that complement each other. The narrative component allows for flexibility in describing the particularities of the patient's condition in natural language, while the standardized component ensures that key informational items are systematically covered.

The standardized component specifies the list of items to be covered and, through instructions presented on the form and in its Manual, provides item definitions and related instructions and guidelines for presence/severity ratings.

Table 2-3 lists the sections included in the narrative and standardized components of the IEF.

In an attempt to illustrate representative features and sections of the IEF, the standardized Symptom Inventory and the diagnostic summary format will be presented next.

Fig. 2-1 shows the list of items included in the Symptom Inventory, which is used in order to parsimoniously map the psychopathology

Table 2-3
Format of the Initial Evaluation Form (1982 Version)

Narrative Component	Standardized Component
	Demographic information Financial/insurance information
Reasons for referral and evaluation	
History of present illness	Psychiatric history markers
History of other psychiatric disorders	
Mental status observations	Symptom Inventory Cognitive Functioning Inventory
Family history	Family history markers
Personal and social history and current social support system and assets	Personal and social history and social support markers
Medical history and examination	Checklist of current physical problems and presence/absence of positive examination findings
Narrative assessment summary, problem list and recommendations, plans for family members	Confidence in the information obtained
	Diagnostic summary and disposition
Evaluator's signatures	Evaluators' codes and signature dates

A supplemental DSM-III Diagnostic Criteria Checklist plan documents the fulfillment of criteria and subcriteria for Axes I and II diagnoses made.

of the subject. This list includes 64 general items, plus 22 supplementary symptoms for children and adolescents. In the actual IEF, each column of syptoms is located on the right-hand side of the page, and the left-hand side contains space for a narrative description of the patient's symptomatology, complementing and enriching the ratings made on the adjacent items of the Symptom Inventory.

The IEF divides the time frame for assessing each item into three levels: "past," "current episode," and "during interview." The box for "never present" is provided as a rating convenience, to be checked only when the symptom in question is judged to have been absent at all times. If a given item could not be explored or the information obtained was inadequate, then "? = unknown" is used for each specified time frame.

Regarding the "past" time frame, a symptom is rated as "y = present" if it is deemed to have been significantly present either during an episode previous to the current one or during a psychiatric illness that is inactive now.

Regarding the "current episode," each symptom is rated as "absent," "mild," "moderate," or "severe" according to its frequency and intensity as follows:

N. Absent: Symptom essentially absent.
1. Mild: Symptom of slight intensity most of the time or of moderate intensity but rarely present.
2. Moderate: Symptom of moderate intensity and present some of the time.
3. Severe: Symptom of marked intensity some of the time or of moderate intensity but continuously present.
? Unknown: Symptom not explored or data inadequate to make a judgment.

"During interview" is typically a temporal subset of the "current episode," since it refers to what is actually observed or convincingly reported as experienced during the interview.

Symptoms are evaluated, taking into consideration the normal baseline for the individual, as well as what would be expected in the general population (with particular emphasis on social and cultural circumstances). The IEF Manual provides brief definitions and additional rating instructions for each of the 86 items of the Symptom Inventory.

Figure 2-2 displays the IEF diagnostic summary format, which is a multiaxial formulation covering all five axes of DSM-III plus a sixth one on current functioning (at expected occupational role, with family, and with other individuals and groups).

For each of the three typological axes (I. Clinical psychiatric syndromes, II. Personality and specific developmental disorders, and III. Physical disorders), the format provides specific spaces for a main formulation of diagnostic terms and codes for alternatives to be ruled out. Several slots are provided in each axis for listing disorders in order of priority for evaluation and care. The coding of each standard diagnostic category includes fields for a five-digit code plus an optional field and code that were developed to identify the category as a "principal" and/or a "provisional" diagnosis. As specified in DSM-III, the first diagnosis in Axis I is assumed to be the "principal" diagnosis unless the first diagnosis in Axis II is qualified as such. Each of the disorders listed in the main formulation sections of Axes I through III can be qualified as "provisional." Axes I and II disorders, diagnosed according to specified DSM-III criteria and terminology, are coded using DSM-III codes consistent with the current International Clas-

	NEVER PRESENT	PAST N=Absent Y=Present ?=Unknown	CURRENT EPISODE N=Absent 1=Mild 2=Moderate 3=Severe ?=Unknown	DURING INTERVIEW Y=Observed or reported as present
1 HYPOSOMNIA difficulty falling or staying asleep, and/or early morning awakening	☐	N Y ?	N 1 2 3 ?	Y
2 HYPERSOMNIA excessive amount of sleep	☐	N Y ?	N 1 2 3 ?	Y
3 APPETITE DECREASED and food refusal	☐	N Y ?	N 1 2 3 ?	Y
4 APPETITE INCREASED	☐	N Y ?	N 1 2 3 ?	Y
5 WEIGHT DECREASED	☐	N Y ?	N 1 2 3 ?	Y
6 WEIGHT INCREASED	☐	N Y ?	N 1 2 3 ?	Y
7 DECREASED LIBIDO lack of sexual interest or activity	☐	N Y ?	N 1 2 3 ?	Y
8 INCREASED LIBIDO	☐	N Y ?	N 1 2 3 ?	Y
9 DISTURBED SEXUAL PERFORMANCE impotence, inhibited orgasm, premature ejaculation, dyspareunia	☐	N Y ?	N 1 2 3 ?	Y
10 ABNORMAL SEXUAL OBJECT OR SITUATION paraphilias	☐	N Y ?	N 1 2 3 ?	Y
11 SEXUAL IDENTITY PROBLEMS	☐	N Y ?	N 1 2 3 ?	Y
12 ALCOHOL USE of concern to individual or significant other	☐	N Y ?	N 1 2 3 ?	Y
13 USE OF OTHER C N S DEPRESSANTS barbiturates, other	☐	N Y ?	N 1 2 3 ?	Y

	NEVER PRESENT	PAST N=Absent Y=Present ?=Unknown	CURRENT EPISODE N=Absent 1=Mild 2=Moderate 3=Severe ?=Unknown	DURING INTERVIEW Y=Observed or reported as present
27 DECREASED MOTOR ACTIVITY	☐	N Y ?	N 1 2 3 ?	Y
28 INCREASED MOTOR ACTIVITY restlessness, agitation	☐	N Y ?	N 1 2 3 ?	Y
29 SOCIAL WITHDRAWAL lack of spontaneous interaction, seclusiveness	☐	N Y ?	N 1 2 3 ?	Y
30 SELF-NEGLECT lack of attention to cleanliness and clothing	☐	N Y ?	N 1 2 3 ?	Y
31 BIZARRE BEHAVIOR idiosyncratic appearance and conduct, mannerisms and posturing	☐	N Y ?	N 1 2 3 ?	Y
32 HOSTILITY belligerence, unco-operativeness	☐	N Y ?	N 1 2 3 ?	Y
33 DISSOCIATIVE SYMP-TOMS narrowing of consciousness	☐	N Y ?	N 1 2 3 ?	Y
34 CONVERSION SYMP-TOMS functional paralysis, anesthesia, seizures, etc	☐	N Y ?	N 1 2 3 ?	Y
35 SLOWED SPEECH AND THOUGHT	☐	N Y ?	N 1 2 3 ?	Y
36 SPEECH PRESSURE OR FLIGHT OF IDEAS speech rapidity and	☐	N Y ?	N 1 2 3 ?	Y

	hypnotics, minor tranquilizers			
14	USE OF OTHER DRUGS stimulants, narcotic analgesics, marijuana, hallucinogens, cocaine	☐	N Y ?	N 1 2 3 ?	Y
15	VIOLENT BEHAVIOR forceful aggressiveness, assaultiveness, destructiveness	☐	N Y ?	N 1 2 3 ?	Y
16	IMPULSIVITY poor impulse control	☐	N Y ?	N 1 2 3 ?	Y
17	OTHER ANTISOCIAL BEHAVIOR cheating, stealing, irresponsibility, lying	☐	N Y ?	N 1 2 3 ?	Y
18	HYPERSENSITIVITY TO CRITICISM or rejection	☐	N Y ?	N 1 2 3 ?	Y
19	EMOTIONAL DISTANCE OR COLDNESS limited capacity to form social relationships	☐	N Y ?	N 1 2 3 ?	Y
20	ECCENTRICITY oddities in thinking, perception, speech, and behavior	☐	N Y ?	N 1 2 3 ?	Y
21	OVERLY DRAMATIC BEHAVIOR attention-seeking and intensely expressed reactive behavior	☐	N Y ?	N 1 2 3 ?	Y
22	SELF CENTEREDNESS grandiose sense and fantasies of self-importance and entitlement	☐	N Y ?	N 1 2 3 ?	Y
23	UNSTABLE AND INTENSE RELATIONSHIPS	☐	N Y ?	N 1 2 3 ?	Y
24	UNDUE DEPENDENCE ON OTHERS allowing others to assume responsibility for self	☐	N Y ?	N 1 2 3 ?	Y
25	UNDUE PERFECTIONISM overconcern with details and work, demandingness	☐	N Y ?	N 1 2 3 ?	Y
26	INTENTIONAL INEFFECTIVENESS indirect resistance to demands for performance	☐	N Y ?	N 1 2 3 ?	Y

	dominance, or abrupt topic changes based on understandable associations, distracting stimuli or word plays				
37	THOUGHT PROCESS DISORGANIZATION loose associations, incoherence, blocking	☐	N Y ?	N 1 2 3 ?	Y
38	GENERAL ANXIETY motor tension, autonomic hyperactivity, apprehensive expectation and scanning	☐	N Y ?	N 1 2 3 ?	Y
39	PANIC ATTACKS discrete periods of sudden onset of intense apprehension or terror with autonomic symptoms	☐	N Y ?	N 1 2 3 ?	Y
40	SITUATIONAL ANXIETY OR PHOBIAS persistent, irrational fear of an object or situation	☐	N Y ?	N 1 2 3 ?	Y
41	DEPRESSED MOOD sadness, dejection, crying	☐	N Y ?	N 1 2 3 ?	Y
42	LOW SELF-ESTEEM	☐	N Y ?	N 1 2 3 ?	Y
43	LABILITY OF MOOD repeated, rapid shifts in mood	☐	N Y ?	N 1 2 3 ?	Y
44	ELATED MOOD euphoria, excitement, expansiveness	☐	N Y ?	N 1 2 3 ?	Y
45	FLAT or INCONGRUOUS AFFECT inappropriate for content of speech	☐	N Y ?	N 1 2 3 ?	Y

Fig. 2-1 (continued)

	NEVER PRESENT	PAST N Absent Y Present ? Unknown	CURRENT EPISODE N Absent 1 Mild 2 Moderate 3 Severe ? Unknown	DURING INTERVIEW Y Observed or reported as present
46 SUSPICIOUSNESS feelings that everything is not as it should be, inappropriate interpretiveness, hyper-vigilance, guardedness	☐	N Y ?	N 1 2 3 ?	Y
47 SOMATIC PREOCCUPATION hypochondriasis	☐	N Y ?	N 1 2 3 ?	Y
48 SUICIDAL INDICATORS death wishes, suicide ideas or attempts	☐	N Y ?	N 1 2 3 ?	Y
49 HOMICIDAL IDEATION	☐	N Y ?	N 1 2 3 ?	Y
50 HOMICIDAL BEHAVIOR	☐	N Y ?	N 1 2 3 ?	Y
51 OBSESSIONS AND COMPULSIONS repetitive, intrusive thoughts or behavior experienced against conscious resistance	☐	N Y ?	N 1 2 3 ?	Y
52 DEPERSONALIZATION experiencing self and surroundings as unreal	☐	N Y ?	N 1 2 3 ?	Y
53 SCHNEIDERIAN SYMPTOMS voices arguing or commenting on one's actions or speaking thoughts aloud, somatic passivity, thought withdrawal, insertion or broadcasting, "made" feelings, impulses, or acts, primary delusional perception	☐	N Y ?	N 1 2 3 ?	Y
54 OTHER AUDITORY HALLUCINATIONS	☐	N Y ?	N 1 2 3 ?	Y
55 VISUAL HALLUCINATIONS	☐	N Y ?	N 1 2 3 ?	Y
56 OTHER HALLUCINATIONS smell, taste, touch	☐	N Y ?	N 1 2 3 ?	Y

	NEVER PRESENT	PAST N Absent Y Present ? Unknown	CURRENT EPISODE N Absent 1 Mild 2 Moderate 3 Severe ? Unknown	DURING INTERVIEW Y Observed or reported as present
65 FIRE SETTING	☐	N Y ?	N 1 2 3 ?	Y
66 TRUANCY	☐	N Y ?	N 1 2 3 ?	Y
67 RUNNING AWAY	☐	N Y ?	N 1 2 3 ?	Y
68 DISOBEDIENCE persistent rule breaking, defiance to authority	☐	N Y ?	N 1 2 3 ?	Y
69 TEMPER TANTRUMS screaming, breath-holding attacks	☐	N Y ?	N 1 2 3 ?	Y
70 SCHOOL REFUSAL	☐	N Y ?	N 1 2 3 ?	Y
71 ELECTIVE MUTISM refusal to speak in social situations	☐	N Y ?	N 1 2 3 ?	Y
72 DISTORTION OF BODY IMAGE	☐	N Y ?	N 1 2 3 ?	Y
73 FEAR OF OBESITY	☐	N Y ?	N 1 2 3 ?	Y
74 PICA persistent eating of non-nutritive substances	☐	N Y ?	N 1 2 3 ?	Y
75 TICS involuntary rapid movements or productions of noises or words	☐	N Y ?	N 1 2 3 ?	Y

57	DELUSIONS OF REFERENCE, PERSECUTION, JEALOUSY, OR GRANDIOSITY	□	N Y ?	N 1 2 3 ?	Y
58	DEPRESSIVE DELUSIONS OR HALLUCINATIONS nihilistic or derogatory content	□	N Y ?	N 1 2 3 ?	Y
59	OTHER DELUSIONS	□	N Y ?	N 1 2 3 ?	Y
60	IMPAIRED SENSORIUM AND ORIENTATION to time, place and person	□	N Y ?	N 1 2 3 ?	Y
61	ACQUIRED INTELLECTUAL IMPAIRMENT deficit in memory, calculation, knowledge, judgement	□	N Y ?	N 1 2 3 ?	Y
62	DEVELOPMENTAL INTELLECTUAL DEFICIT	□	N Y ?	N 1 2 3 ?	Y
63	POOR CONCENTRATION poor attention span, distractibility	□	N Y ?	N 1 2 3 ?	Y
64	LACK OF INSIGHT about presence and nature of psychopathology	□	N Y ?	N 1 2 3 ?	Y

76	STUTTERING	□	N Y ?	N 1 2 3 ?	Y
77	ENURESIS	□	N Y ?	N 1 2 3 ?	Y
78	ENCOPRESIS	□	N Y ?	N 1 2 3 ?	Y
79	PARASOMNIAS e.g. sleepwalking, night terrors	□	N Y ?	N 1 2 3 ?	Y
80	AUTISTIC WITHDRAWAL lack of responsiveness to other people	□	N Y ?	N 1 2 3 ?	Y
81	RESISTANCE TO CHANGE IN THE ENVIRONMENT	□	N Y ?	N 1 2 3 ?	Y
82	PECULIAR SPEECH PATTERN pronominal reversal, metaphoric language, echolalia, bizarre rhythm or intonation of speech	□	N Y ?	N 1 2 3 ?	Y
83	SELF-ABUSIVE BEHAVIOR self mutilation, biting or hitting self, head banging	□	N Y ?	N 1 2 3 ?	Y
84	ODDITIES OF MOTOR BEHAVIOR peculiar posturing, peculiar hand or finger movements, abnormal repetitive movements, walking on tiptoe, etc	□	N Y ?	N 1 2 3 ?	Y
85	DELAYED LANGUAGE ACQUISITION difficulty in comprehending or expressing oral language	□	N Y ?	N 1 2 3 ?	Y
86	DIFFICULTY IN ARTICULATION of speech sounds such as r, sh, f, z, l or ch	□	N Y ?	N 1 2 3 ?	Y

Fig. 2-1 List of items included in the Symptom Inventory.

DIAGNOSTIC SUMMARY

I. Clinical psychiatric syndromes *(Instructions and codes on back of pages 6 and 7)*

Main Formulation:	Codes	Alternatives to be ruled out	Codes
1.			
2.			
3.			
4.			

II Personality and specific developmental disorders *(Instructions and codes on back of pages 6 and 7)*

Main Formulation:	Codes	Alternatives to be ruled out	Codes
1.			
2.			

III. Physical Disorders *(Instructions on back of page 7)*

Main Formulation:	Codes	Alternatives to be ruled out	Codes
1.			
2.			
3.			
4.			

IV. Psychosocial stressors *(Instructions on back of this page)*

A. Ranked list:		Codes
	1.	
	2.	
	3.	
	4.	

B. Overall stressor severity:	1 None	2 Minimal	3 Mild	4 Moderate	5 Severe	6 Extreme	7 Catastrophic	0 Unspecified

V. Highest level of adaptive functioning during the past year *(Instructions on back of this page)*

1	2	3	4	5	6	7	0
Superior	Very Good	Good	Fair	Poor	Very Poor	Grossly Impaired	Unspecified

VI. Current functioning: *(Instructions on back of this page)*

	Superior	Adequate	Slightly Impaired	Moderately Impaired	Markedly Impaired	Unspecified
A. Occupational	1	2	3	4	5	0
B. With family	1	2	3	4	5	0
C. With other indiv. & groups	1	2	3	4	5	0

Fig. 2-2 The Initial Evaluation Form diagnostic summary format.

sification of Diseases, 9th Revision, Clinical Modification (ICD-9-CM). The use of coding consistent with ICD-9-CM facilitates compliance with requirements for diagnostic reporting to appropriate government and third party agencies.

For the diagnosis of current physical disorders and conditions in Axis III, the terms and codes used are those contained in the non-mental disorder sections of ICD-9-CM.

For Axis IV (Psychosocial stressors), slots are provided first for specifying and ranking up to four stressors in decreasing order of importance. These are then coded according to broad categories of stress adapted from those mentioned in the DSM-III Manual. The identification of specific stressors is not only useful for preparing a comprehensive treatment plan, it is also a prerequisite to using the scale of matching stressors provided in the manual for rating overall stressor severity. To facilitate the recording (circling) and visual inspection of this rating, the terms and codes for all levels of the scale are arranged in one line on the format.

Similarly, for Axis V (Highest level of adaptive functioning in the past year), all levels of functioning are specified and arranged in one line to facilitate their circling.

Current functioning (Axis VI) is separately rated for occupational functioning, functioning with family, and functioning with other individuals and groups. This axis seems to be quite useful for clinical management, for considerations such as admission decisions (Mezzich, Evanczuk, Mathias, & Coff, 1982).

The IEF Manual, as well as the back of the diagnostic page of the IEF, provides detailed instructions for rating Axes IV, V, and VI, which are in the same line but are more specific than those included in DSM-III.

A supplemental component of the IEF is the DSM-III Diagnostic Criteria Checklist Plan, a procedure that complements the basic semi-structured procedure by documenting the degree to which the patient meets the criteria and sub-criteria for diagnostic categories formulated in Axes I and II of DSM-III. The procedure first involves retrieving a Diagnostic Criteria Checklist (DCC) for each of the specific diagnostic categories listed in the "main formulation" and the "rule-out" sections of Axes I and II, on the diagnostic page of the IEF. Then, on each DCC, the criteria and subcriteria met by the patient are marked by the evaluator. The completed DCC's are then appended to the IEF and become available for professional inspection and computerization.

CLINICAL MANIFESTATIONS OF SCHIZOPHRENIA

The preceding sections of this article have dealt with general concepts and procedures for psychopathological assessment and diagnosis. This section and the following ones will focus specifically on the evaluation of schizophrenia.

The present section briefly reviews some of the most common psychopathological manifestations described among schizophrenic patients. Their relatively high association with schizophrenia does not imply, however, that they are pathognomonic or exclusive for this disorder. The following sections on diagnostic criteria for schizophrenia will use many of these concepts as elements of the assignment rules for this diagnosis.

Clinical manifestations of schizophrenia prominently include certain disturbances in perception, thought content and process, motor behavior, and affect. The main perceptual disturbances in schizophrenia are hallucinations. These are sensory experiences or perceptions without corresponding external stimuli. They can be subdivided into auditory, visual, and smell, taste, and/or touch. Auditory hallucinations are particularly common in schizophrenia, and they can be subdivided into those that are Schneiderian symptoms and those that represent other auditory hallucinations. The three Schneiderian auditory hallucinations are (1) audible thoughts, in which the patient typically hears his thoughts out loud, just after they have occured in his mind; (2) voices arguing, in which the patient hears two or more voices talking or arguing with each other about him; and (3) voices commenting, in which the patient hears one or more voices commenting on his activities as they occur.

The most prominent thought content disturbance in schizophrenia is the delusion. This is defined as a false belief that is firmly held, despite appropriate argumentation to the contrary, and which is not shared by the individual's cultural group. A useful classification of delusions includes the following: (1) Schneiderian delusions or experiences, which represent ego boundary disorders characterized by the experience that mental activities that belong to the self can leave the self and exist without the self; (2) delusions of reference, persecution, and jealousy; (3) delusions of grandiosity, depressive delusions, and other (e.g., fantastic) delusions.

Thought process disturbances of interest here are the following: (1) Incoherence of speech, which includes distorted grammar, answers not to the point, use of grossly pedantic phrases that obscure the general meaning, and lack of logical connection between one part of a sentence and another or between one sentence and the next; (2) loose associations, characterized by totally unexpected switches of topics, with a very weak or no apparent link between them; and, (3) blocking, which involves pauses in conversation, often in mid-sentence, for a few seconds to a minute or so where, upon questioning, the patient reports that his chain of thought was forgotten or his mind "went blank."

Characteristic disturbances of motor behavior include the following: (1) stupor, which involves considerable reduction in spontaneous movements and lack of responsiveness to the environment; (2) mutism, a functional inhibition of speech and vocalization; (3) purposeless excitement, a wild increase in motor behavior not influenced by external stimuli; (4) mannerisms, which usually involve grimacing or tic-like movements; (5) posturing, involving the adoption of bizarre or uncomfortable positions, or a passive, "waxy" flexibility; (6) negativism, an apparently motiveless resistance to instructions or attempts to be moved; (7) echolalia and echopraxie, which involve imitating the examiner's words or movements, respectively; and, (8) stereotyped behavior, which corresponds to repetitive patterns of moving or walking.

Relatively frequent affect disturbances among schizophrenics include the following: (1) flat or blunted affect, involving a considerable reduction in or lack of signs of affective expression (e.g., the voice may be monotonous and the face immobile); and (2) incongruous or inappropriate affect, in which the subject's affect is discordant with the content of his or her speech or ideation.

DSM-III DIAGNOSTIC CRITERIA FOR SCHIZOPHRENIA

As indicated early in this article, one of the important recent developments in diagnostic methodology is the formulation and use of explicit rules for the assignment of diagnostic categories to subjects under examination. In reviewing explicit diagnostic rules for schizophrenia, it appears appropriate to start with those included in DSM-III, the new American diagnostic system and the first national or international one using such criteria (Table 2-4).

DSM-III recognizes four major syndromic subtypes of schizophrenia (disorganized, catatonic, paranoid, and undifferentiated), as well as a residual one. The diagnosis of one of the subtypes is determined by the manifestations that predominate in the clinical picture.

Table 2-4
Criteria for Obtaining a Diagnosis of Schizophrenic Disorder in DSM-III

A. At least one of the following present during a phase of the illness:

Bizarre delusions (content is patently absurd and has *no* possible basis in fact), such as delusions of being controlled, thought broadcasting, thought insertion, or thought withdrawal

Somatic, grandiose, religious, nihilistic, or other delusions without persecutory or jealous content

Delusions with persecutory or jealous content, if accompanied by hallucinations of any type

Auditory hallucinations in which either a voice keeps up a running commentary on the individual's behavior or thoughts, or two or more voices converse with each other

Auditory hallucinations on several occasions with a content of more than one or two words, having no apparent relation to depression or elation; and/or,

Incoherence, marked loosening of associations, markedly illogical thinking, or marked poverty of content of speech, if associated with at least one of the following:

Blunted, flat, or inappropriate affect,
Delusions or hallucinations, and/or
Catatonic or other grossly disorganized behavior.

B. Deterioration from a previous level of functioning, in such areas as work, social relations, and self-care.

C. Duration: Continuous signs of the illness for at least six months at some time during the person's life, with some signs of the illness at present. The six-month period must include an active phase during which there were symptoms from "A", with or without a prodromal or residual phase, as defined below.

Prodromal phase: A clear deterioration in functioning before the active phase of the illness, not due to a disturbance in mood or to a substance use disorder and involving at least *two* of the symptoms noted below.

Residual phase: Persistence, following the active phase of the illness, of at least *two* of the symptoms noted below, not due to a disturbance in mood or to a substance use disorder.

Prodromal or Residual Symptom

Social isolation or withdrawal

Marked impairment in role functioning as wage-earner, student, or homemaker

Markedly peculiar behavior (e.g. collecting garbage, talking to self in public, or hoarding food

Marked impairment in personal hygiene and grooming

Blunted, flat, or inappropriate affect

Digressive, vague, overelaborate, circumstantial, or metaphorical speech

Odd or bizarre ideation, or magical thinking, e.g. superstitiousness, clairvoyance, telepathy, "sixth sense," "others can feel my feelings," overvalued ideas, ideas of reference; and/or,

Unusual perceptual experiences, e.g. recurrent illusions, sensing the presence of a force or person not actually present.

D. The full depressive or manic syndrome (criteria A and B of major depressive or manic episode), if present, developed after any psychotic symptoms, or was brief in duration relative to the duration of the psychotic symptoms in "A".

E. Onset of prodromal or active phase of the illness before age 45.

F. Not due to any organic mental disorder or mental retardation.

The diagnostic criteria for "disorganized type" include: (1) frequent incoherence, (2) absence of systematized delusions, and (3) blunted, inappropriate, or silly affect.

The diagnostic criteria for "catatonic type" involve the predominance of any of the following in the clinical picture: (1) catatonic stupor (marked decrease in reactivity to the environment and/or reduction of spontaneous movements and activity) or mutism; (2) catatonic negativism (an apparently motiveless resistance to all instructions or attempts to be moved); (3) catatonic rigidity (maintenance of a rigid posture against efforts to be moved); (4) catatonic excitement (excited motor activity, apparently purposeless and not influenced by external stimuli); and, (5) catatonic posturing (voluntary assumption of inappropriate or bizarre posture).

The diagnostic criteria for "paranoid type" require that the clinical picture be dominated by one or more of the following: (1) persecutory delusions, (2) grandiose delusions, (3) delusional jealousy, and/or (4) hallucinations with persecutory or grandiose content.

The diagnostic criteria for "undifferentiated type" include the following elements: (1) a type of schizophrenia in which there are prominent delusions, hallucinations, incoherence, or grossly disorganized behavior; but, (2) the schizophrenia does not meet the criteria for any of the previously listed types, or meets the criteria for more than one.

The diagnostic criteria for "residual type" involve the following requirements: (1) a history of at least one previous episode of schizophrenia with prominent psychotic symptoms; (2) a clinical picture without any prominent psychotic symptoms that necessitated evaluation or admission to clinical care; and, (3) continuing evidence of the illness, such as blunted or inappropriate affect, social withdrawal, eccentric behavior, illogical thinking, or loosening of associations.

The characterization of schizophrenic disorders in Axis I of DSM-III is completed by specifying, through a fifth digit in the diagnostic code, the type of course of illness. These types are the following:

Subchronic. The time from the beginning of the illness, during which the individual began to show signs of the illness (including prodromal, active, and residual phases) more or less continuously, is less than two years but at least six months.

Chronic. Same as above, but greater than two years.

Subchronic with Acute Exacerbation. Reemergence of prominent psychotic symptoms in an individual with a subchronic course who has been in the residual phase of the illness.

Chronic with Acute Exacerbation. Reemergence of prominent psychotic symptoms in an individual with a chronic course who has been in the residual phase of the illness.

In Remission. This should be used when an individual with a history of schizophrenia is now free of all signs of the illness (whether or not on medication). The differentiation of "schizophrenia in remission" from "no mental disorder" requires consideration of the period of time since the last period of disturbance, the total duration of the disturbance, and the need for continued evaluation or prophylactic treatment.

ALTERNATIVE DEFINITIONS OF SCHIZOPHRENIA

The DSM-III criteria listed in the preceding section are probably the most important for general clinical use in the United States, but certainly they are not the only criteria available. Others may have equal or greater validity, and the more familiar the interviewer is with them, the greater will be his competence for appraising schizophrenia.

Schneider's First-Rank Symptoms

Eleven "First-Rank Symptoms" (FRS) were described by Schneider (1959), who considered them pathognomonic for schizophrenia. Of note is the fact that Schneider emphasized presenting symptoms instead of duration of illness. Schneider's system has strongly influenced the British Present State Examination (PSE) and the International Classification of Diseases (ICD). As shown below, Schneider's FRS involve a special class of profoundly psychotic experiences. As the FRS are all subjective mental experiences, their assessment requires considerable skill (Mellor, 1970).

Schneider proposed that a patient with one or more of the following symptoms in the presence of a clear sensorium be considered schizophrenic:

1. The patient hears voices speaking his thoughts aloud.
2. The patient experiences himself as the subject whom hallucinatory voices are discussing.
3. The patient hears hallucinated voices describing his activity as it takes place.
4. Somatic passivity—hallucinated somesthetic experiences.
5. Thought insertion—as though thoughts were put in one's mind by an external force.
6. Thought withdrawal—thoughts are being removed from the patient's mind by an outside agent.
7. Thought broadcast—the passive experience of one's thoughts being magically transmitted to others.
8. Affect, impulses, and motor activity experienced as imposed and controlled from outside one's body.
9. Primary delusional percept—a normal perception that immediately acquires a private and special meaning for the patient.

New Haven Schizophrenia Index

Astrachan, Harrow, Adler, Braver, Schwartz, Schwartz, and Tucker, (1972) developed the New Haven Schizophrenia Index. This group abstracted from the literature specific symptoms felt to be best correlated with schizophrenia. They also noted key exclusionary factors. As shown below, they used a scored system, and emphasized that the diagnosis of schizophrenia required the presence of either delusions, hallucinations, or bizarre thinking. Even after revision of their point system to give greater weight to highly discriminating symptoms, the NHSI appears to be the broadest definition of schizophrenia among those reviewed here.

The New Haven Schizophrenia Index includes the following elements:

1. a. Delusions—not specified or other than depressive (2 points); b. Hallucinations—auditory; c. Hallucinations—visual; d. Hallucinations—other (2 points for b, c, or d)
2. a. Bizarre thinking; b. Autism or grossly unrealistic private thoughts; c. Looseness of association, illogical thinking, overinclusion (2 points for a, b, or c); 2. d. Blocking;* e. Concreteness;* f. Derealization; g. Depersonalization (1 point each for f and g)
3. Inappropriate affect (1 point)
4. Confusion (1 point)
5. Paranoid ideation—self-referential thinking, suspiciousness (1 point)
6. Catatonic behavior: 6. a. Excitement; 6. b. Stupor; 6. c. Waxy flexibility; 6. d. Negativism; 6. e. Mutism; 6. f. Echolalia; 6. g. Stereotyped motor activities (1 point for any one of a through g).

Flexible System

In 1973 Carpenter and Strauss developed a "Flexible System" for the diagnosis of schizophrenia, using data and experience from the WHO (1973) International Pilot Study of Schizophrenia. Using patients evaluated with the Present State Examination (PSE) and ICD-based clinical diagnoses, they performed discriminant function analyses to derive 12 symptoms best correlated with a clinical diagnosis of schizophrenia. Five or six symptoms present is the general recommended cut-off for making a schizophrenic diagnosis, but one can be more strict or more lax, depending on the purposes of the diagnostic task (Table 2-5).

Feighner Criteria

Feighner et al. (1972) proposed operational or explicit criteria for schizophrenia as part of a set of diagnostic criteria for various disorders to be used in psychiatric research. This group, based at that time at Washington University in St. Louis, characteristically used, in addi-

---

*Where the 4th point necessary for inclusion in the sample is provided by 2. d. or e., these symptoms are not scored.

Table 2-5
Carpenter & Strauss Flexible System for the Diagnosis of Schizophrenia

Flexible System	Percent of Schizophrenics Correctly Diagnosed and Nonschizophrenics Incorrectly Diagnosed		
	Minimum Number of Symptoms	Schizophrenic	Nonschizophrenic
Restricted affect	4	91	38
Poor insight	5	81	22
Thoughts aloud	6	63	6
Poor rapport	7	39	1
Widespread delusions	8	20	0
Incoherent speech			
Unreliable information			
Bizarre delusions			
Nihilistic delusions			
Absence of early (1–3 hours) awakening			
Absence of depressed facies			
Absence of elation			

tion to symptomatology, early onset and duration of illness, social disability, and exclusion criteria as elements for the diagnosis of schizophrenia. Their criteria seems to be addressed to identifying schizophrenic patients with a poor prognosis. The Feighner criteria appear to have heavily influenced the design of DSM-III criteria for schizophrenic disorder.

The Feighner criteria consider the following items A through C as necessary for the diagnosis of schizophrenia:

A. Both of the following are necessary: 1. A chronic illness with at least 6 months of symptoms before the index evaluation with out return to premorbid level of psychosocial adjustment; 2. Absence of a period of depressive or manic symptoms sufficient to qualify for affective disorder or probable affective disorder.
B. The patient must have had at least 1 of the following: 1. Delusions or hallucinations without significant perplexity or disorientation associated with them; 2. Verbal production that makes communication difficult because of lack of logical or understandable organization (in the presence of muteness, the diagnostic decision must be deferred).
C. At least 3 of the following for definite, 2 for probable:
    1. Single (never married); 2. Poor premorbid social adjustment or work history; 3. Family history of schizophrenia; 4. Absence of alcoholism or drug abuse within 1 year of onset of psychosis; 5. Onset of illness before age 40.

Taylor and Abrams Criteria

These authors modified the Feighner criteria for schizophrenia on the basis of empirical studies. In one of these, Taylor and Abrams (1975) found that out of 89 patients receiving a clinical diagnosis of schizophrenia, only 11 satisfied the Feighner criteria. Their criteria, in contrast to Feighner's, do not consider early onset of illness nor social disability.

According to Taylor and Abrams' criteria, all of the following must be present for a diagnosis of schizophrenia:

A. Duration of episode greater than 6 months.
B. Clear consciousness.
C. Presence of either delusions, hallucinations, or formal thought disorder (verbigeration, non sequitors, word approximations, neologisms, blocking, and derailment).
D. Absence of a broad affect.

E. Absence of signs and symptoms sufficient to make a diagnosis of affective disease.
F. Absence of alcoholism or drug abuse within one year of the index episode.
G. Absence of focal signs and symptoms of coarse brain disease or major medical illness known to produce significant behavioral changes (e.g. thyroid dysfunction, pernicious anemia, porphyria).

Research Diagnostic Criteria

Spitzer, Endicott, and Robins (1978) developed the Research Diagnostic Criteria (RDC) by making changes in the Feighner criteria and expanding the number of psychiatric disorders covered. Their work was part of a collaborative projecct on depressive disorders sponsored by the National Institute of Mental Health. It makes considerable use of Schneider's First Rank Symptoms, requires a duration of illness of a least two weeks, and carefully excludes patients with a pronounced affective component by placing them in a schizoaffective disorder category. Endicott and Spitzer (1978) subsequently developed the schedule for Affective Disorders and Schizophrenia, a structured interview for making RDC diagnoses.

The Research Diagnostic Criteria for schizophrenia require that stipulations A through C be met for the period of illness being considered:

A. At least two of the following are required for definite and one for probable. (If the symptoms occur only during a period of alcohol or drug abuse or withdrawal from them, do not score here.) 1. Thought broadcasting, insertion, or withdrawal; 2. Delusions of being controlled (or influenced), other bizarre delusions, or multiple delusions; 3. Delusions other than persecutory or jealous, lasting at least one week; 4. Delusions of any type if accompanied by hallucinations of any type for at least one week; 5. Auditory hallucinations in which either a voice keeps up a running commentary on the subject's behavior or thoughts as they occur, or two or more voices converse with each other; 6. Nonaffective verbal hallucinations spoken to the subject; 7. Hallucinations of any type throughout the day for several days or intermittently for at least one month; 8. Definite instances of marked formal thought disorder, accompanied by either blunted or inappropriate affect, delusions, or hallucinations of any type, or grossly disorganized behavior.
B. Either 1 or 2: 1. The current period of illness has lasted at least two weeks from the onset of a noticeable change in the subject's

usual condition; 2. The subject has had a previous period of illness lasting at least two weeks, in which he met the criteria and residual signs of the illness have remained, e.g. extreme social withdrawal, blunted or inappropriate affect, formal thought disorder, or unusual thoughts or perceptual experiences.

C. At no time during the active period of illness being considered did the subject meet the criteria for either probable or definite manic or depressive syndrome to such a degree that it was a prominent part of the illness.

Further subtyping of schizophrenia is done by course (Acute, Subacute, Subchronic, Chronic) and clinical phenomenology (Paranoid, Disorganized, Confusional, Catatonic, and Undifferentiated or Mixed).

Table 2-6 presents a comparative view of the diagnostic criteria listed above, plus those of DSM-III, according to the aspects or elements they consider for the diagnosis of schizophrenia. All seven sets of diagnostic criteria included "characteristic" symptoms of schizophrenia, prominent among which were non-affective and bizarre delusions and derailed thought process. Next in frequency, endorsed by five of the seven criterion sets, was the exclusion of affective (manic or depressive) syndromes. Lower frequencies of endorsement were obtained for duration of illness (present in four of the seven criterion sets), deterioration in social functioning (three of seven), and early onset of illness (two of seven). It is also worth noting that the non-syndromic criteria mentioned last above have been considered as separate axes in several recent multiaxial diagnostic systems. For example, social dysfunction is considered as a separate axis in DSM-III (although in regard to highest level in the past year), and more pointedly as current dysfunction in Strauss' (1975) multiaxial system.

Mezzich et al. (1982) recently found that current dysfunction had, among several axes studied, the highest association with hospitalization decisions both for a general psychiatric population and, specifically, for schizophrenic patients, which denotes the relatively broad distribution of social functioning within this diagnostic group. Duration of illness is considered as a separate axis in the multiaxial diagnostic systems developed by Ottosson and Perris (1973) in Scandinavia, Helmchen (1975) in Germany (Berlin), Strauss (1975) in the U.S., and von Cranach (1977) in Germany (Munich). Age at onset of illness is also included within a time frame in Helmchen's (1975) system.

In light of the diversity of diagnostic criteria sets for schizophrenia, some comparative empirical studies have started to appear in the literature. For example, Overall and Hollister (1979) applied several sets of diagnostic criteria to a group of 166 clinically diagnosed

Table 2-6
Comparative View of Several Diagnostic Criteria According to Aspects Considered for the Diagnosis of Schizophrenia

Criteria Sets	Symptoms	Exclusion Criteria	Duration of Illness	Social Disability	Age at Onset
Schneider's First Rank Symptoms	X				
New Haven Schizophrenia Index	X				
Flexible System	X	X			
Feighner Criteria	X	X	X	X	X
Taylor and Abrams Criteria	X	X	X		
Research Diagnostic Criteria	X	X	X	X	
DSM-III	X	X	X	X	X

schizophrenics. They found that the different criteria, whether narrow or broad, defined only partially overlapping groups and that no objective criteria could precisely map the clinical population of schizophrenia. They suggested that the relative merits of each be examined before any one set is accepted as superior to current diagnosis. Some other studies have compared different sets of diagnostic criteria for schizophrenia by using outcome as an external validating criterion (e.g. Brockington, Kendell, & Leff, 1978).

Mention should also be made of the so-called polydiagnostic approach. This refers to the concomitant use of several diagnostic criteria sets (e.g., Freighner, RDC, DSM-III, etc.) when evaluating an individual. This would also allow for the systematic comparison of various criteria sets in terms of their relations to associated events, social functioning, and illness course and treatment (Strauss & Gift, 1977). This should lead to a more considered appraisal of the condition of schizophrenic patients and enhance their clinical management and prognosis.

CONCLUSION

A thoughtful and well-grounded diagnosis of schizophrenia requires a careful and comprehensive assessment of the subject. These points were explicated through our discussions, early in this chapter, on the employment of systematic approaches to interviewing and evaluation and the use of explicit criteria and a multiaxial framework for diagnostic formulation.

In the preceding section, several criterion sets for the diagnosis of schizophrenia were described. Their potential use is not restricted to the above-described polydiagnostic approach, but it can inform a more considerate appraisal of patients with schizophrenic and related conditions. For regular clinical work, however, the most highly recommended criterion set is that contained in DSM-III. This has not only become virtually the standard diagnostic system in the U.S., but is also reviewed and used with considerable interest in other countries around the world.

The tentative status of the DSM-III criteria for schizophrenia is clearly reflected in its requirement of a duration of illness (including prodromal and active phases) of at least six months. If all other clinical features for the diagnosis of schizophrenia are present, but the duration of illness is between six months and two weeks, a new diagnostic category, schizophreniform disorder, is to be used. For a schizophrenic-looking illness lasting less than two weeks, brief reactive psychosis or atypical psychosis is the label to be used.

One of the principal broad diagnostic categories to be considered in the differential diagnosis of schizophrenia is major affective disorder. DSM-III, as well as several alternative diagnostic systems such as the Research Diagnostic Criteria (Spitzer, Endicott, & Robins, 1978) and the Feighner Criteria (Feighner et al., 1972), provide explicit definitions of affective disorders. One controversial concept, widely recognized but variously defined, is the schizoaffective disorder. Boldly revealing our very limited understanding in this area, DSM-III restricts the use of this category to the case in which the clinician is unable to make a reasonable differential diagnosis between affective disorder and either schizophrenia or schizophreniform disorder.

REFERENCES

Amati A, Del Vecchio M, Kemali D, Perris C, & Vacca L. Communicability and reliability of a multiaxial classification model for the description of psychiatric patients. A pilot international study. Submitted for publication, 1977

American Psychiatric Association. Diagnostic and Statistical Manual of Mental Disorders, (3rd ed.). Washington, D.C. 1980

Astrachan BM, Harrow M, Adler D, Brauer L, Schwartz A, Schwartz C, & Tucker GA. A checklist for the diagnosis of schizophrenia. *British Journal of Psychiatry*, 1972, *121*, 529–539

Brockington IF, Kendell RE, & Leff JP. Definitions of schizophrenia: Concordance and prediction of outcome. *Psychological Medicine*, 1978, *8*, 387–398

Carpenter NT, & Strauss JS. Flexible system for the diagnosis of schizophrenia: Report from the WHO international pilot study of schizophrenia. *Science*, 1973, *182*, 1275–1278

Carpenter WT, Strauss JS, & Bartko JJ. Beyond diagnosis: The phenomenology of schizophrenia. *American Journal of Psychiatry*, 1981, *138*, 948–953

Cooper JE, Kendell RE, Gurland BJ, Sharpe L, Copeland JRM, & Simon R. Psychiatric diagnosis in New York and London. London: Oxford University Press, 1972

Endicott J, & Spitzer RL. A diagnostic interview: The schedule for affective disorders and schizophrenia. *Archives of General Psychiatry*, 1978, *35*, 837–844

Essen-Möller E. On classification of mental disorders. *Acta Psychiatrica Scandinavica*, 1961, *37*, 119–126

Essen-Möller E. Suggestions for further improvement of the international classification of mental disorders. *Psychological Medicine*, 1971, *1*, 308–311

Essen-Möller E, & Wohlfahrt S. Suggestions for the amendment of the official Swedish classification of mental disorders. *Acta Psychiatrica Scandinavica Supplement*, 1947, *47*, 551–555

Feighner JP, Robins E, Guze SB, Woodruff RA, Winokur G, & Munoz R. Diagnostic criteria for use in psychiatric research. *Archives of General Psychiatry*, 1972, *26*, 57–63

Ganguli M, & Saul MD. Letter to the Editor. *Archives of General Psychiatry*, 1982, *39*, 1442–1443

Helmchen H. Schizophrenia. Diagnostic concepts in the ICD-8. In MH Lader (Ed.), Studies in schizophrenia. *British Journal of Psychiatry, Special Publication,* 1975, No. *10,* 10–18

Hempel C. *Aspects of scientific explanation.* New York: The Free Press, 1965

Jaspers K. *Genral psychopathology.* Translated by J Hoenig, & MW Hamilton Chicago: University of Chicago Press, 1963

Kato M. Multiaxial diagnosis in adult psychiatry. Paper presented at the VI World Congress of Psychiatry, Honolulu, Hawaii, 1977

Kendell RE. The role of diagnosis in psychiatry. Oxford: Blackwell, 1975

Mellor CS. First rank symptoms of schizophrenia. *British Journal of Psychiatry,* 1970, *117,* 15–23

Mezzich JE. Patterns and issues in multiaxial psychiatric diagnosis. *Psychological Medicine, 1979, 9,* 125–137

Mezzich JE. Multiaxial diagnostic systems in psychiatry. In HI Kaplan, AM Freedman, & BJ Sadock (Eds.), *Comprehensive textbook of psychiatry,* (3rd Ed.) Baltimore: Williams and Wilkins, 1980

Mezzich JE, Coffman GA, & Goodpastor SM. A format for DSM-III diagnostic formulation: Experience with 1,111 consecutive patients. *American Journal of Psychiatry, 1982, 1139,* 591–596

Mezzich JE, Dow JT, & Coffman GA. Developing an efficient clinical information system for a comprehensive psychiatric institute. I. Principles, design, and organization. *Behavior Research Methods and Instrumentation,* 1981, *13,* 459–463

Mezzich JE, Dow JT, Rich CL, Costello AJ, & Himmelhoch JM. Developing an efficient clinical information system for a comprehensive psychiatric institute. II. Initial evaluation form. *Behavior Research Methods and Instrumentation,* 1981, *13,* 464–478

Mezzich JE, Evanczuk KJ, Mathias R, & Coffman GA. Admission decisions and multiaxial diagnosis. Paper presented at the Annual Meeting of the American Psychiatric Association, Toronto, Canada, May, 1982

Mezzich JE, Keener MA, Kraemer HC, & Worthington DRL. *Comparative reliability of three psychiatric diagnostic systems.* Technical Report. Department of Psychiatry and Behavioral Sciences. Stanford University. Stanford, California, 1978

Ottosson JO, & Perris C. Multidimensional classification of mental disorders. *Psychological Medicine,* 1973 *3,* 238–243

Overall JE, & Hollister LE. Comparative evaluation of research diagnostic criteria for schizophrenia. *Archives of General Psychiatry,* 1979, *36,* 1198–1205

Robins LN, Helzer JE, Croughan J, & Ratcliff KS. National Institute of Mental Health Diagnostic Interview Schedule. Its history, characteristics, and validity. *Archives of General Psychiatry,* 1981, *38,* 381–389

Rutter M, Lebovici S, Eisenberg L, Sneznevskij AV, Sadoun R, Brooke E, & Lin TY. A tri-axial classification of mental disorders in childhood. *Journal of Child Psychology and Psychiatry,* 1969, *10,* 41–61

Rutter M, Shaffer D, & Shepherd M. *A multiaxial classification of child psychiatric disorders.* Geneva: World Health Organization, 1975

Rutter M, Shaffer D, & Sturge C. *A guide to a multiaxial classification scheme for psychiatric disorders in childhood and adolescence.* London: Institute of Psychiatry, 1975

Schneider K. *Clinical psychopathology.* Translated by MW Hamilton. New York: Grune & Stratton, 1959

Spitzer RL, Endicott J, & Robins E. Research diagnostic criteria. *Archives of General Psychiatry,* 1978, *35,* 773–782

Spitzer RL, Skodol AE, Williams, JB, Gibbon M, & Kass F. Supervising intake diagnosis: A psychiatric "Rashomon." *Archives of General Psychiatry*, 1982, *39*, 1299–1305

Stengel E. Classification of mental disorders. *Bulletin of W.H.O.*, 1959, *21*, 601–663

Strauss JS. A comprehensive approach to psychiatric diagnosis. *American Journal of Psychiatry*, 1975, *132*,1193–1197

Strauss JS, & Gift TE. Choosing an approach for diagnosing schizophrenia. *Archives of General Psychiatry*, 1977 *34*, 1248–1253

Taylor MA, & Abrams RA. A critique of the St. Louis research criteria for schizophrenia. *American Journal of Psychiatry*, 1975, *132*, 1276–1280

United States Center for Health Statistics. *The International Classification of Diseases, 9th Revision, Clinical Modification* (ICD-9-CM). Ann Arbor, Michigan, 1978

von Cranach M. *Categorical vs multiaxial classification.* Paper presented at the VI World Congress of Psychiatry, Honolulu, Hawaii, 1977

von Knorring L, Perris C & Jacobsson L. A multi-aspects classification of mental disorders. Experiences from clinical routine work and preliminary studies of interrater reliability. *Acta Psychiatrica Scandinavica*, 1978, *58*, 401–412

Ward CH, Beck AT, Mendelson M, Mock JE, & Erbaugh JK. The psychiatric nomenclature: Reasons for diagnostic disagreement. *Archives of Genral Psychiatry*, 1962, *7*, 198–205

Wing JK, Cooper JE, & Sartorius N. *The measurement and classification of psychiatric symptoms.* Cambridge: Cambridge University Press, 1974

Wing L. Observations on the psychiatric section of the international classification of diseases and the british glossary of mental disorders. *Psychological Medicine*, 1970, *1*, 79–85

World Health Organization. *Report of the International Pilot Study of Schizophrenia. Volume 1. Geneva: Arthor, 1973*

Zeh W. Bemerkugen zu einem Klassificationsvorschlag der psychischen Storungen on Erik Essen-Möller, Lund. Nervenarzt, 1962, *33*, 404–410

Ziskind E. Some nosologic concepts related to mental diseases. *Acta Psychiatrica Scandinavica*, 1965, *41*, 303–312

Zubin J. *Field studies in mental disorders.* New York: Grune & Stratton, 1961

Jesse G. Harris, Jr.

3

Prognosis in Schizophrenia

It has been stated in more than one context that what a person will do in the future can best be predicted from what the individual has done in the past. This common sense principle, substantiated by research in the realm of clinical versus statistical prediction, provides a central theme also for prognosis in schizophrenia. Broadly interpreted, the statement implies that a person whose behavior has been well ordered and invariant over a considerable period of time should exhibit a relatively constant pattern of behavior in comparable situations in the future. Conversely, an individual whose behavior has been highly variable over time or whose emotional or thought pattern has been deviant or unstable should present such a pattern in the future.

The principle of continuity of level or style of functioning from past to present to future, although not always so apparent in the observable symptoms of schizophrenia, is found in research literature to underlie the seeming unpredictability of thought, emotion, and behavioral manifestations in the several forms of schizophrenia and its related disorders. Although it has been known for decades that in any physical or psychiatric disorder, some cases improve, some worsen, and some maintain a relatively constant marginal adjustment for a long period of time, the course of the disorder in schizophrenia follows unusual patterns. Persons who have seemed quite intact and by social, educational, or occupational criteria, normal throughout early life, are found to produce rather abruptly, in late adolescence or in early

SCHIZOPHRENIA
ISBN 0-8089-1640-8

or even mid-adulthood, a confusing array of cognitive, emotional and/or behavioral symptoms.

In some cases, such an individual improves dramatically, never to experience another episode; in other cases the individual regresses within a short interval of time to what ultimately proves to be a chronic state. Other individuals decline gradually over a period of many years, beginning usually in the early years of life. Still others maintain a relatively stable adjustment, focusing and refocusing their cognitive processes on either side of an imperceptible schizophrenic boundary line for many years, while participating to an acceptable degree in the daily interpersonal exchanges of their normal counterparts in society.

All human beings change with time, progressively achieving greater or lesser degrees of personal integration and specificity of behavior, and better or poorer harmony in interpersonal relations, eventually growing older and declining. In schizophrenia, however, the changes occur with a direction and momentum, as if controlled by a special internal gear system for going upgrade, down steep, sharply winding curves, across flat plateaus at lowest possible speeds, and in some cases, as if without gears or even a steering wheel. It is the seeming absence of a self-directing system and the substitution of a controlling mechanism of some other kind from within, but external to the self system, that seem to distinguish the schizophrenic patients from many others in the psychiatric setting, and which also make it difficult to assess the effects of external environmental events.

Predicting the outcome of an initial manifestation of schizophrenic symptoms may be one of the more complex intellectual and research undertakings in the entire realm of psychopathology; and yet, it has been shown in many studies that while symptomatology usually tells us relatively little about the course of the disorder, analysis of past adjustment to life circumstances tells us much about the future. Outcome must always be assessed in relation to the baseline from which the decompensation began. A patient who has achieved significant success in several important realms of endeavor in life prior to decompensation is likely to reach a higher level of functioning on recovery than one whose adjustment was marginal prior to the onset of the episode, even though both may show a decrement.

A comprehensive analysis of the topic of prognosis can best be accomplished by consideration of two separate questions: (1) Who in the general population will become schizophrenic?; and (2) Who among those who become schizophrenic can be expected to return to a state of integration that will permit effective functioning in educational, occupational, sexual, and social realms of endeavor?

The first topic is of more recent origin and has developed from sources that go beyond the clinical study of the individual patient. It has evolved as a consequence of: (1) record keeping on a worldwide basis through the establishment of the World Health Organization and the development of an international system of psychiatric diagnostic nomenclature (World Health Organization, 1973), assisted in this country by extensive refinements and improvements in the *Diagnostic and Statistical Manual of Mental Disorders*—currently DSM-III (1980); (2) the recent attempt to develop a statistical empirical approach to the identification of a predisposition to schizophrenia that is now being applied in exploratory studies of both patient populations and the general normal population; (3) the study of schizophrenia in identical twins; (4) the study of families and relatives of schizophrenic patients; and (5) longitudinal analysis of precursors of adult schizophrenia in childhood. The possible biochemical origins of schizophrenia, which can be assessed adequately only through laboratory studies of individual patients, will not be summarized in this discussion of the problem of prognosis.

The second major topic for this presentation has a history originating in the work of Kraepelin (1907, 1919) at the close of the nineteenth century and departs significantly, as it evolves, from the view that dementia praecox is a metabolic disorder that follows a predetermined downhill course.

THE POTENTIAL FOR A SCHIZOPHRENIC DISORDER

Schizophrenia, in any one of its many diagnostically related forms, is found in slightly less than one percent of the population (median value for studies = .0085), the precise value varying with the method of sampling (Zerbin-Rüdin, 1967, 1972), the methods of arriving at diagnostic decisions, the educational background of the psychiatric staffs, the accuracy and completeness of public records, and with the culture and the nation. If fluctuations occur around this $\frac{0.85}{100}$ ratio worldwide, one might wonder whether biological components that override environmental settings or events are somehow involved. This question cannot be answered even tentatively from available statistical data on the incidence or genetic patterns of the disorder, or answered finally, if ever, by anything short of laboratory investigations of a biochemical or physiological nature. But, reference will subsequently be made to the studies of identical and adoptive twins and to the incidence of schizophrenia among relatives of schizophrenic patients.

In the background of contemporary thinking along biological and hereditary lines is Meehl's (1962) theoretical conception of a schizotaxic individual who has a genetically determined neutral defect, which Meehl believes probably involves a dominant gene. Acknowledging the influence of Rado (1956), Meehl considers the schizotaxic individual to be phenotypically a schizotype (i.e., all schizotaxics are schizotypes), and regardless of child-rearing conditions, which may or may not involve features of the "schizophrenogenic" mother, will acquire to varying degrees through a selective learning process the attributes of cognitive slippage, interpersonal aversiveness, anhedonia, and ambivalence. Many of the mothers may themselves be schizotypes. Additional ingredients, involving polygenetically determined constitutional weaknesses, are a lack of physical vigor, which may contribute to submissiveness in interpersonal relations, and a low threshold for anxiety and stress (Meehl, 1962, 1972; Golden & Meehl 1979). As the list of relevant ingredients lengthens, the underlying genetic formula, already somewhat speculative, becomes more clouded but still provides a conceptualization of the origins of schizophrenia that is consonant with the clinical observations of many professionals in the area of mental health. The more favorable the hereditary background and environment, the more likely it is that the individual will progress through successive stages of life as a well compensated schizotype. In all but rare cases that seem destined to become schizophrenic regardless of events, the additional imposition of stresses of sufficient intensity either within or outside the family, or the occurrence of major unexpected events of overwhelming proportions will result in schizophrenic symptomatology as the preferred mode of maladaptive response.

Golden and Meehl (1979) have attempted to establish an empirical basis for Meehl's conception of a schizoid taxon (i.e., the closely related, but not exact, indicator of membership in the class of schizotaxic individuals) using both artificially generated data and data from a patient population. Conceiving of the relationships among the three categories as inclusive (i.e., all schizotaxics are schizotypes, and only some schizotypes become schizophrenic), Golden and Meehl (1979) have calculated the base rate of the schizoid taxon in a nonpsychotic inpatient population as the value .37. Details of the presentation are to be found also in Meehl and Golden (1982).

Although one study of samples of hospitalized schizophrenic and depressive patients by Miller, Streiner, and Kahgee (1982) failed to produce additional confirming evidence for the Golden and Meehl method of identification, a recent doctoral dissertation by Zita (1982)* conducted at the University of Kentucky has found support for the method, in addition to questioning the appropriateness of interpretations based on the samples used by Miller and associates (1982). Zita found that a group of college students drawn from two different geographic locations, when separated into schizoid and nonschizoid subgroups by application of the Golden and Meehl procedure for assigning probability values to each of the items in a seven item MMPI scale, also showed differences in the expected direction on scales for interpersonal aversiveness (Millon, 1977), ambivalence (Raulin, 1978), cognitive slippage (using an instrument for body-image aberration by Chapman, Chapman, & Raulin, 1978), and dominance (Jackson, 1967). Differences were not found, however, on scales for either social or physical anhedonia (Chapman, Chapman, & Raulin, 1976). It should be taken into account that the items from all of these scales were assembled randomly by Zita into a single comprehensive scale. The study by Zita provides support for the theory from data obtained from a normal population, but with a probability value for the base rate of the schizoid taxon in the general population somewhat lower than that reported by Golden and Meehl (1979), specifically a value of .21 instead of .37. The lower value might be expected on the basis of greater vulnerability in the inpatient population. Using the normal population base rate for schizophrenia divided by the population base rate for the schizoid taxon

$$\left(\frac{0.85}{100}\Big/\frac{21}{100} = 4.05 \text{ percent}\right),$$

Zita estimates that approximately "one person in five is at risk for schizophrenia, and of those at risk, only about one in 25 will ultimately manifest schizophrenic symptomatology."

Golden and Meehl, both well stepped in probability theory and in research design and analysis, anticipate the obvious response of incredulity to their presentation of a seven item scale that they believe might serve psychometrically as a basis for identifying an individual as schizotaxic (i.e., carrying the genetic potential for becoming a schizotype, but capable of maintaining a compensated adjustment if stress is not excessive). The seven items pertain generally to lack of contentment of enjoyment in love, sex, or life in general, lack of inde-

*Zita, DF. An exploration of Meehl's theory of schizoid phenomena: An attempt at construct validation. Unpublished doctoral dissertation, University of Kentucky, 1982.

pendence in activities requiring competence, and sensitivity to the opinions or reactions of others in interpersonal relations. Although any one, or several, of the items could be answered in the scorable direction by a relatively well adjusted person, the essential feature is the summation of scorable items after each has been multiplied by a fraction, indicating the probability of the answer being made by a member of the schizotaxic or of the normal group.

Clearly, a scale of such brevity does not conform to conventional expectations regarding reliability and validity of measurement. Nevertheless, Golden and Meehl (1979) and Zita (1982) have been able to show that high scores on the short scale are found among individuals who produce 2-7-8 MMPI profiles (high points on the Depression, Psychasthenia, and Schizophrenia scales). The very brevity of the seven item scale, as well as the known occurrence of 2-7-8 profiles among psychiatric groups other than schizophrenic patients, might emphasize the need for more empirical data from new sources as a prerequisite to an adequate evaluation of the approach or the empirical findings of Golden and Meehl. If further positive findings are obtained, one might anticipate the use of the method in studies of members of the families and relatives of schizophrenic patients in efforts to predict the incidence of the schizoid taxon among such family constellations.

Although Meehl's initial hypothesis regarding a single dominant gene for schizotaxia, combined with polygenetic determinants of other personal attributes, is sufficiently broad to touch all bases, his view is partially at variance with the conceptions of other investigators who have concentrated on genetic studies of schizophrenia. Rüdin's conclusion in 1916, that genetic patterns in schizophrenia did not follow any simple Mendelian principle, has not deterred further theorizing or interpretation of data on the basis of a single recessive gene (Kallman, 1953) and has not legislated against a polygenetically determined "constitutional resistance to manifestation" trait (Kallman, 1953). Nor has Rüdin's observation induced Slater (1965) to abstain from assuming a partial dominance of a single major locus with alleles or from inferring that homozygosity for the schizophrenic allele should produce schizophrenia, but that heterozygosity should not necessarily result in such a disorder. These interpretations differ from Meehl's to the extent that the genetic ingredients are the determiners of schizophrenia rather than the definers of necessary (but not sufficient) conditions for the production of a schizophrenic disorder. In Slater's view, one type of zygosity will definitely produce schizophrenia. The reader is referred to a concise summary of current viewpoints on genetic conceptions of schizophrenia by Rosenthal (1977) and Kessler (1980), and to a more elaborate discussion of the broader topic of genetics in schizophrenia by Neale and Oltmanns (1980).

Genetic interpretation of schizophrenia is an area of construct theorizing that, at this stage of research, is unsettled. Something complex and somewhat unpredictable apparently is taking place at the level of observation of patients and their relatives, and something complex must be postulated to mirror the empirical observations. A polygenetic interpretation is the broadest and the safest, to the extent that it is least susceptible to disproof. Whether any combination of paired alleles or any combination of loci of gene pairs plays a deterministic role for schizophrenia, as distinct from a partial contributory role, always requiring a primary interaction with environmental events, cannot be determined from existing literature. What can be demonstrated, however, is the degree of relationship of incidence of the disorder among biologically related persons, beginning with identical twins and moving progressively to more remote relatives.

Falconer (1965) has used quantitative genetic methods to determine the heritability of disorders that follow complex genetic patterns. Discarding the concept of susceptibility, which implies only innate tendencies, he introduces the concept of a quasi-normally distributed liability to allow for the effects of environmental circumstance, as well as genetically determined tendencies, toward a disease. He then introduces the concept of threshold at one end of the distribution, in order to separate on his scale of liability the individuals in the general population who possess a disease from those who do not (normals). In his application of these concepts to polygenetically determined disorders, Falconer is able to calculate a mean liability of affected individuals in the population and a mean liability value for relatives, using a normal distribution of liability values and the standard deviation as a measure of variability. The method has been used by Gottesman and Shields (1966, 1976) to calculate a heritability value for liability to schizophrenia.

A cumulative pool of studies of monozygotic and dizygotic twins has developed from the early work of Kallman (1938) and Slater and Shields (1953). Despite the traditional methodological criticisms of identical twin studies, as applied either to psychopathology or to intelligence, the concordance values for schizophrenia have been impressively high in monozygotic twins and, as the data have revealed, higher in cases of severe schizophrenia than in milder forms. It has been only in very recent years, however, that analyses of well controlled adoption studies have provided what most investigators regard as irrefutable evidence for the importance of a genetic transmission that provides the necessary, even if not the sufficient, conditions for the development of some form of schizophrenia. Contributing the most impressive evidence for the genetic argument are Scandinavian studies by Tienari (1963), Kringlen (1967) and Fischer (1973), a series of studies in England by Gottesman and Shields (1966), and in the United States by Pollin and coworkers (1969). A brief overview of these studies is presented in an article by Cancro (1979).

One of the more convincing adoptive studies was conducted by Heston (1966) on a group of schizophrenic women whose children had been placed up for adoption very early in life. Although the prevalence rate for schizophrenia in a control group did not differ from the base rate in the general population, the children of the schizophrenic mothers who were reared elsewhere in foster homes showed a prevalence rate for schizophrenia that did not differ from the rate that would have been expected from other studies if the same children had been reared by their biological (i.e., schizophrenic) mothers.

Independent analyses of data by Rosenthal (1970) and Slater and Cowie (1971), reviewed by Kressler (1980), report estimates for risk among relatives of schizophrenics at 6.7 percent and 8.2 percent, respectively, for siblings if neither parent is affected; 12.5 percent and 13.8 percent for siblings if one parent is affected; 9.7 percent and 12.3 percent for children if one parent is affected; 35 percent and 36.6–45.3 percent for children if both parents are affected; and less than 3 percent by either analysis in second degree relatives (aunts, uncles, nephews, nieces, grandchildren, and first cousins). These values are to be compared with the incidence rate of .0085 in the general population.

Given such findings, it seems only logical that investigators who found it somewhat discouraging to attempt to understand schizophrenic behavior by studying the dynamics and performance in laboratory experiments of adult male schizophrenic patients should have focused on the current life situation of children and adolescents. One of the most comprehensive presentations of the studies of children at risk for schizophrenia as a consequence of being reared in a home in which at least one parent is schizophrenic was presented in a single issue of the *Schizophrenia Bulletin*, published by the National Institute of Mental Health. Although more recent articles have appeared, presentations by Garmezy and Streitman (1974) and by M. Bleuler (1974) provide data, as well as thoughtful discussion of the importance of the family environment in contributing to the onset of a schizophrenic adjustment. Numerous studies are cited in the article by Garmezy and Streitman describing the plight of a child reared in a home in which one or both parents are hospitalized intermittently while attempting to fulfill the role of a parent, presenting in many cases a series of discontinuities as well as maladaptive patterns of child rearing. It is research of this type, aimed at a stage in life which precedes the crystallization of a schizophrenic pattern, that may provide a better understanding of the styles of adjustment by which a child at risk for schizophrenia can remain a well compensated schizotype, instead of becoming overtly schizophrenic.

PREDICTORS OF RECOVERY

The second and more central topic for the care and treatment of schizophrenia is the question, "Who among those who become schizophrenic is capable of reintegrating to a level that permits effective functioning within the family setting or in external settings, both social and occupational?"

Emil Kraepelin, the dominant systematizer of psychiatric nomenclature at the end of the nineteenth century, maintained the conviction that dementia praecox, a term first used by Morel in 1853, was fundamentally a metabolic disorder and, if properly diagnosed from symptomatology, was certain to follow a downhill course. If the patient recovered, it was logically inferred that the diagnosis was incorrect. Although the conception that dementia praecox ran a natural downhill course contributed to a general philosophy of custodial care and treatment of such patients, it should be noted by those of us who have been inclined to think critically of the metabolic interpretation that Kraepelin expressed clearly the need to provide as much freedom to the patient as possible, as well as attentive concern and provision for contact with the outside world. Kraepelin was limited in perspective by the chronic institutionalized population with which he worked.

What Kraepelin did not take adequately into account in his preoccupation with the classification of symptoms was the early life history of the patient as a basis for predicting the future. Nor did Bleuler (1924), who introduced the term schizophrenia, and who focused on dynamic associational processes, emphasize early life adjustment. Bleuler studied the breakdown of associations, ambivalence, autism, and affective disturbance (the four A's), and was influenced by the dynamic aspects of Freud's thinking, but did not concentrate on the long-term development of schizophrenia in early life.

It remained for Meyer (1910) to focus attention on the longitudinal aspects of schizophrenia, the gradual withdrawal and development of faulty or deviant habits of thinking, feeling, and behavior. Although Meyer made no clear distinction between what were later to be regarded as process and reactive schizophrenia, it seemed clear that the environment itself contributed to the nature and course of the disorder. Meyer's conceptions, as well as Sullivan's (1962) contributions, led subsequent investigators to consider the possibility that adjustment in early life might serve not only as a predictor of the future course of development of a schizophrenic disorder, but of recovery, as well.

Interest in the parental environment as a possible important variable in the emergence of schizophrenia was reflected in publications by a number of psychiatrists in the decades of the 1930s, 1940s, and 1950s (e.g., Tietze [1949], and Reichard & Tillman [1950]), each dealing with presumably unhealthy patterns of overprotection, subtle or overt patterns of dominance, or rejection, in either or both parents of the schizophrenic patient.

These partially controlled and partially structured clinical observations led to significant developments in the emerging discipline of clinical psychology, specifically in the area of experimental psychopathology. What had begun as informally gathered descriptive data from case studies, minimally quantified and at times without a control group of any kind, now required the construction of scales susceptible to assessment in terms of reliability, concurrent and predictive validity, and called for the additional application of techniques from the laboratories of experimental psychology.

The studies of patients within the family unit had led to consideration of the whole patient rather than to a collection of symptoms as a primary topic of study. Concern with the whole patient was apparent in the construction of the Elgin Prognostic Scale by Wittman (1941) at the Elgin (Illinois) State Hospital in 1941. The Scale consisted of 30 subscales, each assigned a weighting based on clinical experience, and attempted to cover major areas of life history, mental and physical function, as well as the presenting symptoms and other variables thought to be relevant to schizophrenia (e.g., physiological and anatomical aspects, such as energy level and body type). The Elgin Scale and other prognostic scales have been described comprehensively by Kokes, Strauss, and Klorman (1977) in an excellent summary of the positive and negative research findings with the several prognostic instruments. The Elgin Prognostic Scale had defects of construction, particularly in selection and wording of items, but could be considered the first creditable research instrument that permitted experimental study of the performance of schizophrenic patients on the basis of classification as "process" or "reactive." Reliability of the instrument was found to be high, and studies of its effectiveness as a prognostic indicator of hospitalization by Chapman, Day, and Burstein (1961) helped to establish its reputation as the first of a series of effective prognostic instruments for the experimental and clinical study of schizophrenia. The Elgin Scale was later reduced to an abbreviated 20 item scale by Becker (1955),* and, independently, a 24 item self rating process-reactive scale based on Meyerian and Sullivanian concepts of schizophrenia was developed by Ullmann and Giovannoni (1964), both of which proved to be useful to research studies. One of the interesting findings using the Becker version of the scale was the correlation of Elgin scores with developmental levels of percepts on the Rorschach ink blot technique, the process schizophrenic patients scoring at lower levels of ego development than reactive patients (Becker, 1956).

More than a decade after publication of the Elgin Prognostic Scale, Phillips (1953) constructed what has now become perhaps the most widely used of the prognostic instruments in the context of a study of prediction of improvement with shock therapy in schizophrenic patients. His conception of the effective predictors of improvement focused on early life interpersonal relations and the level of sexual and social maturity achieved by the individual, including marriage and stable family life. The scale was constructed in five sections, each allowing from one to six points for levels of development, with a high score (maximum total of 30 points for the five sections) indicating a greater degree of pathology. An abbreviated form of the Phillips Scale has been developed by Harris (1975) to eliminate redundancy and overlap among scales, and to concentrate on data more readily available in clinical records; this form has been shown to serve as an adequate substitute for the original scale. The abbreviated scale has been found to be among the most effective predictors of symptomatic improvement in a comparative study conducted by Schultz and Herron (1979) using nine different rating scales and three separate criteria. The Abbreviated Phillips Scale was the single best predictor of outcome at three months; marital status was the single best predictor at six months; and overall, the Abbreviated Phillips Scale was the most useful predictor of outcome.

During the decade of the 1950s, a series of studies was conducted involving the application of basic experimental methods to psychopathology (Garmezy, 1968; Garmezy & Rodnick, 1959; Rodnick & Garmezy, 1957). These investigations were concerned with schizophrenia as a motivational phenomenon (i.e., sensitivity to censure or threat, reinstatement of anxiety by cues from early life experience, and consequent decrements or distortions of performance). Studies that initially were designed simply to explore differences between

*Becker, WC. The relation of severity of thinking disorder to the process-reactive concept of schizophrenia. Unpublished doctoral dissertation, Stanford University, 1955.

schizophrenic patients and normal subjects were enhanced by the introduction of the new Phillips Rating Scale of Premorbid Adjustment. Use of the scale enabled each investigator to separate patients into good premorbid and poor premorbid categories and to observe, and usually to predict, differential performance of the two subgroups. In one study, for example, stimulus generalization curves were flattened more in poor premorbid than in good premorbid patients in a task involving movement of a lever by the subject in response to differences in training and test tones under conditions of censure (Garmezy, 1952). In a study of size estimation (Harris, 1957), good premorbid patients tended to underestimate the size of drawings of mother-son relationships, involving content relevant to schizophrenia, while the poor premorbid patients overestimated, apparently exhibiting inadequate perceptual controls. Replication of the size estimation studies by other investigators many years later (Webb, Davis, & Cromwell, 1966), produced similar findings and advanced an interpretation that utilized the scanning phenomenon of Silverman (1964). Good premorbids were scanners (i.e., attempted to take into account analytically the details of the environment in a self-protective way, exhibiting low stimulus redundancy), while poor premorbids were non-scanners (i.e., they focused continuously on a stimulus object in a staring fashion, producing a size enlargement comparable to that observed in young children by Paiget [1950], a phenomenon that diminishes with age). Although the scanning hypothesis seemed at last to explain the size estimation phenomenon as applied to the size underestimation effects of both good premorbid and paranoid patients, questions were later raised by Neale and Cromwell (1968) about this explanation.

These brief examples serve to provide the reader with a glimpse into the type of research that continued for nearly two decades (1950s and 1960s), gathering the usual and expected methodological criticism regarding both small technical matters and interpretations of the performance of subjects (e.g., under what conditions does censure enhance rather than impair performance?). The history of the series of researches involving purposive behavior ran somewhat parallel with the well known series of studies of anxiety in nonclinical subjects as either a facilitator or inhibitor of performance in either simple or complex tasks. Although it seemed for a period that motivational interpretations of schizophrenia might yield entirely to attentional and other central processes as explanations of schizophrenic thought, perception, and behavior, the motivational interpretations, which were related more directly to the life history of interpersonal relations, persist and may yet move back onto stage before the behavioral mysteries of schizophrenia are finally unraveled. It seems plausible that biochemical or central neural processes might serve as background factors for purposive behavior involving distorted interpersonal relations, as well as for more impersonal attentional processes. Neither avenue of research is exclusive of the other.

The Phillips Scale (1953), both original and abbreviated (Harris, 1975), the Elgin Prognostic Scale (1941) and its modifications (Becker, 1955), and the Ullmann-Giovannoni self report scale (1964) are not the only ones that have proven useful in studies of schizophrenia. Kokes, Strauss, and Klorman (1977) have presented a comprehensive review and evaluation of each of the major prognostic scales, including the Zigler and Phillips Social Competence Scale, the Kantor Scales, the Astrup and Noreik Scale, the Vaillant Scale, the Stephens Scale, the Strauss-Carpenter Prognostic Scale, and the Goldstein Premorbid Adjustment Scale (the original references for which can be found in the review article.) A number of these instruments have also been utilized in studies evaluating the relationship of demographic and diagnostic factors to premorbidity in schizophrenia, as summarized by Klorman, Strauss, and Kokes (1977a). An overview of studies of physiological activity in chronic and acute schizophrenic patients and in children at high risk for schizophrenia (i.e., offspring of schizophrenic mothers) has also been provided by Korman, Strauss, and Kokes (1977b). Of particular interest are the partially replicated studies of Mednick, Schulsinger, and Schulsinger (1975) involving a comparison of electrodermal responses during aversive classical conditioning of adolescents at risk for schizophrenia with the responses of normal controls. The findings in these and other studies suggest that high risk children exceed control subjects in amplitude of skin conductance responses to both conditioned and unconditioned stimuli, thus supporting Mednick's hypothesis of autonomic overresponsiveness in the preschizophrenic individual, and permitting predictions of disordered behavior that may over a long period of time eventuate in a diagnosis of schizophrenia.

Other early life correlates of later schizophrenia have been found to be childhood IQ, in a series of studies by Lane and Albee (1968), and schoolroom behavior of boys and girls in the early years (by Watt, 1978).

LONGITUDINAL AND CROSS-CULTURAL STUDIES

As has been true of the course of research in several different areas of psychopathology (e.g., depression, antisocial personality), there is routinely a search for antecedent causes in family pathology, a refined search for a particular pattern of dynamics, a tentative inference that there are many different family patterns involved, an attempt to fractionate family patterns by introduction of another dimension or division of patients (e.g., good and poor premorbidity in schizophrenia), and a belated discovery that socioeconomic, geographic, religious, and other demographic variables are of relevance. Regretfully, it is concluded that specificity of family pattern, however psychopathological, probably accounts for a limited percentage of the variance involved in the production of a schizophrenic disorder.

Family dynamics may be of major significance in individual cases and family pathology may serve as a background factor in most cases of schizophrenia, contributing sufficient stress to produce an episode, but specificity of family pattern has not been established. Perhaps the most striking of the failures to demonstrate persuasively the relevance of a specific pattern of family dynamics is the very plausible, even compelling, double-bind hypothesis of Bateson, Jackson, Haley, and Weakland (1956), as elaborated into a three party system by Weakland (1960). Minimal support has been provided in the research literature after more than 25 years of clinical reference to the hypothesis by the psychotherapist who works daily with schizophrenic patients. The problems of analyzing causality in family research in schizophrenia have been discussed in detail by Dell (1980).

Research has been particularly difficult in this area, as a consequence of the fact that adult male schizophrenic patients in Veterans Administration Hospitals and, secondarily, in state hospitals, have served as the primary sources of data for more than three decades. The data obtained from adult schizophrenic patients regarding sensitivity to the reinstatement of cues from childhood experience must be interpreted through a long chain of chronologically reverse inferences in order to permit reconstruction of the actual early life experiences of the patient. Such difficulties have led to increased interest in those patients who had become schizophrenic during early life and, as previously discussed, to studies of children at risk in a home in which one or both parents have been, or become, schizophrenic.

A recent longitudinal study by Eggers (1978) attempts to address the problem of continuity of personal adjustment from early life. Eggers studied a group of 57 male and female schizophrenic patients, ages 7 to 13, for an average follow-up period of 15 years, and found no relationship between prognosis and either incidence of schizophrenia in the family, family pathology, or even family environment. He did find, however, a significant relationship between prognosis and premorbid personality development. Analyzing for level of remission, he reported that 20 percent of the cases recovered completely,

30 percent achieved a relatively positive adjustment, and 50 percent showed either moderate or poor remission.

In a study of prognosis among young adult schizophrenic patients and antecedent childhood factors, Roff and Knight (1978a) examined the records of 45 male acute schizophrenic patients of mean age 43.7 years, plus early life information at mean ages 10.9 years and 21.7 years. They assessed the long term stability and prediction of outcome in terms of psychotic thinking, affectivity, and social competence. Although the measures of psychotic thinking showed neither stability nor predictive validity, a combined measure of affectivity and social competence showed both temporal stability and a significant relationship to outcome. Childhood data were also related to the adult outcome variables. A second study by Knight, Roff, Barrnett, and Moss (1979) involving a 20-year follow-up of 51 male V.A. patients who were first diagnosed schizophrenic in the military service, confirmed the findings of the first study and provided an opportunity for the investigators to reemphasize their observation that current diagnostic criteria are inadequate because they concentrate too heavily on thought disorder and too little on affectivity and competence in interpersonal relations.

Stephens (1978) reviewed 38 long term follow-up studies of hospitalized schizophrenic patients, and concluded that unspecified schizophrenia of the type described by Kraepelin has a much poorer prognosis than atypical schizophrenia, schizoaffective psychosis, reactive psychosis, or other types that might be generally classified as reflecting good premorbid histories. The author emphasized the necessity of evaluating drug and psychosocial treatment results in terms of prognostic variables. The author also reported no firm evidence that maintenance medication was needed or even beneficial in some patients with good prognoses, a finding that will be debated in other studies to be cited in a subsequent section of the chapter.

Turning now to a set of studies from other countries (Germany, Switzerland, Hong Kong, and Israel), one finds variations in the percentages of patients who are reported as having recovered. Huber, Gross, Schuttler, and Linz (1980) conducted a study of 502 schizophrenic patients admitted to a university psychiatric clinic in Germany from 1945 to 1959 and followed up after an average period of 22.4 years from 1967 to 1973. They reported that 22 percent of the patients showed complete remission, by their criteria, 43 percent showed noncharacteristics remissions, and 35 percent exhibited "schizophrenic deficiency syndrome." They found no support for the hypothesis that presenting symptoms could be used to differentiate true schizophrenia and schizophreniform symptoms. The authors concluded that adequate prognoses could be developed only when several factors with a similar influence on long-term outcome occurred in combination, and when contrary predictors were absent.

Bleuler, Huber, Gross, and Schuttler (1976) reported the results of two studies of the long-term course of 1000 patients in Germany, Switzerland, and the United States in which they found full remission in 25 percent of the cases and spontaneous remission in 20 percent of the cases after one or more acute episodes. It was their observation that what they designated as catastrophic schizophrenia (i.e., acute onset and rapid decline into a chronic state without remission) had become rare. The authors noted that after the fifth year of illness the condition of the patient usually improved, although dramatic changes in 25 percent of the patients continued to occur many years after the first episode. Bleuler and his coworkers found that loss of close relatives and friends, both before and after onset, was more important for female patients than for male patients, and that suicide occurred more frequently than is commonly believed, both early and late in the course of the disorder.

A ten-year follow-up study by Lo and Lo (1977) of 82 Chinese schizophrenic patients in Hong Kong, first evaluated in 1965, and reviewed in 1975, revealed that 65 percent showed lasting remission, mild deterioration only, or no deterioration at all. The indicators for a favorable prognosis were found to be classification as a female patient, short duration of the illness, acute onset, symptoms other than disturbances of emotion or volition, and presence of a supportive relative.

Fallik and Liron (1976) conducted a follow-up study on schizophrenic patients from different social subgroups in Israel. Questionnaires were obtained 7 years after hospitalization from 45 out of 121 schizophrenic patients who had been hospitalized for six or seven years in 1966 and 1967. A parallel set of questionnaires was obtained independently from the psychiatrists who had seen these patients and additional information was obtained from government records. It was found that more than a third of the patients had achieved a good social adjustment, more than a third had achieved a partial social adjustment, and approximately one-fourth remained socially maladjusted with both repeated and persistent hospitalization.

Summarizing this set of studies from different countries in four different areas of the world (United States, Germany, Switzerland, Hong Kong, and Israel), one might infer on a global basis, without reference to specific modes of institutional care or treatment, that between 20 and 35 percent of the patients are likely to achieve a full recovery or at least a very positive social adjustment, and between 50 and 65 percent of the patients show some measure of positive recovery. This leaves from 35 to 50 percent of the patients from different studies moderately to serious impaired. It is difficult to interpret average values from studies conducted in different countries, involving different levels and styles of treatment and different physical, family, social, and cultural environments from which the patients emerge. It does seem reasonable to conclude, however, that not less than 20 to 25 percent of the population of patients with schizophrenia and related disorders will show a remarkable degree of recovery, and not less than 25 percent will have a very poor prognosis, leaving 50 percent of the schizophrenic population with prognoses that vary from study to study, and from country to country, but weighing a bit more heavily in the direction of positive reintegration than in the direction of steady or ultimate deterioration.

An interesting study from Sri Lanka (Waxler, 1979) suggests that schizophrenia has a better prognosis in undeveloped countries than in technologically advanced societies. Waxler conducted a five-year follow-up of 87 first admission schizophrenic patients (mean age 29 years) living in the peasant societies of Sri Lanka (formerly Ceylon). The clinical state and social adjustment of the patients were found to be quite good, and the observations were consistent with those made on samples in Nigeria and India, but different from the findings in industrial societies, such as the United States, Denmark, Great Britain, or the Soviet Union. The beliefs and practices in nonindustrial societies encourage short-term illness and quick return to a normal adjustment, suggesting that cultural differences found among schizophrenic patients may be the result of culturally based self-fulfilling prophecies. The differences found could not be accounted for by sampling, diagnostic methods, types of treatment, or by the family's willingness to tolerate deviance. Explanations were sought in social labeling theory, as contrasted with the medical model of illness, a conceptualization that attributes good prognosis to traditional systems of beliefs, structure of the treatment system (expectation of a short recovery period), and family norms.

A large scale analysis of cross-cultural differences in the short-term prognosis of schizophrenic patients was conducted by Sartorius, Jablensky, and Shapiro (1978). This study involved a two-year follow-up of nearly 1000 of the patients included in an International Pilot Study of Schizophrenia, using standardized assessment instruments and clearly specified criteria. As was found in the study of schizophrenia in Sri Lanka by Waxler (1978), patients in developing (i.e., undeveloped) countries had, on the average, a considerably better course and outcome than schizophrenic patients in the developed countries. Although socioeconomic and other demographic variables and clinical predictors accounted for some of the variance, much was left unexplained. The concepts used in Western societies to describe the psychopathology, the environment, and the history of the patient may not be transferable to the psychiatric setting in markedly different cultures. As has been found in American and European studies, however, clinical diagnosis on initial evaluation may be a good predictor of symptomatology but a poor predictor of length of the psychotic episode, total time during which the patient is psychotic, course of the disorder, or the degree of social impairment.

Returning now to two final longitudinal studies conducted in the United States, Prentky, Lewine, Watt, and Fryer (1980) investigated the prognostic importance of childhood school behavior, home environment, premorbid social competence, and psychiatric symptoms on first admission of 141 patients (59 of whom were schizophrenic) using multiple regression techniques. Outcome was measured by two criteria: days of hospitalization, and "poor," "good," or "poor," "fair," "good" global ratings. Ten of the significant predictors pertained to childhood school behavior or home environment, five dealt with adult social competence and adult avoidance behavior, and only five related to psychiatric symptoms. The most certain indicators of poor prognosis at first admission were the presence of hallucinations and withdrawal in male patients, and perplexity, troubled home environment, and *good* conduct in childhood in female patients. Length of hospitalization was best predicted by adult social competence for all patients. The authors caution against equating the diagnosis of schizophrenia with poor outcome, however, because one-fourth of the patients in the poorest outcome group were not schizophrenic, and one-fourth of the patients in the best outcome group were, in fact, schizophrenic.

Engelhardt and coinvestigators (1982) conducted a 15-year follow-up of 646 chronic schizophrenic outpatients; 20.6 percent had never been hospitalized, 22.0 percent had experienced only crisis admissions, and 57.4 percent had experienced long term hospitalization. A relationship was found in this study conducted in King's County, New York, between previous history of hospitalization and hospitalization during the follow-up period. The authors report that 48 percent of the cohort made little or no use of the inpatient facilities during their lifetime, but for the 52 percent who needed repeated or prolonged access to inpatient facilities, the societal shift toward community outpatient facilities during the past 15 years leaves much to be desired. The most vulnerable group of 371 patients, those who had experienced at least one long term admission to a psychiatric treatment facility prior to the study, revealed a readmission rate to an inpatient facility of 68 percent, with a mean duration of hospitalization of 34.6 months. The authors emphasize the need to design studies that start with a cohort of patients at the time the disorder first appears, or at least before first admission to a hospital. It was found on further analysis that among the group of patients who had never been hospitalized prior to the follow-up study, 60.9 percent had remained in the community continuously for the full 15-year period. Stated in another way, only 39 percent of the individuals diagnosed as schizophrenic, but never previously hospitalized, would be represented in the typical follow-up study that is conducted in the psychiatric hospital setting.

The Relation of Prognosis to Outcome Variables

At this point what is meant by prognosis and outcome must be specified. There are now many empirically based generalizations regarding predictor and outcome variables. The process schizophrenic (or poor premorbid) has been characterized as having a slow insiduous onset, flattened affect, absence of identifiable precipitating factors, and poor outcome. The reactive schizophrenic (or good premorbid) has a more sudden onset, emotional turmoil, more frequent presence of identifiable precipitating factors, and favorable outcome. Paranoid schizophrenics are said to be more intact, and though many become chronic, are said to have a better prognosis. Patients with more intense affect (e.g., schizoaffective) are said to have better prognoses, and acutes better prognoses than chronics. The exceptions are numerous, so much so that Vaillant (1978) concluded in a ten-year follow-up study of remitting schizophrenics that remitting patients are not a discrete type of schizophrenic patients requiring new labels. "Such patients may be more simply classified as schizophrenics who get predictably better after their first admission." Vaillant concludes that prognostic indicators of remission in schizophrenia appear to serve as predictors of remission in other psychoses also, and that in predicting remission, it is not rediagnosis, but the sheer number of favorable factors present that are most useful. Still further, Strauss and Carpenter (1977), in a series of articles, offer the generalization that prior functioning in any one domain of outcome measurement is the best predictor of future functioning in that domain, but not in other domains. The several measures of hospitalization should best predict hospitalization variables in the future, social effectiveness should predict social effectiveness in the future, and similarly for other predictor variables.

Personality Tests and Rating Scales as Predictors of Outcome

One might expect that the Minnesota Multiphasic Personality Inventory (MMPI) should find a place in research on prognosis in schizophrenia, particularly since actuarial systems for diagnosis, accompanied by data on personality, early life history, and outcome of treatment have been extended from the adult clinical population down to the adolescent level (Marks, Seeman, & Haller, 1974).

A recent study by Young, Gould, Glick, and Hargreaves (1980), compared 86 schizophrenic and 47 nonschizophrenic patients randomly assigned to short term (3–4 weeks) versus long term (3–4 months) hospitalization. MMPI scores obtained on intake admission were predictive of outcome (Health-Sickness Rating Scale and the Psychiatric Evaluation Form) for the 26 long term nonschizophrenic patients, but not for any of the other groups. Unreliability of responses apparently reduced the potential for prediction of outcome for the schizophrenic patients. This finding should come as no surprise, in view of the fact that only minor differences were found on the MMPI in an earlier study of good premorbid schizophrenic patients versus poor premorbid patients (Schaefer, 1965), in which the Ma (Mania) scale alone among the basic clinical scales differentiated the group when non K-corrected scales were employed. This finding is not inconsistent with the observation that symptoms of good and poor premorbid patients are often indistinguishable in the early phases of an episode.

In contrast to these findings, Glosz and Grant (1981) analyzed the MMPI records of 41 schizophrenic patients by application of multiple regression techniques to predict length of hospital stay. The two scales with the highest predictive power were the Schizophrenia and Depression scales, but the two scales were inversely related to outcome. A high score on Sc (schizophrenia), Es (ego strength), OH (overcontrolled hostility), or on the MF (Masculine-Feminine) scale was a predictor of a long hospital stay. A high score on D (Depression) as well as number of previous admissions, level of education, or social ties was a predictor of a short hospital stay. It is difficult to compare the findings among the MMPI studies, as well as among investigations using other test instruments, even when the tests are administered on intake, because patients differ greatly in number of days into the current episode, immediately prior medication, previous hospitalization, and in age.

The Rorschach Prognostic Rating Scale (Klopfer and associates [1951]) has also been found in recent years to have prognostic validity in a study of 98 schizophrenic patients, 17 to 31 years of age, by

Newmark and associates (1979). Using several measures of thought disorder as outcome criteria and discriminant function analysis, the authors found practical usefulness for the scale when other demographic and non-test variables were controlled.

Roff and Knight (1978b) evaluated the New Haven Schizophrenia Index, a checklist designed for research purposes, on a sample of 45 male schizophrenic patients for whom follow-up information had been compiled for 22 years. Although the checklist showed high interrater agreement and significant correlations with concurrent measures of thought disorder or psychotic thinking, the checklist was neither stable over time nor did it have predictive validity with regard to outcome. A separate measure of affectivity was shown to have both stability and predictive validity. These findings are not at all at variance with observations reported elsewhere in this chapter that symptom patterns in general are inadequate predictors of outcome, but that an affective component to the disorder may be highly relevant to outcome.

Prognosis and Treatment

Prediction of the effects of treatment constitutes a broad topic covering medication and somatic treatment in general, individual psychotherapeutic relationships, group therapy, and environmental intervention. This commentary is confined to a small number of studies that attempt to investigate the effects of such treatments or interventions on schizophrenic patients in general, and on subtypes of schizophrenic patients, the process and reactive categories, in particular. To reiterate a guiding principle stated early in this chapter, it would seem reasonable to predict that a person who has negotiated major hurdles required by society in early life should have a better chance of returning to a former high level of integration following a schizophrenic episode than one who has never met such challenges with adequate performance or interpersonal effectiveness. And yet, no quantitative method has been developed for evaluating the decrements of performance or adjustment, or the increments of gain on recovery that accompany the psychotic break. The initial decrement and the later remission to reduced levels of functioning are depicted in the pair of curves in Figure 3-1.

It is apparent that the patient with a good premorbid history has reached a higher level of functioning, approximating a normal adjustment, prior to the episode than has the poor premorbid patient, who through the early insiduous encroachments of schizophrenia failed to meet the conventional demands of society during childhood and ado-

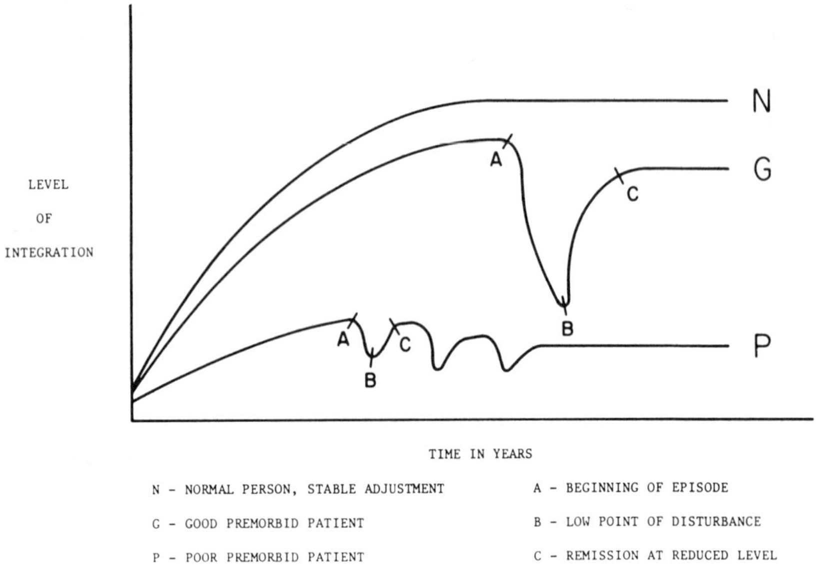

Fig. 3-1. Psychotic episode in good premorbid and poor premorbid patients.

lescence. It is clear also that the good premorbid patient must fall farther from the high plateau into the abyss of a psychotic episode in order to produce symptom patterns that, in many instances, are indistinguishable from those of the poor premorbid patient. From another perspective, the person of poor premorbid adjustment has a shorter vertical distance to descend. Both types of patients may eventually repair, a few with very nearly complete recovery, many at a reduced level of functioning, but each reintegrating toward the plateau that he or she had achieved prior to the schizophrenic episode.

What methods are now available to help the patient whose cognitive, perceptual, affective, or behavioral processes are in disarray to return to a level that approximates the premorbid plateau?

Somatic Treatment

A number of studies that employ somatic methods seek also to identify characteristics of patients that permit differential prediction of success of the treatment. Using a technique that now seems to be somewhat on the wane nationwide, Folstein, Folstein, and McHugh (1973) found improvement with electroshock therapy regardless of diagnostic category, even with schizophrenic patients with first rank symptoms, if the patient had a family history of depression, suicide, or symptoms of worthlessness, hopelessness, or guilt. Although electroshock holds limited appeal as a method of treatment and is seen by some as a category of "last resort," this study is of relevance because it brings into focus the importance of an affective component in predicting a favorable outcome.

The computerized EEG, although classifiable as a diagnostic rather than as a treatment method, has found a place as a prognostic indicator in one study of schizophrenia. Itil (1975) has reported that the more high frequency fast activity waves and the less alpha and slow waves prior to treatment, the more favorable the outcome in response to the major tranquilizers (neuroleptics).

The findings of Itil lead us into a series of studies pertaining to medication in schizophrenia—those using chlorpromazine and related drugs. May and associates (1980, 1981) has measured clinical response at 48 hours and at 28 days, and has concluded that change early in drug treatment is a useful predictor of outcome. Measuring saliva and plasma levels of chlorpromazine, May has shown that chlorpromazine levels in the first 24 hours after the first dose of chlorpromazine showed a significant correlation with clinical improvement; saliva and plasma levels after sustained medication did not show such a relationship with clinical improvement.

Sakurai, Takahashi, Nakahara, and Ikenaga (1980) found that schizophrenic patients who showed high levels of metabolites after a single dose of chlorpromazine tended to have poor clinical improvement with chlorpromazine; those who responded with low levels of the metabolites of chlorpromazine showed good clinical improvement.

Other studies of neuroleptics have been concerned with the effects of discontinuation of drugs, interactions of neuroleptic therapy and other forms of therapy, and the possible beneficial effects of limited intake of neuroleptics. Johnson (1979) reported negative effects of discontinuation of maintenance therapy with neuroleptics over a maintenance dosage period of from one to four years, and concluded that patients could not take "drug holidays." The risks increased significantly after only three months of maintenance dosages. In contrast, Schulz (1980) reviewed six articles on neurleptic and psychosocial treatment of schizophrenia and recommended that patients be allowed postponement of neuroleptic and alternative means of responding to severely disturbed or regressed behavior. The author emphasizes the importance of an involved, responsive staff, and the necessity of presenting to the patient expectations of the highest feasible level of functioning.

Carpenter, McGlashan, and Strauss (1977) conducted an NIH study involving a comparison of patients on sharply limited medication with those who received the "usual" treatment, using one year and two year follow-up criteria. The results were such that the authors recommended further consideration of the feasibility of treating acute schizophrenic patients with minimal use of medication.

In contrast, Goldberg, Schooler, Hogarty, and Rope (1977) insist that neuroleptics are needed for patients with good prognostic signs, and that, in fact, such patients benefit most from the medication. In this multivanate study of patients of both sexes, those who benefit least are: (1) men whose families were disrupted earlier in life; (2) men who lived alone or with extended families whose attitudes toward the study were negative; and (3) men who were irregular in taking the medication. Of considerable interest in this study was the finding that Major Role Therapy, involving social casework plus vocational rehabilitation, was of benefit primarily to asymptomatic patients. Such therapy actually hastened the relapse of severely disturbed inpatients, and this finding was interpreted as an inability on the part of such patients to manage an expanded and enriched cognitive field.

A comprehensive survey of important issues in the drug treatment of schizophrenia has been presented by Davis and coworkers (1980), who reviewed a large number of studies published since 1958, and reached the following conclusions: (1) anti-psychotic drugs are not only effective, but considerably more effective than psychotherapy alone, which produces no better outcome than does a control group; (2) drugs plus psychotherapy may be slightly more effective than drug treatment alone; (3) lack of drug treatment during the initial phase of an acute episode may produce not only less beneficial effects, but harmful effects that can persist for years afterward. These findings cited by Davis and associates (1980) were reported in a series of studies by May and coworkers (1976).

Additional inferences by Davis and coworkers (1980) are that: (4) a type of schizophrenic patient who does not require medication may exist, but has not yet been identified in the work of Klein and Rosen (1973) (chlorpromazine produced negative or mixed effects among asocial patients, but positive effects among non-asocial patients), as contrasted with the findings of Judd, Goldstein, Rodnick, and Jackson (1973) (on placebos, good premorbid, paranoid patients did poorly and, in fact, deteriorated, but good premorbid non-paranoid patients improved); (5) there is an optimal dosage of antipsychotic medication beyond which massive doses produce no further gain; (6) relapses are markedly reduced by antipsychotic medication, as found in a summary of 29 studies; and (7) short term side effects can be controlled, but long term side effects are serious and call for cautious selection of patients.

Buckley (1982) recommends study of the patient's subjective experience as a possible discriminator of patients for whom antipsychotic medication should prove beneficial.

Individual and Group Psychotherapies

Another set of studies deals with individual and group psychotherapy, administered alone or in combination with other methods, including somatic therapy.

Mintz, O'Brien, and Luborsky (1976) studies 100 consecutive schizophrenic outpatients referred to a community mental health center following hospitalization. They randomly assigned 50 patients to group psychotherapy and 50 patients to individual psychotherapy. Criteria employed at a two-year follow-up were rehospitalization and ratings by two clinicians on adjustment and social effectiveness. No differences were found between methods of treatment with regard to predictors of outcome; however, when control for initial status was introduced, mode of treatment was almost as effective as a predictor of later adjustment gains as were other patient variables. The best predictor of hospitalization was the number of previous hospitalizations and the best predictor of adjustment status after two years was pretreatment adjustment level. As one might expect, the patients with good prognostic indicators showed significant improvement.

In a review of group psychotherapy from 1966 to 1975, Parloff and Dies (1977) found no compelling endorsement of the contributions of group psychotherapy to the treatment of schizophrenic patients, juvenile or adult offenders, or narcotic addicts. The authors recommend an abandoment of the goal of demonstrating that global, undefined group therapy is equally effective with all patients or clients, and stress the need for "treatment manuals" that would describe approaches for specific categories of patients.

Investigating the effects of therapist experience and general clinical ability in the treatment of schizophrenia, Tuma, May, Yale, and Forsythe (1978) studied 228 first admission schizophrenic patients without significant prior treatment. Patients received treatment from 38 residents or recently graduated psychiatrists by one of five methods (individual psychotherapy, ataractic drug treatment, individual psychotherapy plus the drug treatment, electroshock, and milieu care). The authors were able to find no evidence for the effects of therapist experience or general clinical ability on outcome. Differences that were found among therapists were related to length of time the therapists kept the patients in the hospital. An additional finding was that drug treatment tended to obscure or override these findings but did not eliminate entirely the effects.

A review of the published studies on the effects of Rogerian therapist-related variables by Marshall (1977), states that although the work of Rogers and Kiesler offers some evidence that genuine and accurate empathy may influence individual therapy with schizophrenics, no conclusions may be drawn from the studies.

Prognosis based on therapist, as distinct from patient, variables is found also in a study by Matthews and Burkhart (1977) of seven "A" therapists and four "B" therapists, as classified by the Whitehorn and Betz Scale (1954). Predicting the effects of the "A" and "B" therapists on 18 schizophrenic and 18 neurotic patients, Matthews and Burkhart expected not only that "A's" would perform better with schizophrenics and "B's" with neurotics, as reported in the literature, but also that "A's" should do at least as well with neurotics as "B's" and should achieve significantly more positive outcomes with schizophrenic patients. Using multivariate analysis of variance for two outcome measures (therapist ratings of patient improvement and number of therapy sessions), the authors found clear support for the hypothesis of the "Super A" therapist. Number of sessions attended proved also to be important in an additional interaction hypothesis. Of particular interest, however, was the finding that ataractic drugs did not modify the effects of the A-B therapist pairings with patients.

In contrast to the findings of Matthews and Burkhart (1977), Young, Gould, Glick, and Hargreaves (1979) evaluated the Whitehorn-Betz A-B therapist variables as predictors of treatment outcome for 141 schizophrenic patients and 94 nonschizophrenic patients randomly assigned to short or long term hospitalization and treated by 47 therapists. The hypothesis of success for A-type therapists with schizophrenics was not confirmed.

Gunderson (1978) has taken a different approach to patient-therapist matching, relying on a set of highly intercorrelated personality variables of the therapists. Studying 50 patients, 85 percent of whom were schizophrenic, seen by either 2 or 3 therapists, Gunderson found that qualities of personality reflecting the capacity of the therapist to function comfortably with a range of strong affects in schizophrenic patients was predictive of the quality of the therapeutic relationship and of the overall clinical outcome.

A final study pertaining to psychotherapy involves an analysis of outcome variance by May, Tuma, and Dixon (1977). The authors pose the question that if psychotherapy makes some patients better and other patients worse, does this account for the lack of differences in mean improvement between psychotherapy and control groups? In a study of 228 hospitalized schizophrenic patients, psychotherapy alone did not increase outcome variance in comparison with the variance of a control group, and, in fact, the outcome variance was found to decrease to a statistically nonsignificant degree. Ataractic drugs alone, psychotherapy plus ataractic drugs, and electroshock therapy reduced the outcome variance to a significant degree. The authors found no clear evidence from this study or from the literature that pscyhotherapy produces any greater outcome variability than that resulting from hospitalization and nursing care alone (control group). The results support the inference that a treatment for schizophrenia reduces outcome variance in proportion to its effectiveness on the specific outcome under investigation.

Impression management theory has now received considerable publicity for approximately two decades. The hypothesis that schizophrenic behavior reflects to a large extent the patient's manipulative management of the environment, specifically the hospital staff, rather than cognitive or emotional deficit was tested on 40 male schizophrenic patients (Watson, Daly, Zimmerman, & Anderson, 1979). Patients with positive attitudes were compared with those with negative attitudes toward the hospital on extent of change in six personality inventories and on length of hospitalization. The results provided no support for the theory. Although the impression management hypothesis has great intuitive appeal, the accumulated research does not provide impressive support for a long-lasting underlying principle, as distinct from a highly time-limited observation in a specific clinical or experimental setting.

Although the general topic of treatment covers content that goes beyond the scope of this chapter, the individual, group, family, and community support systems, as well as special training in social skills are relevant to the recovery of schizophrenic patients. The reader is referred to comprehensive reviews and critiques of studies in these areas by Mosher and Keith (1980) and by Wallace and coworkers (1980).

SUMMARY

This chapter has explored theory and research pertaining to what the author regards as two major subtopics of prognosis in schizophrenia: Who will become schizophrenic?; and, Who among those who become schizophrenic will recover? Meehl's theoretical conception of a genetically predisposed schizotaxic individual who as a phenotypic schizotype is capable of maintaining a well compensated adjustment or of decompensating into a schizophrenic episode, provides a common denominator for a number of genetic conceptions of

Carpenter WT, McGlashan TH, & Strauss JS. The treatment of acute schizophrenia without drugs: An investigation of some current assumptions. *American Journal of Psychiatry*, 1977, *134*, 14–20

Chapman LJ, Chapman, J, & Raulin M. Scales for physical and social anhedonia. *Journal of Abnormal Psychology*, 1976, *85*, 374–382

Chapman L, Chapman J, & Raulin M. Body-image aberration in schizophrenia. *Journal of Abnormal Psychology*, 1978, *87*, 399–407

Chapman LJ, Day D, & Burstein A. The process-reactive distinction and prognosis in schizophrenia. *Journal of Nervous and Mental Disease*, 1961, *133*, 383–391

Davis JM, Schaffer CB, Killian GA, Kinard C, & Chan, C. Important issues in the drug treatment of schizophrenia. *Schizophrenia Bulletin*, 1980, *6*, 70–87

Dell P. Researching the family theories of schizophrenia: An exercise in epistemological confusion. *Family Process*, 1980, *19*, 321–335

Diagnostic and statistical manual of mental disorders, III. Washington, D.C.: American Psychiatric Association, 1980

Eggers C. Course and prognosis of childhood schizophrenia. *Journal of Autism and Childhood Schizophrenia*, 1978, *8*, 21–36.

Engelhardt DM, Rosen B, Feldman J, Engelhardt JO, & Cohen P. A 15-year follow-up of 646 schizophrenic outpatients. *Schizophrenia Bulletin*, 1982, *8*, 493–503

Falconer DS. The inheritance of liability to certain diseases, estimated from the incidence among relatives. *Annals of Human Genetics*, 1965, *29*, 51–76

Fallik A, & Liron R. A follow-up on schizophrenics from various social subgroups seven years after initial hospitalization. *Israel Annals of Psychiatry and Related Disciplines*, 1976, *14*, 229–239

Fischer M. Genetic and environmental factors in schizophrenia. *Acta Psychiatrica Scandinavica*, 1973, Supplement 238.

Folstein M, Folstein S, & McHugh PR. Clinical predictors of improvement after electroconvulsive therapy of patients with schizophrenia, neurotic reactions, and affective disorders. *Biological Psychiatry*, 1973, *7*, 147–152

Garmezy N. Stimulus differentiation by schizophrenic and normal subjects under conditions of reward and punishment. *Journal of Personality*, 1952, *21*, 253–276

Garmezy N. Process and reactive schizophrenia: Some conceptions and issues. In MM Katz, JO Cole, & WE Barton (Eds.), *The role and methodology of classification in psychiatry and psychopathology*. Chevy Chase, Md.: National Institute of Mental Health, 1968

Garmezy N, & Rodnick EH. Premorbid adjustment and performance in schizophrenia. *Journal of Nervous and Mental Diseases*, 1959, *129*, 450–466

Garmezy N, & Streitman S. Children at risk: The search for the antecedents of schizophrenia. Part I. Conceptual models and research methods. *Schizophrenia Bulletin*, 1974, *8*, 14–90

Glosz JT, Jr, & Grant I. Prognostic validity of the MMPI. *Journal of Clinical Psychology*, 1981,*37*, 147–151

Goldberg SC, Schooler NR, Hogarty GE, & Roper M. Prediction of relapse in schizophrenic outpatients treated by drug and sociotherapy. *Archives of General Psychiatry*, 1977, *34*, 171–184

Golden R, & Meehl P. Detection of the schizoid taxon with MMPI indicators. *Journal of Abnormal Psychology*, 1979, *88*, 217–233

Gottesman II, & Shields J. Schizophrenia in twins: 16 years' consecutive admissions to a psychiatric clinic. *British Journal of Psychiatry*, 1966, *112*, 809–818

Gottesman II, & Shields J. A critical review of recent adoption, twin, and family studies of schizophrenia: Behavioral genetics perspectives. *Schizophrenia Bulletin*, 1976, *2*, 360–401

Gunderson JG. Patient-therapist matching: A research evaluation. *American Journal of Psychiatry*, 1978, *135*, 1193–1197

Harris Jr. JG. Size estimation of pictures as a function of thematic content for schizophrenic and normal subjects. *Journal of Personality*, 1957, *25*, 651–671

Harris Jr. JG. An abbreviated form of the Phillips Rating Scale of Premorbid Adjustment in Schizophrenia. *Journal of Abnormal Psychology*, 1975, *84*, 129–137

Heston LL. Psychiatric disorders in foster home reared children of schizophrenic mothers. *British Journal of Psychiatry*, 1966, *112*, 819–825

Huber G, Gross G, Schuttler R, Linz MR, & Frederich-Wilhelms MR. Longitudinal studies of schizophrenic patients. *Schizophrenia Bulletin*, 1980, *6*, 592–605

Itil TM. Computerized EEG: Predictor outcome in schizophrenia. *Journal of Nervous and Mental Disease*, 1975, *160*, 188–203

Jackson D. *Personality Research Form Manual.* Goshen, NY; Research Psychologists Press, 1967

Johnson DA. Further observations of the duration of depot neuroleptic maintenance therapy in schizophrenia. *British Journal of Psychiatry*, 1979, *135*, 524–530

Judd LL, Goldstein MJ, Rodnick EH, & Jackson NLP. Phenothiazine effects in good premorbid schizophrenics divided into paranoid-nonparanoid states. *Archives of General Psychiatry*, 1973,*29*, 207–211

Kallman FJ. *The genetics of schizophrenia.* Locust Valley, NY: J. J. Augustin, 1938

Kallman FJ. *Heredity in health and mental disease.* New York: W. W. Norton & Company, Inc., 1953

Kessler S. The genetics of schizophrenia: A review. *Schizophrenia Bulletin*, 1980, *6*, 404–416

Klein D, & Rosen B. Pretreatment association, adjustment, and phenothiazine treatment among schizophrenic patients. *Archives of General Psychiatry*, 1973, *29*, 480–485

Klopfer, B, Kirkner FJ, Wisham W, & Baker G. Rorschach Prognostic Rating Scale. *Journal of Projective Techniques*, 1951, *15*, 424–428

Klorman R, Strauss JS, & Kokes RF. Premorbid adjustment in schizophrenia: III. The relationship of demographic and diagnostic factors to measures of premorbid adjustment in schizophrenia. *Schizophrenia Bulletin*, 1977, *3*, 214–225

Klorman R, Strauss J, & Kokes R. Premorbid adjustment in schizophrenia: IV. Some biological approaches to research on premorbid functioning in schizophrenia. *Schizophrenia Bulletin*, 1977, *3*, 226–239(b)

Kokes RF, Strauss JS, & Klorman R. Premorbid adjustment in schizophrenia: II. Measuring premorbid adjustment: The instruments and their development. *Schizophrenia Bulletin*, 1977, *3*, 186–213

Knight RA, Roff JD, Barrnett J, & Moss JL. Concurrent and predictive validity of thought disorder and affectivity: A 22-year follow-up of acute schizophrenics. *Journal of Abnormal Psychology*, 1979, *88*, 1–12

Kraepelin E. *Clinical psychiatry*, New York: Macmillan Co., 1907

Kraepelin E. *Dementia praecox*, Chicago: Medical Book Co., 1919

Kringlen E. *Heredity and environment in the functional psychoses.* London: Heineman, 1967

Lane EA, & Albee GW. On childhood intellectual decline and adult schizophrenics: A reassessment of an earlier study. *Journal of Abnormal Psychology*, 1968, *73*, 174–177

Lewine RN, Watt NF, & Fryer JH. A study of childhood social competence, adult premorbid competence and psychiatric outcome in three schizophrenic subtypes. *Journal of Abnormal Psychology*, 1978, *87*, 294–302

Lo WH, & Lo T. A ten-year follow-up stydy of Chinese schizophrenics in Hong Kong. *British Journal of Psychiatry*, 1977, *131*, 63–66

Marks PA, Seeman W, & Haller D. *The actuarial use of the MMPI with adolescents and adults.* Baltimore: Williams & Wilkins, 1974

Marshall KA. Empathy, genuineness, and regard: Determinants of successful therapy with schizophrenics? A critical review. *Psychotherapy: Therory, research, and practice*, 1977, *14*, 57–64

Matthews JG, & Burkhart BR. A-B therapist status, patient diagnosis, and psychotherapy outcome in a psychiatric outpatient population. *Journal of Consulting and Clinical Psychology*, 1977, *45*, 475–482

May PR, Tuma AH, Yale C, Potepane P, & Dixon WJ. Schizophrenia—a follow-up study of results of treatment. II Hospital stay over two to five years. *Archives of General Psychiatry*, 1976,*33*, 481–505

May PR, Tuma AH, & Dixon WJ. For better or worse? Outcome variance with psychotherapy and other treatments for schizophrenia. *Journal of Nervous and Mental Disease*, 1977, *165*, 231–239

May PR, Van Putten T, & Yale C. Predicting outcome of antipsychotic drug treatment from early response. *American Journal of Psychiatry*, 1980, *137*, 1088–1089

May R, Van Putten T, Jenden DJ, Yale C, & Dixon WJ. Chlorpromazine levels and the outcome of treatment in schizophrenic patients. *Archives of General Psychiatry*, 1981, *38*, 202–207

Mednick SA, Schulsinger H, & Schulsinger F. Schizophrenia in children of schizophrenic mothers. In A Davids (Ed.) *Child personality and psychopathology: Current topics, Vol. 2.* New York: Wiley, 1975

Meehl P. Schizotaxia, schizotypy, schizophrenia. *American Psychologist*, 1962, *17*, 827–838

Meehl P. A critical afterword. In I Gottesman & J Shields (Eds.) *Schizophrenia and genetics: A twin study vantage point.* New York: Academic Press, 1972

Meehl P, & Golden R. Taxometric methods. In P Kendall & J Butcher (Eds.), *Handbook of research methods in clinical psychology.* New York: Wiley, 1982

Meyer A. The dynamic interpretation of dementia praecox. *American Journal of Psychiatry*, 1910, *21*, 385–403

Miller H, Streiner D, & Kahgee S. Use of the Golden-Meehl indicators in the detection of schizoid taxon membership. *Journal of Abnormal Psychology*, 1982, *91*, 55–60

Millon T. *Millon Multiaxial Clinical Inventory Manual.* Minneapolis: National Computer Systems, 1977

Mintz J, O'Brien CP, & Luborsky L. Predicting the outcome of pscyhotherapy for schizophrenics: Relative contributions of patient, therapist, and treatment characteristics. *Archives of General Psychiatry*, 1976, *33*, 1183–1186

Mosher LR, & Keith SJ. Psychosocial treatment: Individual, group, family, and community support approaches. *Schizophrenia Bulletin*, 1980, *6*, 10–41

Neale JM, & Cromwell RL. Size estimation in schizophrenics as a function of stimulus presentation time. *Journal of Abnormal Psychology*, 1968, *73*, 44–49

Neale J, & Oltmanns TF, *Schizophrenia.* New York: John Wiley & Sons, 1980

Newmark CS, Konanc JT, Simpson M, Boen RB, & Prillaman K. Predictive validity of the Rorschach Prognostic Rating Sacle with schizophrenic patients. *Journal of Nervous and Mental Disease*, 1979, *167*, 135–143

Parloff MB, & Dies R. Group psychotherapy outcome research, 1966–1975. *International Journal of Group Psychotherapy*, 1977, *27*, 281–319

Piaget J. *The pscyhology of intelligence.* London: Rutledge & Kegan, 1950

Phillips L. Case history data and prognosis in schizophrenia. *Journal of Nervous and Mental Diseases*, 1953, *117*, 515–525

Pollin W, Allen MG, Hoffer A, Stabenau JR, & Hrubec Z. Psychopathology in 15,909 pairs of veteran twins. *American Journal of Psychiatry*, 1969, *126*, 597–609

Prentky RA, Lewine RR, Watt NF, & Fryer JH. A longitudinal study of psychiatric outcome: Developmental variables vs. psychiatric symptoms. *Schizophrenia Bulletin*, 1980, *6*, 139–148

Rado S. *Psychoanalysis of behavior, collected papers.* New York: Grune & Stratton, 1956

Raulin M. Development of a scale for intense ambivalence. (Doctoral dissertation, University of Wisconsin at Madison, 1977.) *Dissertation Abstracts, International*, May, 1978, *38*, (11-B), 5590

Reichard S, & Tillman C. Patterns of parent-child relationships in schizophrenia. *Psychiatry*, 1950, *13*, 247–257

Rodnick EH, & Garmezy N. An experimental approach to the study of motivation in schizophrenia. In MR Jones (Ed.), *Nebraska symposium on motivation.* Lincoln: University of Nebraska Press, 1957

Roff JD, & Knight RA. Young adult schizophrenics: Prediction of outcome and antecedent childhood factors. *Journal of Consulting and Clinical Psychology*, 1978, *46*, 947–952(a)

Roff JD, & Knight R. A schizophrenia checklist: Reliability without stability, concurrent without predictive validity. *Psychological Reports*, 1978, *43*, 791–794(b)

Rosenthal D. *Genetic theory and abnormal behavior.* New York: McGraw-Hill 1970

Rosenthal D. Searches for the mode of genetic transmission in schizophrenia: Reflections and loose ends. *Schizophrenia Bulletin*, 1977, *3*, 268–276

Rudin E. *Zur vererbung and neuentstchung der dementia praecox.* Berlin: Springer Verlag OHG, 1916

Sakurai Y, Takahashi R, Nakahara T, & Ikenaga H. Prediction of response to and actual outcome of chlorpromazine treatment in schizophrenic patients. *Archives of General Psychiatry*, 1980, *37*, 1057–1062

Sartorius N, Jablensky A, & Shapiro R. Cross-cultural differences in the short term prognosis of schizophrenic psychoses. *Schizophrenia Bulletin*, 1978, *4*, 102–113

Schaefer SMJ. MMPI profiles of good and poor premorbid schizophrenic patients. Summa Cum Laude Thesis. University of Minnesota, Minneapolis, 1965

Schultz CL, & Herron WG. Comparison of process-reactive measures in schizophrenia. *Journal of Clinical Psychology*, 1979, *35*, 270–277

Schulz CG. Discussion of neuroleptics and psychosocial treatment. *Schizophrenia Bulletin*, 1980, *6*, 135–138

Silverman J. The scanning control mechanism and "cognitive filtering" in paranoid and nonparanoid schizophrenia. *Journal of Consulting Psychology*, 1964, *28*, 385–393

Slater E. Clinical aspects of genetic mental disorders. In JN Cummings & M Kremer (Eds.), *Biochemical aspects of neurological disorders, Second Series.* Oxford: Blackwell Scientific Publications, Ltd., 1965

Slater E, & Cowie V. *The genetics of mental disorders.* London: Oxford Unviersity Press, 1971

Slater E, & Shields J. *Psychotic and neurotic illness in twins.* Medical Research Council Special Report Series No. 278. London: Her Majesty's Stationery Office, 1953

Stephens JH. Long term prognosis and follow-up in schizophrenia. *Schizophrenia Bulletin*, 1978, *4*, 25–47

Strauss JS, & Carpenter WT. Prediction of outcome in schizophrenia: III. Five year outcome and its predictors. *Archives of General Psychiatry*, 1977, *34*, 159–163

Sullivan HS. *Schizophrenia as a human process.* New York: W. W. Norton and Co., 1962

Tienari P. Psychiatric illnesses in identical twins. *Acta Psychiatrica Scandinavica*, 1963, Supplement 171

Tietze T. A study of mothers of schizophrenic patients. *Psychiatry*, 1949, *12*, 55–65

Tuma SH, May PR, Yale C, & Forsythe AB. Therapist experience, general clinical ability, and treatment outcome in schizophrenia. *Journal of Consulting and Clinical Psychology*, 1978, *46*, 1120–1126

Ullmann LP, & Giovannoni JM. The development of a self-report measure of the process-reactive continuum. *Journal of Nervous and Mental Disease*, 1964,*138*, 38–42

Vaillant GE. A 10-year follow-up of remitting schizophrenics. *Schizophrenia Bulletin*, 1978, *4*, 78–85

Wallace CJ, Nelson CJ, Liberman RP, Aitchison RA, Lukoff D, Elder JP, & Ferris C. A review and critique of social skills training with Schizophrenia patients. *Schizophrenia Bulletin*, 1980, *6*, 42–63

Watson CG, Daly WK, Zimmerman P, & Anderson D. Effects of patient attitude and staff indulgence on improvement in schizophrenics: A test of impression management theory. *Journal of Abnormal Psychology*, 1979, *88*, 338–340

Watt NF. Patterns of childhood social development in adult schizophrenics. *Archives of General Psychiatry*, 1978, *35*, 160–170

Waxler NE. Is outcome for schizophrenia better in nonindustrial societies? The case of Sri Lanka. *Journal of Nervous and Mental Disease*, 1979,*167*, 144–158

Weakland JH. The "Double-Bind" hypothesis of schizophrenia and three-party interaction. In DD Jackson (Ed.), *The etiology of schizophrenia.* New York: Basic Books, 1960

Webb WW, Davis D, & Cromwell RL. Size estimation in schizophrenics as a function of thematic content of stimuli. *Journal of Nervous and Mental Disease*, 1966, *143*, 252–255

Whitehorn JC, & Betz BJ. A study of psychotherapeutic relationships between physicians and schizophrenic patients. *American Journal of Psychiatry*, 1954, *111*, 321–331

Wittman P. A scale for measuring prognosis in schizophrenic patients. *Elgin State Hospital Papers*, 1941, *4*, 20–33

World Health Organization, *The International Pilot Study of Schizophrenia*, Vol. I. Geneva: World Health Organization, 1973

Young RC, Gould E, Glick ID, & Hargreaves W. Personality inventory correlates of outcome in a follow-up study of psychiatric hospitalization. *Psychological Reports*, 1980, *46*, 903–906

Zerbin-Rüdin E. Schizophrenien. In PE Becker (Ed.), *Humangenetik*, Vol. 2, Stuttgart: Thieme, 1967

Zerbin-Rüdin E. Genetic research and the theory of schizophrenia. *International Journal of Mental Health*, 1972, *1*, 42–62

Steven S. Sharfstein

4

Sociopolitical Issues Affecting Patients with Chronic Schizophrenia

Many recent stories in the news media have highlighted both the plight of chronic schizophrenic patients in the community and the impact of large numbers of mentally disabled individuals living in our neighborhoods. The numbers of individuals with chronic mental disorders in and out of institutions are harder to pin down. One analysis reviews the prevalence and statistical literature and estimates that 1.7 to 2.4 million individuals in 1977 suffered from a chronic mental disorder. Of the group, 900,000 were institutionalized (750,000 in nursing homes) and 800,000 to 1.5 million were in the community, intermittently or repeatedly hospitalized for short terms, living with families or on their own in board and care homes, single room occupancy hotels, or literally in the street (Goldman, Gattozzi, & Taube, 1981).

On the upper west side of New York, for example, many former State hospital patients are visible every day, carrying their worldly belongings in paper shopping bags, talking out loud with hallucinated companions, subsisting on a bare minimum. Once deinstitutionalized from the total asylum, most arrive in indifferent or hostile communities to confront a "non-system of care," a bewildering array of federal, state, and local programs making up a fragmentary "patchwork quilt" of services and financing (Sharfstein, Turner, & Clark,

SCHIZOPHRENIA
ISBN 0-8089-1640-8

1978). Many rely on local charity resources and, perforce, the criminal justice system for shelter and a warm meal.

Deinstitutionalization as a deliberate public policy, i.e., discharging and diverting patients from long-term institutional to outpatient community care, has been pursued in earnest by States since 1970. Encouraged by the 1950s development of the major tranquilizer drugs, which control some (but not all) asocial behavioral symptoms, and by increased judicial attention to the civil rights of institutionalized mentally ill patients in the 1960s, advocates of community care strongly pushed for rapid phase out of State mental hospitals. Major federal financing initiatives of the late 1960s, especially Medicaid and Supplemental Security Income (SSI), provided the economic base for deinstitutionalization, as most of these individuals were and remained economically dependent. Further, the ideology and justification of the 1963 federal Community Mental Health Center (CMHC) law proclaimed a more humane and cost-effective alternative in the community.

Social costs of this policy soon surfaced (Arnoff, 1975) and CMHCs came under attack for failing to care for a substantial portion of patients discharged from hospital care (Langsley, 1980). With only one-third of all CMHCs initially envisioned operational, a broad acute-care and prevention mandate, and a reliance on third-party insurance funding, CMHCs seem incapable or unwilling to assume the rehabilitation, social support, and case management services needed by community-dwelling patients with chronic schizophrenia. The issue is compounded by the lack of administrative and clinical coordination with State mental hospitals and the reluctance of community governing boards to make discharged patients residing in their area a high priority population. Therefore, increasingly pervasive public health and social problems have emerged, made worse by federal financing and a federal mental health services program unresponsive to the needs of this group. The 1975 amendments to the CMHC program, Public Law 94-63, tried to remedy the situation by adding additional requirements relating to screening for admission to State mental hospitals, aftercare, and transitional, half-way house services. Yet these mandates were added without appreciable additional federal resources or a cutback on other, previously mandated essential services (Sharfstein, 1978). Two other developments at the federal level attempted to respond to the needs of community-dwelling patients with chronic mental illness. In 1977 the National Institute of Mental Health initiated a modestly funded demonstration program that provided planning and service dollars to and through States to develop comprehensive "community support systems" for the chronically mentally ill (Turner & Tenhoor, 1978). In 1978 the President's Commission on Mental Health issued its report calling for a "national priority" for the chronic patient and suggesting an ambitious agenda of change in service and financing programs. Some of those recommendations became law with the passage of the Mental Health Systems Act of 1980. That law, however, was substantially repealed after the election of Reagan and the passage of the Omnibus Budget Reconciliation Act of 1981. Other, potentially more devastating, cuts have also been put through in life-support welfare programs for these patients.

This chapter will identify the main sociopolitical issues affecting treatment and care for schizophrenic patients in the 1980s. The discussion can be illuminated by a brief historical review of the development of current public policy.

POLICIES OF PUBLIC MENTAL HEALTH CARE

Throughout U.S. history public policies on the treatment and care of economically dependent individuals afflicted by severe mental illness have been shaped by alliances of professionals and social reformers moved by ethical and moral considerations. The tradition began early in the ninteenth century when a small band of physicians formed the first specialty medical society, the Association of Medical Superintendents of American Institutions for the Insane (now known as the American Psychiatric Association), which joined forces with a social reform movement led by Horace Mann and Dorothea Dix. The professionals developed program information and statistics that the reformers used to lobby legislatures to provide public assistance for "the indigent insane" in community after community and State after State.

The Early Years

Dorothea Dix began her prodigious career by petitioning the City of Cambridge to provide heat for inmates of the local jail, many of whom were mentally ill. Soon she was visiting poor houses and jails throughout Massachusetts and, later, the country. Armed with statistics hailing cures by the mode of "moral treatment," she persuaded the Massachusetts legislature to enlarge existing asylums and found new ones. This was in the heyday of the so-called "cult of curability." It was asserted everywhere that properly organized institutions could cure almost every incidence of insanity, allowing the sole qualification that the cases had to be of recent origin. Practitioners competed openly with one another to formulate the most general and optimistic principle, and to announce the most dramatic result. For example, Samuel Woodward, the superintendent of the Massachusetts asylum at Worcester, announced in 1834 that "In recent cases of insanity, under judicious treatment, as large a proportion of recoveries will take place as from any other acute disease of equal severity" (Rothman, 1971, p. 131). He calculated that in his own institution 82.25 percent of the patients recovered. Woodward's tone was still judicious and moderate compared to later assertions. The following year Dr. William Awl of the Ohio asylum announced without qualification one hundred percent cures (Rothman, 1971).

Some comment should be made on the methodology. The percentage of cures was computed from the number of admissions. The same individual was thereby cured more than once in the same year. At Pennsylvania'a Friend's Asylum, for example, 87 persons accounted for 274 recoveries. There was also the practice of including the number of deaths in the figures for recovery, of which Earle in his book on these statistics 25 years later observed: "[this] mathematically demonstrated the curability of *all* the insane" (Rothman, 1971).

Given this alleged cure rate and the indefatigable humanitarianism of Ms. Dix, one after another legislatures were persuaded of the long-term cost benefit of treatment approaches. At one time she almost succeeded in getting the federal government to assume major responsibility for the development of mental hospitals. After seven years of intensive lobbying of the Congress Ms. Dix and her supporters managed to get passed the "12,225,000 acre bill," which provided for proceeds of sales of federal lands to build public mental hospitals. President Franklin Pierce vetoed this bill, however, citing James Madison's explication of the limited powers of the federal government as contrasted to the unspecified powers of the States. In his veto message Pierce detailed his fear that the bill would set a precedent for "the whole field of public beneficience to be open to the care and culture of the federal government." His veto was sustained. Undaunted by this defeat, Ms. Dix continued her efforts and in her 45 years of advocacy, helped establish 32 mental hospitals in 28 of the 33 states of the Republic.

The cult of curability was short-lived. Dr. Isaac Ray and others brought forward in published papers studies that totally discredited these inflated claims. By the 1850s the institutions were taking in far more patients, many from the waves of immigrants coming to the U.S., than could possibly be offered the individual attention called for by moral treatment. Over the ensuing decades asylums that had been devoted to intensive individualized care became human warehouses of the insane. Lifetime stays became commonplace and State mental hospitals assumed the character they would have for the next 100 years; that is, an institutional system of mainly custodial care—not only a system of last resort but also a system of first resort.

Other professional-reformer alliances, such as the movement started by a former mental patient, Clifford Beers, around 1910 attempted to change public policy toward care of the mentally ill. But it took the alarming revelations about the extent of mental disorder in the country, which came out of the examination of men for military service during the Second World War, to galvanize public attitudes and force legislative action. Armed with the new technologies of care provided by the amazing psychotropic drugs and the advances in community-based care, the postwar alliance was able to orchestrate the establishment of a national mental health enterprise that promoted the truly revolutionary policy changes that have transformed public mental health care in the past 25 years (Foley & Sharfstein, 1983).

Post-World War II

The 28 years since 1955 have been the most revolutionary in the history of psychiatric treatment. These years are marked by major change in the scope and diversity of mental health services and providers, in the range and effectiveness of psychiatric treatments, and in the massive migration of severely mentally disabled individuals from the large public asylum back to the community—either to "mini-asylums" such as private nursing and board and care homes or to survive on their own at the fringes.

Decrease in Psychiatric Beds

Today there are a bewildering array of psychotherapies and psychotherapists, of traditional and nontraditional mental health clinics, and of concepts of mental health and mental illness. This was not always the case. In 1955 the vase majority of patients seen in the specialty mental health system were cared for in the public asylum system. In that year the number of residents in State mental hospitals reached a high of 559,000. Over three-quarters of all patient-care episodes* in mental health facilities were inpatient, and inpatient-

*"Patient-care episodes" are defined as the number of residents in inpatient facilities at the beginning of the year (or the number of persons on the rolls of noninpatient facilities) plus the total admissions to these facilities during the year (i.e., new admissions, readmissions, and returns from long-term leave). This index, therefore, provides a duplicated count of persons and is not equal to a true annual-prevalence rate or the annual-prevalence rate for treated mental disorder, which would require unduplicated person counts.

care episodes of State mental hospitals comprised nearly half of all U.S. patient-care episodes (both inpatient and outpatient).

By 1977 the number of residents had fallen to approximately 160,000 and the percent of total patient-care episodes accounted for by State mental hospitals fell to nine percent (Regier & Taube, 1981).

The declining role of the State hospital epitomizes the revolution in society's views on the care and treatment of mentally ill persons. The average length of stay of admissions to State hospitals is one critical change that partially accounts for this massive shift. In 1955 this stay was approximately six months. By 1977, the duration of stay averaged three weeks in State hospitals. Admissions increased up to 1971 and have remained steady since then. Readmissions, the so-called "revolving door" phenomenon, account for 70 percent of all admissions to State mental hospitals. The rate of inpatient episodes per 100,000 population in State hospitals has declined from a high of 502 in 1955 to 266 in 1977 (Witkin, 1980).

There has been a correspondingly dramatic decline in the number of days of inpatient care and also in the number of psychiatric beds. Between 1971 and 1977 the total number of impatient days declined from 153 million to 91 million (40 percent) and the number of beds in inpatient psychiatric settings decreased from 471,800 to 301,011 (36 percent). This decrease in the number of beds is due to a drop in State mental hospital beds from 361,578 to 184,079 (49 percent). Other facilities had increased the number of beds between 1971 and 1977, especially nonfederal general hospitals, where psychiatric unit beds increased from 23,308 to 29,384. Private psychiatric hospital beds also increased from 14,412 to 16,637 (Witkin, 1979).

Despite these shifts, however, public facilities still account for approximately 80 percent of all inpatient days of care and inflation-adjusted expenditures for State mental hospitals remained stable between 1971 and 1975*. The inability to shift State hospital financial and personnel resources with the patients into community settings has increasingly been cited as a major impediment to a humane transition from the institution into the community (Ozorin & Sharfstein, 1978; Sharfstein et al., 1978; Comptroller General of the United States, 1977).

Expansion of Outpatient Services

From 1955 to 1977 there was a four-fold increase in mental health specialty patient-care episodes, from 1.7 million episodes in 1955 to 6.9 million episodes in 1977. This expansion is entirely due to the

---

*Sharfstein, SS. Cost containment and psychiatric care. Unpublished manuscript, 1983.

number of outpatient services established during this period, including community mental health center programs and private office practices (Taube, Regier, & Rosenfeld, 1978). The number of people seen in the private offices of psychiatrists and psychologists in 1975 was approximately 1.3 million, 20 percent of all individuals seen in the specialty mental health sector (Regier, Goldberg, & Taube, 1978).

Growth of Nursing Home Care

A major factor in the decline of psychiatric beds in State mental hospitals was the growth of private nursing homes. Medicare (Title VIII) and Medicaid (Title XIX) amendments to the Social Security Act in 1965 allowed the burden of the costs of caring for the aged mentally ill to shift from the States to the federal treasury.

Between 1954 and 1976 the number of nursing home beds increased over eight times—from 170,000 to 1,407,000. From 1969 to 1973 the number of individuals residing in nursing homes who were 65 and older with a primary diagnosis of mental disorder doubled—from 96,000 to 194,000. During this same period the mentally ill aged in psychiatric hospitals decreased by almost 40 percent (Redick, 1978).

By 1977 the National Nursing Home Survey of the National Center for Health Statistics found that, of the 1.3 million residents of nursing homes surveyed, approximately 290,000 had a primary diagnosis of mental disorders, 100,000 had a secondary diagnosed mental condition, and an additional 400,000 were found to have "senility without psychosis." This number included a large number of under-65 mentally ill individuals who were shifted to nursing homes where they could be supported by Medicaid as long as the homes had not more than 50 percent of their residents with a primary mental disorder (Regier, 1978).

It is increasingly clear from several studies and congressional hearings (Special Committee on Aging, 1976; Scherl & Macht, 1979; Glasscote, Beigel, Butterfield, Clark, Cox, Elpers, Gudenor, Gurel, Lewis, Miles, Raybin, Reifler, & Vito, 1976) that a shift in locus from state mental hospitals to nursing homes has taken place, suggesting that the term "deinstitutionalization" may be a misnomer since many individuals have been "transinstitutionalized" to community "mini-asylums" (Lamb, 1979).

Community Mental Health Care Expansion

In 1963 President Kennedy signed into law the first federal mental health services act, P.L. 88-164, which established the Community Mental Health Centers (CHMC) Program. This Act authorized a total of $150 million over a three-year period to be divided among States for the construction of new community-based facilities. Two years later Congress added an additional $74 million for staffing assistance. The goal was to cover some 2,000 "catchment areas" across the U.S. with a comprehensive, community-based program to which, in the words of Congress, "all Americans should enjoy access" (P.L. 94-63).

As of 1982, 798 CMHCs were operational, far less than the original goal of 2000. The number of needed CMHCs was revised downward in 1970 to 1500. However, 32 percent of all patient-care episodes in the specialty mental health care sector in 1977 took place in federally initiated CMHCs, up from 18.6 percent of all episodes in 1971. CMHCs have accounted for a major part in the growth of day treatment services, which were virtually nonexistent in 1955 (35.6 percent of all such programs in 1977). The strengths and weaknesses of the CMHC Program have been assessed in over 60 evaluation studies and again reevaluated in the 1978 President's Commission on Mental Health (Borus, 1978; NIMH, 1978; Ozarin;, 1977).

Mental Health Services Provided in General Health Settings

The major settings for care of mental disorders are not in specialty mental health facilities, but rather in general health care settings. In 1975, of the total estimated number of individuals with a mental disorder (32 million), approximately 57 percent (19 million) received services only in primary care or outpatient medical settings and general hospital or nursing home settings. About 20 percent of the total (7 million individuals) were seen in the specialty mental health sector (Regier, 1978). It is the trend data from the "specialty" sector that we have focused on; that is, individuals hospitalized in public mental hospitals, psychiatric units in general hospitals and seen in mental health outpatient settings such as CMHCs. The importance of the general health care sector, especially the primary care setting, cannot be over-emphasized as a critical element in the evaluation, treatment, and disposition of the mentally ill. The training of primary care practitioners and the linkages of general health with specialty settings are vital issues of public policy.

The Current Crisis

Clearly, great change has occurred in what is considered to be the most appropriate setting for treatment and the most appropriate roles of a variety of professionals and paraprofessionals, and in recognizing the potential for independent living of persons with chronic mental illness. There have been major improvements in access to care; and a variety of new public and private settings have emerged. The expanded service system today allows a considerable degree of consumer choice in practitioner and practice settings. There is increased integration of mental health with general health care, and as a result greater cost effectiveness for both has emerged. Gone is the system of 19th century asylum psychiatry for the many, and the 1950s' psychoanalytic approach for the few. Today the mental health system is similar to general health in its proportion of outpatient/inpatient care and its emphasis on acute care. While the number of state and county mental hospitals decreased only two percent from 1955 to 1977, the number of beds in these hospitals decreased by 70 percent.

What caused this vast shift in the mental health service system? During the past quarter century the mental health enterprise has, as might be stated by business planners, "expanded and diversified its portfolio." State government was a prime mover in this particular expansion, but it was mostly the federal government, without any specific centralized planning, that promoted the financial opportunities for innovation and a variety of community-based settings for treatment and support. An entirely new system of care has evolved, in large part because of federal leadership and the "seed money" of the federal Community Mental Health Centers Program. Psychiatric units in general hospitals, mostly funded through private third-party insurance and federal Medicaid, and the community mental health centers account for the greatest growth in the facility sector of the specialty mental health system. Federal welfare support through Social Security Titles II and XVI and food stamp programs were essential for many patients who were discharged out of the hospitals to live in community settings. Indeed, the discharge rates from state and county mental hospitals became for policy makers a new cult of curability, with discharge and deinstitutionalization becoming equivalent to cure.

It is clear that enormous advances have occurred in psychopharmacology and community care. Somatic and psychotherapies are more advanced and clearly an improvement as contrasted to the pre 1955 period. Yet, many of the non-medical needs are not being met, and thousands are fending for themselves outside the walls of an asylum, having been abandoned by government and by families.

Have inflated claims for the success of community care created disillusionment in the 1980s similar to that of the 1850s when moral treatment was oversold to the public? The statistics on the change in settings of care, length of stay, and numbers of individuals being deinstitutionalized both camouflaged the major emerging problems now present in many communities and brought into the open the fiscal constraints of the 1980s.

There is tremendous variation among communities in opportunities for treatment and rehabilitation for the chronic patient depending upon socioeconomic class and local economic community traditions. Service opportunities and income supports vary widely, with the poor mentally ill faring very differently in California, Mississippi, Arkansas, and Maine. Nevertheless, almost 800 federally-initiated community mental health centers now cover 54 percent of the country. Although the number of inpatient beds in state hospitals has declined, these public facilities remain a most significant factor for a residual number of severely disabled people who require care and support 24 hours a day, 7 days a week, 52 weeks a year. The number of chronically mentally ill people in communities has increased dramatically and the integration of such patients with health and social service systems varies considerably across the country. The best opportunities for this group of highly vulnerable people occur in those areas that provide an organized system of community mental health and community support. These systems use expanded and modernized state hospital outpatient and day treatment units, inpatient units of general hospitals, and close interaction with psychosocial rehabilitation centers and clubs. Opportunities for housing, ranging from supervised shelter to independent homes, have become a key element in any successful long-term care program. Sustaining high quality care is a difficult task given the fiscal constraints of the 1980s.

The current Administration's intergovernmental policy reminds us of President Pierce's veto message to the Congress in 1854. Cutting back federal involvement from the care and support of the mentally ill will have a profound impact on the opportunities for individuals with chronic mental illness in our communities.

FIVE KEY ISSUES IN THE SOCIOPOLITICAL ARENA OF HEALTH CARE

Opportunities for health and health care depend on the social contexts in which we live, from the quality of community environments to the interactions within the family. We rely on each other for survival, growth, fulfillment, and achievement. Physical and mental health is contingent on the sociopolitical arena in which we live, the particular combination of cultural and economic value systems often called the "social consensus." Society's governmental processes translate these values; they define the lawful boundaries of action and allocate public resources accordingly. Naturally, the practice of medicine both conditions and is conditioned by these factors, and operates within this arena.

The self-evident truth of these assertions as they apply to this subject has recently been forcefully restated by a British self-described "revolutionary-socialist," who noted: "mental illness is a social construction; psychiatry is a social institution, incorporating the values and demands of its surrounding society." This author cogently criticizes the proponents of "anti-psychiatry," Goffman, Szasz, Foucault, and Laing, on many grounds. From a sociopolitical perspective, however, his main argument is that their various approaches to defining away or eliminating mental illness and the practice of psychiatry have been seized upon to justify the current spreading abdication of social responsibility for fellow citizens who are severely disabled (Report to the Secretary, 1980).

One does not have to be a revolutionary socialist to agree with this position: that it is government, especially the national government, that must be persuaded to commit and recommit our society's resources to meet the moral obligation posed by our most vulnerable and dependent individuals. What is called for is a new citizen-professional-reformer alliance that petitions our government and finds the consensual voice that will effectively persuade government to devote resources on behalf of the seriously, mentally ill. What follows are the key issues for this group of former patients, family members, professionals, and reformers as they approach government to enhance opportunities for treatment and support for the chronic schizophrenic.

Current preoccupations with the costs of health care focus more on illnesses and treatments that are not definitive, so called half-way technologies where we can help mental patients be "better but not well" (Klerman, 1977). In contrast to vaccines and antibiotics for infectious disease, these half-way technologies, such as chronic dialysis for kidney disease or neuroleptics for schizophrenia, cost society more as patients live longer and consume more resources from their families, neighbors, and government. Humane and quality delivery of care requires dedicated professional leadership, a caring and informed citizenry, and a government willing to tax its own people to lessen life's inequities. The well must pay for the sick. Care for our approximately 1.5 million schizophrenics has never before been so dependent on such leadership and social will.

In this complex, multifaceted society, we see many contradictory forces and values that determine basic life opportunities for our mentally ill citizens. Ours is a capitalist, competitive society. The value of independence, autonomy, and individualistic achievement can overwhelm the collective responsibilities we bear toward the infirm and destitute. Our political tradition relies on professional and citizen leadership to mitigate some of these inequities. The basic issues are often front page news—the stories of bag ladies freezing in doorways and grate people dying in our streets.

Prior to deinstitutionalization, financing policies were based on the "economies of scale" of large State and county mental hospitals. Total asylums served as the locus of long-term care for the chronically mentally ill for years and for lifetimes, providing in one financing package not only mental health care but also food, clothing, shelter, and in some instances, social services and rehabilitation. It is obvious that the successes and failures of deinstitutionalization are greatly affected by funding policies. To over-simplify a bit, in place of the previous policy of economies of scale, the tendency has been to shift toward an implicit policy of "let the other person (or agency) pay." Among the most significant factors pushing toward reducing long-term psychiatric hospitalization has been the financial pressure of rising hospital costs and the opportunity for State mental health agencies to save money by transferring costs of long-term mental health care to federally-subsidized SSI and/or Medicaid programs.

The Public Health Service stated as a matter of policy that

> in the future, the term 'deinstitutionalization' will be used as a neutral term rather than as a goal. This (phenomenon) has occurred, is occurring, and will continue to occur throughout the country for a combination of reasons. In itself, it is neither 'good' nor 'bad.' It is clear that many people remaining in large impersonal institutional facilities could be better cared for in appropriately conceived and managed community programs. It is also clear that unless such facilities are developed, moving people out of institutions into a haphazard nonsystem of 'community' settings is no solution. (Report to the Secretary, 1980, p. 1–6).

Clearly, reliance on hospitals for long-term care of the chronically mentally ill is diminishing for many valid reasons, among the most important being the negative consequences of long-term institutionalization and the increasing attention to human and civil rights of the mentally disabled. What is also clear, however, is that existing funding policies—federal, State and local—are poorly designed to meet the basic and special needs of chronically disabled people in the community.

Existing funding patterns are a hodge-podge of conflicting formulas, planning jurisdictions, eligibility requirements, etc. Both responsibility and resources for care of the chronically mentally ill are fragmented among three levels of government and among a wide range of mental health and human service agencies, with no single agency having either the mandate or the resources for providing comprehensive assistance to the mentally disabled in the community. Cutbacks in the federal support system create pressure on State and local government to pick up the slack.

Deinstitutionalization raises a number of specific financing problems that have emerged relative to the goal of developing comprehensive community support systems for the chronically mentally ill.

How can emergency services best be funded to encourage use of the least restrictive setting and the least obtrusive means? At present, financial coverage for alternatives to inpatient hospitalization for mental health treatment is very limited. Particularly lacking is coverage for home care, assistance to families to cope with mental disability at home, coverage for in vivo crisis intervention and treatment, or coverage for some of the promising forms of alternative community treatment as described in recent research (Stein & Test, 1980). Even coverage for traditional outpatient care is limited, particularly under Medicare Part B, which provides reimbursement only for direct physical services. Those services receive either 50 percent of a visit or a flat fee, whichever is less, with a limit of $250 annually. State and federal incentives toward unnecessary hospitalization need to be thoroughly reexamined and amended where appropriate. In the process, special demonstrations or waiver projects should be developed to explore the costs and benefits of alternatives to more traditional methods of crisis mental health treatment.

How should the living arrangements for the chronically mentally ill be financed? One of the less recognized functions formerly serviced by public mental hospitals was providing shelter for mentally ill and disabled persons on a temporary, transitional, or long-term basis. The problem of temporary special living arrangements has been mentioned above. Equally problematic in a deinstitutionalized service system is the question of what types of transitional and long-term living arrangements are needed, and what agency or agencies should pay. Recognizing the need for a broad spectrum of special living arrangements offering varying degrees of supervision, rehabilitation, treatment, and/or support, it is unclear which kinds of programs and/or facilities should be conceptualized under the health or mental health rubric, which types should be regarded as rehabilitative or social service concerns, and which types should be seen primarily as housing programs. Most importantly, individuals should have choices of living environments, including opportunities to live in their own homes with family or friends. Care must be taken to avoid financing policies that encourage stereotyping of patients or unnecessarily restrict choices (Black, 1977).

How should daytime rehabilitative and supportive programs be financed? One of the most critical needs of the chronic patient in the community, in addition to continuing mental health treatment and stabilization of periodic crises, is some place to go and something to do on a daily basis. At present, however, the mandate as to who should develop such programs is unclear, and the resources for their development are severely limited. Health insurance often restricts reimbursements to such programs, as does social insurance.

Community mental health day-care or partial hospitalization programs are one way of meeting some of the needs in this area. Such programs may be planned with either a treatment, rehabilitative, or supportive focus. In some instances, partial hospitalization programs have become the focal point within a CMHC for development of comprehensive psychosocial rehabilitation services similar to the Fountain House and Horizon House programs. This trend should be encouraged.

It should be noted in designing financing for day programs that chronic patients, while they need continuing mental health care, also need opportunities to move away from the patient role into more normal social roles such as worker, club member, and citizen. Thus, care must be taken to avoid designing and financing programs that unnecessarily perpetuate the patient role. Also, careful consideration should be given to the possible advantages of separating the treatment and rehabilitative services from the residential setting, since it is more normative in our society to live in one location and to engage in work, education, or other daily activities in another location.

How should long-term rehabilitative and supportive work opportunities be financed? It is ironic to observe that recent reform efforts relative to institutional peonage and the recent deinstitutionalization trend have, in effect, created a situation in which chronically mentally ill or disabled persons now may have less opportunity to do any useful work (especially in a recessionary economy) than they did before these reform efforts began. It has been documented that having a work role in society is often closely correlated with successful community tenure. Yet, we have not found workable methods to provide such roles in society for people with marginal productive capacity. Black has pointed out that some other industrialized countries have already developed systems for providing long-term sheltered work for their handicapped. In the United States, however, it was estimated nine years ago that we need seven times the number of substitute places in the workaday world than we had in sheltered workshops (Housing and Urban Development Report, 1982). That was before the deinstitutionalization trend released additional thousands of marginally employable persons into communities that were ill equipped to provide for them. Some chronic patients with limited employment capability still may be able to work in specially designed work spaces in regular commerce and industry, as has been demonstrated by the transitional employment programs developed on a scattered basis throughout the country. Methods should be sought to subsidize the organization and supervision of such arrangements on an indefinite duration basis, without time limits, for those who have reached their highest level of functioning.

Also, additional attention must be given to financing rehabilitation services for those chronic patients who are not expected to become even partially employable but who nonetheless can benefit from training in self-care, socialization, and the skills of daily living. Some specific form of financing for independent living rehabilitation may be required.

How can financing methods be modified to facilitate rather than impede coordination of services for the chronically mentally ill? It has been frequently observed that the current fragmented funding patterns (federal, state, and local, across a wide range of health, mental health, and human service agencies) constitute major impediments to developing integrated, comprehensive service clusters adapted to the needs of the chronically mentally ill. The fragmented thinking of many of these patients is mirrored by the thought-disordered financing of the system. We need to examine the extent to which state mental health agencies can successfully provide leadership in working with a broad range of "mainstream" agencies—vocational rehabilitation, social services, income maintenance, medical assistance, and housing—to improve and better coordinate opportunities and services for the severely mentally disabled adult.

LONG-RANGE SOCIOPOLITICAL ISSUE TO BE RESOLVED

It may ultimately be necessary or desirable to make fundamental changes in the allocation of responsibility and resources for care of the chronically mentally ill in the United States if we are to close the gap between existing knowledge and value systems and the conditions that now exist. Major redefinition of the roles and responsibilities of federal, state, and local government and of the health, mental health, and human service systems may be required. National health insurance, long on the national agenda and still awaiting debate and action, may be the vehicle for these necessary redefinitions.

The interface between mental health and other human services is a particularly critical area that needs careful scrutiny in current long-range planning for national health insurance. The National Conference on Social Welfare (Black, 1977) almost 10 years ago proposed a model for a comprehensive insurance system that should include the following kinds of services: (1) Diagnostic and Treatment Services including ambulatory diagnosis, evaluation, and treatment, and acute inpatient care (24-hour or day/night treatment). (2) Specialized and Extended Health Services including skilled nursing, intermediate or other 24-hour care that includes and organized program of health services, home health care, day care, outreach or followup visits by multidisciplinary health care personnel to provide health supervision, health counseling, and education, and therapies to patients in their own homes and in various types of community settings, and medications.

In addition, the following social services provide critical support for maintaining functioning for the chronic patient.

(3) Supportive Services including many kinds of human services such as meals on wheels, transportation, special education, vocational counseling and training, homemaker services, chore and shopping assistance, protective services, supervised living arrangements, recreation and leisure-time activities, and maintenance.

In the National Conference on Social Welfare's proposal, national health insurance would cover those health and health-related services identified in Categories 1 and 2. Costs of other supportive services in Category 3, particularly those required by individuals needing long-term care for chronic physical and mental disorders, would be borne by compatible financing arrangements outside of the health insurance system, including the patient's own resources and public and private programs that provide income maintenance, social services, supervised living, education, housing and vocational rehabilitation. The integration of these services is depicted in Table 4-1.

In addition to paying special attention to the unique needs of the chronically mentally ill in planning for national health insurance, the needs of this population must also be given careful consideration in relation to welfare reform. Balance must be sought in developing a policy that responds promptly and effectively to both the crisis and long-term needs of the population, but does not reinforce unnecessary

Table 4-1
Integrated Comprehensive Health Support Services

Financed by National Health Insurance		Financed by Other Human Service Support Sources
1 Diagnostic and Treatment Services	2 Specialized and Extended Health Services	3 Supportive Services

Individuals may enter the health care systems through 1 or 2 or 3

dependency. Both incentives and services oriented toward improving and enhancing functional capacities and productivity are necessary. Assuring such services may ultimately call for some form of social insurance to complement health insurance.

In the last 30 years State and federal mental health and social policy leaders working together have shown courage and moral vision. They developed a vision of the needs of a vulnerable population for whom improvement but not cure could be expected. They developed opportunities for life support of such people in the community and promoted some very innovative programs throughout the 1960s and 1970s. Even in the face of hostile administration, impoundment of funds, and budget vetoes, this leadership was able to sustain these programs until 1980. The current national administration is a turning point, due to the electoral mandate of 1980 and the view that there is too much government involvement with our lives and choices. The federal Community Mental Health Centers Program, a small proportion of the total cost of mental health care, has been transferred to the States through a so-called block grant. The responsibility for community mental health, its fiscal base, has shifted from Washington to the states. The States face inadequate tax bases, tax revolts, and cutbacks in federal welfare support, such as those going on right now with the SSI program.

Indeed, the safety net of social welfare supports generally has been holed dramatically. The current triennial review of individuals on the permanent disability rolls (Report of the Task Force, 1975) is leading to the dismissal of approximately three to four thousand mentally disabled individuals from this federal welfare program every month. Additional cutbacks in the food stamp programs, housing subsidies, and Medicaid are creating a fiscal crisis for the chronically mentally ill. These social welfare cuts, in contrast to the treatment and rehabilitation cuts instituted through the block grants, are particularly devastating.

One cannot expect the severely mentally disabled to pull themselves up by their own bootstraps. Sick people are now wandering in the streets or finding themselves in unsafe circumstances in modern-day alms houses like single room occupancy hotels; some of them are being reincarcerated in our criminal justice system. They are invisible persons in our midst, seen but not noticed hallucinating in our fast-food emporia, sleeping on top of sidewalk grates. In terms of cycles of reform and retreat, have we returned to Dorothea Dix's plea? These people are ill, they don't belong in jails or scrabbling at the grim margins of twentieth century "outdoor relief." They do not deserve to be penalized for being ill or accused of being shiftless and lazy.

Appropriate and sustained treatment and rehabilitation of the seriously and chronically ill is the base of a humane health and social policy. These patients are not an effective political constituency for voting or payment purposes and the cost-effectiveness of treating them is marginal at best. But a grave moral issue is at stake here. As much for our own sake as for theirs, we need a renewed sociopolitical consensus that provides for the needs of the schizophrenic patient, both the clinical needs and the life support needs.

ACKNOWLEDGMENT

The views expressed herein are those of the author and do not represent the official position or opinion of the American Psychiatric Association.

REFERENCES

Arnoff FN. Social consequences of policy toward mental illness. *Science,* 1975, *188,* 1277–1281

Borus JF. Issues critical to the survival of community mental health. *American Journal of Psychiatry* 1978, *135,* 1029–1035

Black BJ. Substitute permanent employment for the deinstitutionalized mentally ill. *Journal of Rehabilitation* 1977, *43,* 32–35

Comptroller General of the United States (Report to Congress). *Returning the mentally disabled to the community: Government needs to do more.* Washington, D.C.: U.S. General Accounting Office, Publication HD-76-152, 1977

Foley HF, & Sharfstein SS. *Madness and government: Who cares for the mentally ill?* Washington, D.C.: American Psychiatric Association, 1983

Glasscote R, Beigel A, Butterfield A, Clark E, Cox B, Elpers R, Gudeman JE, Gurel L, Lewis R, Miles D, Raybin J, Reifler C, & Vito E. *Old folks at homes.* Washington, D.C.: American Psychiatric Association, 1976

Goldman HH, Gattozzi AA, & Taube CA. Defining and counting the chronically mentally ill. *Hospital and Community Psychiatry,* 1981, 32, 21–27

Housing and Urban Development Report on shelter and basic living needs of chronically mentally ill individuals, DHHS, June 1982

Klerman GL. Better but not well: Social and ethical issues in the deinstitutionalization of the mentally ill. *Schizophrenia Bulletin,* 1977, *3* 617–631

Lamb RH. The new asylums in the community. *Archives of General Psychiatry,* 1979, *36,* 129–134

Langsley DG. The community mental health center: Does it treat patients? *Hospital and Community Psychiatry,* 1980, *1,* 815–819

National Institute of Mental Health: *Community mental health centers: The Federal Investment,* DHEW Publication No. (ADM) 78-677. Washington, D.C. DHEW, 1978

Ozarin LD. Community mental health: Does it work? Review of the evaluation literature. In WE Barton & CJ Sanborn (Eds.), *An assessment of the community mental health movement.* Lexington, MA.: Lexington Books, 1977

Ozarin LD, & Sharfstein SS. The aftermath of deinstitutionalization: Problems and solutions. *Psychiatric Quarterly,* 1978, *50,* 128–132

President's Commission on Mental Health. *Report to the President.* Washington, D.C.: U.S. Government Printing Office, 1978

Redick RW. *Patterns in use of nursing homes by the aged mentally ill.* Statistical Note 107, Division of Biometry and Epidemiology, NIMH, 1974

Regier DA. *Memorandum #41, Nursing home residents with mental disorders or senility, U.S. 1977,* Division of Biometry and Epidemiology, NIMH, 1978

Regier DA, Goldberg ID, & Taube CA. The deFacto U.S. mental health services system. *Archives of General Psychiatry,* 1978, *35,* 685–693

Regier DA, & Taube CA. The delivery of mental health services—where and by whom? In S Arieti & HKH Brodie (Eds.), *American handbook of psychiatry.* New York: Basic Books, 1981

Report to the secretary. *Toward a national plan for the chronically mentally ill.* DHHS (ADM) 81–1077, 1980

Report of the Task Force. *The impact of national health insurance on services to the mentally ill and mentally disabled.* National Conference on social welfare, Institutes on Health and Health care Delivery: Columbus, Ohio, June 1975

Rothman D. *The discovery of the asylum.* Boston: Little, Brown & Co., 1971

Scherl DJ, & Macht LB. Deinstitutionalization in the absence of consensus. *Hospital and Community Psychiatry,* 1979, *30,* 599–604

Sharfstein SS. Will community mental health survive in the 1980s? *American Journal of Psychiatry,* 1978, *135,* 1363–1365

Sharfstein SS, Turner JE, & Clark HW. Financing issues in the delivery of services to the chronically mentally ill and disabled. In JA Talbott (Ed.), *The chronic mental patient.* Washington, D.C.: American Psychiatric Association, 1978

Special Committee on Aging, U.S. Senate: *Nursing home care in the United States: Failure in Public Policy.* Supporting Paper #7, U.S. Government Printing Office #67–4750, 1976

Stein L, & Test MA. Alternative to mental hospital treatment I. Conceptual model, treatment program, and clinical evaluation. *Archives of General Psychiatry* 1980, *37* 392–397

Taube CA, Regier DA, & Rosenfeld AH. *Mental disorders in health, United States*—1978, DHEW Publication No. (PHS) 78–1232, Hyattsville, Maryland, 1978

Turner JE, & Tenhoor WS. The NIMH community support program: Pilot approach to a needed social reform. *Schizophrenia Bulletin* 1978, *4*, 319–348

Witkin MJ. *Provisional patient movement and selective administrative data, state and county mental hospitals, inpatient services by state: United States 1976.* Statistical Note No. 153, Division of Biometry and Epidemiology, NIMH, 1979

Witkin MJ. *Trends in patient care episodes in mental health facilities, 1955–1977*, Statistical Note 154, Division of Biometry and Epidemiology, NIMH, 1980

John M. Davis
Ben Gierl

5

Pharmacological Treatment in the Care of Schizophrenic Patients

HISTORY

The first reported use of neuroleptic medication for the treatment of schizophrenic patients was by Delay and Deniker in 1952 using chlorpromazine. Chlorpromazine was initially tested as an antihistamine and was noted to have sedative properties. Around the same time, the French surgeon Laborit, in an attempt to reduce autonomic response to surgical stress, noted that chlorpromazine had the interesting property of producing an apparent state of tranquilization. Also at this time, reserpine was introduced as a pharmacological agent in Western psychiatry, although it had been used in the form of the plant *Rouwolfia serpentina,* from which it is derived, by native doctors in India. The rather specific relief of florid schizophrenic symptoms that chlorpromazine and reserpine provided was a breakthrough in the treatment of schizophrenia.

Prior to 1956, psychiatric hospitals primarily provided custodial care, and with the advent of widespread use of phenothiazines, positive treatment was available. We have reviewed eight typical long-term studies of schizophrenic patients hospitalized before antipsychotic drugs were discovered (Astrup, Fossum, & Holmboe, 1962; Beck, 1968; Faergeman, 1963; Hastings, 1958; Langfeldt, 1969; Ren-

SCHIZOPHRENIA
ISBN 0-8089-1640-8

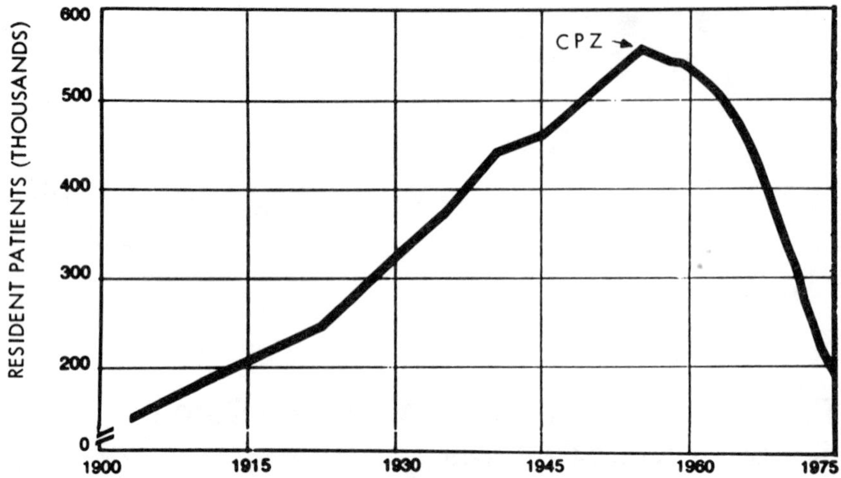

Fig. 5-1. Number of hospitalized patients from 1900 to 1975.

nie, 1939; Rupp & Fletcher, 1939–40; Stalker, 1939). In the years following 1956, a population shift (see Fig. 5-1) occurred as patients were discharged from mental institutions. This coincided with the implementation of treatment with phenothiazines. The vigorous application of other therapies, such as group therapy, psychotherapy, milieu therapy, and occupational therapy, were also made possible by the control of psychotic symptoms with effective medication treatment.

We believe the fate of many patients was altered by the large scale application of antipsychotics. Through maintenance medication many schizophrenics were able to remain out of the hospital and function adequately in the community. Of course, some had to be relocated to nursing homes and boarding homes. Today, the treatment of psychotic illness is largely accomplished through community mental health centers and wards in general hospitals where neuroleptic treatment can be started immediately and effective treatment accomplished in a short time. Since patients do not have to be transferred to distant mental hospitals in most cases, their social support networks and vocational responsibilities are maintained so they can be restored to a functional state sooner.

EFFICACY

Skeptical investigators challenged the efficacy of neuroleptics and raised the possibility that the positive results observed in patients were due to a placebo effect or to ancillary psychosocial therapy. There was considerable controversy for some time about the real effectiveness of these medications. Controlled studies have, with refinement of methods, supported neuroleptic efficacy with solid empirical data. The methodology of testing psychotropic medication and other treatments has been an important advancement in the field of psychiatry. As can be seen in Figure 5-2, about 70 percent of schizophrenic patients showed substantial improvement with an antipsychotic drug and almost none showed a worsening of their condition. With placebo, however, only about 25 percent showed a similar improvement and about 45 percent worsened (Cole, Goldberg, & Davis, 1966).

The placebo effect is thought to work by the power of expectation of improvement. Although there is certainly some measurable improvement in some patients receiving a placebo, this generally is seen in no more than 20–40 percent. A good double-blind study involves the use of a pill administered by a doctor or nurse who is "blind" to whether the pill is placebo or active drug and remains blind in rating its effectiveness. This type of study controls the therapist bias, spontaneous improvement, and effects of other treatments. Another aspect of rigorous treatment evaluation is the random assignment of patients to placebo or active medication, thus preventing placement of preselected patients in one of the groups.

Chlorpromazine and other antipsychotic drugs have been studied in the past 30 years in hundreds of double-blind controlled studies (Cole et al., 1966; Davis, 1965), with the majority demonstrating that antipsychotics in therapeutic doses are superior to placebo in the treatment of acute and chronic schizophrenia. The time course of improvement has been used to compare the effectiveness of different phenothiazines (Fig. 5-3) (Cole et al., 1966). In the average case, most of the improvement is seen in the first 6 weeks, although further treatment gains are made during the subsequent 12–18 weeks. There are dramatic individual differences in rate of response. There is no evidence that one class of neuroleptics is superior to any of the others. In addition, all subtypes of schizophrenia respond equally well to each class of neuroleptics (Goldberg, Mattson, Cole, & Klerman, 1967; Goldberg, Frosch, Drossman, Schooler, & Johnson, 1972).

Assertions that excited schizophrenics respond better to a sedating phenothiazine, such as chlorpromazine, and that withdrawn patients respond best to an alerting phenothiazine, such as fluphenazine ortrifluoperazine, have not stood up to the test of cross validation.

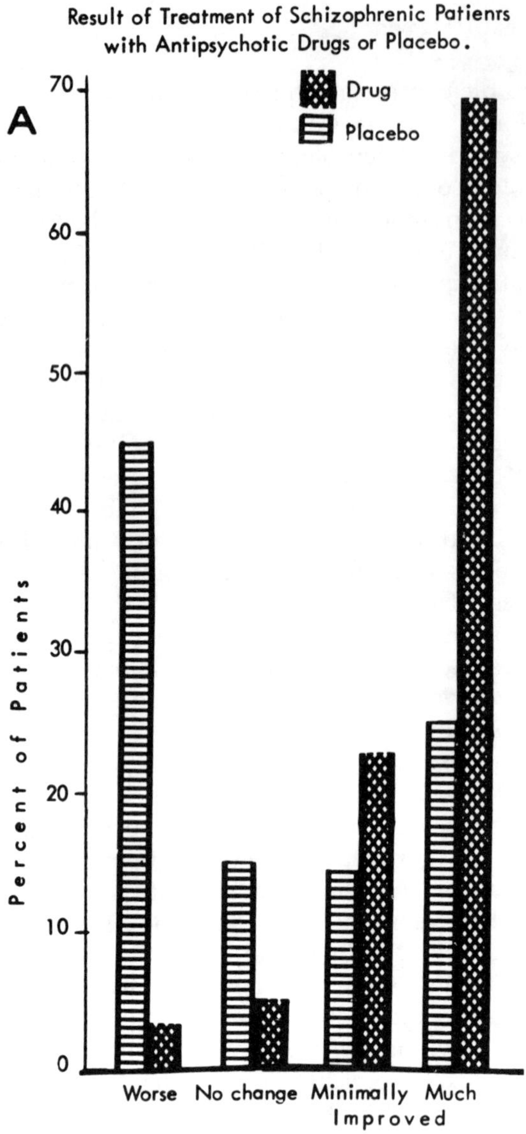

Fig. 5-2. Results of treatment of schizophrenics with antipsychotic drugs or placebo presented as the percent of patients who are much improved, minimally improved, do not change, or become worse, as determined by a reanalysis (Davis, 1976) of data in NIMH Collaborative Study No. 1 (Cole, Goldberg, and Davis, 1966). (From Davis JM. Recent developments in the drug treatment of schizophrenia. *American Journal of Psychiatry*, 1976, *133*, 208–214(6). With permission.)

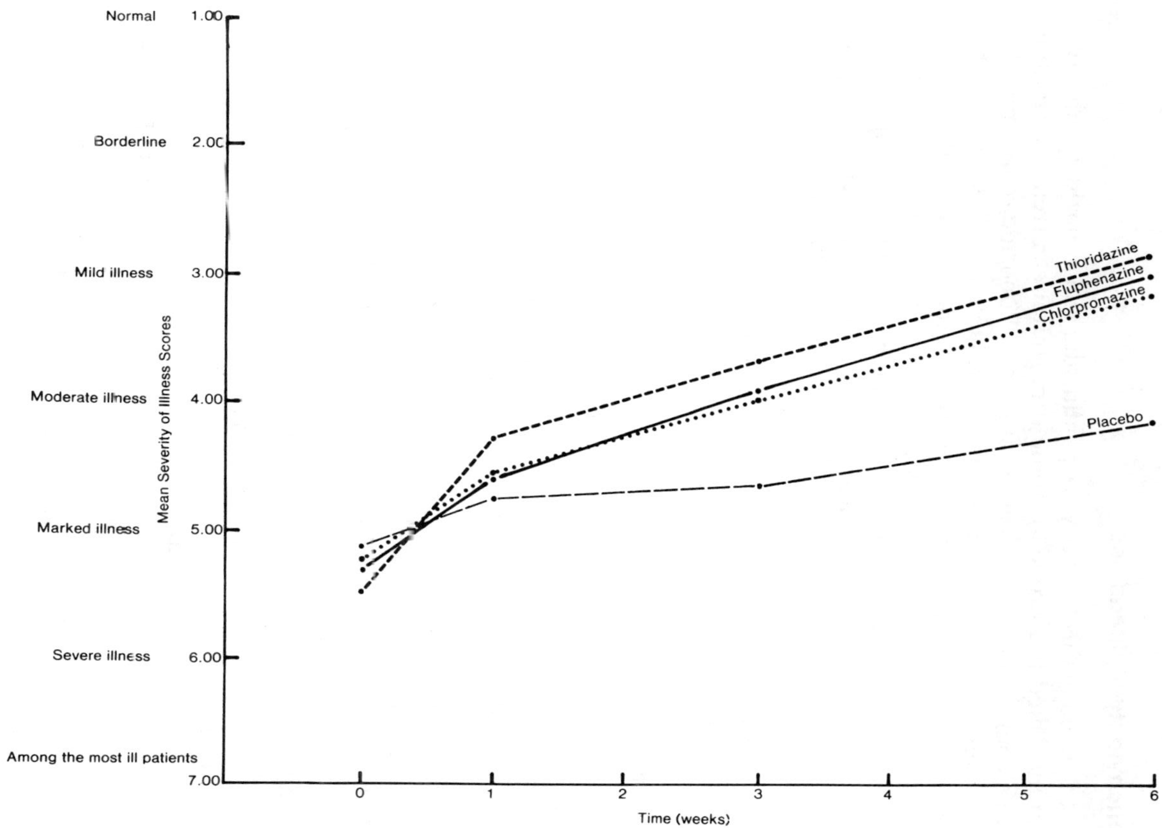

Fig. 5-3. Severity of illness over time in patients treatment with phenothiazines. (Data from NIMH-PSC Collaborative Study 1).

DRUG CLASSES

Diphenylbutyrylpiperidines

Included in this category are penfluridol and pimozide; both have been marketed in Europe for some time, but are currently available in this country only for research purposes. Pimozide represents one of the purest dopamine antagonists available and is supported by research literature as effective in treating both acute and chronic schizophrenia. It is, without a doubt, an effective maintenance drug. Penfluridol is administered orally and has a duration of action of close to one week, making its clinical efficacy equivalent to either oral or depot fluphenazine (Quitkin, Rifkin, Kane, Ramas-Loren, & Klein, 1978). This is something the other orally administered neuroleptics do not have that may increase medication compliance that is often a problem with maintenance medication.

Dihyroindolones

Molindone (Moban, Endo Pharmaceuticals) is a member of this category. Six controlled studies revealed it to be about as effective as other neuroleptics with no significant difference in efficacy for the 200 patients studied (Clark, Huber, Sakata, Fowles, & Serafetinides, 1970; Freeman & Frederick, 1969; Gallant & Bishop, 1968; Itil, Polvan, & Ucok, 1970; Ramsay, Ban, Lehmann, Saxena, & Bennett, 1970; Simpson, Amin, & Edwards, 1971). It does not cause weight gain and does not antagonize the antihypertensive effect of guanethidine.

Dibenzodiazepine

The Dibenzodiazepine clozapine is an important drug both theoretically and practically. It is no longer available for research in this country because of the more frequent occurrence of agranulocytosis than is seen with other antipsychotics. Clozapine does not appear to act upon corpus striatum neurons and therefore does not cause EPS or tardive dyskinesia (Shopsin, Klein, Aaronson, & Collora, 1979). This gives impetus to the search for a selective agent acting specifically in the mesolimbic system that would be a significant advancement in neuroleptic treatment. Since the major significant side effect of neuroleptics is tardive dyskinesia, it is important that clozapine be made available for clinical treatment in the United States. It is hard to equate a rare but life threatening side effect such as agranulocytosis, to a more commonly occurring, moderately serious, but not life-

Table 5-1
Comparison of Benefit of Loxitane with Other Neuroleptics

Drug	Number Improved	(%)	Number Treated
Loxitane	270	63	429
Other neuroleptics	267	62	428

threatening side effect as tardive dyskinesia. Clozapine could be extremely useful for patients who have tardive dyskinesia yet need an antipsychotic drug. It is hoped that clozapine will be made available for clinical use in the United States in the future.

Dibenzoxazepine

Loxapine (Loxitane, Lederle) belongs to the dibenzoxazepine category, which is structurally close to the benzodiazepine antianxiety medications (Filho, Caldiera, & Bueno, 1975). It is equal in efficacy with standard drugs in both acute and chronic schizophrenia. Table 5-1 presents a summation of 23 studies, tabulated by Davis, Janicak, Chang, and Klerman (1982), comparing loxapine with other neuroleptics.

CLINICAL ISSUES

Dosage Levels

As shown in Table 5-2, it is the dose of medication given and by inference the amount that gets to the site of action in the brain that determines a large part of the effectiveness seen. A dose sufficient to be effective must be given for a sufficient length of time to have effect. There is a wide range of dosage used for the different neuroleptics; this can be appreciated by examining Table 5-3. In order to have a standard of comparison, chlorpromazine dosage equivalence is frequently used to communicate the relative dose of another neuroleptic. It is important to keep in mind that the dosage amount shown is only an approximate number. For any given patient this may vary substantially. Relative potency means the dosage indicated has a clinical effect equal to 100 mg of chlorpromazine; hence a low number means a more potent drug. Haloperidol and thiothixene are high potency drugs and have dosages in the 2–5 mg range. Chlorpromazine and thioridazine are low potency. Different potency groups differ in their

Table 5-2
Effectiveness of Different Dose Levels of CPZ

	Percentage of Studies in Which Chlorpromazine Was		
Dose mg/day	More effective than a placebo	Slightly more effective than a placebo	Equal to a placebo
300 or less	42	23	35
301–400	50	38	13
401–500	80	0	0
501–800	100	0	0
800 or more	100	0	0

side effect profiles but not in clinical efficacy per se if adequate dosing is possible. A neuroleptic may be limited by the side effects it causes and the patient's tolerance of the side effects.

Symptom Reduction

For accurate communication, a uniform description of symptoms is necessary. This is shown in Table 5-4 for thought disorder. Uniformity of description ensures that the same phenomenon is given the same label by various observers using the same procedures and cri-

Table 5-3
Dose Equivalence

Drug	Dose
Chlorpromazine	100
Triflupromazine	28.4 ± 1.8
Thioridazine	95.3 ± 8.2
Prochlorperazine	14.3 ± 1.7
Perphenazine	8.9 ± 0.6
Fluphenazine	1.2 ± 0.1
Trifluoperazine	2.8 ± 0.4
Acetophenazine	23.5 ± 1.5
Carphenazine	24.3 ± 2.7
Butaperazine	8.9 ± 1.1
Mesoridazine	55.3 ± 8.3
Piperacetazine	10.5
Haloperidol	1.6 ± 0.4
Chlorprothixene	43.9 ± 13.9
Thiothixene	5.2 ± 1.3

Table 5-4
Thought Disorder

Symptom	Example
Contamination	On the Rorschach form Card I, a patient stated: "A butterfly holding the world together because I see on both sides patterns of a map."
Incoherence	I don't quite gather. I know one right and one left use both hands but I can't follow the system that's working."
Neologisms	A patient reports that he was "accused of mitigation."
Illogical thinking	A patient gave her family an IBM card she punched in order to overcome communication difficulties.
Loosening of associations	"I'm tired. All people have eyes. Do you have glasses? I'm thirsty, can I have a glass of water?"
Poverty of content	"Well, er . . . not quite the same as, er . . . don't know quite how to say it. It isn't the same being in the hospital as er . . . working er . . . the job isn't quite the same, er . . ." (Wing, 1971).
Condensation	(E) What does this saying mean: "One swallow doesn't make a summer." (S) "You can't enjoy everything in life just tasting the fruit one time."
Idiosyncratic word usage	I have menu three times a day."
Clangs	On asking a patient the meaning of travesty, he reports, "I think of the treasury and the dynasty."
Concreteness	On asking a patient in what way are an orange and a banana alike, he reports that "you peel them."
Overinclusion	On asking the similarity between an orange and a banana, he reports, "They come from the earth."

Reprinted from *Practical Clinical Psychopharmacology,* WE Appleton and JM Davis. Copyright 1980 by Williams and Wilkins, Co. With permission.

teria. Much work has gone into developing uniform diagnostic and rating scales and other tools for quantifying symptoms and their severity.

Although earlier investigators made claims to certain symptoms being specific to schizophrenia (i.e., Bleuler's four A's: autism, ambivalence, loosening of thought association, and affective disturbance; and Schneider's first-rank symptomatology), there are no symptoms specifically pathognomonic of schizophrenia. Antipsychotics benefit all the symptoms of schizophrenia. They also have a normalizing effect on the state of motor activity, as shown by a slowing down of excited, agitated schizophrenic patients and some speeding up in retarded or catatonic states. As implied by the name *neuroleptic,* these drugs are primarily effective for psychotic symptoms. Neuroleptics are not sedatives as such; those with greater sedative effect are not more effective antipsychotics, and they do not work through the mechanism of sedation.

There have been many studies examining the effects of drug treatment on schizophrenic thinking, and they generally have shown a substantial improvement with medication (Hurt, Holzman, & Davis, unpublished data; Schooler & Goldberg, 1972; Shimkunas, Gynther, & Smith, 1966; Spohn, Lacoursiere, Thompson, & Coyne, 1977; Wahby, Donlon, & Meadow, 1981). Overall, cognitive performance is greatly improved after antipsychotic treatment. These patients are able to read, talk, and concentrate relatively normally even though they are receiving medication. This generally coincides with the observed reduction in other symptoms of schizophrenia.

Holzman, Hurt, and Davis (unpublished) measured the change in schizophrenic symptoms and thought disorder before and after drug treatment. The results indicated that antipsychotic drugs produced a marked reduction in the various symptoms of schizophrenia along with improvement of the thought disorder. The disordered thinking improved within the same time course and to the same degree as the schizophrenic symptoms (Fig. 5-4).

Others have studied the cognitive and psychological changes related to neuroleptic administration with chronic schizophrenics. Spohn et al. (1977) administered a variety of psychological tests designed to measure attentional, perceptual, and psychophysiological parameters, and accompanying psychological dysfunctions in schizophrenia. Following a six-week placebo washout period, patients were randomly placed either on placebo or on chlorpromazine. The effect of the medication was to enhance their abilities of concentration and attention. With a reduction in the patients' previous overestimation and fixation time on perceptual tasks, they increased the accuracy of their percep-

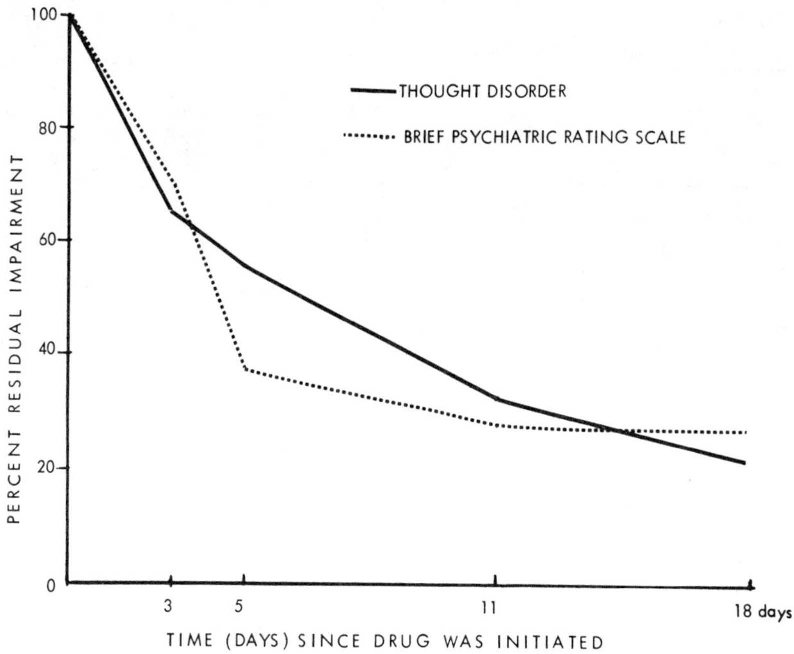

Fig. 5-4. Response to antipsychotic medication (haloperidol) in schizophrenic patients as measured by the Holzman Thought Disorder Index and the Brief Psychiatric Rating Scale (BPRS). On each measure, psychopathology is assigned a value of 100 percent prior to drug treatment and then improvement is expressed as the percent of 100 percent on these two indices at assessment time. The rate of improvement of BPRS and of thought disorder parallel each other, and at the end of the three-week study, the extent of improvement is approximately equal the residual psychopathology present at that time being reduced from 100 percent to 25 percent (Hurt, Holzman, and Davis, unpublished data).

tual judgements. With medication there also was a normalization of the autonomic dysfunction that has been documented as common in schizophrenia. This means that the medication normalizes processes that were speculated to be associated with the psychological abnormalities thought to underlie schizophrenia. It is still not known what the biological or psychological cause of schizophrenia is, so how the medication affects the causative process cannot be specified. What we do know is that neuroleptic medication normalizes psychomotor behavior and perceptual and autonomic dysfunctions, and reduces hallucinations and thought disorder symptoms. Neuroleptics decrease projection, suspiciousness, hostility, resistiveness, and ideas of refer-

Table 5-5
Effect of Phenothiazines on Symptoms in Schizophrenia

	V.A. Study No.1	V.A. Study No. 3	Kurland 1966	NIMH-PSC No. 1	Gorham and Pokorny. 1964 vs. Group Psychotherapy
Fundamental symptoms					
Thought disorder	+ +	+ +	+ +	+ +	+ +
Blunted affect-indifference				+ +	+
Withdrawal-retardation	+ +	+ +	0	+ +	+ +
Autstic behavior-mannerisms	+ +	+ +	0	+ +	+
Accessory symptoms					
Hallucinations	+ +	+ +	+	+	0
Paranoid ideation	0	+ +	0	+	+
Grandiosity	0	0	0	0	+
Hostility-belligerence	+ +	+ +	H.R.*	+	+
Resistiveness-uncooperativeness	+ +	+ +	H.R.	+ +	+ +
Nonschizophrenic symptoms					
Anxiety-tension agitation	0	0	H.R.	+	0
Guilt depression	+ +	0	0	0	0
Disorientation				0	
Somatization					0

From Cole, JO, Goldberg, SC, & Davis, JM. Drugs in the treatment of psychosis: Controlled studies. In P Solomon (Ed.), *Psychiatric drugs.* New York: Grune & Stratton, 1966. With permission.
+ + Sympton areas showing marked drug-control group differences; +, those showing significant but less striking differences; 0, areas not showing differential drug superiority.
* H.R.: heterogeneity of regression found on analysis of co-variance of the measures indicated. (This invalidates this particular statistical procedure, but does not mean that there was no drug effect. Cole, Goldberg, and Davis, 1966.)

ence, and so, with the above beneficial results, may restore coherence and normalcy to cognitive processes (see Table 5-5).

Mechanism of Action

All clinically effective antipsychotics block the neurotransmitter dopamine at postsynaptic membrane receptor sites in the central nervous system (Carlsson, 1978; Horn & Snyder, 1971). This occurs at all three major sites of dopamine transmission in the brain: the mesolimbic system, the corpus striatum, and the hypothalamus-pituitary system. It is the dopamine blockade in the mesolimbic system that is thought to be responsible for the antipsychotic effect of these agents. Corpus striatum dopamine blockade is thought to cause the extrapyramidal side effects (EPSE), including Parkinsonian symptoms, associated with these drugs. As Parkinson's disease involves a dopamine deficiency somewhat reversible with dopamine administration, one can understand how these side effects are produced by the blockade of dopamine. With central dopamine receptors blocked by the antipsychotic agents, dopamine synthesis is increased and some tolerance to EPSE develops over the course of a few weeks treatment. These effects are the basis for the dopamine hypothesis of schizophrenia. This hypothesis is supported by the finding that blockade of dopamine receptors as measured by dopamine binding in vitro is parallel with the potency of antipsychotic compounds in man. In other words, the dose necessary to help schizophrenia corresponds quantitatively with the dose necessary to block dopamine binding in vitro (Creese, Burt, & Snyder, 1976; Seeman, Chau-Wong, Tedesco, & Wong, 1975; Seeman, Lee, Chau-Wong, & Wong, 1976; Snyder, Creese, & Burt, 1975). Although this theory does not fully explain the biochemical basis of schizophrenia, the dopamine receptor blocking property has proved helpful in finding drugs to treat schizophrenia. For example, an isomer of flupenthixol that blocks dopamine receptors is a potent antipsychotic in humans, but another flupenthixol isomer that does not block dopamine receptors is ineffective in schizophrenia (Johnstone, Crow, Frith, Carney, & Price, 1978). Another finding supporting blockage of dopamine at the receptor site as the reason neuroleptics have their beneficial effect, is that blocking dopamine synthesis with alpha-methylparatyrosine reduces the amount of neuroleptic agent necessary for a beneficial effect in schizophrenia (Carlsson, 1978). Other agents that decrease the level of dopamine (reserpine and tetrabenazine) have antipsychotic properties, but are less effective than phenothiazine derivatives (Davis, 1965). These agents act through non-selective interference with the storage of biogenic amines such as serotonin, norepinephrine, and dopamine, by compromising the integrity of the storage vesicles. It also has been found that apomorphine has an antipsychotic effect, presumably because it stimulates presynaptic receptors and thus effects reduced dopamine synthesis and release (Corsini, DelZompo, Maconi, Chianchetti, & Mangoni, 1977; Smith, Tamminga, Haraszti, Pandey, & Davis, 1977; Tamminga, Schaffer, Smith, & Davis, 1978).

If decreasing dopaminergic activity benefits schizophrenic patients, increasing dopaminergic activity should aggravate their disorder. Stimulants such as amphetamine, methylphenidate, and cocaine are potent dopamine releasers and also block the presynaptic reuptake of dopamine. In large doses, these drugs can cause a paranoid schizophrenic-like episode in both addicts and normal subjects. In patients with schizophrenia, Janowski, El-Yousef, Davis, and Serkerke (1973) showed that small intravenous doses of methylphenidate produced a marked worsening of the preexisting psychotic symptoms in patients with active symptoms; catatonic schizophrenics become more catatonic and hebephrenic schizophrenics more hebephrenic. This may be a different phenomenon from that seen in nonschizophrenics given large doses. All this is consistent with the dopamine hypothesis of schizophrenia; although the evidence is impressive, it is not conclusive.

Plasma Levels

Most clinicians find a great variability in the dose requirements of schizophrenics. Some patients respond well to low dose treatment, but will fail to improve, or may even deteriorate, with higher doses. Others fail to respond when given low to moderate doses, but show considerable improvement on higher doses. Blood levels have been studied in an attempt to explain this discrepancy as they may reflect a convenient measure of the amount of drug available to the CNS receptor site due to the pharmacokinetic factors involved. Blood levels should reflect the amount of drug absorbed. Absorption may be decreased in oral administration because the drug may bind to other substances in the gastrointestinal (GI) tract. Drugs metabolized by the liver may also be considerably degraded on the first pass after GI absorption. This may be circumvented by using other modes of administration.

The following equation has been worked out to represent the blood concentration relationship for a fixed dose of drug given at specific time intervals (Greenblatt & Koch-Weser 1975).

$$\bar{C}_\infty = 1.44 \times \frac{fD \times t_{1/2B}}{V_d \times T}$$

$\bar{C}_\infty$ represents the average steady-state concentration of the drug in the blood, fD is the absorbed dose, $t_{1/2B}$ is the elimination half-life, V_d is the apparent volume of distribution of drug in the body, and T is the dosage interval. It is important to recognize that not all drugs fit the above pharmacokinetic model, but in terms of general principles, drug concentration in the blood is a function of dose times half-life divided by volume of distribution times dosage interval. Both volume of distribution and half-life can be different in different patients.

The volume of distribution may differ greatly between lean persons and obese persons. Most neuroleptics are highly lipophilic. The metabolism rate may be genetically influenced or influenced by other medications, alcohol, or nicotine competing for the same liver enzymes. This drug-drug interaction has been well documented with other compounds. We have shown that phenobarbital decreases chlorpromazine blood levels, presumably by inducing liver microsomal enzymes that metabolize chlorpromazine more rapidly through an entirely different mechanism (Curry, Janowsky, Davis, & Marshall, 1970).

Only the drug free in plasma will be available for transfer across the membrane, such as into the red blood cell or the central nervous system (across the blood-brain barrier). Plasma protein binding may be decreased in malnutrition and plasma proteins can be altered by disease. If drugs compete for binding sites, higher free plasma levels can occur. The theoretical advantage to using a red blood cell level is that it may be a better model for the brain level as only a drug that has crossed a membrane will be measured.

If clinical response depended only upon getting a sufficient amount of drug to the receptor site, one would expect to see a simple, classical sigmoid curve representing the dose-response curve. The top portion of Figure 5-5 shows the lack of clinical response with small doses of drug (low plasma level) and the improving clinical response as the drug amount reaching the receptor is increased. With increased dosage, a plateau occurs above which increasing the dosage further has no benefit. The adverse effects of medication, which seem to increase as plasma levels increase, are represented by the middle section of Figure 5-6. As for the total clinical benefit to the patient, as plasma level increases, the patient improves until improvement levels off—this is the optimal benefit level. Any further increases in plasma level result in detrimental side effects that may outweight the beneficial therapeutic effect. The dose-response curve, therefore, is an inverted U-shaped curve (bottom of Fig. 5-6). This was demonstrated by Casper, Garver, Dekirmenjian, Chang, and Davis (1980) by measuring red blood cell levels of butaperazine. The situation is much more complex for neuroleptics such as chlorpromazine, which are extensively metabolized into compounds having different pharmacologic properties and different therapeutic and side effects. As shown by Cohen, Herschel, and Soba (1980), different patients show varying proportions of chlorpromazine and thioridazine metabolites; this correlates with different therapeutic and side effects being seen between individuals given the same drug. There is evidence from several laboratories that patients with low plasma levels fail to have an adequate clinical response and also evidence that there may be patients who fail to respond with high plasma levels (Curry, Janowsky, Davis, & Marshall, 1970; Curry, Marshall, Davis, & Janowsky, 1970; Davis,

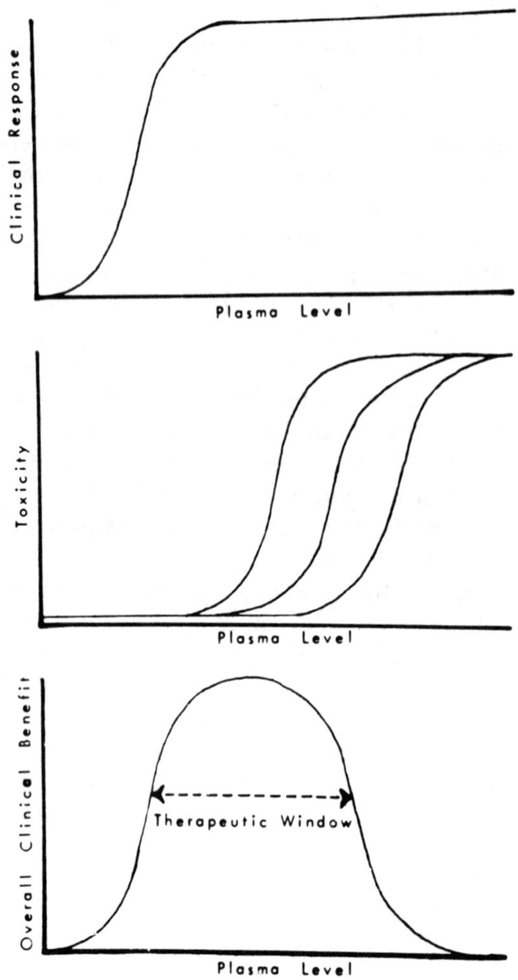

THEORETICAL CONCEPT OF THERAPEUTIC WINDOW

Fig. 5-5. Schematic hypothetical relationship between plasma level and clinical response; between plasma level and toxicity; and between plasma level and overall clinical benefit (From Davis JM, Ericksen SE, & Dekirmenjian H. Plasma levels of antipsychotic drugs and clinical response. In MA Lipton, A DiMascio, & KR Killian (Eds.), *Psychopharmacology: A generation of progress*. New York: Rarer Press, 1978.)

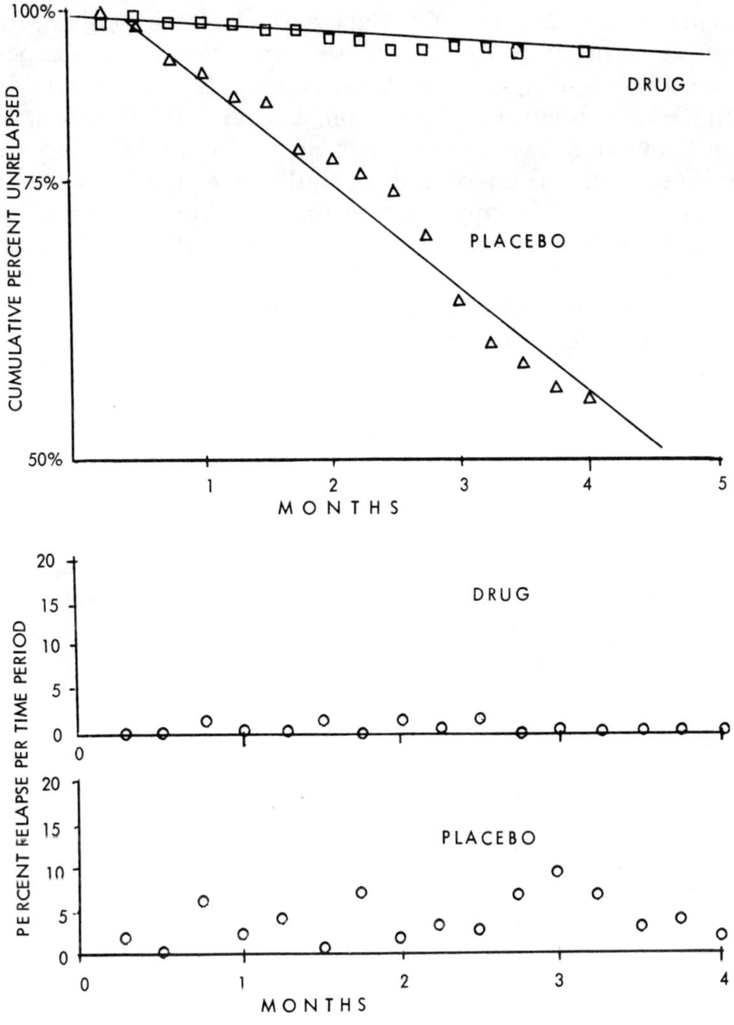

Fig. 5-6. Reanalysis of data presented by Caffey et al. (1964). Top panel presents cumulative percent of schizophrenics unrelapsed on drug or placebo vs time. Bottom panel presents the percent of patients who relapsed in each time period (number of patients relapsing vs number of patients unrelapsed at the beginning of that period).

Eriksen, & Dekirmenjian, 1978; Garver, Davis, Dekirmenjian, Jones, Casper, & Haraszti, 1976; Garver, Dekirmenjian, Davis, Casper, & Eriksen, 1977; Smith, Dekirmenjian, Crayton, Klass, & Davis, 1979; Smith, Dekirmenjian, Davis, Crayton, & Evans, 1977; Smith, Tamminga, Crayton, & Davis, 1979; Wode-Helgodt, Borg, Fryo, & Sedvall, 1978; Wode-Helgodt, Encroth, Fryo, Gullberg, & Sedvall, 1977). This can be understood by appreciating that sometimes a drug that is stimulatory to the receptor site in lower concentrations may be inhibitory at higher concentrations. Much more research is necessary with consideration of the metabolites and primary compounds together in analysis of the therapeutic and adverse side effects. Because the level of medication at the receptor site itself cannot be measured in the alive subject, it is necessary to make inferences from what can be measured. Plasma or red blood cells level may be endorsed as reasonable parameters: plasma chlorpromazine level has been shown to correlate with cerebrospinal fluid chlorpromazine level ($r = 0.9$) by Sedvall (1979) and Wode-Helgodt et al. (1977, 1978). At the present time clinicians must use their clinical judgement in adjusting dosage of neuroleptics and observing therapeutic response and side effects, while allowing sufficient time for a response to be observed on what seems an appropriate dose.

High Dose Neuroleptic Treatment

Due to the variability of dosage needed for a response in some patients and the failure of response to conventional dosages by a certain percentage of schizophrenics (about one-sixth), the question arises of using higher than normally recommended doses in order to get remission of symptoms. It is clear that massive doses (megadoses) of the more potent neuroleptics can be given, as is frequently reported in case histories.

The hypotheses that a high initial dosage produces a more rapid improvement and a better result after three weeks treatment than occurs with normal doses, were tested by Ericksen, Hurt, Chang, and Davis (1978). They used 60 mg of intramuscular haloperidol for 5 days in the experimental group while the control group received 15 mg orally each day of the study. After the first 5 days, the high dose group was tapered to 15 mg of haloperidol. On comparison after 5 and 21 days, the therapeutic results for both groups were identical. The high dose group had more side effects, especially dystonias. This finding has been replicated with trifluoperazine (Stelazine, Smith, Kline, & French) (Goldberg et al., 1972); and 80 and 600 mg per day of fluphenazine (Prolixin, Squibb) (Donlan, Meadow, Tupin, & Wahby, 1978).

Using 20 and 80 mg per day of fluphenazine, Neborsky, Janowsky, Munson, and Depry (1981) found no benefit from high doses over more moderate doses.

Prien and Cole (1968) found a low dose of chlorpromazine, 300 mg daily, to be less effective than a 2000 mg dose; this finding fits the dose-response curve, which shows low doses being below the optimal therapeutic response point. Clark, Ramsey, Ragland, Rahhal, Serafetinides, and Costiloe (1970) supported the finding that 300 mg or less of chlorpromazine is probably below the effective therapeutic dose for chronically ill patients. Moderately high neuroleptic doses may be beneficial, if a satisfactory response is not seen with lower dosage, especially with the high potency neuroleptics that can safely be tolerated. In acutely agitated patients, higher doses may be needed to achieve an initial response than will be necessary later to maintain remission from the illness; this can be conceptualized as a shifting of the dose-response curve to the right.

When megadose therapy is considered, it is probably best to use thiothixine; extensive clinical studies support it as causing no undue toxicity. High-dose chlorpromazine use is limited by sedation. Thioridazine dosage should not exceed 800 mg/day because of pigmentary retinopathy having been seen at these doses. In general, no advantage is seen with high-dose treatment, except with treatment resistant patients, when high doses should be considered useful as these patients may be extremely fast metabolizers or have other pharmacokinetic or pharmacodynamic factors making them relatively insensitive to the drug.

Maintenance Treatment

After a patient has responded to medication and is restored to near the prepsychotic level of functioning, it is necessary to consider medication maintenance. There may be considerable resistance to this by the patient or his or her family as it clearly reminds them that the illness has not been cured permanently. It is known from more than 35 double-blind studies that neuroleptic maintenance prevents relapse. Table 5-6 presents 33 of these studies conducted over several months of follow-up. Of these 3609 patients, 20 percent relapsed on drug, whereas 53 percent relapsed on placebo. Using the Mantel test combining the data from all 33 studies, a chi-square of 470.3 with $df = 1$ was obtained significant to $p < 10^{-100}$ (far beyond the usual ranges obtained in statistical analysis). It is clear that patients relapse over time when off neuroleptics.

Table 5-6
Antipsychotic Prevention of Relapse

Study	No. of patients	Relapse on placebo (%)	Relapse on drug (%)	Difference in relapse rate (placebo-drug) (%)
Caffey	250	45	5	40
Prien	762	42	16	26
Prien	325	56	20	36
Schiele	80	60	3	57
Adelson	281	90	49	41
Morton	40	70	25	45
Baro	26	100	0	100
Hershon	62	28	7	21
Rassidakis	84	58	34	24
Melynk	40	50	0	50
Schauver	80	18	5	13
Freeman	94	28	13	16
Whitaker	39	65	8	57
Garfield	27	31	11	20
Diamond	40	70	25	45
Blackburn	53	54	24	30
Gross	109	58	14	44
Englehardt	294	30	15	15
Leff	30	83	33	50
Hogarty	361	67	31	36
Troshinsky	43	63	4	59
Hirsch	74	66	8	58
Chien	31	87	12	94
Gross	61	65	34	31
Rifkin 1977	62	68	7	61
Clark	35	78	27	51
Clark	19	70	43	27
Kinross-Wright	40	70	5	65
Andrews	31	35	7	28
Westedt	38	63	38	25
Cheung 1981	28	62	13	48
Levine, PO	33	59	33	26
Levine, IM	34	30	18	12

From Davis, JM. Overview: Maintenance therapy in psychiatry: I. Schizophrenia. *American Journal of Psychiatry* 1975, *132*, 1237–1245
Summary statistics, $p < 10^{-100}$ (Chi square = 470.3: df = 1)

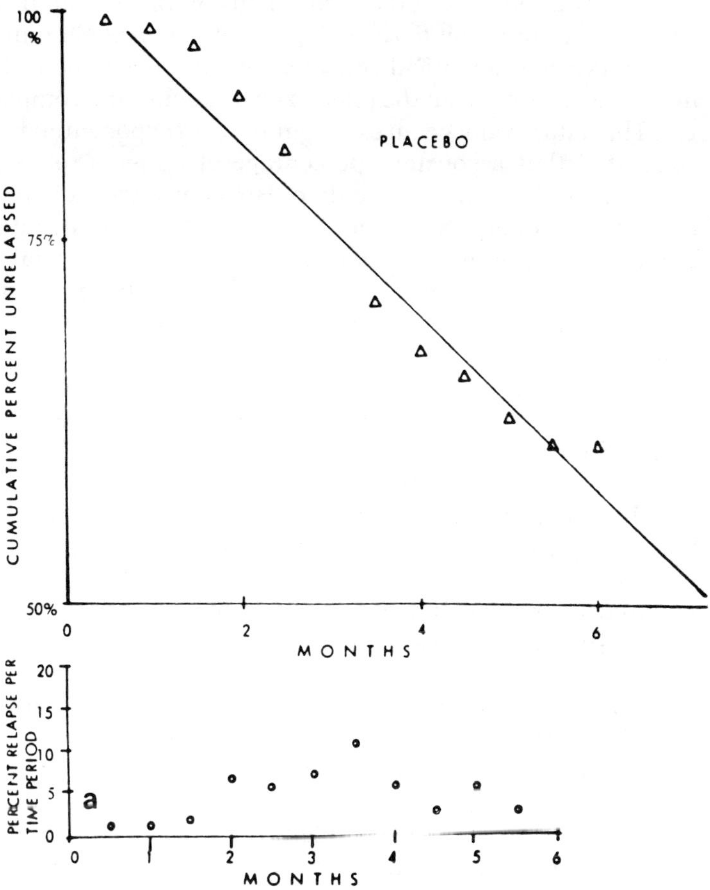

Fig. 5-7. Reanalysis of data of Prien and Cole (1968). Top panel presents cumulative percent of patients unrelapsed vs time. Bottom panel presents the percent of patients relapsing per time period (number of patients relapsing in a given time period divided by number of patients as yet unrelapsed at the beginning of that time period).

The relapse rate expressed as a percentage of patients relapsing per unit of time is presented in Figures 5-6 and 5-7 using data from two well controlled studies (Caffey, Diamond, Frank, Grasberger, Herman, Klett, & Rothstein, 1964; Prien & Cole, 1968). A semi-log plot of relapse over time yields a constant ratio relationship. The rate of relapse demonstrated by patients was first proposed by Davis (1975, 1976b) to be expressed as an exponential function. This corrects for the fact that each month a smaller absolute number of patients has not relapsed and remains in the study. Thus, with a constant relapse rate, the number of patients relapsing decreased exponentially each month. Similar mathematical consideration applies to half-life ($T_{1/2}$) of drugs being cleared from the plasma or to calculating compounded interest. The data produced an excellent fit to an exponential function and suggested that a constant percentage of patients relapse each month. Expressed this way, the data of Hogarty and Goldberg (1973) and Hogarty, Goldberg, Schooler, and Ulrich (1974) indicate neuroleptics reduce relapses by a factor of 2.5, which is a substantial degree of prophylaxis. This rate applies to patients who have a history of chronic relapsing schizophrenia and holds constant over an 18-month followup period. (Fig. 5-8)

It was reported that half of the patients who relapsed stopped taking their medication. If all relapsed patients had stopped taking their medication prior to relapsing, the protective benefit of neuroleptics would be twice 2.5, a 5-fold difference. One cannot determine, however, how many patients stopped medication because of becoming psychotic. Caffey et al. (1964) found the rate of medication dropout varied from 1.5 to 15 percent. Maintenance medication may need to be increased in times of greater stress in order to prevent relapse. Compliance studies show few patients take all their medication exactly as prescribed.

How long does this rate of relapse remain constant? There may be a certain point after which all those at risk of relapse have been eliminated, leaving some patients who will never relapse. Because so few patients in any study have not relapsed after months off medication, it is difficult to make generalizations about them. They might represent a different group than those suffering from a recurrent form of schizophrenia. Even after two years of medication maintenance free from psychosis, patients then discontinued from medication had a relapse rate similar to that initially seen in the placebo group (Hogarty, Ulrich, Mussare, & Aristigueta, 1976). It would be useful to be able to predict those who need medication maintenance; however, there is no clear evidence that any great number of chronic schizophrenics can be maintained off medication without relapsing.

Goldberg, Schooler, Hogarty, and Roper (1977) investigated schizophrenics who did and did not relapse while on medication when given psychotherapy or just brief contact with a psychotherapist. They found that those schizophrenics with good prognostic signs seemed to profit most from drug treatment. Patients asymptomatic with respect to psychotic symptoms of schizophrenia seemed to benefit most from psychotherapy compared to patients with a degree of psychosis who did poorly in psychotherapy. This is thought to mean that since psy-

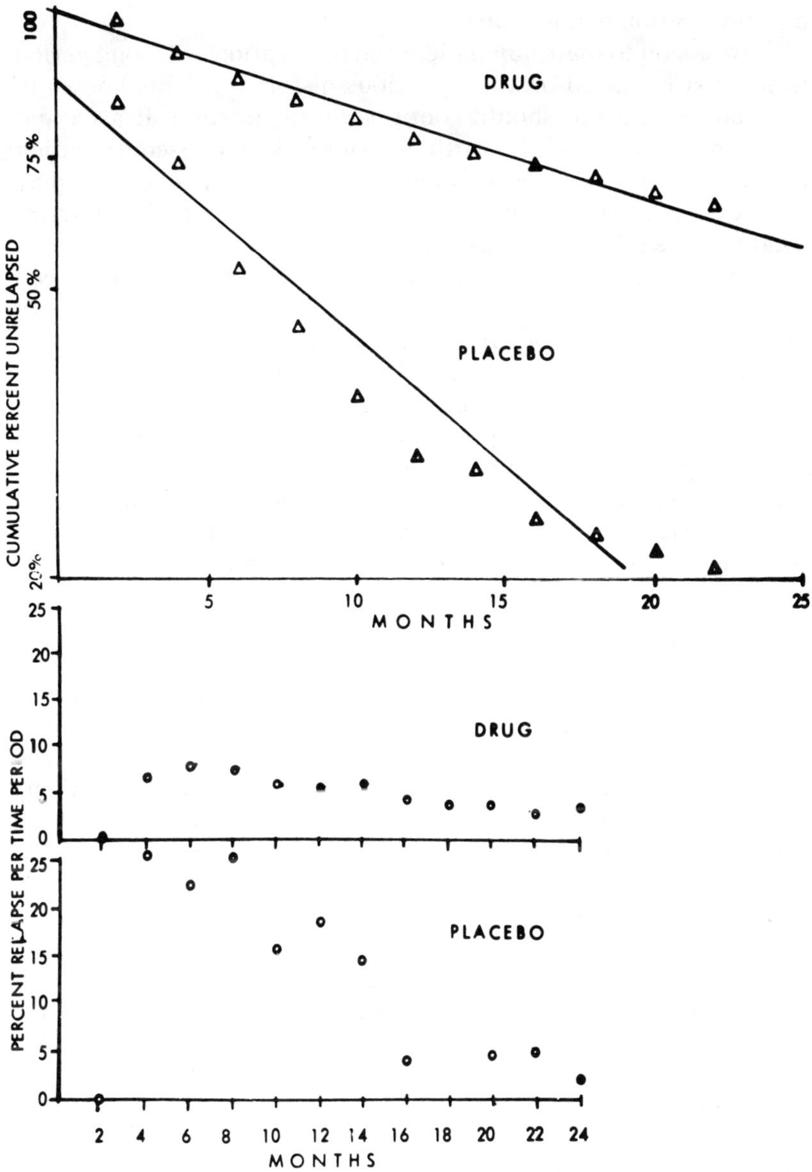

Fig. 5-8. Reanalysis of data of Hogarty and Goldberg (1973,1974). Top panel presents cumulative percent of patients unrelapsed on drug and placebo. Bottom panel presents percentage of patients relapsing per time period (number of patients relapsed divided by number of patients as yet unrelapsed at beginning of that particular time period).

chotherapy urges patients to become more responsible and more outgoing socially, it may induce a stress with which a patient in borderline compensation cannot cope.

The decision to maintain patients on medication for a long period of time must be based on their previous history; patients known to relapse off medication should continue on medication. If a patient had one episode of psychosis with no prior sickness, discontinuation of the neuroleptics with close follow-up in the next year or two may allow the patient to avoid the risks of long term medication. Careful clinical appraisal should be used in gauging the stresses of a schizophrenic patient taking medication, as the maintenance dose may need to be increased when increased anxiety is noted. Such anxiety may warn of impending psychotic recurrence that can be deterred by quickly increasing the neuroleptic. Generally, one would adjust the dose downward over time as longer periods go by with stable or improved functioning following the psychotic episode. The value of supportive pscyhotherapy should be appreciated as it benefits most patients who also are on medication. A patient on medication should not be seen as "just a medication patient," as this is a one-dimensional way of viewing the multidimensional problem of schizophrenia.

Depot Therapy

Two depot neuroleptics are available, fluphenazine enanthate and fluphenazine decanoate. Many attempts have been made to determine which of these two is superior. Van Praag and Dols (1973) studied patients in acute schizophrenic psychosis by randomly assigning them to receive an injection of one of these depot medications every four weeks. Patients could receive supplemental chlorpromazine or antiparkinsonian medication as needed. They found more patients receiving fluphenazine enanthate required antiparkinson drugs, especially during Weeks one and two. Fewer patients receiving prolixin decanoate required chlorpromazine during Weeks three and four, suggesting a longer lasting antipsychotic effect. A slight advantage or no antipsychotic difference has been found by other investigators (Del Guidice, Clark, & Gocka, 1975; Hogarty, Schooler, Ulrich, Mussare, Ferro, & Herron, 1979; Kane, Quitkin, Rifkin, & Klein, 1978; Levine, Schooler, Serene, Escobar, Gelenberg, Mandel, Somer, & Steinbook, 1980, pp. 483–4; Schooler & Levine, 1978; Schooler, Levine, & Severe, 1979). Donlon et al. (1978) also found EPSE to be slightly less with prolixin decanoate.

The ideal use of depot medication is long term maintenance. Of course, one wishes to minimize the potential for tardive dyskinesia by using as low a dose as possible; this logically should minimize the risk. Kane, Rifkin, Quitkin, and Klein (1979b), using random assignment of partially remittent outpatient schizophrenics to low (1.75–5.0 mg bi-weekly) or standard dosage (12.5–50 mg bi-weekly) groups, confirmed a lower incidence of abnormal involuntary movement in low dose group. they found, however, that the cumulative relapse rate was significantly higher in low dose group.

A newer depot medication, pipofiazine palmilate, was tested by French investigators (Simon, Fermanian, Ginestet, Goujet, & Peron-Magnam, 1978) and found equal in effectiveness to oral medication and fluphenazine decanoate. Quitkin et al. (1978) compared the efficacy of penfluridol, an orally administered neuroleptic given once weekly, with fluphenazine decanoate and observed them to be equally effective. Haloperidol decanoate injections once monthly were reported to be at least as effective as oral haloperidol (Darondel & Fengler, 1981; Meco, Casacchia, Attenni, Iafrate, Ecari, & Argenta, 1981; Roose, 1981). The dosage of the monthly haloperidol decanoate was calculated by oral dosage of haloperidol multiplied by a factor of 20. The dosage of haloperidol decanoate used in these 3 studies was 75–200 mg every 4 weeks. The dosage of fluphenazine decanoate is usually calculated from the oral dose of fluphenazine multiplied by a factor of 4.

Antidepressants and Antipsychotics

Adding antidepressants to neuroleptics in schizoaffective patients is indicated when there is an admixture of affective and schizophrenic symptoms (Brockington, Kendall, Kellett, Curry, & Wainwright, 1978; Casey, Hollister, Klett, Lasky, & Caffey, 1961; Hanlon, T., Nussbaum, Wittig, Hanlon, D., & Kurland, 1964; Hanson, Elley, Cristensen, Larsen, Naestoft, & Hviddcrg, 1979; Michaux, Kurland, & Agallianos, 1966; Prusoff, Williams, Weissman, & Astrachan, 1978, 1979).

An antidepressant may be necessary for treating a *post psychotic depression,* so called because it occurs after the florid psychotic symptoms are no longer the major problem. While maintaining these patients on the neuroleptic, antidepressant medication can be added, in doses comparable with those used for uncomplicated depression, with favorable results. Having diagnosed a typical schizophrenic psychosis does not rule out the possible need for an antidepressant if the typical neurovegetative symptoms of depression are later manifested.

Unfortunately, adding tricyclic antidepressants to antipsychotics does not produce an appreciable effect in extremely retarded or chronic, burned-out schizophrenics. One must be careful to distingush the "negative" schizophrenic symptoms from depressive symptoms; this can be done by looking for the neurovegetative symptoms of depression. A time of high risk for suicide is also the time of reconstitution following a psychotic episode; unfortunately, this also coincides with the time of discharge from the hospital.

SIDE EFFECTS

It is in their side effect profiles that neuroleptics differ most. The neuroleptics, if given in adequate dosage, which ranges widely because of the broad range of potency, are equally effective. Sometimes the dosage range of the medication is limited by the side effects experienced, so one drug may not be able to be given at an effective dosage while another may be tolerated at a dosage adequate for achieving clinical efficacy. We will attempt to generalize about groups of medications with similar pharmacological mechanisms rather than speak to each individual drug. It should be kept in mind that any single neuroleptic is potentially capable of causing any of the possible side effects listed for neuroleptics in the *Physicians's Desk Reference.*

Patients manifesting drug side effects may present to other physicians without even mentioning that they are taking psychotropic drugs (Hollister, 1964), so it is important to warn patients of side effects and to ask to be called if side effects are noted as they often can be handled before an emergency room visit is necessary.

Autonomic Effects

The low potency (high dosage for efficacy) neuroleptics are more likely to cause both anticholinergic and antiadrenergic side effects. Manifestations of the autonomic nervous system effects are dry mouth and throat, flushing of skin, nasal congestion, mydriasis or miosis causing blurred vision, urinary retention, paralytic ileus, constipation, mental confusion, and postural hypotention. Anticholinergic effects result in dry mouth, a frequent complaint that may be partially relieved by rinsing out the mouth frequently with water. Constipation, if developing, should be rectified with administration of a cathartic; if unresolved, a bowel obstruction may develop. Urinary retention is a particular concern in elderly males with prostatic hypertrophy; it may require catheterization for relief and increases the risk of a urinary tract infection. Generally, after the early stage of treatment, a tolerance to the autonomic side effects is developed, which is reassuring to patients.

Postural hypotension is a potentially serious side effect, especially if causing symptoms, and can be documented by measuring a patient's blood pressure from lying down to standing and finding a drop of 15–20 mm mercury. Hypotensive episodes may suddenly result in a fall, which for an elderly patient is especially risky as it may result in a fracture or subdural hematoma. Generally, patients felt to be at risk for autonomic side effects should be warned to proceed with caution and rise from a sitting or lying position gradually and only if they have no feelings of dizziness or faintness. These are precisely the types of instructions a severely agitated psychotic patient is not going to follow. The clinician is therefore advised to avoid using low potency neuroleptics for these patients. Intramuscular injections of chlorpromazine are known to be associated with a risk of precipitating a hypotensive crisis; this is far less likely to occur with haloperidol (Man & Chen, 1973) or other high potency neuroleptics. The risk of neuroleptic-induced orthostasis is greatest in those with preexisting orthostasis. For mild hypotension, the patient may be placed in a supine position with the feet elevated above the head. For a severe drop in blood pressure, a vasopressor agent such as norepinephrine (noradrenaline) intravenously is necessary. One cannot give epinephrine (adrenalin); it would worsen the hypotension because of neuroleptic blockade of the alpha-adrenergic autonomic nervous system receptor sites that leaves the beta-adrenergic sites available to effect vasodilation, not the desired vasoconstriction.

Electrocardiographic change can occur from neuroleptics, especially thioridazine. These changes generally consist of broadened, flattened T-waves and an increased P-R interval. It is by no means clear that this predisposes the patient to sudden death, a rare event. Levenson, Beard, and Murphy (1980) list the following cardiac conditions as contraindication for antipsychotic medication: history of strokes-Adam's attacks, idiopathic hypertrophic subaortic stenosis, and symptomatic orthostatic hypotension.

Extrapyramidal Side Effects

EPSE are the major problem in the use of high potency (low dosage requirement) neuroleptics primarily because these drugs lack the anticholinergic effects that the low potency drugs have. Because neuroleptics effect the caudate nucleus by blocking dopamine transmission and disturbing the balance between that and the cholinergic system, the result is relative over-activity of the cholinergic system. This causes symptoms such as acute dystonic reactions, a pseudoparkinson syndrome, and akathisia, in from 15 to 50 percent of those treated. Dystonic reactions can occur within hours of a single dose of an antipsychotic drug. They present as spasms of the face, neck (torticollis), back, or extraocular muscles (oculogyric crisis). These painful spasms can be relieved by anticholinergic drugs such as benzotropine mesylate (Cogentin, Merek Sharp & Dohme) or diphenhydramine (Benadryl, Parke-Davis) administered intravenously or intramuscularly. Akathisia is experienced as a compulsion to move. Patients constantly pace and move their legs in a restless manner that is difficult to differentiate from psychotic agitation except with a trial of anticholinergic medication. Drug-induced parkinsonism is characterized by akinesia, muscle rigidity, tremor, drooling, mask-like facies, shuffling gait, and loss of associated movements. This can be quantified by movement of the wrist to test for cogwheeling rigidity. Patients with underlying Parkinsonism are worsened dramatically with this side effect, which for them greatly limits the use of high potency neuroleptics.

Tardive Dyskinesia

An extrapyramidal syndrome called tardive dyskinesia may appear late in neuroleptic treatment or even after neuroleptics are discontinued. Tardive dyskinesia is an involuntary movement disorder characterized by buccofacio-mandibular movement, sucking and smacking of the lips, with jerky or athetoid movements of the arms, truck, or legs (Crane, 1968). These movements may be decreased by increasing the neuroleptic dose. However, since symptoms will reappear after a few months treatment with the increased dosage or become more severe than initially observed upon subsequent decrease of the dosage, this is not a recommended treatment. These symptoms vary during the day and seem to be worse with emotional stress, psychomotor stimulants, or anticholinergic medication; the symptoms disappear with sleep. Tardive dyskinesia is hypothesized to be a supersensitivity condition of striatal dopamine receptors that have increased in number because of the chronic blockade of dopamine by neuroleptics (Lemberger & Crabtree, 1979).

Tardive dyskinesia is the most significant risk with long-term medication. Its symptoms occur in 20 percent of patients who have received long-term antipsychotic medication and 5 percent of the controls; so, presumably, the incidence of tardive dyskinesia is 15 percent (20 percent − 5 percent) (Smith, Tamminga, Haraszti, Pandey, & Davis, 1977). The great majority of patients with tardive dyskinesia have relatively mild movement disorders that constitute only a minor social diability. There is no doubt that patients with moderate or severe tardive dyskinesia experience a substantial social disability. Patients taking neuroleptics should be examined for emergence of this condition. It often is first manifested as a vermicular (worm-like) tongue movement. If this or other symptoms suggesting tardive dyskinesia are seen, the neuroleptics should be stopped, if possible, as the symptoms may resolve after some time off neuroleptics, but otherwise may prove to be irreversible. Frequently, the discontinuation of neuroleptics is not possible without a relapse of the psychosis, with reinstitution of neuroleptic therapy being mandated. When it comes to discontinuing neuroleptics, many patients, when warned of tardive dyskinesia, prefer to risk its occurrence and potential exacerbation because of the symptomatic relief they desire from psychotic symptoms and because they are not distressed by these socially embarrassing involuntary movements. Anticholinergic drugs worsen, while cholinomimetic drugs benefit, tardive dyskinesia (Tamminga, Smith, Eriksen, Chang, & Davis, 1977).

There is currently no effective treatment for tardive dyskinesia, although much research has been directed at finding effective agents. The emphasis, then, must be on prophylaxis. All patients on neuroleptics should be carefully monitored, every three months or so, for early signs such a rhythmic, vermicular movements of the tongue. Since there is some evidence that early diagnosis makes reversibility more likely, early discontinuation of neuroleptics should be considered whenever tardive dyskinesia is suspected.

THE ROLE OF PSYCHOTHERAPY IN THE TREATMENT OF SCHIZOPHRENIA

There has always been a difference of opinion as to the efficacy of psychotherapy in the treatment of schizophrenia. Theories on exactly what constitutes the disorder of schizophrenia range from considering it to be a purely psychological disorder to considering it to be a purely biological disorder for which psychotherapy has no part to play in treatment. It is important to recall that while we have shown neuroleptics to be helpful in symptom reduction, they are not expected to induce social skills or warm, empathic human relationships beyond reducing symptoms that interfere with social functioning, thus allowing a return to preexisting social skills. Psychotherapy can reduce intrapsychic conflict and help in dealing with social and personal issues. This way of thinking about the two treatments suggests a role for both in what has been referred to as the Dual Mechanisms Theory.

Prior to the discovery of phenothiazines, the natural course of illness of schizophrenia had been thought to be one of progressive deterioration, most likely necessitating long-term custodial care. As most studies have clearly demonstrated the benefit of phenothiazines, which are a mainstay in the treatment of any psychotic illness, one might wonder if withholding them does not constitute permanent harm to the patient. May and his coworkers suggest this may be the case when phenothiazines are withheld while psychotherapy is tried (May 1968; May, Tuma, & Dixon, 1976, 1981; May, Tuma, Yale, Potepan, & Dixon, 1976). First admission schizophrenics were randomly assigned for 6 to 12 months to one of four groups (1) phenothiazine, (2) psychotherapy, (3) phenothiazine and psychotherapy, or (4) neither treatment. The maximal improvement was produced by phenothiazines, either alone or in conjunction with psychotherapy. These groups had an increased release rate, shortened stay in the hospital, decreased necessity for the use of sedatives or hydrotherapy, and an improved clinical state as rated by the Menninger Health Sickness Scale (see Table 5-7).

Of greater interest are the follow-up findings of the May study, made 3–5 years after discharge from the initial hospitalization. (Fig. 5-9) After the initial experimental period of 6–12 months, all groups of patients received standard treatment. Patients who had received psychotherapy only during the initial study had about twice as many days in the hospital after their index admission as patients who had received phenothiazines or phenothiazines plus psychotherapy.* In the subgroup of patients initially rated as undergoing successful treatment, those who had received psychotherapy plus drugs during the initial study had poorer interpersonal relationships with persons outside of the family and significantly poorer social adjustments during the first two follow-up years than patients who received drugs alone. Similarly, those who receive psychotherapy alone did significantly worse than those who received neither therapy† (May, Tuma, & Dixon, 1981).

---

*Admittedly, the psychotherapy treatment was limited because of the small amount of additional time spent with patients and the relative lack of experience of the psychotherapist. Yet, it was found that the therapist's general clinical ability and experience were not related to outcome (May,1968).

†The investigators speculate that the comparatively poor results produced by psychotherapy do not indicate a "direct toxic effect," but may result from the psychotherapy patients' longer hospital stay, which may have "fostered chronicity and social disarticulation." Also, patients who received psychotherapy during the initial study were, perhaps, less likely to receive drugs or social casework during the follow-up period (May, Tuma, & Dixon, 1981).

Table 5-7
Assessment of Outcome in Schizophrenic Patients Treated with and without Antipsychotic Drugs and Psychotherapy

	No Drugs		Drug	
	No psychotherapy	Psychotherapy	No psychotherapy	Psychotherapy
Percent released	59	64	95	96
Nurses' rating MACC total	38	38	48	48
Menninger nurses health-sickness rating	26	23	29	30
Nurses' idiosyncratic symptoms (125-X)*	37	29	66	74
Therapists' rating on symptom rating sheet (50-X)*	22	21	27	27
Analysis rating of insight	3.4	3.3	3.7	4.1

From May PRA. *Treatment of Schizophrenia: A Comparative Study of Five Treatment Methods.* New York: Science House, 1968. With permission.
* A higher number reflects greater improvement. In order to have the two scales fit with this convention, we subtracted scores from an arbitrary constant.

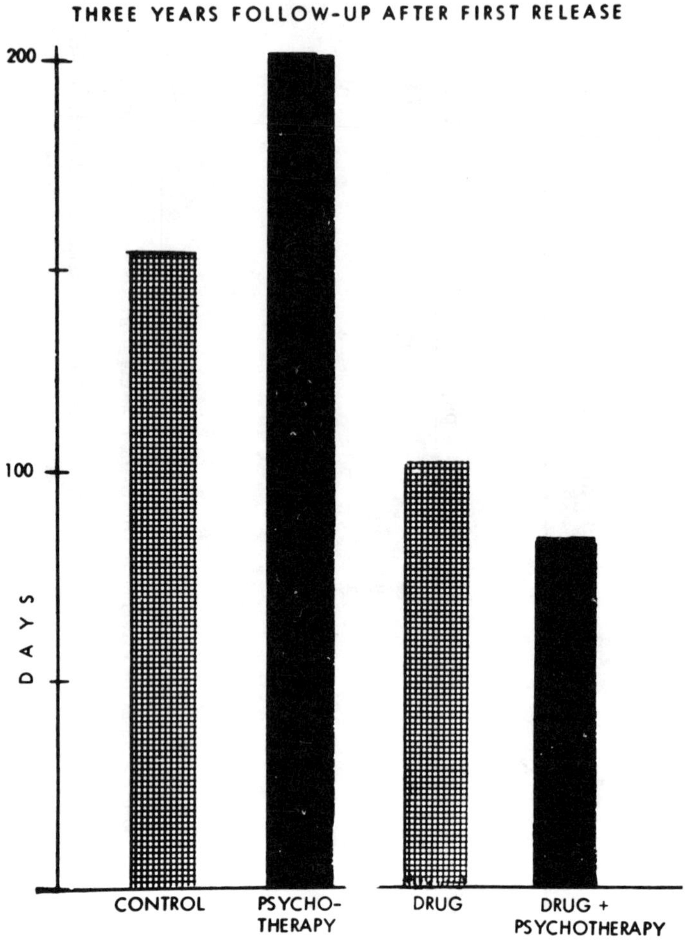

Fig. 5-9. Cumulative days in hospital during three-year period following release from hospitalization for first psychotic episode. Patients received either drug, psychotherapy, drug plus psychotherapy, or neither treatment during the first 6–12 months of the initial admission period.

There may be implications that drug treatment alters the natural history of schizophrenia in a beneficial way by preventing the harm of a prolonged psychotic experience. The effect persisted over a 3–5 year follow-up period after the initial period of drug or no-drug. As another group study demonstrated, the experimental group receiving medication after six months of social therapy only had a worse result than either the drug only or drug plus psychotherapy groups. Even if given drugs later, patients initially deprived of drugs never caught up with the initial drug-treated group (Greenblatt, Solomon, Evans, & Brooks, 1965). Perhaps, when drugs were withheld, social deterioration occurred due to the long hospitalization, or the antipsychotic drugs interrupted some sort of biochemical process that leads to deterioration. Table 5-8 summarizes some well conducted studies that allow some comparison of random assignment to psychotherapy.

As expected, neuroleptics are uniformly more effective than nondrug treatment. Other conclusions drawn from the studies in Table 5-8 are that neuroleptics do not interfere with psychotherapy for schizophrenics, as was once feared by analysts, but are a necessity if psychotherapy is to be helpful. For first hospitalization for an initial schizophrenic illness, withholding antipsychotic treatment for 6–12 months may have a long-lasting detrimental effect as the patients never catch up with or do as well at staying out of the hospital as patients given drugs initially. Drugs and psychotherapy together may help patients use the improvement with drugs to make a better adjustment. An adequate medication regimen combined with combined with family psychotherapy produced better results in outpatients than less-than-adequate dosing combined with family therapy. Family therapy does not reduce the need for antipsychotics. In outpatients taking maintenance medication group therapy may not add much symptomatic improvement, but it may benefit a schizophrenic's insight. Not enough has been learned about how to measure the meaning of the patient-therapist relationship and what goes on within that relationship to correlate gains from therapy with any course-of-illness changes.

SUMMARY

We believe neuroleptics are responsible for positive results in the treatment of many schizophrenics and that patients not treated with drugs have a worse prognosis; this is supported by many studies discussed above. No other treatment has proved as effective for schizophrenia as neuroleptics. No one neuroleptic has thus far been demonstrated to be superior to any other for any particular patient as based upon symptoms or subtypes of schizophrenic illness. There is no etiological cure for schizophrenia, only symptom control with neuroleptics; social or psychological therapy may be helpful in furthering the patient's insight and social adjustment. Before psychotherapy can be effective, the more severe symptoms of schizophrenia must be controlled with neuroleptic medication; medication also must be continued over time if relapse is to be prevented.

Table 5-8
Select Studies Comparing Psychotherapy and/or Pharmacotherapy Results in the Treatment of Schizophrenics

Principal Authors	Year	Design, Results, and Critique
Individual Therapy Studies		
Greenblatt, Solomon, Evans, and Brooks	1965	Drug and nondrug groups subdivided into intensive and minimal social therapy groups. In both social therapy groups, drugs helped especially when started initially. Social therapies helped patients use the improvement with drugs to facilitate discharge and adjustment. Those not given drugs for the first six months never caught up with the initial drug group. This suggests a harmful effect of not receiving drug initially.
Rogers, Gendlin, Kiesler, and Truax	1967	One-half of matched groups and acute and chronic state hospital patients receiving unspecified treatment were assigned to psychotherapy. Psychotherapy had no effect on the schizophrenic symptoms, but it decreased the need to deny their own experiences and increased the appropriateness in emotional expression. There was a problem of controlling for initial differences in ego strength with the comparison groups used.
Rosen	1947, 1953	Impression given of analytic techniques producing improvement in 37 cases of deteriorated schizophrenia. Horwitz, Polatin, Kolb, and Hock (1958) in a five-year follow-up, identified 19 of these patients and found 7 not diagnosed initially as schizophrenic. Of those considered schizophrenic, 75% had two to five admissions to a mental hospital during a ten-year follow-up, which contradicted Rosen's report.
Grinspoon, Ewalt, and Shader Messier, Finnerty, Botvin, and Grinspoon	1972, 1976 1969	A crossover-random assignment of a drug-placebo crossover design for chronic schizophrenics receiving intensive psychoanalytically-oriented therapy demonstrated a beneficial synergetic effect of drug and therapy with deterioration when switched to placebo.

Table 5-8 (continued)

Hogarty, Goldberg, and Schooler 1974b Hogarty, Goldberg, Schooler, and Ulrich 1974a	Psychotherapy in combination with drug or placebo was found to have no effect on the number of relapses. There was a large drug-placebo difference. With those receiving drug who failed to relapse, psychotherapy resulted in improved functioning in "relationships in and out of the home." Psychotherapy without drugs did not improve social functioning.
May 1968 May et al. 1976a, 1976b, and 1981 (see Table 5-1 and Figure 5-4)	First admission schizophrenics were treated with psychotherapy alone, phenothiazine alone, both together, or neither. The group getting psychotherapy alone did no better than those getting neither drugs or therapy. Drugs alone or with psychotherapy increased the release rate, shortened the hospital stay, decreased the necessity for the use of sedatives or hydrotherapy, and produced beneficial changes in the clinical state. The presence or absence of psychotherapy did not significantly alter the outcome. However, the therapists were not very experienced, and the psychotherapy group only received 24-hours more contact than the drug-alone group so this may not reflect a fair test of psychotherapy.
Family Therapy Studies	
Goldstein, Rednick, Evans, May, and Steinberg 1978	Following a two-week admission, acute schizophrenic patients did best on moderate doses of fluphenazine decanoate (25 mg every 2 weeks) and family therapy than on low dose with family therapy or either dose without family therapy. This supports the idea that family therapy and adequate drug therapy combined have more to offer than either alone.
Group Therapy Studies	
O'Brian, Himm, Ray, Pierce, Luborsky, and Mintz 1972	Random assignment to group or individual therapy on discharge from a state hospital while on medication yielded no difference in readmission rate, but group patients did better on social factors and symptomatic ratings on 12 and 24-month follow-up.
Claghborn, Johnston, Cook, and Itschner 1974	Outpatient schizophrenics on maintenance medication while in a group did not improve symptomatically, but made gains in insight, as demonstrated in projective tests, compared to those not given group treatment.

The positive effect of physical (drug) treatment suggests a significant organic impairment or imbalance upon which these drugs impact. Further research should help clarify the exact organic impairment or types of impairment that result in the symptomatic behavior that we now call schizophrenia. Hopefully, more specifically acting drugs that are free from the side effects that present drugs have will be synthesized, but at present, the neuroleptics available are the best we have as a basic treatment for schizophrenia.

REFERENCES

Astrup C, Fossum A, & Holmboe R. *Prognosis in functional psychoses.* Springfield: C.C. Thomas, 1962

Beck MH. Twenty-five and thirty-five year follow-up of first admissions to mental hospital. *Canadian Psychiatric Association Journal,* 1968, *13,* 219–229

Brockington I, Kendell R, Kellett J, Curry S, & Wainwright S. Trials of lithium, chlorpromazine and amitriptyline in schizoaffective patients. *British Journal of Psychiatry,* 1978, *133,* 162–168

Caffey EM, Diamond LS, Frank TV, Grasberger JC, Herman L, Klett CJ, & Rothstein D. Discontinuation or reduction of chemotherapy in chronic schizophrenics. *Journal of Chronic Disease,* 1964, *17,* 347–358

Carlsson A. Antipsychotic drugs, neurotransmitters, and schizophrenia. *American Journal of Psychiatry,* 1978, *135,* 164–173

Casey FJ, Hollister LE, Klett CJ, Lasky JJ, & Caffey EM. Combined drug therapy of chronic schizophrenics. Controlled evaluation of placebo. Dextro-amphetamine, imipramine, isocarboxazid and trifluoperazine added to maintenance doses of chlorpromazine. *American Journal of Psychiatry,* 1961, *117,* 997–1002

Capser R, Garver DL, Dekirmenjian J, Chang S, & Davis JM. Phenothiazine levels in plasma and red blood cells. *Archives of General Psychiatry,* 1980, *37,* 301–305

Claghorn J, Johnston E, Coot T, & Itschner I. Group therapy and maintenance treatment of schizophrenia. *Archives of General Psychiatry,* 1974, *31,* 361–385

Clark ML, Ramsey HR, Ragland RE, Rahhal DK, Serafetinides EA, & Costiloe JP. Chlorpromazine in chronic schizophrenia. Behavioral Dose-response relationship. *Psychopharmacologia,* 1970, *18,* 260–270

Cohen BM, Herschel M, & Soba A. Antimusearinic and antiadrenergic activity of chlorpromazine, thioridazine and their metabolities. *Psychiatric Research,* 1980, *1,* 199–208

Cole JO, Goldberg SC, & Davis JM. Drugs in the treatment of psychosis: Controlled studies. In P Solomon (Ed.), *Psychiatric drugs.* New York: Grune & Stratton, 1966

Corsini GU, DelZompo M, Maconi S, Chianchetti C, & Mangoni A. Sedative, hypnotic and antipsychotic effect of low doses of apomorphine in man. In E Costa & GL Gessa (Eds.), *Symposium on non-striatal dopaminergic neurons.* New York: Raven Press, 1977

Crane GE. Tardive dyskinesia in patients treated with major neuroleptics: A review of the literature. *American Journal of Psychiatry,* 1968, *124,* (Suppl.), 37–42

Creese I, Burt DR, & Snyder SH. Dopamine receptors and average clinical doses. *Science,* 1976, *191,* 545–546

Curry SH, Janowsky DS, Davis JM, & Marshall JHI. Factors affecting chlorpromazine plasma levels in psychiatric patients. *Archives of General Psychiatry*, 1970, *22*, 209–215

Curry SH, Marshall JHI, Davis JM, & Janowsky DS. Chlorpromazine plasma levels and effects. *Archives of General Psychiatry*, 1970, *22*, 289–296

Darondel A, & Fengler B. Open study of haldol decanoate in psychotic syndromes. *Proc. III World Congress of Biological Psychiatry*, June, 1981

Davis JM. Efficacy of tranquilizing and antidepressant drugs. *Archives of General Psychiatry*, 1965, *13*, 552–572

Davis JM. Overview: Maintenance therapy in psychiatry: Schizophrenia. *American Journal of Psychiatry*, 1975, *133*, 1237–1245

Davis JM. Comparative doses and costs of antipsychotic medication. *Archives of General Psychiatry*, 1976, *33*, 858–861 (a)

Davis JM. Recent developments in the drug treatment of schizophrenia. *American Journal of Psychiatry*, 1976, *133*, 208–214 (b)

Davis JM, Ericksen SE, & Dekirmenjian H. Plasma levels of antipsychotic drugs and clinical response. In MA Lipton, A DiMascio, & KR Killiam (Eds.), *Psychopharmacology: A generation of progress*. New York: Raven Press, 1978

Davis JM, Janicak, P, Chang S, & Klerman K. Recent advances in the pharmacological treatment of the schizophrenic disorders. In L Grinspoon (Ed.), *Psychiatry 1982 Annual review*. Washington, D.C.: American Psychiatric Association Press 1982

Delay J, & Deniker P. LeTraitement des psychoses par une methode neurolytique derivee de l'hibernotherapie. In J. Boudouresques & J Bonnal (Eds.), *Congres des medicins aliensites et neurologistes de France*, Vol. 50. Paris: Masson & Cie Libraries de L'Academie de Medecine, 1952

Del Guidice J, Clark W, & Gocka E. Prevention of recidivism of schizophrenics treated with fluphenazine enanthate. *Psychosomatics*, 1975, *16*, 32–36

Donlon PT, Meadow A, Tupin JP, & Wahby M. High vs. standard dosage fluphenazine HCl in acute schizophrenia. *Journal of Clinical Psychiatry*, 1978, *39*, 800–804

Ericksen SE, Hurt SW, Chang S, & Davis JM. Haloperidol dose, plasma levels, and clinical response: A double-blind study. *Psychopharmacology Bulletin*, 1978, *14*, 15–16

Faergeman PM. *Psychogenic psychoses*. London: Butterworth & Company, 1963

Filho VV, Caldiera MVN, & Bueno JR. The efficacy and safety of loxapine succinate in the treatment of schizophrenia: A comparative study. *Current Therapeutical Research*, 1975, *18*, 476–490

Garver DL, Davis JM, Dekirmenjian H, Jones FD, Casper R, & Haraszti J. Pharmacokinetics of red blood cell phenothiazine and clinical effects. *Archives of General Psychiatry*, 1976, *33*, 862–866

Garver DL, Dekirmenjian H, Davis JM, Casper R, & Ericksen S. Neuroleptic drug levels and therapeutic response: Preliminary observations with red blood cell bound butaperazine. *American Journal of Psychiatry*, 1977, *134*, 304–307

Goldberg SC, Frosch WA, Drossman AK, Schooler NR, & Johnson GFS. Prediction of response to phenothiazines in schizophrenia: A cross-validation study. *Archives of General Psychiatry*, 1972, *26*, 379–384

Goldberg SD, Mattson N, Cole JO, & Klerman GL. Prediction of improvement in schizophrenia under four phenothiazines. *Archives of General Psychiatry*, 1967, *16*, 107–117

Goldberg SC, Schooler N, Hogarty G, & Roper M. Prediction of relapse in schizophrenic outpatients treated by drug and sociotherapy. *Archives of General Psychiatry*, 1977, *34*, 171–184

Goldstein MJ, Rodnick E, Evans J, May P, & Steinberg M. Drug and family in the aftercare of acute schizophrenics. *Archives of General Psychiatry,* 1978, *35,* 1169–1177

Greenblatt M, & Koch-Weser J. Clinical pharmacokinetics, Parts 1 and 2. *New England Journal of Medicine,* 1975, *293,* 702, 964–970

Greenblatt M, Solomon MH, Evans AS, & Brooks GW. *Drug and social therapy in chronic schizophrenia.* Springfield: Charles C. Thomas, 1965

Grinspoon I, Ewalt JR, & Shader RI. *Schizophrenia: Pharmacotherapy and psychotherapy.* Baltimore: Williams & Wilkins, 1972

Hanlon TE, Nussbaum K, Wittig B, Hanlon DD, & Kurland AA. The comparative effectiveness of amitriptyline, perphenazine, and their combination in the treatment of chronic psychotic female patients. *Journal of New Drugs,* 1964, *4,* 52–60

Hanson LB, Elley J, Cristensen TR, Larsen NE, Naestoft J, & Hvidderg FF. Plasma levels of perphenazine and its major metabolites during simultaneous treatment with anticholinergic drugs. *British Journal of Clinical Pharmacology,* 1979, *7,* 75

Hastings DW. Follow-up results in psychiatric illness. *American Journal of Psychiatry,* 1958, *114,* 1–111

Hogarty GE, & Goldberg SC. Drugs and sociotherapy in the aftercare of schizophrenic patients. *Archives of General Psychiatry,* 1973, *28,* 54–64

Hogarty GE, Goldberg SC, & Schooler NR. Drugs and social therapies in the after care of schizophrenic patients: III. Adjustment of nonrelapsed patients. *Archives of General Psychiatry,* 1974, *31,* 609–618(b)

Hogarty GE, Goldber SC, Schooler NR, & Ulrich RF. Drugs and sociotherapy in the aftercare of schizophrenic patients. *Archives of General Psychiatry,* 1974, *31,* 603–608 (a)

Hogarty GE, Schooler NR, Ulrich R, Mussare F, Ferro P, & Herron E. Fluphenazine and social therapy in the aftercare of schizophrenic patients. *Archives of General Psychiatry,* 1979, *36,* 1283–1294

Hogarty G, Ulrich R, Mussare F, & Aristigueta N. Drug discontinuation among long term successfully maintained schizophrenic outpatients. *Diseases of the Nervous System,* 1976, *37,* 494–500

Hollister LE. Complications from psychotherapeutic drugs. *Clinical Pharmacological Therapy,* 1964, *5,* 322.

Horn AS, & Snyder SN. Chlorpromazine and dopamine: Conformational similarities that correlate with the antischizophrenic activity of phenothiazine drugs. *Proceedings of the National Academy of Sciences of North America* 1971, *68,* 2325–2328

Horwitz WA, Polatin P, Kolb IC, & Hoch PH. A study of cases of schizophrenia treated by direct analysis. (sic), 1958, *114,* 780—–783

Janowsky DS, El-Yousef MK, Davis JM, & Sekerke HJ. Provocation of schizophrenic symptoms by intravenous administration of methyphenidate. *Archives of General Psychiatry,* 1973, *28,* 185–191

Johnstone EC, Crow TJ, Frith CD, Carney MWP, & Price JS. Mechanism of the antipsychotic effect in the treatment of acute schizophrenia. *Lancet,* 1978, *1,* 848–851

Kane J, Quitkin F, Rifkin A, & Klein DF. Comparison of the incidence and severity of extrapyramidal side effects with fluphenazine enanthate and fluphenazine designate. *American Journal of Psychiatry,* 1978, *135,* 1539–1542

Kane J, Rifkin A, Quitkin F, & Klein DF. A pilot study of low dose fluphenazine decanoate in outpatient schizophrenics. *Psychopharmacology Bulletin,* 1979, *15,* 78–80 (a)

Kane J, Rifkin A, Quitkin F, & Klein DF. Low dose fluphenazine decanoate in maintenance treatment of schizophrenia. *Journal of Psychiatric Research,* 1979, *1,* 341–348 (b)

Langfeldt G. Schizophrenia: Diagnosis and prognosis. *Behavioral Science,* 1969, *14,* 173–182

Lemberger L, & Crabtree RE. Pharmacologic effects in man of a potent, long acting dopamine receptor agonist. *Science,* 1979, *205,* 1151–1153

Levenson AJ, Beard OW, & Murphy ML. Major tranquilizers and heart disease: To use or not to use. *Geriatrics,* 1980, *35,* 55–61

Levine J, Schooler N, Serene F, Escobar J, Gelenberg A, Mandel H, Somer R, & Steinbook R. Discontinuation of oral and depot fluphenazine in schizophrenic patients after one year of continuous medication. In E Cattabeni (Ed.), *Long term effects of neuroleptics.* New York: Raven Press, 1980

Man PL, & Chen, CH. Rapid tranquilization of acutely psychotic patients with intramuscular haloperidol and chlorpromazine. *Psychosomatics,* 1973, *13,* 59–63

May PRA. *Treatment of schizophrenia: A comparative study of five treatment methods.* New York: Science House, 1968

May PRA, Tuma AH, & Dixon WJ. Schizophrenia: A follow up study of results of treatments. I. Design and other problems. *Archives of General Psychiatry,* 1976, *33,* 481–486

May PRA, Tuma AH, & Dixon WJ. Schizophrenia: A follow up study of the results of five forms of treatment. *Archives of General Psychiatry,* 1981, *38,* 776–784

May PRA, Tuma AH, Yale C, Potepan P, & Dixon WJ. Schizophrenia: A follow-up study of results of treatment. II. Hospital stay over two to five years. *Archives of General Psychiatry,* 1976, *33,* 481–486

Meco G, Casacchia M, Attenni M, Iafrate A, Ecari U, & Argenta G. Haloperidol decanoate: An open study in acute and chronic schizophrenic outpatients. *Proceedings III World Congress of Biological Psychiatry,* p. 300, 1981

Messier M, Finnerty R, Botvin C, & Grinspoon L. A follow up study of intensively treated chronic schizophrenic patients. *American Journal of Psychiatry,* 1969, *125,* 1123–1127

Michaux MJ, Kurland AA, & Agallianos D. Chlorpromazine-chlordiazepoxide and chlorpromazine-imipramine treatment of newly hospitalized acutely ill psychiatric patients. *Current Therapeutic Research,* 1966, Suppl. *8,* 117–152

Neborsky R, Janowsky D, Munson E, & Depry D. Rapid treatment of acute psychotic symptoms with high and low dose haloperidol. *Archives of General Psychiatry,* 1981, *38,* 195–199

O'Brien C, Hamm K, Ray B, Pierce J, Luborsky I, & Mintz J. Group vs. individual psychotherapy with schizophrenics. *Archives of General Psychiatry,* 1972, *27,* 474–478

Prien RF, & Cole JO. High dose chlorpromazine therapy in chronic schizophrenia. *Archives of General Psychiatry,* 1968, *18,* 482–495

Prusoff BA, Williams DH, Weissman MM, & Astrachan BM. A controlled clinical trial of amitriptyline added to perphenazine in the treatment of depressed schizophrenics. *Psychopharmacology Bulletin,* 1978, *15,* 80–81

Prusoff BA, Williams DH, Weissman MM, & Astrachan BM. Treatment of secondary depression in schizophrenia. *Archives of General Psychiatry,* 1979, *36,* 569–579

Quitkin F, Rifkin A, Kane J, Ramos-Lore JR, & Klein, DF. Long-acting oral versus injectable antipsychotic drugs in schizophrenia. *Archives of General Psychiatry,* 1978, *35,* 889–892

Rennie TAC. Follow-up study of five hundred patients with schizophrenia admitted to the hospital from 1913 to 1923. *Archives of Neurological Psychiatry,* 1939, *42,* 877–891

Rogers CR, Gendlin EG, Kiesler DJ, & Traux CB (Eds.). *The therapeutic relationship and its impact: A study of psychotherapy with schizophrenics.* Madison: University of Wisconsin Press, 1967

Roose K. Monthly haloperidol decanoate as a replacement for maintenance therapy. *Proceedings from III World Congress of Biological Psychiatry,* p. 410, 19811

Rosen, JN. *Direct analysis: Selected papers.* New York: Grune & Stratton, 1953

Rosen JN. The treatment of schizophrenic psychoses by direct analytic therapy. *Psychiatric Quarterly,* 1947, *21,* 117–119

Rupp CG, & Fletcher E. A five to ten-year follow-up study of 641 schizophrenic cases. *American Journal of Psychiatry,* 1939–40, *96,* 877—888

Schooler NR, & Goldberg SC. Performance tests in a study of phenothiazines in schizophrenia: Caveats and conclusions. *Psychopharmacology,* 1972, *24,* 81–98

Schooler NR, & Levine J. Fluphenazine and fluphenazine HCl in the treatment of schizophrenic patients. In P Deniker, C Radouca-Thomas, & A Villeneuve (Eds.) *Proceedings of the meeting of the Collegium International Neuro-Psychopharmacologicum.* Oxford: Pergamon Press, 1978

Schooler NR, Levine J, & Severe JB. Depot fluphenazine in the prevention of relapse in schizophrenia: Evaluation of a treatment regimen. *Psychopharmacology Bulletin,* 1979, *15,* 44–47

Sedvall G. Neuroendocrine correlates in schizophrenia. In E Muller & A Agnoli (Eds.), *Neuroendocrine correlates in neurology and psychiatry.* Amsterdam: Elsevier Press, 1979

Seeman P, Chau-Wong M, Tedesco J, & Wong K. Brain receptors for antipsychotic drugs and dopamine: Direct bindings assays. *Proceedings of the National Academy of Sciences of the United States of America. 1975, 72,* 4376–4380

Seeman P, Lee T, Chau-Wong M, & Wong K. Antipsychotic drug doses and neuroleptic/dopamine receptors. *Nature,* 1976, *261,* 717–719

Shimkunas AM, Gynther MD, & Smith K. Abstracting ability of schizophrenics before and during phenothiazine therapy. *Archives of General Psychiatry,* 1966, *14,* 79–83

Shopsin B, Klein M, Aaronson, & Collora M. Clozapine chlorpromzine and placebo in newly hospitalized acutely schizophrenic patients. *Archives of General Psychiatry,* 1979, *36,* 657–664

Simon P, Fermanian J, Ginestet D, Goujet MA, & Peron-Magnan P. Standard and long-acting depot neuroleptics in chronic schizophrenics; An 18-month open multicentric study. *Archives of General Psychiatry,* 1978, *35,* 893–897

Smith RC, Dekirmenjian H, Crayton J, Klass D, & Davis JM. Blood levels of neuroleptic drugs in non-responding chronic schizophrenic patients. *Archives of General Psychiatry,* 1976, *36,* 579–584(a)

Smith RC, Dekirmenjian H, Davis JM, Crayton J, & Evans H. Plasma Butaperazine levels in long-term chronic non-responding schizophrenics. *Communications in Psychopharmacology,* 1977, *1,* 319 (a)

Smith RC, Tamminga C, Crayton J, & Davis JM. Relationships of butaperazine blood levels to plasma prolactin in chronic schizophrenic patients. *Psychopharmacology,* 1979, *66,* 29–33 (b)

Smith RC, Tamminga C, Haraszti J, Pandey GN, & Davis JM. Effects of dopamine agonists in tardive dyskinesia. *American Journal of Psychiatry,* 1977, *134,* 763

Spohn HE, Lacoursiere K, Thompson K, & Coyne L. Phenothiazine effects of psychological and psychophysiological dysfunction in chronic schizophrenia. *Archives of General Psychiatry,* 1977, *34,* 633–644

Snyder SH, Cresse I, & Burt DR. The brain's dopamine receptor: Labelling with ^{3}H-haloperidol. *Communications in Psychopharmacology,* 1975, *1,* 663–673

Stalker H. Prognosis in schizophrenia. *Journal of Mental Science,* 1939, *85,* 1224–1240

Tamminga CA, Schaffer MH, Smith RC, & Davis JM. Schizophrenic symptoms improve with apomorphine. *Science,* 1978, *200,* 567–568

Tamminga CA, Smith RC, Ericksen SE, Chang S, & Davis JM. Cholinergic influences in tardive dyskinesia, *American Journal of Psychiatry,* 1977, *134,* 769

Van Praag H, & Dols LCW. Fluphenazine enanthate and fluphenazine decanoate: A comparison of their duration of action and motor side effects. *American Journal of Psychiatry, 1973, 130,* 801–804

Wahby M, Donlon PT, & Meadwo A. Cognitive changes in acute schizophrenia with brief neuroleptic treatment. *American Journal of Psychiatry,* 1981, *138,* 1307–1310

Wode-Helgodt B, Borg S, Fyro B, & Sedvall, G. Clinical effects and drug concentrations in plasma and cerebrospinal fluid in psychotic patients tested with fixed doses of chlorpromazine. *Acta Psychiatrica Scandinavica,* 1978, *58,* 149–173

Wode-Helgodt B, Encroth P, Fyro B, Gullberg B, & Sedvall G. Effect of chlorpromazine treatment on prolactin levels in cerebrospinal fluid and plasma of psychotic patients. *Acta Psychiatrica Scandinavica,* 1977, *56,* 280–293

Gary J. Tucker
Richard B. Ferrell
Trevor R. P. Price

6

The Hospital Treatment of Schizophrenia

In 1911, Bleuler published his landmark monograph on schizophrenia. It is not only a most refreshing book but humbling as well. Even more remarkable is its pertinence to those who currently treat schizophrenic patients. The complexities of the diagnosis of schizophrenia as well as the efficacy of pharmacologic treatment of schizophrenia have been covered in other sections of this book. Our task will be to delineate the management of acute schizophrenics during a short term hospital stay. This chapter could also be titled "The Hospital Treatment of Psychosis," because the principles of treatment of any psychotic process are very similar. As one begins to review the literature on the hospital treatment of schizophrenia it quickly becomes apparent that there is a tremendous literature relating to diagnosis, etiology, prognosis, and pharmacotherapy of schizophrenic patients but very few articles on hospital management and treatment. Bleuler's book is a good example. This monograph is a total of 489 pages. There are 850 references. The number of pages devoted to therapy are 17! It is a testament to Bleuler that these 17 pages still contain useful information for the modern clinician. For example, Bleuler states in the first paragraph of the section on therapy

> . . . except for the treatment of truly psychogenic disorders, the therapy of schizophrenia is one of the most rewarding for the physician who does not ascribe results of this natural healing process of psychosis to his own intervention (Bleuler, 1950).

SCHIZOPHRENIA
ISBN 0-8089-1640-8

Further on, he cautions, as any good physician would, that in treating a disease that is difficult to treat and whose etiology is unclear, one should pay attention to the patient's physical hygiene, sleep, and nourishment, and avoid various toxic excitements. He also counsels that "strong affects" as well as idleness should be avoided, as all of these facilitate the disease process. These are sound general principles for any physician and, for that matter, for the treatment of most diseases.

Considering hospital treatment specifically, Bleuler notes

> . . . the institution as such does not cure the disease . . . it may be valuable from an educational viewpoint and may alleviate acute, agitated states . . . it carries with it the danger that the patient may become too estranged from normal life, and . . . relatives get accustomed to the idea of the institution (Bleuler, 1950).

Following are Bleuler's fundamental rules of treatment that are still useful today:

1. "The aim of the patient's education must be the development of self control" (Bleuler, 1950). Bleuler notes that this includes control of symptoms by patients. He states that many patients can be taught to suppress their symptoms.
2. "The first goal should be the proper utilization of time" (Bleuler, 1950),
3. "Punishments should not consist in hurting the patient, but rather withholding the 'candy' " (Bleuler, 1950),
4. "A special task of institutional education is of helping the patients to get accustomed to freedom" (Bleuler, 1950).

Perhaps most importantly, he states "the principle rule is that no patient must ever be completely given up, the doctor must always be prepared to take action, and to offer the patient the chance to abandon his pathological way of thinking" (Bleuler, 1950). This last comment is the most crucial to those who undertake the treatment of the schizophrenic patient.

THE HOSPITAL ENVIRONMENT

Approximately 63 years after the publication of Bleuler's book we outlined additional principles about the ideal hospital environment. We called this *the reactive environment* (Maxmen, Tucker, & LeBow, 1974). "A reactive environment may be defined as one in which the unit's overall structure maximally utilizes and coordinates the entire staff's efforts toward the rehabilitation of the patient's particular behavior problems so that ultimately he becomes a longstanding and productive member of society." The importance of this concept rests in that all hospitals operate, at least temporarily, as total environments for the patient. It is within this unique experience of a total environment that the strength of hospital treatment is evident. It is in this environment that the hospital staff can observe the patient's behavior and symptoms that have caused the hospital stay in the first place. Indeed, this focus on the patient's behavior provides a more rehabilitative, pragmatic model of therapy than one that rests on any single etiologic theory of schizophrenia. Also, close adherence to specific etiological models often limits the interventions available to the staff for treatment. When one focuses on the patient's behavior it is clear that pragmatic considerations have high priority. Modern treatments available to schizophrenic patients range from pharmacology to psychotherapy to behavior therapy, etc. This highlights the need for each patient to have an individually designed plan of treatment, which implies more than simply establishing a ritualized "individualized treatment plan." It requires that accurate observations of each patient be made and that specific therapeutic techniques be designed to fit each patient's needs. Consequently, the modern hospital must have many therapeutic techniques available so that treatment can be modified for each patient. The appropriate hospital environment does not aim at producing a standardized product. Neither should it attempt to process each patient through the same program. It should address the patient's needs, strengths, and requirements and provide a therapeutic program with these factors in mind.

We have come to believe that the best types of hospital activities are those that will carry over into the patient's life after hospitalization. It is important for the entire staff, if they are to react consistently and therapeutically toward the patient, to be aware of which activities are appropriate for each patient and which types of behavior should be encouraged. Staff observations are extremely important, in that the patient's behavior in the hospital and his relations with patients, staff, and visitors, provide important data for further designing and prescribing treatment.

It is the job of the staff to utilize its' near total observation of the patient during each day to develop plans that are revised as needed and directed at the patient's specific maladaptive behaviors. Specific elements that are important in this effort are a behavioral focus, treatment designed to fit the patient's individual needs, clear and attainable rehabilitation goals, and an early focus on the patient's aftercare needs.

SPECIFIC THERAPEUTIC APPROACHES TO THE SCHIZOPHRENIC PATIENT

Perhaps the oldest form of treatment of schizophrenia has been the psychosocial approach. Recently, Van Putten and May, after an exhaustive review of studies of milieu treatment, concluded

> . . . the evidence from controlled studies suggests the current methods of milieu therapy given in the hospital add little to the treatment of the ordinary schizophrenic patient once gross neglect is corrected and adequate chemotherapy is used. (Van Putten & May, 1976).

Gunderson takes some exception to this statement and notes that these studies have been primarily done on chronic patients. He raises the question: what is the effective milieu in an acute population? Carpenter, Mosher, and Rappaport all report studies that show positive effects of milieu treatment (Gunderson, 1980, 1983).

Units that have been successful in the exclusive use of psychosocial treatments for schizophrenics seem to have the following characteristics: (1) a high staff to patient ratio; (2) they are relatively small; (3) all staff seem to have equal amounts of responsibility for the patient; (4) there is a cultural belief in such units that the patients should assume many social responsibilities; and (5) most of these units take the viewpoint that psychosis is often a growth experience that should be understood, lived through, and accepted. Also, it was noted that: almost all of these units were set up as units that were nontraditional and could be looked upon as a counter-cultural approach to the prevailing medical attitude about effective treatments for the schizophrenic process (Gunderson, 1980, 1983). Gunderson also quotes a series of studies by Spadoni and Smith, Fairweather, and May that show little or no effect of milieu treatment alone for the schizophrenic. While debate of "either/or" goes on, it is apparent that psychosocial and milieu treatment of schizophrenics has been practiced for centuries. The quality, atmosphere, organization, and effectiveness of any treatment setting and the morale of the staff will certainly affect the outcome for patients. It is of note that there was a remarkable study by Klaf and Hamilton, (1961) who compared the schizophrenic patients admitted to the Maudsley Hospital in 1850 and 1950. They found that there were no major differences in outcome for the schizophrenic patients—a slightly longer stay in 1850 but not remarkably longer with the major difference being the content of the patients' delusions and hallucinations, e.g. in 1850 there was more concern with religion and in 1950 there was more concern with politics and sex (Klaf & Hamilton, 1961).

Etiologic theories of schizophrenia generate concepts of cure. If the theory of illness relates to the family then only the resolution of the family problems and the understanding of these family problems on the part of the patient fulfill the therapist's criteria for cure. For example, although Strauss and Carpenter present a very humane and "eclectic" theory about the etiology of schizophrenia, in their discussion of the treatment of the schizophrenia patient, their criteria of cure are evident in their emphasis of five major treatment issues: (1) conveying a sense of security, (2) contact with the patient, (3) psychological insight, (4) establishing a collaborative relationship, and (5) developing mutual expectations with the patient (Strauss & Carpenter, 1981). Aside from the fact that one would hope to establish this type of relationship with any patient (and the dictates of being a good physician mandate this type of care), there is little evidence that these principles are any more effective or necessary than other concepts, or for that matter no talking at all, just drug use, or ECT. Almost all of us who have consulted at or visited a wide range of hospitals have seen recovered patients who have had no psychotherapy at all, just somatic treatments.

Frank, in 1961, clearly delineated the basic principles of psychosocial therapy that seem a reasonable way to characterize the relationship, that at best, are mutually satisfactory for both therapist and the schizophrenic patient in the hospital setting. These include (1) An emotionally charged relationship with a helping person—this seems to be a useful factor in assisting the patient during the experience of hospitalization, (2) A plausible explanation of the causes of the problem is useful for most patients although there are some studies that show that the resolution of the psychotic process varies from person to person, with some completely sealing over as if the process never happened, and others integrating it into some type of theoretical psychological framework, (3) Provision in the hospital setting and in the relationship of some experience of success, and (4) the use of some qualities of the therapist's personality to strengthen the clients' expectations of help (Frank, 1961).

THE TREATMENT MILIEU

The hospital setting and the interaction of staff and patient are the matrix for treating the acute schizophrenic in the hospital. We believe these environmental factors can neither be ignored nor looked to as the exclusive treatment of the patient, but must be seen as a part of the treatment and as the setting in which treatment takes place.

Principles that apply to the psychotherapeutic and psychosocial treatment of the patient also apply to the use of medications. While it is true that psychopharmacologic agents are an effective treatment for psychosis (May, 1968), they are only a part of hospital treatment. There is also no question that some patients admitted to the hospital in an acute psychotic state, who are accurately diagnosed and treated exclusively with neuroleptic drugs, will improve in a matter of weeks regardless of what treatments they are given in addition to the drugs. A major question in the treatment of schizophrenic patients that most studies fail to answer is: what is the outcome of this long term or perhaps lifelong illness? While many of the treatments, especially drugs, seem to be effective in the short term, it is the long term, the 10 to 20 year period, over which we are lacking in information on effective treatment. Recently, long term followup studies by Manfred Bleuler (1974) and Huber, Gross, and Schuttler (1979) intimate a better prospect for some functioning outside of an institution for the schizophrenic patient. With the use of DSM-III diagnostic criteria for schizophrenia, however, which define a more chronic population, the question of treatment outcome at this point becomes almost more a matter of emotional and religious belief than scientific investigation. With the major treatments currently available for the schizophrenic patient, it is apparent that we have not yet discovered the "magic bullet" for schizophrenia, yet we have been basically effective in the short term treatment of this condition. Techniques of treatment that almost all clinicians use intuitively for these patients have evolved over the years.

ACUTE MANAGEMENT OF THE SCHIZOPHRENIC PATIENT (The psychotic patient)

With increasing precision of the diagnostic process more attention has been paid to specific treatment interventions. In part the diagnostic process and treatment revision goes on throughout hospitalization. There are, however, a limited number of presentations of acute schizophrenic psychosis. Andreasen recently, called attention to this fact when she noted that patients often present with either negative symptoms (e.g., withdrawal, apathy, and uncommunicativeness) or with positive symptoms (e.g., agitation, hallucinations, and delusions)(Andreasen, 1982). Even though these conditions seem so distinct, the initial management of these patients is similar regardless of positive or negative symptoms. The issues that confront the clinician with the introduction of any patient into a hospital setting are made vividly evident by the acutely psychotic patient; however, some distinctions in treatment technique will subsequently be made.

Bowers clearly outlined the experience of the acute schizophrenic patient. They are often sleep deprived, feel bombarded by many perceptual stimuli, struggle with tremendous feelings of ambivalence, and are quite disorganized (Bowers, 1974). We can easily imagine what it must mean to a person in such a condition to be moved rapidly from an environment that may be either threatening or frightening, but at least familiar, into an entirely new hospital environment surrounded by strangers. The first task of the therapist in such a setting is to give a feeling of safety to the patient by assuring them that they are in a place where they will be helped to feel better and not "changed," that no one is there to hurt them, and that they were wise to enter the hospital to get some respite from the things that have been so bothersome to them and to their family.

Another symptom of the acute schizophrenic that is often evident on admission is the intense ambivalence so well described by Bleuler (1950). The patient recognizes that he needs to be in the hospital, discusses this quite reasonably with the therapist and staff, and then half an hour later presents himself at the nursing station saying he has to leave. Whether this is fear or simple perplexity is unclear, but it is certainly perplexing to the staff. Coupled with this is the negativism often shown by these patients. This negativism may be a reflection of ambivalence, but whatever the cause it can lead to immobilization of the patient. Perhaps these two symptoms, ambivalence and negativism, more than any others, make schizophrenic patients difficult for staff to treat. Perhaps the best approaches for these symptoms are non-confrontation, understanding, and an awareness that they are part of the illness, and that if the patient could behave in a more agreeable manner he would not need to be in the hospital in the first place. Another useful way of dealing with these symptoms is to offer reassurance that the patient is doing the right thing, that he is trying to help himself, and that he is safe there.

Whether the patient has predominantly negative or positive symptoms, the only variation in management relates to those patients with positive symptoms who are extremely agitated or perhaps actively hallucinating. These patients should be placed in a less stimulating environment rather than being put in the middle of the day room or in group therapy. This may also be a useful approach for some withdrawn patients with negative symptoms. Perhaps the most therapeutic thing the hospital staff and therapist can do is to "be with the patient." While this is extremely difficult for the staff to do for prolonged periods, especially with agitated patients, certainly the fact that someone is sitting with them and being with them in a nonthreatening, friendly, and supportive manner, is extremely useful and most reassuring to most patients. Similarly, the physician, during the early part of the admission, can often best spend his time by making many brief, five to ten minute contacts with an agitated or disorganized patient scattered throughout the entire day rather than trying to sit down for an hour to obtain a history, or to give the patient a "therapeutic experience." The conduct of these brief contacts is usually one of reassurance, identification of who the therapist is, where the patient is, and precisely what is expected of the patient at this point; specifically, that he or she should begin to feel better.

It is also during this early phase of hospitalization that the major part of the psychological and medical diagnostic evaluation of the patient is undertaken. Diagnostic information is gathered by observing the patient's interaction with others, and through necessary laboratory measures. Important data is gained by observation of the patient's sleep patterns, eating habits, and general fluctuations in behavior during this initial period in the hospital. While medications can always be instituted, it is usually best to delay these as long as possible in order to have the clearest observations of the patient's behavior. It should be remembered that important criteria for the early use of medication are the amount of pain the patient seems to be experiencing and the ability to keep the patient in the hospital. Often medications do not greatly interfere with the diagnostic process. The major problem is that if a rapid response occurs, one is never sure if it is the medication or a natural resolution. It is also important, early in hospitalization, to gather as much information about the onset of the illness from those who were with the patient when the illness began. This is necessary in order to understand some of the stresses or precipitants that may be related to the onset of illness.

SPECIFIC STAFF-PATIENT INTERACTIONS

Neuroleptic drugs are considered to be a mainstay in the treatment of acute schizophrenic illness, but compassionate physicians, nurses, and other persons caring for patients with serious illness do not consider prescribing or dispensing medicine top be sufficient treatment. Thoughtful and considerate reassurance, support, and direction are important in the treatment of all persons, but these are especially necessary in the treatment of persons with psychotic illness.

Fear, which largely derives from that special sense of uniqueness and estrangement that accompanies all illness and from uncertainty about the future, should be expected as a routine feature of acute schizophrenic illness. Fear is fed by apprehension and uncertainty about what is happening inside one's own body and mind. Fear is particularly terrifying if symptoms are experienced as life threatening or if they are experienced as tearing at the fabric of one's self as may be the case, for example, with symptoms such as hallucinations, delusional thoughts or perceptions, disorganized thinking, or unfamiliar aggressive or sexual impulses. Among all persons with serious illnesses, those with serious mental syndromes or illnesses such as schizophrenia are at a particular disadvantage because it is the function of the central nervous system that is compromised. Those who care for psychotic individuals must be aware of and understand this dysfunction. This understanding should be reflected in the person to person care given to schizophrenic individuals and in the hospital environments in which such care is given.

The interaction between those who are ill and those who are giving care is dynamic in nature. Those giving care act and speak in certain ways and they allow patients to act and speak in certain ways. What those giving care say is important, what they do is important, but what patients are allowed to say and do is most important. This is the case in the care of nearly all ill persons; what is said to patients is almost never as important as what the patient is allowed to say. If the patient with schizophrenia is able to experience the environment as safe and secure and the caregivers as allies, then fear and anxiety may be expressed directly as such, but sometimes hostility, aggressiveness, or agitation will be the closest emotional approximations that the patient can muster. It must be remembered that hospitalization is often experienced as yet another threat to a person's autonomy in addition to the effects of illness itself. Whatever its attributes may be, the hospital presents the patient with an environment substantially different from that to which he is accustomed and this at a time when adaptive capacity is severely compromised. It is always important for patients to be reassured as far as possible that they will be treated with respect, taken seriously, cared for with intelligence and understanding, and that they will not be in danger of physical harm. These reassurances should be conveyed to patients by words and actions and never assumed to be understood. Family members and friends should be encouraged to support these messages.

Delusions in schizophrenia are often persecutory in nature, but they are sometimes grandiose, somatic, or simply bizarre. The response to delusional thinking should be matter of fact, empathetic, and respectful of the individual's integrity. Humoring the patient, "playing along with" the delusion, or, on the other hand, being derisive, angry, or annoyed with delusional thinking are not helpful. Rational arguments create distance between patient and caregiver and seldom have any countervailing positive effects. The most useful response usually consists of three steps. The first of these is to acknowledge and understand that the patient actually believes what he says he believes. The second is to politely register disagreement with the content of the delusional belief or perception. The third step, which is as important as the first two, consists of an expression of understanding of the emotional effects of the delusional belief. Thus, an appropriate response to a persecutory delusional statement might be as follows: "I understand that you believe that you are in danger of being harmed. I don't actually believe that this is true but I do understand that you probably feel quite frightened." This kind of statement invites the patient to elaborate on how he or she feels and avoids a futile argument about the content of the delusion. The patient can then be reassured that while he or she and the caregiver may disagree about the content of the delusion, they do both understand something about its emotional effects and at the least can be allied in helping the patient to feel less fearful. Disagreement with the content of the delusion will usually not antagonize patients. Not all delusional thinking is cast in concrete. Some delusional beliefs may be loosely held and, especially in these instances, patients are often reassured by the knowledge that others are not perceiving things as they are.

A similar three-step approach is appropriate when patients are experiencing hallucinatory phenomena. Schizophrenic hallucinations are usually auditory and are often threatening. They can usually be responded to in the same three step manner. First, the reality of the phenomenon for the patient is acknowledged and then the patient is reassured that not everyone is experiencing the same reality. Most importantly, the affective content and significance of the hallucination are acknowledged and understood.

It is often said that patients with schizophrenia require protection from excessive stimulation. This may be true in many instances, but on the other hand, a dearth of stimulation may be equally bad. What is needed is an environment in which contact with others is frequent and supportive, but does not place high demands on the patient for emotional, verbal, or intellectual performance. Above all, the interpersonal and environmental treatment of schizophrenic patients should be directed to the needs of the individual as much as possible. As a general rule patients whose illness is mostly characterized by negative symptoms such as withdrawal and negativism, may be best served by an environment that engages them and presents them with well modulated social stimulation that invites responsiveness. Patients whose illness is characterized by positive symptoms, such as delusions and hallucinations may require an environment in which demands and stimulation are more muted and subdued.

It is simply common sense not to ask for sustained, high level intellectual or verbal performance from persons whose thinking is disorganized. While a high level of contact with patients in the nature of "being with" them is important, long or heavy conversation is seldom advisable.

The "laying on of hands" is usually regarded as "un-psychiatric" but it is an important part of therapeutic art in the rest of medicine. In severe psychiatric illnesses, as in all illness, a warm handshake or a socially appropriate gentle touch or squeeze of the forearm or shoulder may be enormously comforting. It is always possible of course that frightened, hostile, or aggressive patients may experience such contacts as assaultive and therefore such contact should be used with great care and judgement. Usually there are sufficient nonverbal cues in the initial handshake and greeting to permit a decision as to whether or not such contact will be perceived as comforting.

Aggressiveness should always be dealt with a firm setting of limits consonant with the safety of the individual patient, other patients, and staff members. The interests of frightened or disorganized psychotic individuals are not served by their feeling that hostile feelings and aggressive impulses that they are experiencing are likely to result in loss of control of behavior on their part. Patients who have schizophrenia should be reassured that although it is understood that they are ill, their illness is not a license for ill-mannered, nasty, or assaultive behavior. They should be further assured that if they feel that self control is in jeopardy, help is available from personal contact with staff members and additional medication if necessary. The more they are in contact with such patients the more staff members will be able to recognize the borderline between encroaching upon the patient's "space" and sense of autonomy on the one hand, and undue avoidance of the patient on the other.

MID STAGES OF HOSPITALIZATION

During the first few weeks of hospitalization most of the acute symptoms have subsided and the patient is usually able to engage his environment more actively. The coordination of staff through various meetings assures that the patient is being treated in a consistent manner by all of the staff. The observations that the staff make of the patient interacting with other patients, family, and relatives, friends who come to visit, and staff themselves, are very useful data for planning therapeutic interactions with the patient and for determining what is stressful for each patient. During this period, an exhaustive assessment should be made of the patient's strengths and weaknesses, particularly in the interpersonal area. How much of this interpersonal activity is encouraged depends on the patient's attention span and his ability to participate with others in activities and group therapies.

The utilization of the patient's time in the hospital is important and most of this time should be used to allow the staff to make observations of the patient in different settings and also to provide some activity whereby the patient can learn something about himself that might be useful in life outside of the hospital. During this time it is worthwhile to aid the patient in understanding some of the possible causes of his illness or at least some things in his life that upset him. Often, again following Bleuler's principles, and educational approach is important. The patient can learn to recognize particular danger signals, especially difficult environmental stresses or situations that may lead to relapse. If medication is effective, this may be a time the patient can be taught to increase or decrease medication on his own. Also, he can be taught to be aware of specific repetitive trains of thought or thought contents that seem to be particularly upsetting for him and that may connote recurrence of the illness process. Similarly, sleep patterns should be observed by the patient and the patient told that as his sleep pattern changes this may indicate a change in his health. Assessment should also be made as to where the patient would best live after hospitalization. Is the relationship with the family one that should be encouraged or is it one that, for clear clinical reasons, should be discouraged? We must be very careful in this area because we often forget that the patient may need the support of a family and that there may be few others who will extend themselves to support this particular person. Consequently, recommendations for separation from the family must be done diplomatically, delicately, and allow for return to the family if separation proves unsatisfactory. Assessments of vocational skill or ability to concentrate on such things as school work can also be undertaken. It cannot be emphasized enough that the evaluation of the patient is ongoing and that the diagnostic process continues. Even though one is clear on the idea of a schizophreniform process, it is still possible that a schizophreniform disorder exists with an underlying attention deficit disorder, or that a neurologic disorder is mimicking a functional psychosis (Bellak, 1979). The diagnostic process must go on continually during hospitalization and the clinician must continue to make careful observations of the patient's behavior.

THE ROLE OF THE FAMILY IN THE CARE OF ACUTELY ILL SCHIZOPHRENIC PATIENTS

Ill persons are best cared for when proper attention is given to the effects of illness on the social and family life of the individual and vice versa. This is especially true of schizophrenia, which is an illness process affecting the thinking and the emotional life of the afflicted person. We contend that the care of schizophrenic patients is best accomplished when members of their family are reasonably included in diagnostic and therapeutic efforts as opposed to attempting to treat the patients in isolation from those who are important to them. Hospitalization in Western society separates patients from families and care should be taken to limit the discontinuity in the social fabric of patients' lives caused by this separation (Mosher & Gunderson, 1979).

Some patients may specifically insist that relatives or friends not be included in their care or even advised of their illness and hospitalization. Such requests should be taken seriously, but whenever possible permission should be sought to include trusted family members in discussions of treatment. For our purposes family is defined as those persons who live with or who are in extremely close daily contact with the patient. Such persons will usually be relatives, but the concept of family may be extended to include close friends as well.

There are three important ways in which family members can provide help in the care of schizophrenic patients. The first of these is in giving information about the patient's history of health and illness. The second is in providing support, advice, and comfort to the patient, especially during the acute phase of the illness. The third is direct participation in family therapy, which may or may not be indicated.

Psychotic individuals who are frightened, hallucinating, delusional, or disintegrated in their thinking are not in the best position to give cogent medical and psychiatric histories. Clinicians must often then rely directly on family members for this information. Included here are the history of the present illness plus information concerning previous episodes of a similar or different nature, previous medical or surgical illness, and social and vocational history. Schizophrenia is often best understood when placed in the perspective of a lifetime of development. Parents of patients are usually in the best position to give historical particulars of prenatal life, infancy, childhood social, cognitive, and physical development and school history.

Family members are also an important source of information as treatment proceeds. They have the advantage of knowing the patient both in health and illness while hospital staff usually see patients only when they are ill. Relatives can often recognize subtle improvement or worsening in symptoms or general function, which might escape physicians and nurses. They should be encouraged to freely offer such observations. As recovery proceeds family members are often in the best position to advise staff as to when the patient has reached his normal functional level. This kind of observation will assist staff members in not mistaking quirks in personality or other preexisting idiosyncratic traits for residual signs of illness.

If dismissal from the hospital is anticipated by brief trial visits to home, the family members will have the opportunity to make further observations in the home environment.

After hospitalization, family members can further assist both patient and therapist or physician by being aware of any early signs of recurring illness. Family members can probably be most helpful to schizophrenic patients simply by consistently offering their genuine support and encouragement. This is as would be the case for any ill person, but with schizophrenia such encouragement is especially important in helping patients overcome negativism and fear. In the most practical terms this includes encouraging the patient to remain in the hospital, to cooperate with diagnostic tests or to take prescribed medication, and to participate in treatment as much as possible. It may sometimes be difficult for relatives to maintain consistency about the importance of treatment, especially if patients are begging to be taken home from the hospital. Guilty feelings may further complicate matters. Many people believe that mental illness is the product of faulty relationships and while this idea may have some validity, little is usually accomplished by family members believing that they are personally responsible for their relative's illness. Efforts should be made to reassure them on this point.

It is sometimes difficult for anyone to believe that symptoms of mental illness are in fact symptoms, and not the result of some intentional maleviolence on the part of the patient. Family members have no immunity to this difficulty and it is therefore important that they be reminded of the differences between the patient's usual personality and behavior and unpleasant or disagreeable behavior that may occur as a result of illness. This will allow them to keep the illness in perspective and not to unnecessarily blame the patient for being less agreeable than usual.

Family members are often afraid of saying the wrong thing. Even if they do not volunteer this fear it is worthwhile to assure them that schizophrenia is not caused or made worse by someone saying the "wrong" thing, and that in talking with an ill person, their own common sense is as good a guide as any as to what should or should not be discussed. As a general rule, persons in the middle of psychotic illness should not be asked to make major decisions that will affect them for the rest of their lives. Neither is this a good time for family members to bring up long ignored family problems expecting that they be immediately solved. If such problems are to be addressed, this should be done later in the course of recovery. On the other hand, it is usually not helpful for families to treat patients condescendingly or to try to pretend that they are not concerned or upset. Such pretense is usually quite transparent even to persons who are psychotic.

Friends and relatives often wonder whether or not or for how long to visit. Usually visiting probably does more good than harm although seriously ill patients may tolerate short visits better than long ones. If patients seem distressed by visits, or signs and symptoms consistently seem to worsen after visits, then visits may at least temporarily be shortened or made less frequent. If such ill effects are seriously upsetting either to patients or relatives or both, then it may be advisable to temporarily cease visits altogether. There seems to be no better rule to follow than this kind of common sense approach.

The questions of whether or not children should visit may arise because of concern for their welfare. Visiting a psychotic relative, especially a parent, may be too upsetting for some children, especially younger ones. On the other hand, however, not visiting may allow them to imagine a situation much worse than that which actually exists. Simply asking the child whether or not they wish to visit has been proposed as the best approach concerning visits to patients with other serious illness (Cassem & Stewart, 1977). This probably holds as well for children visiting schizophrenic patients. Children often comprehend more than adults think they do and may prove to be less upset by illness than adults expect them to be.

When illness occurs, patients and families alike want to know what is wrong and what to expect. Candor is almost always a good policy but this should always be tempered with understanding of what use patients and close relatives are likely to make of information given to them. This is especially true with diagnoses such as schizophrenia, which have a strongly negative emotional charge. If the diagnosis is not yet clear then it is important to inform the family as to what the differential diagnostic possibilities are. If additional diagnostic testing is indicated then the nature of these tests and their purposes should be explained to both patient and family. At some point during hospitalization it is a good idea to review with patients and their families the history and results of tests and examinations and the conclusions to which these data point. Timing of this discussion depends, of course, on the clinical status of the patient.

It is important to remember that friends and relatives may feel some guilt about their possible role in causing the patient's illness. These feelings should be openly addressed by indicating that schizophrenia is a disorder of unknown cause, although like all illness, it is presumed to be the result of many factors operating in conjunction with one another. It is extremely unlikely that any single factor is by itself responsible for causing the schizophrenia. It should be understood that schizophrenia is a serious illness, that its treatment is not likely to be brief, and that symptoms are likely to linger to some extent for a considerable period of time. Although schizophrenia is widely understood to be a chronic illness, it is worth pointing out that statistical trends do not define the course of any individual case. Thus, while complete recovery can never be guaranteed, improvement is always a reasonable and attainable goal. Families should be given to understand that while the causes of schizophrenia are incompletely understood and while our treatments are not as good as we would like them to be, we and they should remain hopeful for improvement and remission.

The expected benefits as well as the possibility of unwanted effects of treatment should be discussed with the patients and families. Exhaustive discussion of every possible side effect is more mystifying than helpful.

Before discharge from the hospital it is often instructive for the patient, family, and staff to allow the patient to have passes of increasing lengths of time, to the environment in which he or she will be living after hospitalization. These passes frequently highlight sources of stress that are best dealt with prior to discharge. They sometimes point out sources of future support and assistance also.

It is also important not to decrease or change the patient's medication at the time of discharge, as this is a time of stress and change for the patient, and one will never be certain if a behavioral change is related to the change in medication or the problems associated with discharge from the hospital. Another crucial concept to convey to the patient is the importance of returning to the hospital should there be a need, rather than fearing to return to the hospital as a "failure," for unfortunately the care of most schizophrenics usually will require several rehospitalizations.

Perhaps it is best to conclude as we began by remembering Bleuler's words

> . . . the principle rule is that no patient must ever be completely given up, the doctor must always be prepared to take action, and to offer the patient the chance to abandon his pathological way of thinking (Bleuler 1950).

REFERENCES

Andreasen NY, & Olsen S. Negative vs. positive schizophrenia. *Archives of General Psychiatry*, 1982, *39;* 789–794

Bellack L. *Psychiatric aspects of minimal brain dysfunction in adults.* New York: Grune & Stratton, 1979

Bleuler E. *Dementia praecox.* Translated by J. Zinkin. New York: International Universities Press, 1950

Bleuler M. The long term course of schizophrenic psychosis. *Psychological Medicine*, 1974, *4*, 244–254

Bower M. *Retreat from society.* New York: Human Sciences Press, 1974

Cassem NH, & Stewart RS. Management and care of dying patients. In ZJ Lipowski, DR Lipsitt, & PC Whybrow (Eds.), *Psychosomatic medicine.* New York: Oxford University Press, 1977

Frank J. *Persuasion and healing.* Baltimore: Johns Hopkins Press, 1961

Gunderson JG. A reevaluation of milieu therapy for non-chronic schizophrenic patients, *Schizophrenia Bulletin,* 1980 *6,* 64–69

Gunderson J. If and when milieu therapy is therapeutic for schizophrenics. In JG Gunderson, O Will, EL Mosher (Eds.), *Principles and practice of milieu therapy,* New York: Jason Arensen, 1983

Huber G, Gross G, & Schuttler R. *Schizophrenia.* Berlin: Springer/Verlog, 1979

Klaf FS, & Hamilton JG. Schizophrenia—A hundred years ago and today. *Journal Mental Science,* 1961, *107,* 819—827

Maxmen JS, Tucker GJ, & LeBow M. *Rational hospital psychiatry.* New York: Brunner/Mazel: 1974

May PRA. *Treatment of schizophrenia.* New York: Science House, 1968

Mosher LR, & Gunderson JG. Group, family milieu and community support systems treatment for schizophrenia. In Bellak L (Ed.), *Disorders of the schizophrenic syndrome.* New York: Basic Books, 1979

Strauss JS, & Carpenter WT. *Schizophrenia.* New York: Plenum, 1981

Van Putten T, & May PRA. Milieu therapies of the schizophrenias. In LJ West, ED Fluin (Eds.), *Treatment of schizophrenia: Progress and prospects.* New York: Grune & Stratton, 1976

Peter A. Magaro
John A. Talbott
Ira Glick

7

The Inpatient Care of Chronic Schizophrenia

The chronic schizophrenic has always been with us. When we had the will to assume responsibility for those not able to support themselves and the resources to support our ideals, we created institutions. They consisted not only of large state hospitals mounted on hills overlooking our cities, the setting most commonly brought to mind when thinking of mental institutions, but other settings, such as country cottages in rural societies, ashrams in more tribal societies, wards in private hospitals, or private homes in residential neighborhoods.

Today, especially, the state hospital is not the only setting housing chronic schizophrenics. Social, legal, and legislative pressures have brought about the movement of all types of chronic patients, the majority being diagnosed as schizophrenics, out of state hospitals into non-traditional institutions such as nursing homes, homes for the aged, boarding homes, and the rooms and doorways of the slums (Lerman, 1981). This process of moving patients from state hospitals into other facilities began in 1955 and became known as deinstitutionalization. This social movement will be briefly discussed since it has been driven by a particular concept of mental illness and has produced a new form of habitation for the chronic schizophrenic patient.

The decade of the 1950s saw the formation of an optimistic vision of mental illness. Two great events occurred at the same time. The first was the advent of the community psychiatry movement and the

SCHIZOPHRENIA
ISBN 0-8089-1640-8

second was the development of effective psychopharmacological agents. The Mental Health Act of 1952 and President Kennedy's address to Congress in 1963 suggested a radically new approach to the care and treatment of mental illness. This new approach stressed prevention through alleviating the social ills, including mental illness. Johnson's Great Society embodied these principles in its formulation of social goals by giving official recognition to the social model and by diverting the greater portion of the nation's mental health resources toward the implementation of the Community Mental Health Center Act of 1963. Rising hospital costs during the 1960s also encouraged the community center approach and the elimination of public hospitalization.

By the 1960s, federal entitlement programs, such as Medicaid, Medicare, and Supplementary Security Income (SSI), were introduced and states were thus able to shift the burden of funding for chronic patients to these federal auspices. Where previously the state funded 100 percent of public institutions, federal welfare programs allow the state to only fund from 50 to 100 percent of the cost of traditional and nontraditional facilities (Lerman, 1981). Thus, the chronic patient no longer was funded for treatment only in state hospitals, but could be supported in a variety of private or not for profit community agencies. SSI deserves specific mention since it specified that the intellectual, physical, or emotional disabilities of the chronic schizophrenic required special care.

A number of legal actions in the 1960s and 1970s also helped propel patients out of institutions into the community. Wright vs. Stickney in 1972 in Alabama ruled that the state hospital failed to provide adequate treatment for committed patients and validated their rights to due process. State hospitals were thus required to provide treatment or discharge patients. The Supreme Court also ruled in O'Connor vs. Donaldson (1975) that any hospital patient required treatment. Rouse vs. Cameron (1966) in the District of Columbia found that a patient had a statutory right to treatment because it is implied in the 1964 District of Columbia Mentally Ill Act. In 1968, Nason vs. Bridgewater State Hospital in Massachusetts provided the ruling that confinement without treatment denied patients due process of law and also confirmed that each individual required an individualized treatment program.

As would be expected, these changes dramatically affected the census of public mental hospitals nationwide. The census began to decline for the first time in over one hundred years. The forces that brought about this dramatic shift include: (1) the community mental health philosophy that it was better, cheaper, and more humane to treat and care for the chronic mentally ill in community settings nearer their homes, families, jobs, and neighborhoods, than in far distant "warehouses"; (2) the technological innovations in the delivery of mental health services in both social (e.g., open doors, therapeutic communities) and, most importantly, pharmacological (e.g., phenothiazine medication) areas; (3) the pressure of civil libertarian forces both within psychiatry and from legal advocates; and (4) the economic advantages to state government to shift the responsibility of funding the chronically ill from state to largely federal auspices, through the provision of Medicaid, Medicare, and SSI (Talbott, 1981).

The resultant shift in the locus of treatment and care of chronic schizophrenics was characterized both by transinstitutionalization (from state hospitals to nursing homes) and depopulation (of state hospitals to no planned alternative), which forced thousands of patients into a variety of substandard community residences or onto the streets. Over the past decade, an increasing number of contributions have appeared in professional journals focusing upon the many problems engendered by deinstitutionalization (Anthony, 1977, 1980; Bachrach, 1980; Binner, 1974). There has also been almost a decade of legislative inquiry that has heard complaints about the condition of the chronic patient in the community (Senate Subcommittee on Long-term Care, 1975; Comptroller General Report, 1977; the President's Commission on Mental Health, 1978; HEW Task Force Report, 1979). All of these reports express disappointment with deinstitutionalization without adequate community support.

Characteristics of the chronic schizophrenic patient will now be discussed and some information on the prevalence of the condition will be presented. We recognize, however, that there are two main groups of chronic mental patients; those who left the state hospital during deinstitutionalization and those who stayed behind. We will present information on both of these groups, including treatment results.

DEFINITION AND CHARACTERISTICS OF THE CHRONIC MENTAL PATIENT

The Committee on Psychopathology of the Group for the Advancement of Psychiatry (1982) defines a chronic patient as a person with a psychotic diagnosis accompanied by severe disabilities in social and vocational role functioning lasting at least two years. Dorwart (1980) lists some characteristics of the patients who still inhabit state facilities: they need a high level of care and are potentially destructive, withdrawn, actively psychotic, and possibly dangerous to themselves.

A more detailed description of the chronic patient who is still residing in state hospitals can be derived from the descriptions of the patients who participated in hospital treatment programs for chronic patients (e.g., Paul & Lentz, 1977). The patients averaged 17 years in the hospital, were usually diagnosed as process schizophrenic, approximately 50 percent had received ECT, and approximately 33 percent had received insulin shock therapy. All had received medication for a long period of time, and only 15 percent had received any contact, even a letter, from friends of relatives in the previous year. In most cases, they had no vocational or housekeeping skills, could not reliably care for themselves, and had few interpersonal or communication skills. They behaved in a bizarre fashion most of the time and were sometimes assaultive. To summarize, these individuals seem to be deviant in many ways, have little contact with reality, and have few of the skills needed to function in society.

INCIDENCE AND MOVEMENT OF CHRONIC PATIENTS

An accurate estimate of the number of chronic patients is very difficult to obtain because it depends upon an estimate of the number of all types of patients in a variety of settings. Such information is either unavailable, incomplete (board and care homes), or gathered by different agencies using different methods. Thus, estimates become a matter of which data are examined and how revealing are the reasons for being in a particular setting (Kiesler, 1982b). With this warning, however, we will proceed to present some attempts at deriving an incidence figure. The estimate of the number of chronic patients has widely varied from approximately 1 percent of hospitalized patients in the U.S. (Kraft, Binner, & Dickey, 1967) to a 10 percent estimate in Switzerland (Bleuler, 1978). Goldman, Gattozzi, and Taube (1981) estimate 1 percent of the U.S. population, between 1.7 and 2.4 million, suffer from chronic mental illness, 10 percent of whom reside in state and county hospitals, while another 40 percent are in nursing homes.

In 1970, the United States Census reported that over 900,000 patients were residing in homes for the aged and of this number, over 600,000 were residing in homes that were not known to provide skilled nursing care (Lerman, 1981). In 1977, it was estimated that from 360,000 to 500,000 mental patients resided in board-and-care facilities. These are non-medical, supervised living settings. These facilities therefore have the second largest population of chronic mental patients (Lerman, 1981). All together, there are over one million institutionalized and mainly chronic schizophrenic mental patients in the country.

When considering chronic inpatient facilities, we find that the vast majority of chronic patients are treated in the public sector (Goldman et al., 1981). From 1950 to 1970, homes for the aged and dependent, serving the aged, mentally ill, retarded, and disabled, increased 133 percent (Kramer, 1977). These facilities are not state owned but have become a large scale private medical business. Seventy-seven percent of nursing home facilities are privately owned and account for 67 percent of all nursing home resident beds. Twenty-five to 30 percent of these homes and 35 percent of their beds are owned by large nursing home chains (Comptroller General Report, 1977). It has been estimated that the federal expenditures for mental health services through Medicaid is four million dollars and over half of that amount goes to the care of mental patients in nursing homes (Kiesler, 1982b). Obviously, deinstitutionalization did not mean becoming independent in the community after leaving institutions.

Another statistic to consider is the number of admissions to resident mental health facilities. While the patient population in state hospitals declined 47 percent from 1950 to 1970, annual admissions increased. Admissions in 1955 were 178,000 while 375,000 admissions occurred in 1974 (Bassuk & Gerson, 1978). This did not only occur in state hospitals. The number of mental patients admitted to private and not for profit hospitals increased 34 percent from 1968 to 1975 (Lerman, 1981). In fact, facilities without psychiatric units contain 40 percent of the total psychiatric episodes, making them the most popular site for mental hospitalization (Kiesler, 1982b). When data from such institutions are added to the total admission figures of other institutions, such as state hospitals, we find that hospitalization has steadily increased for the past 15 years (Kiesler, 1982a; 1982b).

A related trend in the movement of patients involves readmission to a facility after being discharged. This data is even more difficult to ascertain because it is not totally independent of admission information, especially in some data sources that do not separate first admissions from subsequent admissions. One report notes that readmission to state hospitals increased from 47 percent in 1969 to 54 percent in 1972 (Comptroller General Report, 1977). Thus, although a large segment of the chronic population was discharged from the hospital, many more patients began entering and reentering for brief periods of time, resulting in the phrase the "revolving-door" patient. Whatever the exact incidence of chronic mental patients, it does seem clear that nontraditional settings now outnumber traditional ones in terms of number of chronic mental patients housed. Treatment of the chronic schizophrenic must thus be considered in both traditional and nontraditional centers.

TREATMENT OF THE CHRONIC SCHIZOPHRENIC IN NONTRADITIONAL INSTITUTIONS

The chronic schizophrenic in the nontraditional inpatient setting may have been the highest functioning chronic patient in terms of the initial pool of state hospital patients, but he or she is still not accepted by the community (Jones, 1979). A point repeatedly made in discussion of the chronic patient is that placement in itself is not treatment. The simple shuffling of people into different social settings under the guise of treatment is no longer sufficient. At the same time, just as treatment and rehabilitation programs have always been a secondary function of a state hospital (Bachrach, 1976), current funding programs of nontraditional treatment settings are creating a situation where no rehabilitative treatment is provided. The available funding, such as social security, medicaid, and medicare, for patients in the community only pays for basic care exclusive of treatment and thus, the government policy works against providing treatment (Bachrach, 1979; Lerman, 1981; Mechanic, 1969). The nursing home, therefore, receives the chronic patient from a custodial setting and provides custodial and asylum functions, similar to the former functions of state hospitals. In one study, there were only 7.5 hours of psychiatric services a week per 100 patients, and fewer than 10 full or part-time psychiatric treatment staff (Shadish, Straw, McSweeney, Koler, & Bootzin, 1981). Such meager treatment figures may actually represent an overestimation when psychiatric treatment time is defined or the nature of psychiatric staff is clearly specified.

There have been almost no reports of treatment effectiveness in nontraditional settings, especially those serving the chronic schizophrenic. Kraus (1981) presents an experiment in California where a nursing home was funded to provide psychiatric care. The state recognized that the Medicaid reimbursement rate of $15.52 per patient day for nursing home care was not sufficient to provide more than custodial care to a docile, institutionalized population of chronic patients. An alternative to acute hospitalization at $100 per day and the state hospital at $65 per day was needed. A contract with a nursing home for an additional $6.50 per patient day for 40 patients was negotiated, enabling the home to hire additional psychiatric aides and occupational therapists. They then found that symptomatology decreased over a 6 month period for 75 percent of the patients admitted. The program adopted a rehabilitation model and was granted additional funding of $3.19 per day for Special Rehabilitation programs for nursing homes. The program has not been formally evaluated, but it does suggest a treatment program for chronic patients that can be administered in a nursing home at minimal cost compared to state facilities. The major recommendation from such work would be that funding sources should finance rehabilitation service beyond custodial and nursing care in any inpatient setting. The evaluation of treatment effectiveness at these new facilities serving chronic patients is still being awaited.

TREATMENT OF THE CHRONIC PATIENT IN TRADITIONAL SETTINGS

Several research questions have been asked about the treatment of the chronic patient in the traditional state and county hospital. These questions have focused on differences in the modality, length, and level of alternative treatments.

Hospital Versus Alternatives

Kiesler (1982b) evaluated the research examining the effect of hospitalization in a state mental institution relative to alternatives (usually community treatments). Using a criteria of only including studies employing random assignment of patients to conditions, 10 studies were considered to arrive at a conclusion that the effects of alternative care were consistently more positive than hospitalization in mental institutions. Of most importance was the documentation of the finding that once admitted to a mental hospital people were more likely to be readmitted than if randomly assigned to another treatment and never admitted to a hospital. Braun, Kochansky, Shapiro, Greenberg, Gudeman, Johnson, and Shore (1981) also reviewed a number of outcome studies and concluded that any alternative to hospitalization was superior. Smith and Hart (1975), however, have shown that a community mental health center was not superior to a state hospital in terms of decreasing the number of social disabilities, cost, or reduction in the number of individuals becoming chronic. In all of these studies there are serious methodological problems that only allow a suggestion about the effects of hospitalization relative to other alternatives. None of the studies specifically isolated the chronic schizophrenic.

Short Versus Long Hospital Stay

Length of stay studies have consistently demonstrated no advantage for most chronic schizophrenics treated for long (e.g., greater than 30 days) rather than short (under 30 days) hospitalizations in terms of symptomatology, rate of rehospitalization, and quality of life. Short stays are also obviously far less costly. The controlled studies of short versus long—hospitalization have been reviewed by Riessman, Rabkin, and Struening (1977) and Mattes et al. (1977a; 1977b).

Herz and associates (1976; 1977) excluded patients who were a danger to themselves or others and those without families; in effect, excluding the patient most likely to remain in a state hospital (i.e., had the poorest prognosis). Patients were randomly assigned to standard inpatient care (60 days), brief hospitalization (11 days) plus day outpatient care upon discharge, or brief hospitalization only. When Herz and associates assessed their patients after one year, they found those assigned to brief hospitalization plus day care showed the least psychopathology, while those who had received standard care showed the most. There also were significant differences in symptom levels between groups, with the longer term patients exhibiting more symptomatology; but, this effect disappeared after the second year. They also found differences in role-functioning at follow-up that favored the brief-hospitalization groups. Such patients were more likely to be working at each follow-up point. For example, at two years, 40 percent of the standard-hospitalization group were employed compared to 55 percent of the brief-stay group and 57 percent of the brief-stay/day-care group. Furthermore, more of the standard-care group were judged as failing to perform any occupational role, including student or housekeeper, as well as wage earner.

Mattes and associates (1977a; 1977b) also studied a diagnostically mixed sample of patients. Their patients were assigned to either short-term wards with a 90 day stay or to long-term wards with a mean stay of six months, based on administrative criteria that they argued were an approximation of random assignment. They too found that short-term patients showed more improvement at discharge. Three years after discharge there were few between-group differences, but long-term patients were rated by relatives as having less pathology, and this effect was accounted for by a tendency for patients receiving individual psychotherapy to be rated less symptomatic by their relatives (long-term patients were more likely to receive this mode of posthospital care). It is not clear whether the participation in individual therapy influenced symptoms or created a rating bias among patients' relatives, since the groups did not differ on other measures. Another potentially important finding was that among patients who were rehospitalized, long-term patients tended to be rehospitalized more often and for longer periods.

Glick and Hargreaves (1979) included patients who were voluntarily admitted to a research unit of an academic medical center, which was also a part of the California State Hospital system. The randomly assigned patients to either short-term inpatient care (21–28 days) or to long-term hospitalization (3–4 months). The sample was stratefied by diagnosis into patients with schizophrenic disorders, affective disorders, and other non-schizophrenic diagnoses. After one year, with no post-hospital care being provided, the schizophrenics treated for a longer time were doing significantly better on two global measures than the short-term patients. Discrete symptom scales failed to differentiate the groups, however, and there was no difference in rehospitalization data. The long-term group received significantly more psychotherapy after discharge, as well as medication at significantly higher dosage levels than controls. The authors concluded that their work with patients and their families during the longer hospitalization period effectively encouraged acceptance of the need for continued psychotherapy and medication. After two years, the clinical global scale again favored the long-term group, but the relationship was less strong than at one year. On further analysis, the investigators found that long-term hospitalization produced a better outcome only in those schizophrenic patients whose prehospital functioning had been relatively good. For those that had relatively poor prehospital functioning, longer hospitalization appeared to be detrimental to outcome. In contrast to the findings for the schizophrenics, one and two-year follow-ups of the nonschizophrenic long and short-term groups revealed no significant differences in global ratings, severity of symptom measures, or social and work adjustment.

These studies, when taken together, indicate equal benefits for "brief" versus "standard" hospitalization, although some diagnostic differences seem to be crucial. For instance, Gunderson (1983) suggests that for some schizophrenic patients, longer rather than briefer stays are preferable. The rationale is that specific subgroups may, in fact, respond differently to hospital-stay strategies. The confounding, or interactive, influences of medication and outpatient programs are troublesome in the studies thus far. It does seem that chronic patients require a setting that is intensive and highly structured, and thus studies not meeting such criteria may be expected not to produce positive results. Finally, certain groups of patients in these studies are unrepresented (for example, involuntary patients) or underrepresented (for example, patients without families). The findings to date may not apply equally well to these patients. This is a serious problem when speaking of the chronic schizophrenic who remains in the state hospital today. However, recognizing such cautions, Riessman, Rabkin, and Struening (1977) concluded their review of this literature with the opinion that it is now incumbent upon the clinician to justify the use of a hospital stay of more than 60 days.

This conclusion rests upon the adequacy of nonhospital services. Most psychiatric patients who require hospital treatment may be effectively treated in a relatively short-term setting, as long as day treatment and supportive residential placement are readily available. In fact, with adequate outpatient resources, hospitalization can be avoided altogether for many patients who would formerly have been hospitalized (Riessman & Rabkin, 1977).* We are not sure, however, that this applies to the chronic schizophrenic who may require longer-term hospitalization to accomplish a specific task or to resolve a focused, solvable problem (Reibel & Herz, 1976).

Pharmacological Treatment

The chronic schizophrenic who is receiving medication as part or the whole of his treatment is involved in a maintenance program. In most cases, symptoms are in remission and the patient is maintained on a once-daily nighttime dosage to achieve improved compliance, better absorption, and few extrapyramidal side effects (Lipton & Burnett, 1980). Patients maintained in the hospital for long periods of time are considered to require such treatment to prevent the reoccurrence of symptoms.

A major problem with the continued administration of medication to the chronic schizophrenic is that a significant number do not improve clinically and/or they develop extrapyramidal side effects (Lehmann, 1975). The most disconcerting side effect associated with antipsychotic drugs is tardive dyskinesia. It has been estimated that the mean prevalence rate in response to neuroleptic medication among longstaying psychiatric patients is around 15 percent (Fann, Davis, & Janowsky, 1972). Not all long-term patients exhibit this problem but a certain subset seem to be at risk, although the characteristics of that subset is not known. The seriousness of the condition, besides its disfiguring nature, is that it is extremely difficult to reverse or treat

---

*Riessman CK, & Rabkin JG. Hospital vs. home care programs for psychiatric patients: Summary of published findings. Unpublished, 1977.

(Jeste & Wyatt, 1979). The following quote by Lipton and Burnett (1980, p. 340) summarizes our present understanding of the condition:

> The availabile evidence thus suggests a strong association between drug use and TD. Whether or not predisposing organicity relates to the development of TD is of little relevance to the patient and his clinician who are faced with disfiguring and health-impairing oral-facial dyskinesia. Rehabilitation of such patients is frequently most difficult, and treatment often is unavailing. The development of involuntary buccolinquo-facial tics, tongue "fly-catching" movements, grunting and other peculiar sounds, smacking and sucking lip movements, chewing and jaw deviations, furrowing of the forehead, rapid perseverative eye blinking, and choreoatheototic movements of the trunk and extremities should be anticipated in all patients on long-term neuroleptic regimes (Kobayshi, 1976)—especially in those who are to be maintained on neuroleptics for longer than three months. Probably for all such patients informed consent, and/or relatives' consent for those who are refractory to treatment of their psychosis, should be obtained if neuroleptic treatment is to be continued for more than three months (Ayd, 1977). Reasonable standards of prevention would appear to include the reduction of drug dosages, drug holidays, and periodic reevaluation of the necessity for continued drug prescriptions.

Balancing such negative side effects of a maintenance medication program are the results that indicate high relapse rates with patients withdrawn from medication (Prien & Klett, 1972), although this conclusion has been debated (Davis, 1975; Tobias & McDonald, 1974). It has been reported that while neuroleptics do prevent relapses in a subgroup of schizophrenics, others may do as well without maintenance medication (Gardos & Cole, 1976). The usual suggestion is that dosage be lowered after remission to the point where there is no reoccurrence of symptoms and that chronic patients be given a drug-free trial to determine if they can remain stabilized even without maintenance medication. Such a procedure would decrease the probability of detrimental side effects and also identify those patients requiring maintenance medication.

It should also be noted that medication should not be considered as the total treatment for a chronic patient. There is a body of literature that suggests medication in conjunction with other treatments may be the treatment of choice (Gunderson, 1977, Hogarty, Goldberg, Schooler, & Ulrich, 1974; Lipton & Burnett, 1980). We will discuss this modality interaction effect as we consider the results of therapy interventions.

Individual and Milieu Therapy

Rogers and associates (1967) employed inexperienced therapists to treat chronic schizophrenics for two hours a week for 2½ years. They found favorable results after a year and a half for those who received therapy. The measures indicated more self awareness and greater time out of the hospital. There were also differences in rate of release and time in the hospital a year after treatment, although these results did not reach significance. Karon and Vanderbos (1981) also found positive changes with acute schizophrenics treated by experienced therapists 3 to 5 times a week and then once a week for up to a year of treatment in individual therapy employing a psychoanalytic model. The therapy group spent less time in the hospital, was better clinically, and exhibited less of a thought disorder.

Greenblatt, Solomon, and Evans (1965) assigned chronic schizophrenics from Boston State Hospital to intensive milieu therapy at Massachusetts Mental Health Center. They received six months of individual therapy and milieu therapy divided into drug and no drug groups. Patients receiving drugs in either milieu or custodial treatment showed the most improvement, although there were some interaction effects of drugs and therapy. The concluded that the effects of intensive milieu therapy were additional to effects of medication.

In contrast to these positive results for individual therapy or a combination of therapy plus medication are the studies finding medication to be superior to individual or milieu therapy. Grinspoon, Ewait, and Shader (1972) also transferred chronic patients from the same hospital to the Massachusetts Mental Health Center and treated them with intensive analytic psychotherapy for a two year period. Half of the patients received drugs. They found that intensive milieu therapy and individual therapy had no advantage over custodial treatment at a two year and five year follow-up. There was a trend, however, for more patients to be living outside the hospital when they were treated with milieu therapy.

May (1968) compared the conditions of therapy plus medication, therapy without medication, medication alone, electroconvulsive therapy (ECT), and milieu therapy. Each resident or staff psychiatrist practiced each of the five treatments to control for therapist dimensions. Therapy was administered to acute patients by inexperienced therapists for two hours a week during six months of hospitalization. Medication seemed to produce the major effect on symptoms; psychotherapy without drugs was less effective than psychotherapy with drugs, or drugs alone. May (1975) reiterated the finding that psychotherapy was not essential to the inpatient treatment of chronic schizophrenia, but added that this result may not apply to chronic schizophrenics in an outpatient setting where group psychotherapy is more effective than individual treatment and drugs alone are not sufficient to prevent relapses.

Mosher and Gunderson (1972) considered the nature of a ward milieu program and concluded that a highly-structured, highly-organized, highly-expectant milieu that stresses adaptive skills, while suppressing symptoms and maladjustive behavior, was helpful in the hospital treatment of chronic schizophrenia. Sanders, Smith, and Weinman (1967) were one of the first to confirm this hypothesis when they treated chronic schizophrenics in a milieu therapy program at the Philadelphia State Hospital. Patents were placed in three cottages with varying degrees of structure: minimal, partially structured, and maximally structured. The maximally structured cottage had a therapeutic community with patient government, group therapy, and high interactions. The partially structured cottage had a therapeutic community and other interventions as found in the maximum cottage except for group therapy. The minimal therapeutic community had no interaction program. A control condition entailed patients being assigned to the traditional wards. The major interest was in the experimental groups assigned to cottages that differed in the degree and kind of social interaction. The patients selected were the better adjusted chronic patients who would not be in the hospital today. They had an average age of 45, 82 percent were schizophrenic, and their average length of hospitalization was 6–8 years. The groups were then split into old and young (median age of 45) and length of illness (median length 12 years for males). They measured awareness of others, interaction with others, and spontaneous social behavior. Their results showed that older, more chronic, patients improved most in the most structured cottage. Less structured situations helped the younger patients, but not as clearly. In fact, younger patients were reported to exhibit a less favorable response to the socio-environmental treatment. The major effect, however, was that a structured cottage produced more positive effects than unstructured, and older patients improved more than younger patients in all areas of community adjustment.

Fairweather et al. (1969) tended to confirm this result when a combination of group therapy, structured work activities, and shared responsibility for group living conditions produced the greatest degree of change in terms of level of ward behavior, with longer-term psychotics. Fairweather (1964) also reported that with three levels of chronic patients the most chronic improved the least with a high decision-making treatment program. Small group programs had no appreciable effect on the community adjustment of the chronic patients. A conclusion that could be drawn from such studies is that while a high decision-making program is beneficial to acute patients, the most intensive structured program is required for the most chronic patient, possibly defined as those currently in the state hospital.

Paul and Lentz (1977) present a comparative study of three treatments, social learning, milieu therapy, and "traditional" treatment, in a state hospital. Patients were assigned randomly to the three treatment settings. The patients in the study were those left in the hospital after deinstitutionalization and could be considered rejected by community settings such as community mental health centers and nursing homes. The goal of the program was to rectify the deficiences of the chronic patient through improving interpersonal skills and role performance as required in vocational and housekeeping tasks, reducing bizarre behavior, and providing aftercare, defined as having at least one supportive person in the community. The program was a 24 hours a day, 7 days a week comprehensive treatment program requiring extensive patient-staff interaction. Eighty-five percent of each patient's working hours were devoted to programs designed for skill acquisition, as compared to the custodial control ward, where 64 percent of the time was unstructured and only 10 percent of activities were structured. The rest of the time was allocated to medication and meals.

Psychosocial treatment (40 patients) resulted in 36 being discharged to board-and-room homes, while others achieved independent living status. Of the 31 milieu therapy patients, 22 were discharged, to independent living. The custodial ward had the least number of patients discharged. In regard to rehospitalization over the next year, fewer than 10 percent of the psychosocial patients, compared to 30 percent of those in the milieu program and 50 percent of those treated "traditionally," returned to the hospital.

In summarizing the effectiveness of intensive hospital programs, we can conclude that chronic patients exposed to such treatment are discharged from the hospital more often than those in custodial treatment. Many of the studies evaluating therapeutic communities, however, contain methodological problems. Reviews (Paul, 1967; Sanders et al., 1967) examining the empirical data derived from all types of milieu therapy programs, including the early "total push" approaches (e.g., Martin, 1950; Miller & Clancy, 1952; Rashkis & Smarr, 1957), have generally agreed that "the general milieu therapy literature is characterized by a paucity of solid evidence and a plethora of equivocal results" (Paul, 1969, p. 87). One study (Sanders et al., 1967), however, with nearly adequate controls yielded interesting results and the Paul and Lentz (1977) study yielded very positive results regarding the effects of two types of milieu programs. The most successful treatment in the Paul and Lentz (1977) study, the social learning program, was based upon learning principles that have been directly incorporated into many token economy programs, which we will now review.

Token Economy Programs

Ayllon and Azrin (1965) utilized a token economy program (TEP) to improve occupational performance, personal care, and social skills. The program was very successful for individual patients and spawned a major treatment modality directed toward the chronic patient. The basic mechanism of the program was the delivery of tokens by the staff to patients contingent upon the performance of preselected responses. The tokens very quickly acquired the status of conditioned reinforcers that were later exchanged for real-life benefits (e.g., snacks).

Atthowe and Krasner (1968) conducted a 2-year TEP on a closed VA hospital ward populated by male chronic schizophrenics and brain damaged patients. At the beginning of the project, the ward housed 12 bedwetters who were awakened periodically during the night and taken to the toilet. In addition, they were rewarded with tokens the following morning if their bed remained dry. At the end of the project period there were no bedwetters on the ward. It is not clear, however, whether the awakenings or token reinforcement were responsible for the improvements observed. In the same program, Atthowe and Krasner also managed to reduce the number of "infractions" of the morning routine of getting out of bed, making the bed, and leaving the bed area, by giving tokens to each patient daily following a "no infraction" morning. Beginning with a baseline average of 75 "infractions" per week for the entire ward, infractions were reduced to an average of 9 per week by the end of a 9-week period. Lloyd and Garlington (1968) reported similar results focusing upon several types of self-care behaviors, including quality of facial makeup, hair combing, neatness and cleanliness of clothing, attendance at a morning pay station, bedmaking, and breakfast and luncheon eating habits.

Steffy, Hart, Craw, Torney, and Marlett (1969) worked on alleviating meal-time problems. Of their 34 patients, 16 had problems of either refusing to enter the dining room or disrupting mealtime operations. Before the project began, an average of 16 patients missed each dining room meal. Treatment involved stopping urging patients to come to the dining room to eat and forcible eviction of violent or argumentative patients. The time allowed between announcement of the meal and the closing of access to the dining room was gradually reduced from 20 minutes to 5 minutes. At this point, tokens were given to patients just before they entered the dining room. The time between token delivery and entry to the dining room was then gradually increased to 30 minutes. Within 2 weeks the average number of patients missing each meal had dropped to 2 from the baseline number of 16. Winkler (1970), Shean and Zeidberg (1971), and McReynolds and Coleman (1972) also reported positive results with chronic patients in regard to feeding and self-care behaviors.

Another behavioral deficit usually found in chronic psychiatric patients is reduced social responsivity. Shaefer and Martin (1966) divided chronic women patients into two groups that had equal "apathy" scores. Time sample observations made on two subsequent occasions after the introduction of a selective token reinforcement for interactional behavior found the token reinforcement group to reduce apathy in these patients. Atthowe and Krasner (1968) also successfully increased social responsiveness in their Palo Alto TEP.

Grip and Magaro (1971) published the first report of a quantitative comparison of behavioral changes, using four different rating scales for chronic patients treated in a TEP and in a traditional hospital. They compared chronic women patients on one TEP ward and three traditional wards. After six months of treatment, those patients on the control ward showed no positive changes but the TEP patients demonstrated marked improvement in social responsiveness. Gorham et al. (1970) also report significant improvements in three social interaction behaviors included in the Perry Point Nursing Evaluation Scale (PPNES), after nine months of TEP treatment. Shean and Zeidberg (1971) also confirmed improvement in social responsivity under TEP treatment using standardized rating scale data.

Although the TEP is often viewed as an effective treatment approach for overcoming various behavioral deficits, especially those associated with self-care and social responsiveness, TEPs have also been reported to be effective in ameliorating behavioral excesses. Included in this category are violent and aggressive behaviors and bizarre behaviors associated with psychosis. The Steffy et al. (1969) study discussed earlier reduced aggressive behaviors associated with meal schedules. Winkler (1970) reported a decrease in behavioral excesses such as violence and screaming, as well as apathy and a general lack of responsiveness to the ward environment.

Atthowe and Krasner (1968) reported the first data on numbers of patients returned to the community after treatment in a TEP; 24 of their original 86 patients were discharged and 8 were transferred to more active and discharge-oriented wards during the first year that the TEP was in operation. These figures compare favorably with the same ward's 11 discharges and zero transfers in the 11 months preceding the TEP. The authors also report that 11 of the 24 who were discharged returned to the hospital within 9 months. They do not say whether the discharged patients went to boarding homes, to their families, or lived alone, nor do they indicate whether or not any changes in hospital discharge policies occurred during the period.

Steffy et al. (1966) made an "all out" effort at the end of the project year to secure placements outside the hospital for their patients. Sixteen of their original 34 patients were placed in community nursing homes and 3 were sent to other wards in the hospital. In the 2 years following placement, 4 of the 16 sent to the community had returned to the hospital. The "all out" effort itself may have been responsible for the discharge of these patients, regardless of whether or not they had received TEP or any other kind of treatment.

Lloyd and Abel (1970) also provide a detailed analysis of the movement of TEP patients from the hospital. During its 27 months of operation, their TEP had treated 39 men and 13 women patients. Thirteen of the 52 patients were out of the hospital at the time the report was submitted. The authors also indicate that those patients who had been discharged had been in the hospital a shorter length of time. No data are provided comparing this discharge rate with other or previous rates of discharge for the ward or hospital in general. The primary goal of the TEP developed by Heap et al. (1970) was the restoring of patients to their communities. Of the 478 patients, 68 percent had been discharged or furloughed, 14 percent of whom were returned for more treatment. During the same time period, the return rate for the hospital at large was approximately 50 percent following a discharge or furlough rate of approximately 54 percent.

CLINICAL REASONS FOR TREATING CHRONIC SCHIZOPHRENICS IN AN INPATIENT SETTING

It seems clear that some chronic schizophrenics can be treated in a residential facility. Even those (or perhaps, especially those) who have been left behind after the "better" patient has been sent to community mental health centers and nursing homes can benefit from such care. If one is looking at symptom reduction, however, the treatment of choice is community care as long as day treatment and supportive residential services are available but those are big "ifs." Such conditions often only exist in the minds of the clinicians and planners. Hence, most pragmatists now look to the total mental health system, including its state hospitals for the treatment of the chronic patient.

The Group for the Advancement of Psychiatry Committee on Psychopathology (1982) proposes that the hospital can best provide the total care required by the chronic patient, whereas a prior committee on Psychiatry and the Community recommended an ongoing pursuit of adequate community care. In either case, Talbott (1981) lists the specific services required by the chronically ill: medical, psychiatric, social, housing, nutritional, income maintenance, employment training, vocational, and social rehabilitation. All of these services are taken for granted in the hospital but often are not readily available in the community.

The Psychopathology Committee's (1982) argument rests upon the conclusion "that one cannot prevent chronicity, nor cure dependent chronic mental patients, many of whom will need indefinite care" (p. 1). They consider the benefits of hospital care to come from six main areas: (1) structure, containment, and support, (2) total comprehensive services, (3) relief for the community and the family, (4) asylum for the patient, (5) clarification of diagnosis and prognosis, and (6) research.

Structure, containment, and support refer to providing a structural environment with a strong hierarchy of authority that compensates for the patient's disorganization. The environment is predictable, and thus consistent. Such an environment also allows for quick containment of individuals who are out-of-control by removing the unacceptable burdens of self control. The Committee also sees a benefit in regulating the level of stimulation, somehow assuming that stimulation actually can be varied in an institution and it can be varied in regard to individual patients in a group setting.

All inpatient admissions of chronic patients require the clinician to be clear as to the reasons for the hospitalization, the goals the admission is intended to achieve, and the optional plans envisioned if the target goals are not reached. Admissions that are "fishing expeditions" or hoped for magical solutions for the "tough cases" are irresponsible and bound to fail. There are also specific contraindications to the admission of the chronic patient. These include repeating a treatment that has already failed, using the hospital because nothing else works, attempting to make major characterological changes, attempting to try a new medication without any positive indications for its success, trying to convince patients to change their living situations, treating the patients' unwillingness to follow treatment plans, and sheltering malingerers or patients facing legal charges.

The hospital possesses some advantages in the quest for excellence of care for the chronic patient. One of the first advantages is determining the diagnosis. Primary to the establishment of any effective treatment program is the concurrence on a specific diagnosis. Since withdrawal, depression, lack of spontaneity, etc. are common to chronic schizophrenia, chronic affective disorders, chronic institutionalization, and organic mental conditions, this is one series of differential diagnoses that must be considered from the start, because the required interventions flow from the diagnosis: e.g., socialization for institutionalization; appropriate medication for affective disorders, and elimination of organic factors, if possible, for organicity. In addition, many chronic mentally ill persons have received diagnoses years before, and regardless of either current thinking about nomenclature or changes in symptoms, the diagnosis are reapplied thoughtlessly year after year. Also, Axis II or III diagnoses may be more treatable, and thus provide the critical wedge in a seemingly unbudgeable schizophrenic condition.

Another reason for admission to a hospital is to utilize the most productive treatment for each individual. An element of such a prescription is the evaluation of what treatment has or has not worked in the past. The patient may not be on an optimal psychopharmacological regimen and may need readmission to reequilibrate medication. Either too much (indicated by the occurrence of undesirable side effects or the inability to perform the social coping functions necessary to community survival) or too little medication (indicated by reemergence of psychotic symptoms, inability to function optimally, or behavior that is upsetting or disorganized) may indicate the need for readmission.

It is clear that psychotropic drugs are necessary, but not sufficient, for the treatment of chronic schizophrenia. They are necessary, in that they appear to reduce symptomatology (especially the so-called positive signs of schizophrenia such as hallucinations, delusions, ideas of reference, etc.), but not sufficient to normalize social and vocational functioning. The question of dosage and compliance has become paramount. In recent years, the current clinical guideline is to use as low a dosage as possible to maintain symptom remission and prevent rehospitalization. Needless to say, adequate doses over an adequate duration (minimum of six weeks but probably at least two months on one medication before deciding that a patient is drug resistant) must be carried out. The vexing clinical question is "Even if massive doses do produce some improvement over what is obtained with lower doses, is it worth the problem of increased risk of tardive dyskinesia if the clinical improvement is not substantial enough to permit return to the community?" (Klein, Gittleman, Guitkin, & Rifkin, 1980, p. 9). Empirically, in most inpatient settings, the benefits of medication may outweigh the risk of tardive dyskinesia. That is, unless some patients are maintained on drugs, they relapse and are rehospitalized (or continually symptomatic) so that the potential risk of tardive dyskinesia does at times not outweigh the necessity for the drug.

Chronic schizophrenics also may need the hospital to obtain treatment that is not available or easy to administer in community settings. Some chronic patients, for example, are unprepared or ill prepared to survive in the community and require hospitalization to enable them to learn the skills of everyday living that ensure such survival in our complicated contemporary society. Such skill training should usually be circumscribed (e.g., instruction about transportation systems, self-care, etc.) so that the target for discharge can be clearly achieved. Without such skills, patients are predisposed to become overtly psychotic, homocidal, or suicidal, and present a danger to themselves or others. Such behavior endangers either the patient or others, and may be prevented by longer-term treatment, usually utilizing a highly-structured behavioral modification or social learning program with an end toward modifying specific behaviors. Possibly this is the most pressing reason for considering the place of the state hospital in the mental health system.

Critical to the community retention of chronic schizophrenics is their ability to communicate, get along with others, and develop networks of support (Greenblatt, Becerra, & Serafetinida, 1982). Hospitalization may allow for full development of socialization skills by providing the opportunity to target specific deficits and areas that need improvement, and begin remediation of those areas. Referral to ongoing socialization programs can then follow. A good example of such treatment is reported in the social skill training of Goldstein et al. (1966) who report positive results with chronic schizophrenics. Bellack, Hersen, and Turner (1976) also report that social skill training with chronic patients concentrating on assertive behavior through role playing procedures produced improvement in assertive behavior that generalized to other situations.

On a more long-term basis, skills may be taught that require a large time investment and are not readily performed in the community setting, where there is difficulty in having the patient maintain an appointment schedule. Magaro and DeSisto (1981), for instance, present a treatment system that requires the rehabilitation of developmental deficits from early reflexes to later social skills. A controlled environment is possibly the only place where such long-term treatment can be completed, especially when the goal of treatment is to modify cognitive processes (Magaro, 1980). Structure is required in such programs but structure also may be required during certain periods (e.g., following the death of a close family member or spouse) when other treatment (e.g., increased medication) would not be helpful. In either case, treatment, whether psychotherapeutic, somatic, or behavioral, is sought within the structure of and making use of the supervision available in inpatient settings.

Rehabilitation or social learning in severely impaired chronic schizophrenics therefore may be a major indication for hospitalization. Persons who have been institutionalized for many years, have severe ego deficits, or who cannot function at even a minimal level because of their mental disability may require a long-term structured experience in order to progress to another facility or setting, even a half-way house or group home.

Finally, inpatient care can be critical to families and community support systems who cannot care for the chronic schizophrenic 365 days a year. Such "respite care" has been found to be extremely useful to families of the mentally retarded but is currently an underutilized, underoffered, and underreimbursed service for the mentally ill.

CONCLUSION

Services for chronic schizophrenics in this country have seen radical shifts in the concept of the ideal treatment setting for the chronic patient. Until the 1950s, hospitals were the locus of treatment and care, but subsequently, and especially during the late 1960s, some individuals maintained that there was no need for any hospitals for the mentally ill (James, 1980); and only recently has it been realized that there is a need for asylum for some small percentage of our chronic patient population (Lamb, 1979).

By asylum, we do not mean to imply a building or institution, but rather a function. It is possible that both board and care homes and "L-facilities" have performed this function of asylum, custody, or supervised sheltered care. We also wish to be clear that we do not think that such asylum functions need to be operated by the state. There is good evidence that while they could be funded by the state, because of their tertiary role in the mental health system, they could also be operated by local governmental units and located in the community. There are also strong arguments, however, for the settings to be operated by private enterprise (Magaro, Gripp, & McDowell, 1978).

Certainly, the future of inpatient hospital treatment for chronic schizophrenics depends in large part on two factors—reimbursement and scientific research. With the beginning understanding of differential therapeutics (Frances & Clarkin, 1983), it is becoming increasingly obvious that the practices of both professionals and third-party payers will be governed more and more by answers to the question, "What treatment works for which patients in what settings?" Certainly, more sophisticated methods of delineating different subgroups of chronic schizophrenics must be continued.

It is also clear that while we are miles ahead of where we were a few decades ago, there is still no "cure" in sight for the basic disorder or disorders. As has often been pointed out, scientific advances take place in leaps and bounds and quite spottily, and just as no one would have predicted the current state of understanding in treating many formerly devastating cancerous conditions, no one can predict which mental disorder will come under control next or when. Waiting around for the millenium, however, is an inadequate response to the current problem. Given what we do know about the contemporary care and treatment of chronic schizophrenia, we are not implementing even the little knowledge available (Department of Health and Human Services Report, 1981). For example, continuity of care, use of short-term hospitalization, the necessity of combining psychosocial and psychopharmacological interventions, the necessity of seeing a hospital episode as just one part in the patient's lifetime experience with a mental disorder, and the need to forge a true mental health system. While we await the "cure" for those suffering from chronic schizophrenia, there is plenty of work in simply bringing about their "care."

REFERENCES

Anthony WA. Psychological rehabilitation: A concept in need of a method. *American Psychologist,* 1977, *32,* 658–662

Anthony WA. A rehabilitation model for rehabilitating the psychiatrically disabled. *Rehabilitation Counseling Bulletin,* 1980, Sept., 6–20

Atthowe JM, & Krasner L. Preliminary report as the application of contingency response procedures (token economy) on a "chronic" psychiatric ward. *Journal of Abnormal Psychology,* 1968, *73,* 37–43

Ayllon T, & Azrin NH. The measurement and reinforcement of behavior of psychotics. *Journal of Experimental Analysis of Behavior,* 1965, *8,* 357–383

Bachrach LL. *Deinstitutionalization: An analytic review and sociological perspective.* DHEW Pub. No. (ADM) 79-351. Washington, D.C.: Superintendent of Documents, U.S. Government Printing Office, 1976

Bachrach, LL. Planning mental health services for chronic patients. *Hospital and Community Psychiatry,* 1979, *39,* 387–393

Bachrach LL. Is the least restrictive environment always the best? Sociologic and semantic implications. *Hospital and Community Psychiatry,* 1980, *31,* 97–103

Bassuk EL, & Gerson S. Deinstitutionalization and mental health services. *Scientific American,* 1978, *238,* 46–53

Bellack AS, Hersen M, & Turner SM. Generalization effects of social skills training in chronic schizophrenics: An experimental analysis. *Behavior Research and Therapy,* 1976, *14,* 391–398

Binner PR. *Output value analysis: An overview paper presented at the Information and Feedback Conference.* York University, Toronto, Canada, 1974

Bleuler M. *The schizophrenic disorders.* New Haven: Yale University Press, 1978

Braun P, Kochansky G, Shapiro B, Greenberg S, Guademan JE, Johnson S, & Shore MF. Overview: Deinstitutionalization of psychiatric patients: A critical review of outcome American studies. *American Journal of Psychiatry,* 1981, *138,* 736–749

Committee on Psychopathology, Group for the Advancement of Psychiatry. *The positive aspects of long-term hospitalization in the public section for chronic psychiatric patients.* New York: Mental Health Materials Center, 1982

Comptroller General Report. *Report to Congress by the Comptroller General of the United States. Returning the mentally disabled to the community: Government needs to do more.* Washington, D.C.: Department of Health, Education and Welfare, 1977. Publication #(HRD) 76-152

Davis JM. Overview: Maintenance therapy in psychiatry: I. Schizophrenia. *American Journal of Psychiatry,* 1975, *132,* 1237–1245

Dorwart P. Deinstitutionalization: Who is left behind? *Hospital and Community Psychiatry,* 1980, *31,* 336–338

Fairweather GW (Ed.), *Psychology in treating mental illness. Experimental approach.* New York: Wiley, 1964

Fairweather GW, Sanders DH, Maynard H, & Cressler DL. *Community life for the mentally ill: An alternative to institutional care.* Chicago: Aldine, 1969.

Fann WE, Davis JM, & Janowsky DS. The prevalence of tardive dyskinesias in mental hospital patients. *Diseases of the Nervous System,* 1972, *33,* 182–186

Frances A, & Clarkin J. *Differential therapeutics.* In press, 1983

Gardos G, & Cole, JO. Maintenance antipsychotic therapy: Is the cure worse than the disease? *American Journal of Psychiatry,* 1976, *133,* 32–36

Glick LD, & Hargreaves WA. *Psychiatric hospital treatment for the 1980's.* Lexington, MA: Lexington Books, 1979

Goldman HH, Gattozzi AA, & Taube CA. Defining and counting the chronically mentally ill. Hospital and Community Psychiatry, 1981, *32,* 21–27

Goldstein AP, Heller K, & Sechrest LB. *Pshchotherapy and the psychology of behavior change.* New York: Wiley, 1966

Gorham DC, Green LW, Caldwell LR, & Bartlett ER. Effects of operant conditioning techniques in chronic schizophrenics. *Psychological Reports,* 1970, *27,* 223–234

Greenblatt M, Becerra RM, & Serafetinida EA. Social networks and mental health: An overview. *American Journal of Psychiatry,* 1982, *139,* 977–984

Greenblatt M, Solomon M, & Evans A. *Drug and social therapy in chronic schizophrenia.* Springfield, IL: Charles C. Thomas, 1965

Grinspoon L, Ewait J, & Shader R. *Schizophrenia: Pharmacotherapy and psychotherapy.* Baltimore: Williams & Wilkins, 1972

Gripp RF, & Magaro PA. A token economy evaluation with control ward comparisons. *Behavior Research and Therapy,* 1971, *9,* 137–149

Gunderson JG. Drugs and psychosocial treatment of schizophrenia revisited. *Journal of Continuing Education in Psychiatry.* 1977, *8*(25), 4–5

Gunderson J. *National institute of mental health.* U.S. Department of Health & Human Services, Vol. VIII, 1983

Heap RF, Boblitt WE, Moore CH, & Hard JF. Behavior milieu therapy with chronic neuropsychiatric patients. *Journal of Abnormal Psychology,* 1970, *76,* 349–354

Herz MI, Endicott J, & Spitzer RL. Brief vs. standard hospitalization: The families. *American Journal of Psychiatry,* 1976, *133,* 795–801.

Herz MI, Endicott J, & Spitzer RL. Brief hospitalization: A two year follow-up. *American Journal of Psychiatry,* 1977, *134,* 502–507

HEW Task Force Report. *On the report of the president from the president's commission on mental health.* Washington, D.C.: Dept. of Health, Education and Welfare, 1979. Publication #(ADM) 79-848

Hogarty GE, Goldberg SC, Schooler NR, & Ulrich RF. Drug and sociotherapy in the aftercare of schizophrenic patients. II. Two-year relapse rates. *Archives of General Psychiatry,* 1974, *31,* 603–608

James JF. State hospitals should be replaced. In JA Talbott (Ed.), *State mental hospitals: Problems and potentials.* New York: Human Sciences Press, 1980.

Jeste DV, & Wyatt RJ. In search of treatment for tardive dyskinesia: Review of the literature. *Schizophrenia Bulletin,* 1979, *5,* 251–293

Jones M. Community care for chronic mental patients: The need for a reassessment. *Hospital and Community Psychiatry,* 1979, *30,* 387–393

Karon BP, & Vanderbos GR. *Psychotherapy of schizophrenia: The treatment of choice.* New York: Jason Aronson, 1981

Kiesler CA. Mental hospitals and alternative care: Noninstitutionalization as potential public policy for mental patients. *American Psychologist.* 1982 *37,* 349–360 (a)

Kiesler CA. Public and professional myths about mental hospitalization. *American Psychologist,* 1982, *37,* 1323–1339 (b)

Klein DF, Gittelman R, Quitkin F, & Rifkin A. *Diagnosis and drug treatment of psychiatric disorders: Adults and children,* 2nd ed. Baltimore: Williams & Wilkins, 1980

Kramer M. *National institute of mental health, Series B,* No. 12, 1977

Kraft AM, Binner PR, & Dickey BA. The community mental health program and the longer stay patient. *Archives of General Psychiatry,* 1967, *16,* 64–70

Kraus RT. A nursing home model. In J Talbott (Ed.), *The chronic mentally ill.* Human Sciences Press, 1981

Lamb, HR. The new asylum in the community. *Archives of General Psychiatry,* 1979, *36,* 129–138

Lehmann HE. Psychopharmacological treatment of schizophrenia. *Schizophrenia Bulletin,* 1975, *13,* 27–45

Lerman P. *Deinstitutionalization: A cross problem analysis.* U.S. Dept. of Health and Human Services, DHHS Publication No. (ADM) 81-987, 1981

Lipton MA, & Burnett GB. Pharmacological treatment of schizophrenia. In L Bellak (Ed.), *Disorders of the schizophrenic syndrome.* New York: Basic Books, 1980

Lloyd KE, & Abel L. Performance in token economy psychiatric ward: A two year summary. *Behavior Research and Therapy,* 1970, *8,* 1–9

Lloyd KE, & Garlington WK. Weekly variations in performance on a token economy psychiatric ward. *Behavior Research and Therapy,* 1968, *6,* 407–410

Magaro PA. *Cognition in schizophrenia and paranoia: The integration of cognitive processes.* Hillsdale, NJ: Lawrence Erlbaum, 1980

Magaro PA, & DeSisto M. A developmental treatment program for the chronic patient. *American Journal of Psychotherapy,* 1981, *35,* 47–60

Magaro PA, & Giardina P. Comparing custodial and democratic treatment progress. *Hospital & Community Psychiatry,* 1970, *21,* 118–119

Magaro PA, Gripp R, & McDowell DJ. *The mental health industry: A cultural phenomenon.* New York: John Wiley & Sons, 1978

Martin MA. A practical treatment program for a mental hospital "back" ward. *American Journal of Psychiatry,* 1950, *10,* 758–760.

Mattes JA, Rosen B, & Klein DF. Comparison of the clinical effectiveness of "short" versus "long" stay psychiatric hospitalization: II. Results of a 3-year posthospital follow-up. *Journal of Nervous and Mental Disease,* 1977, *166,* 387–394 (a)

Mattes JA, Rosen B, Klein DF, & Millan D. Comparison of the clinical effectiveness of "short" versus "long" stay psychiatric hospitalization: III. Further results of a 3-year posthospital follow-up. *Journal of Nervous and Mental Disease,* 1977, *165,* 395–402 (b)

May PKA. *Treatment of schizophrenia: A comparative study of five treatment methods.* New York: Science House, 1968

May PKA. Schizophrenia: An overview of treatment methods. In A. Freedman, HI Kaplan, & BJ Sadock (Eds.), *Comprehensive textbook of psychiatry. II.* Baltimore: Williams & Wilkins, 1975

McReynolds WT, & Coleman J. Token economy: Patient and staff changes. *Behavior Research and Therapy,* 1972, *10,* 29–34

Mechanic D. *Mental health and social policy.* Englewood Cliffs, NJ: Prentice-Hall, 1969

Miller DH, & Clancy J. An approach to the social rehabilitation of chronic psychotic patients. *Psychiatry,* 1952, *15,* 435–443

Mosher L, & Gunderson J. Special report on schizophrenia. *Schizophrenia Bulletin,* 1972, *7,* 10–52

Paul GL. Strategy of outcome research in psychotherapy. *Journal of Consulting Psychology,* 1967, *31,* 109–118

Paul GL, & Lentz RJ. *Psychosocial treatment of chronic mental patients.* Cambridge: Harvard university Press, 1977

Preliminary Report to the President. *The president's commission on mental health, Vol. I.* Washington, D.C., 1978

Prien RF, & Klett CJ. An appraisal of the long-term use of tranquilizing medication with hospitalized chronic schizophrenics: A review of the drug discontinuation literature. *Schizophrenia Bulletin,* 1972, *1,* 64–73

Rashkis HA, & Smarr ER. Drug and milieu effects with chronic schizophrenics. *Archives of Neurology and Psychiatry,* 1957, *78,* 89–94

Reibel S, & Herz MI. Limitations of brief hospital treatment. *American Journal of Psychiatry,* 1976, *133,* 518–521

Riessman CK, Rabkin JG, & Struening EL. Brief versus standard psychiatric hospitalization: A critical review of the literature. *Community Mental Health Review,* 1977, *2,* 1–10

Rogers CR, Gendlin EG, Kiesler DJ, & Trauzz LB. *The therapeutic relationship and its impact: A study of psychotherapy with schizophrenics.* Madison: University of Wisconsin Press, 1967

Sanders R, Smith RS, & Weinman BS. *Chronic psychosis and recovery.* San Francisco: Jossey-Bass, 1967

Senate Subcommittee. *On long term care of the Special Committee on aging and the U.S. House of Representatives Subcommittee on health and long term care of the Selection Committee on aging: Proprietary home health care. Joint hearing.* Washington, D.C.: Superintendent of Documents, 1975

Shadish WR, Straw RB, McSweeney AJ, Koler DL, & Bootzin RR. Nursing home care for mental patients: Descriptive data and some propositions. *American Journal of Community Psychology,* 1981, *9,* 617–633

Shaefer HH, & Martin PL. Behavior therapy for apathy of hospitalized schizophrenics. *Psychological Reports,* 1966, 1147–1158

Shean GD, & Zeidberg Z. Token reinforcement therapy: A comparison of matched groups. *Journal of Behavior Therapy and Experimental Psychiatry.* 1971, *2,* 94–105

Smith WG, & Hart DW. Community mental health: a noble failure? *Hospital and Community Psychiatry,* 1975, *26,* 581–583

Steffy RA, Hart S, Craw M, Torney D, & Marlett N. *Learning techniques to the management of rehabilitation of severely regressed chronically ill patients: Preliminary findings.* Paper presented at Ontario Psychiatric Association, Ottawa, Canada, 1966

Talbott JA. *The chronic mentally ill. Treatment, programs, systems.* New York: Human Sciences press, 1981

Tobias LL, & MacDonald ML. Withdrawal of maintenance drugs with long-term hospitalized mental patients: A critical review. *Psychological Bulletin,* 1974, *81,* 107–125

Toward a National Plan for the Chronically Mentally Ill: Report to the Secretary by the Department of Health and Human Services Steering Committee on the Chronically Mentally Ill. Washington, D.C.: Public Health Service, USDHHS, (ADM) 81-1077, 1981

Winkler RC. Management of chronic psychiatric patients by token reinforcement system. *Journal of Applied Behavior Analysis,* 1970, *3,* 47–55

Raymond F. Luber

8

Partial Hospitalization

The marked growth in the utilization of partial hospitalization programs for the treatment of a wide variety of psychiatric disorders can be directly related to the passage of The Mental Retardation Facilities and Community Mental Health Centers Construction Act of 1963. In the years immediately following the passage of this Act, which made partial hospitalization a mandated service in federally funded projects, the modality experienced a 700 percent increase in the number of programs and a 1400 percent increase in the number of patients served (Taube, 1973). This growth has continued in recent years, at a somewhat less dramatic rate.

At least two interesting historical developments have influenced the evolution of partial hospitalization. The first relates to purpose or function. The first documented partial program was established in Moscow, Russia in 1933 (Dzhagarov, 1937). It was developed as a pragmatic necessity rather than a theoretical or academic exercise: the First Psychiatric Hospital was experiencing an acute shortage of inpatient beds. Consequently, "the day infirmary for the mentally ill" was established as a substitute or alternative for full-time hospitalization and, reportedly, treated over 1200 patients in 4 years.

In the Western world, partial hospitalization developed under a slightly different emphasis. Some practitioners, such as Bierer (1951), advocated the "alternative" use of the modality. The main emphasis in the West, however, was initially on partial hospitalization as a

SCHIZOPHRENIA
ISBN 0-8089-1640-8

transitional treatment modality. Thus, Cameron (1947) developed a program in Montreal, Canada that was conceptualized as an extension and supplement for full-time hospitalization. Bierer (1951) also established a program in London that was intended to close the gap between the inpatient department and the outpatient department. Thus, almost from its inception, partial hospitalization has been conceptualized as having dual functions: an alternative to inpatient treatment and a transition between inpatient and outpatient treatment. This historical duality is reflected in the actual utilization of partial hospitalization today.

A second interesting and significant development relates to the varying therapeutic approaches that developed in early programs and continue to influence treatment formats in current programs. For example, in Russia the primary therapeutic emphasis was on work, in Canadian programs on psychotherapy, and in England on socialization via the social club model. This tripartite emphasis on work, psychotherapy, and socialization is reflected today in the composition of individual programs or the components incorporated, in varying combinations, in other programs.

Although the literature indicates that partial hospitalization has been successfully utilized in the treatment of a wide range of psychiatric disorders (Luber, 1979), the largest single category is undoubtedly schizophrenia, including acute and chronic episodes in both children and adults. As will be discussed subsequently, significant evidence exists demonstrating the efficacy of partial hospitalization in the treatment of schizophrenic disorders, although opinions differ regarding the setting and/or methodology for this treatment.

Finally, several theoretical and pragmatic advantages of partial hospitalization should be mentioned briefly. First, empirical data exist to support the contention that partial hospitalization can, for a certain patient population, provide treatment that is equally or more effective than inpatient treatment at about one-half the cost. Apart from the obvious desire to provide the most efficacious treatment possible, the potential cost savings represented by partial hospitalization are a significant advantage.

A second advantage of this modality can be seen in the flexibility of programming that is possible without the usual restrictions imposed by inpatient care and the limited contact that is typical of outpatient treatment regimes. The usual partial hospitalization program operates five days per week, six hours per day. Within this structure, a wide variety of therapeutic approaches can be utilized in a comprehensive and consistent manner. In addition, the program itself can be tailored to meet individual needs as much as possible, ranging from the days utilized to the types of treatment offered.

Third, partial hospitalization offers the possibility of providing effective treatment without completely destroying the individual's contact with social and environmental systems. This may be particularly significant in light of the current emphasis on deinstitutionalization and the need to maintain many individuals with schizophrenic disorders largely in the community setting. In addition, this approach may provide a method of diluting the "social breakdown syndrome" (Chen, Healey, & Williams, 1969), which often develops as a result of hospitalization even for a short duration.

Finally, partial hospitalization may be an advantageous approach because of the decreased amount of social stigma that seems to be attached to this form of treatment. The fact that partial hospitalization is less restrictive, less disruptive, and more acceptable to patients and their families (Zwerling & Wilder, 1964) appears to contribute to this situation. This more positive attitude may, in turn, lead to a more successful treatment outcome because patients will be more amenable to therapeutic interventions offered through the program.

The remainder of this Chapter will consider more specific issues related to the care and treatment of the schizophrenic patient in partial hospitalization, including current research findings, clinical guidelines for treatment procedures, and important clinical issues related to the use of the treatment modality.

RESEARCH REVIEW

In recent years a number of comprehensive reviews of research relative to major aspects of partial hospitalization have appeared in the literature (Hersen, 1979; Herz, 1982; Mason, Louks, Burmer, & Scher, 1982). Research in the area has dealt with a number of significant issues including the following:

1. The utilization and effectiveness of partial hospitalization as an alternative to inpatient treatment
2. The utilization of partial hospitalization in conjunction with short-term inpatient treatment
3. The effectiveness of partial hospitalization as an alternative to traditional outpatient approaches
4. Studies related to the issues of program evaluation and the effectiveness of individual program components
5. Cost effectiveness studies

6. The factors effecting the utilization of partial hospitalization

This section will consider those studies and research findings that are particularly relevant to issues related to the care and treatment of schizophrenia. It should be pointed out, however, that significant data is somewhat limited. Although the descriptive literature on partial hospitalization shows that a large percentage of patients treated in the modality are diagnosed as schizophrenic, few studies control for diagnosis when investigating and reporting outcome results. It should also be noted that in most cases research in partial hospitalization is aimed at demonstrating the utility of the modality in the continuum of mental health services rather than as the primary psychiatric treatment modality (Luber, 1979). This is, in this area as in most others, an effort is being made to determine the most effective match of patients and treatments in order to provide the best possible outcome.

Short Term Inpatient Treatment

Several studies have been conducted in recent years related to the goals and length of hospitalization (Caffey, Galbrecht, & Klett, 1971; Glick, Hargreaves, & Druers, 1976; Herz, Endicott, & Spitzer, 1977). A review of the literature related to brief versus standard psychiatric hospitalization (Reisman, Rabkin, & Struning, 1977) concluded that the research to date consistently demonstrates that brief hospitalization is a feasible alternative to standard hospitalization; moreover, few or no differences seem to be evident in the relative effectiveness of the two treatments over a two year period of followup.

There is some indication that these findings are generally applicable to the subpopulation identified as schizophrenic. For example, Caffey et al. (1971) studied 201 newly admitted schizophrenic men in 14 different Veteran's Administration hospitals. One condition of the study involved the accelerated discharge of patients followed by one year outpatient treatment by the same staff. This group averaged 29 days of hospitalization as compared to 83 days for the standard group; most importantly, no difference in outcome between the two groups was discovered. Thus, the investigators concluded that short term treatment is effective because, while readmission rates were similar to those of long term patients, total time in the community was longer due to the brevity of initial treatment.

In addition, a series of well designed studies related to brief versus standard hospitalization have been conducted by Herz and his colleagues (1971, 1975, 1976, 1977, 1979). Since the most common diagnosis among study patients (63 percent) was schizophrenia, an effort was made to determine if diagnosis could be utilized as a predictive criterion for successful use of short term hospitalization treatment. Results indicated that the number of pervious admissions and a diagnosis of schizophrenia were synergistic and associated with poor outcome; however, in contrast to other studies (Glick et al., 1976), the investigators concluded that "there was no evidence that schizophrenic patients had superior outcomes when treated with the standard approach" (Endicott, Cohen, Nee, Fleiss, & Herz 1979, p. 712). Finally, in summary, Herz (1977) states:

> As a result of these studies, we believe that if hospitalization is necessary, in general it should be utilized only to control acute symptoms. Once this is accomplished, patients should be transferred to other treatment modalities which are less restrictive to autonomous functioning and which are more suited to maintaining and encouraging healthy areas of functioning, such as day and outpatient care (p. 105).

Previous studies have indicated that approximately 50 percent of the patients treated in the short term model will need some form of transitional treatment, such as partial hospitalization, for an average of 45 days following hospitalization (Herz, 1982). There is currently little evidence indicating that diagnosis itself is a significant determinent in the effective utilization of this approach; nor, is there any significant evidence that demonstrates that improvements accomplished through standard hospitalization treatment have any significant effect on post-hospital adjustment (Anthony, Buell, Sharratt, & Althoff, 1972). Obviously, since brief hospitalization is less expensive, its utilization with partial hospitalization can represent significant cost savings without sacrificing effective treatment outcome.

Alternative to Inpatient Treatment

In summarizing the research in the area of partial hospitalization versus inpatient treatment, it is possible to state that an impressive amount of empirical support has been gathered for the contention that day treatment can be a viable alternative to inpatient treatment for a substantial number of patients. Two factors are involved in this situation. First, studies indicate that patients treated in day hospitals are likely to show greater appropriate role functioning in the community than their hospitalized counterparts; and, second, although inpatients generally show a greater decrease in symptomatology in initial stages of treatment than day patients, these differences tend to equalize over time. Of course, a major area of interest involves the question of which particular patients are most suitable for this alternative. Unfortunately, data at this point in time can only indicate trends. Nevertheless, several studies of importance should be mentioned.

Wilder, Levin, and Zwerling (1966) conducted a two year followup study of 189 patients admitted to inpatient treatment and 189 patients treated in a day hospital program; random assignment of patients was made to the two treatment conditions. The investigators concluded that "the day hospital was a feasible treatment modality and was generally as effective as the inpatient service in the treatment of acutely disturbed patients for most or all phases of their hospitalization" (p. 1101). In addition, an important finding in this study indicated that the interval between readmissions was significantly longer for day hospital patients than for inpatients; thus, day patients spent considerably more time in the community than inpatients.

This study was sufficiently large to provide outcome data related to diagnosis and treatment effectiveness. Of particular interest were the following findings:

1. Schizophrenic women seemed to do better in their post-hospital adjustment when treated in the one "day" hospital; this was reflected in the fact that 93 percent were in the community at followup (versus 69 percent of those treated as inpatients).
2. Schizophrenic male day patients tended to be hospitalized earlier and more frequently than inpatients.
3. Patients with the poorest prognosis for treatment in the day hospital *as an alternative to inpatient services* tended to be schizophrenic men (italics added).

Finally, the investigators (Zwerling & Wilder, 1964) in an earlier report on the efficacy of partial hospitalization treatment with various diagnostic categories, stated that:

> our attention has been called to what we feel to be the unusually good outcome in the cases of patients diagnosed as "paranoid schizophrenia," undifferentiated or mixed schizophrenia and psychotic depressive reactions in all diagnostic categories (pp. 183–184).

A comparative study by Washburn and his colleagues (1976) is also of importance. Although outcome data by diagnostic categories was not obtained, it is significant that 50 percent of the 93 female patients followed in the study were diagnosed as schizophrenic. Patients were evaluated over a 2 year period on 5 separate dimensions with results favoring day hospital treatment in all areas; after 24 months, however, the general advantage of day treatment was "overcome" and inpatients evidenced comparable gains. This study demonstrated the superiority of day over inpatient treatment in the following areas: (1) community functioning; (2) subjective distress; (3) family burden; (4) total hospital cost; and, (5) days of attachment to the program.

Michaux et al. (1970, 1973) reached somewhat different conclusions regarding the effectiveness of partial hospitalization as an alternative to inpatient treatment for the schizophrenic population. Unfortunately, however, this was not a controlled study and did not involve the randomization of patients to treatment conditions. This may limit the general applicability of the results.

In general, the investigators concluded that inpatients treatment was especially useful for "quick symptom relief" while day treatment enabled patients "to make lasting gains in social adjustment and eventually in symptomology" (1973, p. 651). More specifically, in regard to the schizophrenic population, the investigators concluded that full time hospitalization was superior to day treatment in the reduction of such symptoms as excitement, impaired functioning, anxious intrapunitiveness, and paranoia; both schizophrenics and nonschizophrenics showed significant improvement in conceptual disorganization in both treatment conditions. Again, however, these gains tended to equalize over time. In this study, at 12 month followup assessments, no significant differences were observed in symptomatology or relapse.

Finally, Herz, Endicott, Spitzer, and Mesnikoff (1971) also generated data favoring day hospital treatment over inpatient care on practically every dependent measure used. Although this was a well controlled study, the number of subjects in each condition (45) was insufficient to analyze by subgroups including diagnosis. Nevertheless, the obvious superiority of day treatment was demonstrated. Also, it is interesting to note the investigators' speculation regarding the possible reasons for this outcome:

> Day care apparently avoids the regressive feature associated with "total institutionalization." In addition, day patients have a greater opportunity to maintain healthy areas of functioning, including the preservation of social and instrumental roles (p. 1379).

In conclusion, it can be stated with reasonable confidence that partial hospitalization can be effectively utilized as an alternative to inpatient treatment. Moreover, specific data indicate that this alternative is, indeed, viable for the treatment of schizophrenic women; unfortunately, little reliable data exists with regard to other subgroups in this diagnostic category.

Cost Effectiveness Studies

In addition to therapeutic outcome, the question of cost-effectiveness is of significance when considering the utilization of partial hospitalization as an alternative to inpatient treatment or in conjunction with short term hospitalization. In summary, it can be said that cost-effectiveness studies have demonstrated the efficacy of partial hospitalization for a number of patients who are potential candidates for inpatient treatment, resulting in considerable financial savings over the entire course of treatment. Indeed, controlled studies have shown that the use of partial hospitalization can reduce such costs by up to 50 percent (Endicott, Herz, & Gibbon, 1978; Washburn et al., 1976), and that these initial cost savings can be maintained during followup treatment (Longabaugh, Fink, & Stout, 1975).

Two additional studies in this area are important. First, Guilette, Crowley, Savitz, and Goldberg (1978) conducted a pilot study funded by the Aetna Insurance Company. The purpose of the investigation was to determine whether providing insurance coverage for day hospitalization on the same basis as was provided for inpatient treatment would be a feasible means of controlling the cost of psychiatric care. In brief, the investigators concluded that the use of partial hospitalization for the 31 patients studied would have saved the insurer nearly $255,000 over the period of treatment, which averaged 88.5 calendar days.

Secondly, a study conducted by Krowinski and Fitt (1978) concluded that a cost saving of approximately $749 per patient could be achieved by treatment in partial hospitalization while maintaining greater therapeutic gains than inpatient treatment. Specifically, the study concluded that "it tends to be less expensive to treat patients in partial hospitalization than in full hospitalization when admission-to-discharge costs are computed"; and, "when costs of readmission are included, the data indicates that patients treated in partial hospitalization incur less expense than patients admitted to inpatient facilities" (pp. 18–19). In the areas of both treatment efficacy and cost savings, partial hospitalization has been demonstrated to be a viable alternative to inpatient care and a useful adjunct to short term hospitalization.

It should be pointed out that partial hospitalization is not the only alternative to hospital treatment, which has been investigated and found to be effective. A subsequent chapter in this volume (Test, Chapter 13) discusses Community Support Programs. One such program was developed and studied in relation to the treatment of chronically disabled psychiatric patients (Stein & Test, 1980; Test & Stein,

1980; Weisbrod, Test, & Stein, 1980). This investigation also clearly demonstrated the viability of treating patients outside the more traditional hospital setting. Such an approach should not be viewed as a "competitive model" for partial hospitalization. Rather, it should be seen as another available and empirically supported option in the effort to provide the most effective treatment possible. Unfortunately, the obstacles to the implementation of both alternatives seem to be similar and involve issues and questions other than those of treatment efficacy. Mendel and Allen (1978) define these barriers in an interesting way when they state:

> It has become perfectly clear that professional comfort, economic forces, and social and cultural resistences have much more to do with the continuation of the hospital as the central health care delivery system than does science or considerations of patient care (p. 182).

At the very least, this statement demarcates the fact that there are, indeed, significant barriers to be overcome in the future if alternative treatment approaches are to be widely implemented on more than experimental research levels.

Alternative to Outpatient Treatment

Since approximately 1975, a major emphasis in the treatment of psychiatric patients has been the movement toward deinstitutionalization. As defined by the National Institute of Mental Health, the elements involved in this concept include:

1. The prevention of inappropriate hospital admissions through the provision of community alternatives for treatment.
2. The release to the community of all institutionalized patients who have been given adequate preparation for such a change.
3. The establishment and maintenance of community support systems for noninstitutionalized people receiving mental health services in the community (Braun, Kochansky, Shapiro, Greenberg, Gudeman, Johnson, & Share, 1981, p. 739).

The effects of this widespread approach are as yet unclear. One study, however, suggests that for a large majority of patients, being "in the community" means little more than social isolation (Solomon, Baird, Evenstine, & Escobar, 1980). In this context, research related to the use of partial hospitalization as an alternative to traditional outpatient treatment is important. Unlike some other areas, data regarding the effectiveness of partial hospitalization with the schizophrenic population are available. Several studies will be briefly cited.

Guy, Gross, Hogarty, and Dennis (1969) conducted a controlled comparison between partial hospitalization and outpatient treatment. The results of this study indicated that for schizophrenic patients the day hospital was the treatment of choice; this was especially true for those patients with schizoaffective diagnostic characteristics. Specifically, the symptom constellation that improved through day hospital but not outpatient treatment included communication and accessibility; that is, these individuals were less withdrawn, hostile, and suspicious and were more cooperative than their counterparts treated in the outpatient clinic.

An earlier study (Meltzhoff & Blumenthal, 1966) also favored day hospital treatment. Specifically, partial hospitalization was demonstrated to be superior in the treatment of the marginally adjusted schizophrenic patient. Thus, over the 18 months of the study, day patients had significantly fewer readmissions and remained the same or improved in the areas of self-concept, relationship with the family, and general mood; the outpatient group, however, declined in all of these areas.

Two additional studies have produced data related to partial hospitalization and diagnosis. First, Erickson (1972) examined the effects of treatment duration and diagnosis (schizophrenic and non-schizophrenic) and types of improvement. At discharge, both groups showed improvement with regard to alcohol abuse, depression, confusion, and anxiety, while schizophrenics also improved in the area of interpersonal involvement. Interestingly, long-stay patients (4 months vs. 2 months) showed greater improvement than short-stay patients in both groups. On the other hand, Davis, Lorei, and Caffey (1978) found less improvement among schizophrenics than non-schizophrenics in their study of 34 Veterans Administration Day Hospital programs. They concluded, however, that performance at admission was a better predictor of outcome than background or demographic variables.

Finally, Linn et al. (1979) conducted a two year Veterans Administration hospital study comparing partial hospitalization and outpatient treatment for an exclusively schizophrenic population. Ratings of symptomology and role functioning were made at admission and at 6, 12, 18, and 24 months. Results indicated no difference in readmission rates (with a trend favoring day hospital patients) and a significant improvement in role functioning favoring day hospital patients. In the area of symptomology, day hospital patients showed significantly better improvement in conceptual disorganization, hostility, hallucinatory behavior, uncooperativeness, and unusual thought content. Also, there were no statistically significant differences in the cost of the two treatments.

Based on post hoc analysis, the investigators also attempted to differentiate between "good result" and "poor result" programs. Although these results may be less reliable due to design problems, their general conclusion is worth noting and will be discussed in more detail later:

> In regard to the large number of chronic schizophrenics discharged from mental hospitals, there is evidence that day treatment that is of a supportive and perhaps long-term nature, can help to prevent relapse, enhance functioning and decrease symptoms (p. 1066).

As was stated earlier, the largest single category of patients reported in the literature to be treated in partial hospitalization was the schizophrenic, both acute and chronic. To date, there is supportive evidence for the utilization of this treatment modality with this patient population.

Summary

From this brief review it can be seen that significant empirical data regarding the effectiveness of partial hospitalization has been accumulated in several areas. Questions are still unanswered. Overall, however, it appears clear that partial hospitalization has significant advantages both in the areas of cost effectiveness and treatment efficacy; this includes the treatment of acute and chronic phases of schizophrenia. In addition, partial hospitalization has certain advantages in terms of program flexibility and the reduction of social stigma that support its potential effectiveness.

It is also true, however, that partial hospitalization is a generally underutilized treatment modality. It appears that a major reason for this underutilization relates to professional biases and a variety of non-clinical factors that affect referral to and use of partial hospitalization programs. The interested reader is referred to Luber (1979) for a more comprehensive description of this problem.

Finally, available data support the contention that partial hospitalization provides several treatment advantages related to the avoidance of problems generally associated with more traditional, restrictive forms of treatment. Specifically, partial hospitalization provides minimal disruption to the individuals' involvement in significant social systems (i.e., family, peer group, job, etc.), increases the amount of time in the community and outside institutional settings, and provides demonstrated increases in the individual's ability to function socially.

CLINICAL ISSUES

Goals of Treatment

What are the treatment goals for schizophrenics in a partial hospitalization program? To some extent the answer to this question is derived from the broader question "What are the goals of mental health services in general?" In part, this question is also related to such considerations as the duration of the problem being experienced by the individual (i.e., acute or chronic), the age of the individuals being treated (children, adolescents, adults), and the nature of the treatment system of which the particular program is a part. Consequently, treatment goals tend to be individualized to particular programs in particular settings. This section will attempt to delineate some of the issues involved in determining adequate goals for the treatment of a schizophrenic population in partial hospitalization and derive some general principles for deciding this issue. The reader is encouraged to review the citations listed in this section for a more detailed delineation of the issues discussed.

According to the "Standards and Guidelines for Partial Hospitalization" developed by the American Association for Partial Hospitalization (Casarino, Wilner, & Maxey, 1982), four possible functions for partial hospitalization can be identified. These functions, representing conceptual treatment goals, include:

1. Resolution or stabilization of short-term or crisis situations for decompensating clinical conditions which if not arrested would require 24 hour hospitalization.
2. Habilitation or rehabilitation of mentally disabled persons with long-standing social or vocational deficits resulting from or related to their mental illness . . . Habilitation or rehabilitation of vulnerable individuals with the residual or resolving disability following the acute phase of a major psychiatric illness.
3. Maintenance of individuals outside of the hospital through supportive and rehabilitative services designed for individuals with profound social, vocational and primary role deficits . . .
4. Diagnosis of those individuals for whom extended or direct observation is necessary to determine functioning and interaction, to identify problem areas, and to formulate a treatment plan (p. 10).

It is apparent that, at the present time, the majority of partial hospitalization programs are designed to perform the habilitation/rehabilitation and maintenance functions regardless of the diagnostic categories being treated; however, the stabilization function is becoming more prominent, with the programs being developed to serve as true alternatives to inpatient treatment.* Casarino et al. have described general treatment goals derived from these functions along the following lines:

1. Resolution: the elimination or relief of dysfunction and the return to premorbid levels within the family, community and vocational/educational settings;
2. Habilitation/Rehabilitation: the restoration of functioning to a level consistent with independent living, the maximum reduction of mental disability and enhancement of productivity;
3. Maintenance: the reduction of mental and functional disabilities so as to avoid the necessity for hospital treatment (p. 11).

Although these functions and goals are rather broad they highlight two significant points: (1) Individual partial hospitalization programs should be designed to perform a specific function; and, (2) Program goals should be derived from the needs of the individuals being treated; these goals are generally based on functioning levels rather than diagnosis alone. Similar functions for partial hospitalization reflecting comparable treatment goals have been described elsewhere also (APA/CHAMPUS, 1979; Weiss & Dubin, 1982; West, Casarino, DiBella, & Gross, 1980.

In regard to the treatment goals for the acutely ill schizophrenic (stabilization function), research results previously cited clearly indicate that the remission of symptoms involving conceptual disorganization, hostility, suspiciousness, self-concept, and mood can be effectively achieved in a partial hospitalization program; in addition, they can be achieved without the total disruption generally associated with hospitalization. Further, significant symptom reduction can be achieved through the use of partial hospitalization in conjunction with short term hospitalization when institutional care is unavoidable.

Several years ago, Hogarty (1971) pointed out a problem that is still relevent for the use of partial hospitalization as a stabilization treatment for the acutely ill schizophrenic: the need for "ongoing, comprehensive aftercare programs to maintain remission and increase social restoration . . ." (p. 199). Although significant developments

---

*Meliest S, & Chinen L. A major victory: How to successfully negotiate a contract for day hospital services. Unpublished manuscript, 1982

have occurred since this observation was initially made, it remains a primary concern. A possible consideration could be the utilization of two partial hospitalization programs (or one program with two distinct components), the first to stabilize the acute situation and the second to consolidate, maintain, and enhance the initial treatment gains. Such an arrangement could effectively utilize the unique aspects of partial hospitalization in the continued treatment of the schizophrenic patient while avoiding institutionalization.

As was stated earlier, the largest documented population being treated in partial hospitalization is the chronic schizophrenic. There is currently significant disagreement regarding the type of treatment and the treatment goals that are most appropriate for this particular population (Allen & Mendel, 1982; Bachrach, 1982; Goldberg, 1980; Klein, 1980; Mosher & Keith, 1980; Solomon, 1980). Allen and Mendel (1982) effectively point out that goals for traditional treatment models are frequently oriented to the "cure" or correction of structural (biological) deficits ("magic cure" model), the learning of specific skills or the experience of personal dignity and motivation (environmental model), or the engagement in a competitive employment situation (vocational rehabilitation model). As has been noted elsewhere (Turner & TenHoor, 1978, however, the "myths" of rehabilitation and reintegration may actually have contributed to worsening the plight of chronic patients by establishing unrealistic goals for patients and unrealistic expectations for care-givers and society in general. Perhaps an alternative perspective, which more realistically recognizes the limitations, deficits, and potential of chronically disabled individuals, is needed.

Such an approach has generally been referred to as a "supportive model" (Allen & Mendel, 1982; Hogarty, 1971; Mosher & Keith, 1980; Stein & Test, 1980). Usually the key concepts in this model involve the maximizing of functioning and the minimizing of dysfunction and stress rather than "cure," "training," or "employment." It must be recognized that in all probability not all chronic patients have equal rehabilitation potential; consequently, program goals measured by such criteria as competitive employment, high level social functioning, and participation in society's mainstream may not be universally realistic (Bachrach, 1982).

For many chronic schizophrenic patients treated in partial hospitalization programs, the goals of symptom relief and the maximizing of social functioning may be necessary initial steps to the more complex goal of mainstreaming in society; for other patients, however, these may represent the maximum potential for change. Consequently, in the latter instance, partial hospitalization may be viewed as an effective but long term modality that can provide the massive and continuing amounts of supportive and restorative services needed to sustain these individuals at a reasonable cost (Klein, 1980). Unfortunately, from fiscal, administrative, and theoretical perspectives, this program function does not have widespread support. This may, in part, be due to the assumption that supportive partial hospitalization programs are non-change producing and perpetual in duration. This, of course, need not be the case. Indeed, it would be expected that such a partial hospitalization program would demonstrate successful outcome by at least reducing the amount of institutional or treatment-system support needed to maintain the individual. This would make it possible to move the patient to less intense and concentrated modes of treatment.

In summary, the goals for the treatment of schizophrenic patients in partial hospitalization are dependent on the nature of the problems being treated. In acute episodes, symptom relief is a primary concern; however, this must be directly correlated with an aftercare regime designed to consolidate, maintain, and enhance treatment gains. For the chronic schizophrenic patient, partial hospitalization may be viewed as a rehabilitative modality and as a supportive service with a primary goal of maintenance, depending on the needs and potential of the patients being served.

Program Structure

Although partial hospitalization programs are generally quite diverse in their treatment approaches, two principle rationales for programming have tended to predominate: the therapeutic milieu and the behavioral or educational approaches (Luber, 1979). Washburn (1979) defines the primary process variables of a milieu operated in a partial hospitalization program as containment, support, structure, involvement, validation, and negotiation. Similarly, Eckman (1979) defines the principle of a behaviorally oriented partial program as altering "the patient's primary presenting problems rather than to directly bring about a change in personality or to treat underlying conflicts" (p. 26). As with treatment goals, there is currently some controversy over the efficacy of particular program structures for schizophrenic patients (Gunderson, 1980).

In considering program structure it seems reasonable to view the deficits of the individuals being treated. In general, acutely disturbed schizophrenic patients tend to reflect symptoms in the spheres of perception, attention, and information processing; chronic schizophrenic patients, while they may evidence problems in these areas, also demonstrate severe deficits in interpersonal functioning and life management skills. In light of these charcteristics, the primary assumption of the milieu approach (i.e., that the milieu itself will stimulate interaction and progress toward resocialization) may be questioned in regard to the treatment of a schizophrenic population (Hersen & Luber, 1977). It may, indeed, be more effective and appropriate to provide specific, detailed, and structured programming in an attempt to meet the treatment needs of this population.

The study conducted by Linn et al. (1979) presented some interesting conjectures regarding the effective ingredients of a partial hospitalization for chronic schizophrenic patients. In general, for this population, the investigators suggested that a program that is "less intensively personal and more object focused" produces better outcome; they minimized the effectiveness of more traditional individual and group psychotherapy. Again, it must be noted that due to the post hoc nature of these findings they should be regarded as indicative not conclusive. The study does point to the probability that program structure plays a significant role in the effectiveness of partial hospitalization for schizophrenics.

This, of course, is not to say that elements of the milieu approach as it is generally practiced today do not contribute to effective treatment in partial hospitalization. Indeed, as Gunderson (1980) points out in his review, certain characteristics of the treating environment tend to have positive effects on outcome for nonchronic schizophrenics, especially in terms of community tenure. Several of these elements are central to the milieu approach including autonomy, practical orientation, order and organization, focus on personal problems, and open expression of angry feelings. In addition, effective milieus seem to be characterized by a high staff/patient ratio, responsibility distributed among all staff, and a high premium placed on participation of all individuals in the milieu. Many of these elements are characteristic of partial hospitalization programs irrespective of their basic treatment orientation or structure.

The question regarding program structure basically involves whether the goals of treatment should be permitted to "spontaneously develop" or should be "programmed in " when treating a schizophrenic population. The experience of this author and available research data seem to support the latter. Whether dealing with the acute or chronic patient, the goal of treatment involves reintegrating the individual into society and the community to whatever extent possible. Community living requires the individual to provide a large amount of structure for his own life. This structure ranges from self-care to scheduling activities. Many of these skills can be successfully taught to schizophrenic patients in structured, educationally oriented approaches. In addition, the experience of a structured environment in a partial hospitalization program can be a key element in helping the individual develop and achieve personal goals. It seems crucial to assist this type of individual to develop a personal structure that will be of assistance in living in the less structured, less supportive, and, perhaps, less sympathetic community environment.

Consequently, from the perspective of both the patient population and available research data, a program structure that provides a maximum of support and addresses specific skill deficits exhibited by patients appears to be the most reasonable and effective approach in partial rehabilitation.

Program Components

Several specific treatment components utilized in partial hospitalization with a schizophrenic population have been evaluated in recent years. This section will briefly discuss some of these elements; again, the reader is directed to the sources cited for a more detailed consideration of these items.

Token Economy

The token economy has generally been considered an effective "management" technique, especially in inpatient settings. Its use and effectiveness as a therapeutic strategy and as a means to provide an overall program structure in an outpatient setting such as a partial hospitalization program is less clear. Nevertheless, the use of the token economy has produced some positive results in terms of attendance and participation in partial hospitalization programs (Eckman, 1979). There also appears to be some evidence that the token economy may serve a different function when it is utilized in this setting.

In a study conducted with a schizophrenic population in a partial hospitalization program, Turner and Luber (1980) generated evidence that the token economy may serve as an information feedback loop. In other words, the therapeutic effect of the token economy is to provide participants with immediate, concrete, non-threatening feedback regarding their progress both in individual groups and in the program as a whole.

In light of these results and the apparent utility of providing overall program structure in the treatment of a schizophrenic patient population, some form of the token economy would be an effective ingredient in partial hospitalization programming. This ingredient would provide more than simply "behavioral management" functions. In addition, it would provide useful feedback and an opportunity to develop realistic self-evaluation skills in participants. Such skills should enhance the ability of the patient to function up to the level of his or her individual capabilities.

Social Skills Training

An exceptionally comprehensive and complete review of social skills training with schizophrenic patients is presented by Wallace, Nelson, Liberman, Aitchison, Lukoff, Elder, and Ferris (1980). This critique amply defines the areas of weakness (both in terms of treatment methodology and research) and accomplishment. Social skills training is an integral element in the majority of partial hospitalization programs today (Eckman, 1979; Hersen & Luber, 1977), especially in those treating a primarily chronic schizophrenic population (Bellack & Hersen, 1979; Bellack & Hersen, 1978).

In general, social skills training encompasses a wide range of behavioral patterns from basic survival skills (such as planning and preparing meals and laundering clothes) to more complex interactional and life management skills (such as acquiring and maintaining friends, budgeting, and the use of leisure time). Conceptually, it is assumed that because chronic schizophrenic patients generally evidence extensive deficits in these areas, their ability to cope with the natural environment is very limited even with the effective use of psychotropic medications; consequently, the individual is less likely to improve his or her "quality of life" and more likely to require full-time custodial care of one kind or another. Social skills training is aimed at remediating these deficits and establishing the ability for more independent community functioning.

Typically, social skills training is conducted in a group setting, utilizes role playing and similar techniques, and, frequently, incorporates videotaping as an instructional, feedback, and evaluation tool (Beidel, Bellack, Turner, Hersen, & Luber, 1981; Williams, Turner, Watts, Bellack & Hersen, 1977). Training is usually conducted in a highly structured format and emphasizes the following general principles:

1. Provide a clear rationale to the patient concerning the relevence of the skills to be learned in order to develop a learning incentive.
2. Skills should be taught slowly, concretely, and in small basic components; these components are then combined to form the overall desired behaviors.
3. Repetition of the correct performance of a behavior is necessary for learning.

4. Reinforcement of every positive attempt or approximation of the skill is provided.
5. Proven training procedures (e.g., instruction, modeling, role playing, etc.) are used.
6. Reasonable goals for treatment based on the specific individuals involved are established.

As Wallace et al. (1980) point out, ample evidence exists to demonstrate the effectiveness of training in modifying and improving specific social skills. In addition, there is evidence that these skills are maintained post-treatment. Nevertheless, an area of concern remains that of the generalization of social skills acquired in treatment to everyday life situations. On the basis of current knowledge, it seems clear that the generalization of newly acquired behaviors must be programmed into the actual treatment procedure; it does not appear that generalization is a "spontaneous" result of treatment. It also appears that increased attention must be paid to the cognitive aspects of training (e.g., thoughts and feelings) if generalization is to be maximized.

In summary, social skills training is an integral and effective treatment component for schizophrenic patients in a partial hospitalization program. Such training can help individuals cope more successfully with the environment, function in a more independent manner, and, thus, improve the quality of life. See Chapter 9 for a further discussion of social skills in general.

Life Management Training

Related to the interpersonal skills generally included under the rubric of social skills training are the life management and activities of daily living skills necessary to function independently in the community. A substantial portion of partial hospitalization programming generally involves the teaching of such skills.

As with deficits in the area of interpersonal skills, it is important to adequately assess the nature of life management skill deficits. That is, it is necessary to determine whether skills have never been acquired or whether there is an inability to execute learned skills due to additional factors such as depression, anxiety, etc. Learning and performance deficits require different approaches for remediation.

The general categories of behaviors considered in life management training include skills such as personal care (cooking, nutrition, grooming), time management (recreational activities, use of leisure time), vocational assessment, and bureaucratic systems (the function and utilization of community systems such as banks, utilities, and welfare offices). The objective of training in these areas is to provide the individual with the minimal skills required to survive at an acceptable level in the community (Hersen & Luber, 1977). The basic training principles cited in the discussion of social skills are also applicable in this area.

Problem Solving Training

As has been pointed out elsewhere, individuals are constantly faced with complex problems that must be resolved effectively if they are to function adequately in society. This is difficult even for those with adequate cognitive functioning; for those experiencing a breakdown in the cognitive process characteristic of schizophrenia, such tasks often result in confusion and an increased inability to cope with the situations of daily life.

A standard problem solving technique has been discussed widely in the literature (D'Zurilla & Goldfried, 1971; Kanfer & Goldstein, 1975) and is being increasingly incorporated into the partial hospitalization treatment program. Briefly, five steps are generally incorporated into this procedure:

1. General orientation
2. Problem definition and formulation
3. Generation of alternatives
4. Decision making
5. Verification of choices

One study has reported on the utilization of this treatment with a small group of partial hospitalization patients with a diagnosis of schizophrenia (Noblit, Luber, & Vargas, 1982). The study, although somewhat limited, indicated two important findings:

1. Patients of this diagnostic type cognitively mastered the elements of the problem solving technique after 4, 2-hour training sessions.
2. Generalization of learning (the application to concrete interpersonal situations) was quite limited.

Again, the investigators suggest that generalization procedures must be incorporated into the overall training process if the technique is to be fully effective.

Despite these difficulties, it seems reasonable to conclude that problem solving training in a systematic, structured form can be a useful component for the treatment of schizophrenia in a partial hospitalization program. In addition, the learning of this technique might add to the effectiveness of social skills training by incorporating the behavioral cognition aspect described by Wallace et al. (1980).

Family Therapy

As in several other areas, there seems to be some uncertainty regarding the utility of family therapy in the treatment of the schizophrenic (Keith, 1980; Mosher & Keith, 1980). Evidence does, however, point to the effectiveness of some family therapy approaches with this population.

For example, Anderson, Hogarty, and Reiss (1980) describe a psycho-educational approach to family therapy that has produced some initially encouraging impressions regarding its effectiveness with a schizophrenic population. The broad objectives of the program are to increase family understanding of the schizophrenic illness, reduce family stress, enhance social networks, and diminish long-term issues that contribute to family stress. The model is described as basically concrete, supportive, and educational in nature.

More specifically related to partial hospitalization, Luber and Wells (1977) described an educational model for multiple family therapy used in a partial hospitalization setting with a predominantly schizophrenic population. This short-term (seven sessions), educational model utilized a variety of therapeutic techniques and was designed to remove the focus from the so-called "identified patient" and place problems in the context of the family as a whole. Outcome results indicated that the model was useful from several perspectives: (1) it served as an inducement for some families to enter long-term family therapy; (2) the needs of those families requiring only short-term intervention were met and, (3) problems requiring longer and more specific intervention were identified.

From several perspectives, family therapy is an important program component in partial hospitalization treatment. First, it is commonly held by a variety of orientations that the identified patient is frequently a reflection of a disturbed family system (Luber & Anderson, in press). Many professionals are convinced that effective treatment is unlikely to be achieved if this pathological system is not changed or the individual is not assisted in coping with the system in some direct way. Consequently, it is common for partial hospitalization programs to consider the family as an "extended population" to be incorporated into the treatment process (Lefkovitz, 1979).

From another perspective, it is useful to incorporate families in the treatment process as an aid in the generalization of treatment gains. As has been indicated previously, it is clear that many behavioral and cognitive changes can be accomplished through partial hospitalization treatment; generalization of these changes, however, does not appear to be spontaneous. Family members, cognizant of the treatment procedures utilized in the partial program, can be effective extensions of these procedures; they can be utilized to assist in the observation, reinforcement, and evaluation of treatment methods.

Finally, the incorporation of families into the treatment program can be a distinct service to the families themselves. Whether the affected individual is experiencing an acute or chronic episode, family members are themselves frequently experiencing a variety of feelings including guilt, fear, anger, resentment, disappointment, frustration, etc. Such feelings increase the difficulty the family has in coping with their own lives. Participation in programs such as supportive, educational multiple family therapy can be of distinct benefit.

In summary, family treatment approaches that emphasize a supportive, educational orientation are a basic component of partial hospitalization treatment for a schizophrenic population.

Other Program Components

A variety of other group activities and treatment components are frequently incorporated into partial hospitalization programming. In general, these elements are directed at further development and reinforcement of the interpersonal and daily living skills needed for community living.

For example, when treating a school-age population an integral part of partial hospitalization programming involves basic educational/academic preparation. An increasing number of partial programs designed specifically for an adolescent population are being developed, frequently including a substantial subpopulation of schizophrenic patients (Lahey & Kupfer, 1979). As with other populations, the aim of treatment is to reintegrate the individual into the mainstream of both the school system and the community. Thus, in many cases, partial programs for adolescents are conducted in conjunction with educational systems or contain a full academic component comparable to that provided in the usual school setting. Such a program requires a high degree of coordination between educational and treatment staffs to insure continuity and uniformity of care (Herzka, 1982). This reflects, however, the unique flexibility and adaptibility of partial hospitalization that permits the modality to be utilized with a number of specialized populations.

In addition to the components already discussed, partial hospitalization programs often utilize other discussion/interaction group activities. These include the expressive therapies (art, poetry, and music) designed to provide expanded methods for individuals to formulate and articulate thoughts, feelings, and emotions (Luber, 1973). Current Issues groups discussions are utilized to assist individuals become aware of and conversant with national and local issues that impact on their lives; an activity of this type is designed to help provide individuals with the information and skills necessary to participate in normal types of conversations and interactions.

The Theme Centered Group is another commonly utilized program component (Hersen & Luber, 1977). This type of group discussion operates under a formalized set of rules designed to teach participants the acceptable procedures for participating in interactions involving more than two people; special emphasis is generally placed on such techniques as not monopolizing a discussion and remaining relevent to the topic being discussed rather than on eliciting emotional responses and reactions.

Finally, most programs incorporate a number of recreation/craft activities. These should be designed to explore and develop areas of interest that individuals might utilize during their leisure time; this usually includes a component to familiarize participants with community resources available for leisure-time utilization.

Again, the emphasis is basically pragmatic and practical in attempting to provide individuals with skills and resources that can be incorporated realistically into their daily living.

THE UNDERUTILIZATION OF PARTIAL HOSPITALIZATION

Despite the increasing evidence in support of the cost efficiency and treatment efficacy of partial hospitalization, the modality remains significantly underutilized in proportion to the increased use of other outpatient services. Several investigators over the past few years have examined this situation and reached some startling conclusions regarding non-clinical factors that seem to impact on the utilization of partial hospitalization (Luber, 1979). In summary, it appears that factors such as insufficient insurance coverage, attachment to previously utilized mental health services, lack of awareness regarding the existence and/or purposes of partial hospitalization, transportation difficulties, and certain attitudinal biases on the part of mental health professionals (especially potential referral resources) have as much to do with the underutilization of partial hospitalization as issues of treatment efficacy.

In the area of "attitudinal biases" on the part of psychiatric professionals, the following seem to be the most consistent and significant biases based on current data:

1. New professionals, especially psychiatric residents, tend to emphasize possible problems that might be encountered rather than possible benefits that might accrue when considering referrals to partial hospitalization; in other words, they tend to view the possible referral from an initially negative perspective.
2. More experienced professionals, especially those who have not had direct experience with partial hospitalization, tend not to accept the modality as adequate for "intensive treatment," a term that appears to have no commonly accepted definition.
3. Professionals tend to emphasize the "severity of symptoms" as the basic criterion for inpatient hospitalization when, in reality, there may be no differences in symptomatology between inpatients and partial hospitalization patients.
4. Professionals support inpatient treatment as a means to separate the patient and family and, thus, "learn more about the patient" while providing "intensive" treatment; however, several studies cited previously indicate that, generally, inpatients demonstrate no better clinical outcome than day patients, raising the question whether anything useful in improving clinical outcome is actually achieved by hospitalization; and, indeed, research findings indicate that inpatient treatment has an insignificant effect on post-hospital adjustment (Stein & Test, 1980).

In conclusion, a reasonable amount of evidence exists to indicate that the underutilization of partial hospitalization is related to certain personal and professional biases as much as to issues related to psychopathyology and financial considerations. It appears that attitudinal factors rather than treatment considerations frequently control the referral process and influence final treatment decisions. In most cases, these subjective factors have a detrimental effect on referrals to partial hospitals. This, of course, raises the question whether all patients, including schizophrenics, have equal access to the most appropriate treatment for their needs and clinical condition.

REFERENCES

Allen C, & Mendel W. Chronic illness and staff burnout: Revised expectations for change in the supportive-care model. *International Journal of Partial Hospitalization*, 1982, *1*, 191–201

Anderson C, Hogarty G, & Reiss D. Family treatment of adult schizophrenic patients: A psycho-educational approach. *Schizophrenia Bulletin*, 1980, *6*, 490–505

Anthony W, Buell G, Sharratt S, & Althoff A. Efficacy of psychiatric rehabilitation. *Psychological Bulletin*, 1972, *78*, 447–456

APA/CHAMPUS National Advisory Committee. *Partial Hospitalization Guidelines.* American Psychiatric Association, September, 1979

Bachrach L. Assessment of outcomes in community support systems: Results, problems and limitations. *Schizophrenia Bulletin,* 1982, *8,* 39–60

Beidel D, Bellack AS, Turner S, Hersen M, & Luber R. Social skills training for chronic psychiatric patients: A treatment manual. *JSAS Catalogue of Selected Documents in Psychology,* May, 1981

Bellack AS, & Hersen M. Chronic psychiatric patients: Social skills training. In M Hersen & A. Bellack (Eds.) *Behavior therapy in the psychiatric setting.* Baltimore: Williams & Wilkins, 1978

Bellack AS, & Hersen M. (Eds.) *Research and practice in social skills training.* New York: Plenum, 1979

Bierer J. *The day hospital: An experiment in social psychiatry and syntho-analytic psychotherapy.* London: Washburn & Sons, 1951

Braun P, Kochansky G, Shapiro R, Greenberg S, Gudeman J, Johnson S, & Shore M. Overview: Deinstitutionalization of psychiatric patients, a critical review of outcome studies. *American Journal of Psychiatry,* 1981, *136,* 736–749

Caffey E, Galbrecht C, & Klett C. Brief hospitalization and aftercare in the treatment of schizophrenia. *Archives of General Psychiatry,* 1971, *24,* 81–86

Cameron D. The day hospital. *Modern Hospital,* 1947, *69,* 60–62

Casarino J, Wilner M, & Maxey J. American association for partial hospitalization (AAPH) standards and guidelines for partial hospitalization. *International Journal of Partial Hospitalization,* 1982, *1,* 5–22

Chen R, Healey J, & Williams H. *Partial hospitalization: Problems, purposes and changing objectives.* Topeka: RR Sanders, 1969

Davis J, Lorei T, & Caffey E. An evaluation of the veteran's administration day hospital program. *Hospital and Community Psychiatry,* 1978, *29,* 297–302

Dzhagarov M. Experience in organizing a day hospital for mental patients. *Neuropathology and psychiatry,* 1937, *6,* 137–147

D'Zurilla T, & Goldfried M. Problem solving and behavior modification. *Journal of Abnormal Psychology,* 1971, *78,* 107–126

Eckman T. Behavioral approaches to partial hospitalization. In R Luber (Ed.), *Partial hospitalization: A current perspective.* New York: Plenum 1979

Endicott J, Cohen J, Nee J, Fleiss J, & Herz M. Brief vs. standard hospitalization: For whom? *Archives of General Psychiatry,* 1979, *36,* 706–712

Endicott J, Herz M, & Gibbon M. Brief versus standard hospitalization: The differential costs. *American Journal of Psychiatry,* 1978, *125,* 707–712

Erickson R. Length of stay and adjustment and role skill changes of day hospital patients. *V.A. Newsletter: Resident Psychology.* 1972, *14,* 31–33

Glick I, Hargreaves W, & Drues J. Short versus long hospitalization: Prospective controlled study: IV. One-year followup results for schizophrenic patients. *American Journal of Psychiatry,* 1976, *133,* 509–514

Goldberg S. Drug and psychosocial therapy in schizophrenia: Current status and research needs. *Schizophrenia Bulletin,* 1980, *6,* 117–121

Guillette W, Crowley B, Savitz S, & Goldberg F. Day hospitalization as a cost-effective alternative to inpatient care: A pilot study. *Hospital and Community Psychiatry,* 1978, *29,* 525–527

Gunderson J. A reevaluation of milieu therapy for nonchronic schizophrenic patients. *Schizophrenia Bulletin,* 1980, *6,* 64–69

Guy W, Gross M, Hogarty G, & Dennis, H. A controlled evaluation of day hospital effectiveness. *Archives of General Psychiatry,* 1969, *20,* 329–338

Hersen M. Research considerations. In R. Luber (Ed.) *Partial hospitalization: A current perspective.* New York: Plenum, 1979

Hersen M, & Luber R. Use of group psychotherapy in a partial hospitalization service: The remediation of basic skill deficits. *International Journal of Group Psychotherapy*, 1977, *27*, 361–376

Herz M. Research overview in day hospital. *International Journal of Partial Hospitalization*, 1982, *1*, 33–45

Herz MI, Endicott J, & Gibbon M. Brief hospitalization: Two-year follow-up. *Archives of General Psychiatry*, 1979, *36*, 710–715

Herz M, Endicott J, & Spitzer R. A study of brief hospitalization: Initial results. *American Journal of Psychiatry*, 1975, *132*, 413–418

Herz M, Endicott J, & Spitzer R. Brief versus standard hospitalization: The families. *American Journal of Psychiatry*, 1976, *133*, 795–801

Herz M, Endicott J, & Spitzer R. Brief hospitalization: Two-year followup. *American Journal of Psychiatry*, 1977, *134*, 502–507

Herz M, Endicott J, Spitzer R, & Mesnikoff A. Day versus inpatient hospitalization: A controlled study. *American Journal of Psychiatry*, 1971, *127*, 107–118

Herzka H. Zurich's day clinic for child and adolescent psychiatry: Setting and possibilities. *International Journal of Partial Hospitalization*, 1982, *1*, 89–98

Hogarty G. The plight of schizophrenics in modern treatment programs. *Hospital and Community Psychiatry*, 1971, *22*, 197–203

Kanfer F, & Goldstein A. *Helping people change: A textbook of methods.* New York: Pergamon Press, 1975

Keith OF. Psychosocial treatment of schizophrenia, or psychosocial help for people with schizophrenia? *Schizophrenia Bulletin*, 1980, *6*, 122–130

Klein D. Psychosocial treatment of schizophrenia, or psychosocial help for people with schizophrenia. *Schizophenia Bulletin*, 1980, *6*, 122–130

Krowinski W, & Fitt D. *Report to capital blue cross.* Reading Hospital and Medical Center, 1978

Lahey B, & Kupfer D. Partial hospitalization for children and adolescents. In R Luber (Ed.), *Partial hospitalization: A current perspective.* New York: Plenum, 1979

Lefkovitz P. Patient population and treatment programming. In R Luber (Ed.), *Partial hospitalization: A current perspective.* New York: Plenum, 1979

Linn M, Caffey E, Klett J, Hogarty G, & Lamb H. Day treatment and psychotropic drugs in the aftercare of schizophrenic patients: A veteran's administration cooperative study. *Archives of General Psychiatry*, 1979, *36*, 1055–1066

Longabaugh R, Fink E, & Stout R. A one-year followup comparison of day hospital transfer and inpatient sample with respect to the cost effectiveness of psychiatric care. *Butler Hospital Treatment Evaluation Series: Report No. 11*, Providence, R.I., 1975

Luber R. Poetry helps patients express feelings. *Hospital and Community Psychiatry*, 1973, *24*, 387

Luber R (Ed.), *Partial hospitalization: A current perspective.* New York: Plenum, 1979

Luber R, & Anderson C. *Family intervention with psychiatric patients.* New York: Human Sciences Press, 1983

Luber R, & Wells R. Structured, short-term multiple family therapy: An educational approach. *International Journal of Group Psychotherapy*, 1977, *27*, 43–58

Mason J, Louks J, Burmer G, & Scher M. The efficacy of partial hospitalization: A review of recent literature. *International Journal of Partial Hospitalization*, 1982, *1*, 251–270

Meltzhoff J, & Blumenthal R. *The day treatment center.* Springfield: Charles C. Thomas, 1966

Mendel W, & Allen R. Rescure and rehabilitation. In L Stein & MA Test (Eds.), *Alternatives to mental hospital treatment.* New York: Plenum, 1978

Michaux H, Chelst M, Foster S, & Prium R. A controlled comparison of psychiatric day treatment with full-time hospitalization: An interium report. *Current Therapeutic Research,* 1970, *12,* 627–638

Michaux H, Chelst M, Foster S, Prium R, & Dasinger E. Post-release adjustment of day and full-time psychiatric patients. *Archives of General Psychiatry,* 1973, *29,* 647–651

Moser L, & Keith S. Psychosocial treatment: Individual, family, group and community support approaches. *Schizophrenia Bulletin,* 1980, *6,* 10–40

Noblit P, Luber R, & Vargas L. An evaluation of problem solving training for partial hospitalization patients. *International Journal of Partial Hospitalization,* 1982, *1,* 67–76

Reisman A, Rabkin J, & Struning E. Brief versus standard psychiatric hospitalization: A critical review of the literature. *Community Mental Health Review,* 1977, *2,* 2–10

Solomon E, Baird R, Everstine L, & Escobar AJ. Assessing the community care of chronic psychotic patients. *Hospital & Community Psychiatry,* 1980, *31,* 113–116

Stein L, & Test M. Alternatives to mental hospital treatment: I. Conceptual model, treatment program and clinical evaluation. *Archives of General Psychiatry,* 1980, *37,* 392–397

Taube C. *Day care services in community mental health centers.* Statistical Note No. 96, Survey and Reports Section, National Institute of Mental Health, Rockville, MD, 1973

Test M, & Stein L. Alternatives to mental hospital treatment: III. Social Cost. *Archives of General Psychiatry,* 1980, *37,* 409–412

Turner J, & Ten Hoor W. The NIMH community support program: Pilot approach to a needed social reform. *Schizophrenia Bulletin,* 1978, *4,* 319–343

Turner S, & Luber R. The token economy in day hospital settings: Contingency management or information feedback? *Journal of Behavior Therapy and Experimental Psychiatry,* 1980, *11,* 89–94

Wallace C, Nelson C, Liberman R. Aitchison R, Lukoff D, Elder J, & Ferris C. A review and critique of social skills training with schizophrenic patients. *Schizophrenia Bulletin,* 1980, *6,* 43–63

Washburn S. Organization of the therapeutic milieu in the partial hospital. In R Luber (Ed.), *Partial hospitalization: A current perspective.* New York: Plenum 1979

Washburn S, Vannicelli M, Longabaugh R, & Scheff B. A controlled comparison of psychiatric day treatment and inpatient hospitalization. *Journal of Consulting and Clinical Psychology,* 1976, *44,* 665–675

Weisbrod B, Test M, & Stein L. Alternatives to mental hospital treatment: II. Economic cost-benefit analysis. *Archives of General Psychiatry,* 1980, *37,* 400–405

Weiss K, & Dubin W. Partial hospitalization: State of the art. *Hospital and Community Psychiatry,* 1982, *33,* 923–928

West O, Casarino J, DiBella G, & Gross R. Partial hospitalization: Guidelines for standards. *Psychiatric Annals,* 1980, *10,* 43–55

Wilder J, Levin G, & Zwerling I. A two-year follow-up of acute psychotic patients treated in a day hospital. *American Journal of Psychiatry,* 1966, *122,* 1095–1101

Williams M, Turner S, Watts J, Bellack AS, & Hersen M. Group social skills training for psychiatric patients. *European Journal of Behavioral Analysis and Modification.* 1977, *4*, 223–229

Zwerling I, & Wilder J. An evaluation of the applicability of the day hospital in the treatment of acutely disturbed patients. *Israel Annals of Psychiatry and Related Professions*, 1964, *2*, 164–185

Randall L. Morrison
Alan S. Bellack

9

Social Skills Training

Social dysfunction is a hallmark of schizophrenia. Poor social functioning is currently considered to be as critical to the etiology and persistence of the schizophrenic disorders as the prominent psychotic symptomatology such as thought disturbances, delusions, and hallucinations (e.g., Goldsmith & McFall, 1975; Hersen & Bellack, 1976a; Liberman, 1982; Ziegler & Phillips, 1961, 1962). Deterioration of social relations is one of the defining diagnostic criteria for schizophrenia specified in DSM-III (American Psychiatric Association, 1980), and social isolation or withdrawal and marked impairment in major life role functioning are listed as prominent prodromal and residual symptoms. Clinical observation documents that schizophrenics are not simply withdrawn, but that they frequently appear to be "odd" and unable to relate in a "normal" manner. Even when gross psychotic symptomatology is pharmacologically controlled or in remission, schizophrenic patients can be expected to have marked difficulties in social interactions (Serban, 1975; Strauss, Carpenter, & Bartko, 1974). Owing to these difficulties, schizophrenics often fail to become integrated into a natural social network that may assist them in coping with social demands and other life stressors (Gleser & Gottschalk, 1967; McClelland & Walt, 1968). The schizophrenic's family is often the only network of which he or she is part. The interactional pattern of families of schizophrenics, however, is often deviant and frequently may provide additional stress on the patient, which he or she lacks

SCHIZOPHRENIA
ISBN 0-8089-1640-8

the necessary interpersonal skills to resolve (Brown, Birely, & Wing, 1971; Vaughn & Leff, 1976).

Given that the social disability of schizophrenic patients is a well established fact, it is not surprising that considerable attention has been devoted to ameliorating social skills deficits in these patients. Indeed, social skills training has become one of the most widely used psychosocial interventions in the treatment of schizophrenia. Our primary concern in this chapter will be to evaluate the status of social skills training with schizophrenic patients.

THE NATURE OF SOCIAL SKILL

The concept of social skill has undergone a transition in the psychologic and psychiatric literatures from an emphasis on enduring personality traits to the recognition of the situational specificity of interpersonal responding. Despite increasingly sophisticated functional analyses of interpersonal functioning, however, no consensus has been reached regarding a precise definition of social skill. On an everyday basis, most persons have a general sense of what is meant by the term, and there is frequently good agreement among friends and colleagues regarding which acquaintances are unskilled. There has, however, been remarkable difficulty deriving an acceptable definition of the term social skill to be used in guiding scientific efforts in this area. Numerous definitions have been proposed. Argyris (1965) referred to social skill as comprising those behaviors that contributed to a person's effectiveness as part of a larger group of individuals. Weiss (1968) defined it in terms of communication, understanding, interest, and rapport between the speaker and the listener. Trower, Bryant, and Argyle (1978) suggested that

> A person can be regarded as socially inadequate if he is unable to affect the behaviour and feelings of others in the way that he intends and society accepts. Such a person will appear annoying, unforthcoming, uninteresting, cold, destructive, bad-tempered, isolated or inept, and will generally be unrewarding to others (p.2).

The definition provided by Libet and Lewinsohn (1973) states that social skill involves "the complex ability to emit behaviors which are positively or negatively reinforced and not to emit behaviors which are punished or extinguished by others" (p. 304). Hersen and Bellack (1977) defined social skill as

> an individual's ability to express both positive and negative feelings in the interpersonal context without suffering consequent loss of reinforce-

> ment. Such skill is demonstrated in a large variety of interpersonal contexts . . . and involve[s] the coordinated delivery of appropriate verbal and nonverbal responses. In addition, the socially skilled individual is attuned to the realities of the situation and is aware when he/she is likely to be reinforced for his/her efforts (p. 512).

Each of these definitions provides a general sense of what social skill connotes, but none is entirely satisfactory. For the most part they are broad and vague, and fail to specify critical motoric responses that contribute to, or unequivocally demonstrate, social skill. While no one definition has proved acceptable, there is clearly general agreement regarding what the concept of social skill refers to. First, interpersonal behavior is assumed to depend on learned performance abilities. This is consistent with the use of the term *skill,* and derives from the behavioral model. In contrast to the presumption of the personality model regarding a more- or -less inherent capability to perform effectively, the behavioral model emphasizes that response capability is required through learning, and consists of an identifiable set of behavioral components such as voice intonation and the use of social reinforcers. These learned response components comprise a behavioral repertoire that the individual can use in social encounters. Those individuals who, as a result of faulty learning experiences, lack particular skills are said to have social skills deficits. These deficits are considered to be definable, measurable, and subject to remediation through training.

The second generally accepted notion regarding social skill refers to the situational specificity of socially skilled behavior. This perspective is obviously consistent with a behavioral orientation to social functioning in that it recognizes the impact of environmental factors on responding. Few, if any, aspects of interpersonal behavior are appropriate (or inappropriate) across all contexts. The individual who shouts and screams encouragement to his teammates during an athletic contest would not be sanctioned for the use of a similar voice volume (or vocabulary) when interacting with those same persons at his neighborhood church.

> The acceptable form of eye contact, interpersonal (spatial) distance, voice intonation, posture, etc., vary according to sex, age, status, degree of familiarity, and the cultural background of the interpersonal partner, as well as with the context of the interaction" (Bellack & Morrison, 1982, p. 720).

The interpersonally skilled individual has thus acquired a behavioral repertoire to be used in social encounters, as well as the ability to perceive relevant parameters of interpersonal contexts and concomitantly select and emit the most appropriate responses for the particular context. The notions of situational specificity and learned performance abilities are central to current strategies for social skills training.

SOCIAL SKILLS TRAINING

As with any effective treatment program, social skills training must be tailored to the specific needs of the individual patient. Hence, training must be preceded by a careful, systematic assessment. The clinician should consider four questions: (1) Does the patient have an interpersonal dysfunction? (2) Is the dysfunction associated with a social skill deficit? (3) Under what circumstances does the dysfunction occur? and (4) What is the specific nature of the patient's skill deficits? These questions are ordered hierarchically and serve as something of a decision tree. They provide progressively more specific information that determines the suitability of social skills training for the patient, as well as identifying the appropriate content of training. The answers to the first three questions determine whether the subsequent question needs to be addressed, and if so, delimit their focus.

Does the Patient Have an Interpersonal Dysfunction?

We have previously referred to the role of social competence in schizophrenia. It is clear that many, if not most, schizophrenics have significant impairments in social functioning. The more chronic the history, the more likely the patient is to have severe deficits. These difficulties are not universal, however. Particularly, many acute patients achieve satisfactory adjustments when in remission. Social skills training should not be routinely prescribed on the basis of schizophrenic diagnosis.

This initial question is the most general. It can typically be answered by clinical staff based upon interviews with the patient and/or significant others, by direct observation of the patient interacting with others, or even by chart review. The staff simply need to be attuned to interpersonal behavior and have a general conception of the range of normative functioning. As will be seen below, the term *interpersonal functioning* encompasses a broad range of behaviors. Subsidiary questions to help focus staff attention include: Does the patient make others feel uncomfortable? Is the patient able to initiate and maintain a conversation? Can he or she express feelings? Can he or she avoid being mistreated? Can he or she get others to respond positively? Is he or she socially isolated?

Is the Dysfunction Associated With a Skill Deficit?

Given that the patient has an interpersonal dysfunction, the next step is to determine (to the extent possible) whether or not the difficulty is tied to social skill deficits, as opposed to some non-skill factors. The literature on non-psychotic populations indicates that social functioning can be affected by a variety of factors other than social skill, including social anxiety (Arkowitz, 1977), depression (Weissman, Paykel, Siegel, & Klerman, 1971), and dysfunctional cognitions such as negative expectancies and self-critical thoughts (Bellack, 1979). These factors could also be expected to affect the social functioning of schizophrenics. In fact, recent research has pointed to a strong relationship between depression and social competence in some patients (Glazer, Prussoff, John, & Williams, 1981; Klein & Williamson, 1981). Moreover, given the severity and breadth of dysfunctions associated with schizophrenia, still other factors might well be implicated. Andreasen (1982; Andreasen & Olsen, 1982) has highlighted the significance of "negative" symptoms, such as avolition, anhedonia, and flattened affect. These phenomena would certainly limit social functioning and lead to poor role performance regardless of whether the patient had the specific skills needed to respond effectively. So-called "positive" symptoms could also lead to maladaptive social behavior, either by frightening others or by disrupting the patient's attention. Similarly, Liberman and his colleagues (Liberman, 1982; Liberman, Wallace, Falloon, & Vaugh, 1981) have recently underscored the possibility that the perceptual and information processing deficits characteristic of schizophrenia may also interefere with social functioning.

Given the diversity of factors impinging on social performance, social skills could play one of three different roles: (1) social failure could be a direct consequence of social skill deficits; (2) social failure could result from non-skill factors despite the presence of adequate skills in the repertoire; or (3) social failure could result from several interacting factors, one of which is social skill deficits. These alternatives have major implications for the applicability of social skills training. In the first case, skills training would clearly be the treatment of choice. In the second case, skills training could have indirect benefits, at best (e.g., practice interactions could reduce social anxiety). Given the limited resources available in most settings, it would be inappropriate to administer skills training to the patient with this pattern. The third case (skills deficts interacting with some other parameter) is apt to be the most common among schizophrenics. Hence, skills training will often be appropriate, in conjunction with medication and social supports.

There is no definitive test for determining the presence of skill deficits. There are, however, several guidelines that can help in the assessment process. First, social skills (and deficits) are situationally specific. No one is uniformly skilled or unskilled. Rather, people tend to be skillful in some situations and deficient in others. Therefore, a global pattern of asociality suggests that non-skill factors are involved. Second, in the absence of specific training, skill deficits should be stable. A patient who performs effectively during remission (or otherwise exhibits adequate performance) probably has the requisite skills in his or her repertoire. Both of these patterns can be ascertained by careful interviewing of the patient and family members, and examination of the case history.

Under What Circumstances Does the Dysfunction Occur?

Once it is determined that the patient does have skill deficits, the next step is to ascertain the specific circumstances in which the difficulties occur. As indicated above, social skills are situationally specific. For example, chronic psychiatric patients have been shown to be differentially assertive with males and females, with familiar and unfamiliar people, and in situations requiring expression of critical as opposed to positive feelings (Eisler, Hersen, Miller, & Blanchard, 1975; Hersen, Bellack, & Turner, 1978). Thus, some patients will have difficulites in assertion with family members but not with peers, while others will exhibit the opposite pattern, and others still a different pattern. Some will be unable to initiate conversations with potential sexual partners while they are quite adept with the same sex peers; others will be able to initiate conversations, but be unable to proceed toward intimacy. To be most effective, training should be tailored to the patient's specific pattern of deficits. The more the intervention is tailored for an individual or small group of patients, the more critical it is to identify the precise situational parameters governing performance.

What Is the Specific Nature of the Patient's Skill Deficits?

As indicated above, social skills are comprised of an extensive set of verbal and non-verbal response elements, which are combined into complex repertoires. Social skills training impacts on the repertoires

Table 9-1
Components of Social Skill

Expressive Elements
Speech Content
Paralinguistic Elements
Voice
Pace
Pitch
Tone
Nonverbal Behavior
Proxemics
Kinesics
"Eye Contact"
Facial Expression
Receptive Elements (Social Perception)
Attention
Decoding
Knowledge of Context Factors and Cultural Mores
Interactive Balance
Response Timing
Turn Talking
Social Reinforcement

(e.g., conversational skill) by teaching the patient how to effectively perform the various component elements. Consequently, assessment must identify both the problematic repertoires and the respective elements. The interested reader is referred to Bellack and Hersen (1979), Harper, Weins, and Matarazzo (1978), and Trower et al. 1978, for a more detailed analysis of these issues.

Some of the most important components of social skill are listed in Table 9-1. *Expressive Elements* are those parameters responsible for sending messages to others. Speech is the predominant vehicle for transmitting information. Speech content is, thus, the most important parameter. *Paralinguistic Elements* refer to voice quality. These play a central role in qualifying verbal content. The same phrase can take on dramatically different meaning as a function of the voice characteristics with which it is delivered. This dimension is commonly employed by clinicians in assessing flattened or inappropriate affect. *Nonverbal Behavior* entails everything the person does with his or her body during the interaction. These parameters also play an important role in the interpretation of speech content. Moreover, they transmit vital messages independent of any spoken words. Facial expression is, perhaps, the most important feature in the expression of emotions.

Kinesics, or body movements, include illustrative gestures (e.g., banging hand on table), as well as nervous mannerisms (e.g., foot tapping, fidgeting). Proxemics refers to interpersonal distance and posture, for which there are well-defined social rules (e.g., men do not embrace in public, but women do). Eye contact or gaze plays a central role in initiating and maintaining social contact, dominance, affection, and many other aspects of social interchange.

We have previously referred to the primary role of Receptive Elements in the context of social perception as it relates to situational specificity. Specifically, the individual must first attend to the cues provided by the interpersonal partner; these include all of the expressive elements described above. The information so received must then be effectively decoded. Then, the individual must match his or her response to the demands of the situation. Social perception requires extensive knowledge about cultural mores and the significance of numerous expressive cues and response patterns in diverse settings (Morrison & Bellack, 1981).

This issue is underscored by the final category: Interactive Balance. Effective interpersonal performance entails something of a ballet between the participants. There is a constant ebb and flow, governed by various conventions and the particular responses of each person in the interaction. No response is skillful at all times or in all situations. In fact, unskilled people often differ from their skilled peers more in their response timing than the objective quality of their responses (Fischetti, Curran & Wessberg, 1977).

Given the diversity of social relationships, the list of compound skill repertoires is exhaustive. The empirical literature has not yet documented which repertoires are most critical for patients to achieve an adequate social adjustment. The clinician must therefore use his or her judgment to determine which areas are apt to be most relevant for the individual patient. We have focused most extensively on conversational skills and assertiveness. Other topics frequently requiring attention are job interview skills, telephone skills, heterosocial skills, and skills required to be effective with medical and social service personnel. As will be detailed below, skills training focuses on one small segment of behavior at a time. Thus, each repertoire must be broken down into sub-areas. This is illustrated in Tables 9-2 and 9-3 for conversational skills. The General repertoire is subdivided into three segments: Initiating, Maintaining, and Terminating conversations. As shown in Table 9-2, each of these sub-repertoires consists of a variety of components that involve somewhat different skills. While some of the elements overlap, each sub-repertoire is sufficiently different (and complex) to require independent training. Moreover, as

Table 9-2
Conversational Skills

Initiating Conversations	
	Initiating a Brief Conversation with an Acquaintance
	Initiating a Brief Conversation with a Stranger
	Social Telephone Calls
Maintaining Conversations	
	Asking Questions
	Providing Information
	Social Reinforcement
	Social Perception
Ending Conversations	
	Timing
	How to Break-Off
	Goodbyes
	Judging When the Partner Wants to Leave

illustrated in Table 9-3, each of these subsidiary skills must be further divided into a set of small, discrete responses. This process may seem somewhat pedantic. But, most patients will have attentional deficits and be easily frustrated by failure experiences. Only by focusing on small, manageable units can the trainer insure the success experiences needed to maintain patients' interest and facilitate skill development.

The data needed to determine the patients' specific skill deficits can best be secured by direct observation. Clinical staff who have frequent contact with the patient can be trained to systemmatically observe him or her intereacting with others on an inpatient unit or in a partial hospital setting. It should be underscored that observers should be well trained to attend to specific response parameters, as

Table 9-3
Steps in Initiating a Brief Conversation with an Acquaintance

1. Make Contact
   e.g., Smile and say, "Hello (Name)."
2. Ask a General Question
   e.g., "How have you been?"
3. Ask a Specific Question or Answer a Question from the Other Person
4. Give a Reason for Leaving and Say Goodbye
   e.g., "I have an appointment . . ."

the natural tendency is to form global reactions (e.g., socially skilled or unskilled). Frequently, it will not be possible to observe the patient in all relevant areas (e.g., interactions with family members, strangers, in heterosocial situations). The best strategy for resolving this problem is role playing. A pertinent situation is first described to the patient, and the clinician assumes the role of the other person in the interaction. The patient is then instructed to interact with the clinician as if the situation were really happening. For example, "Imagine that you are at home watching television. You were really enjoying the program. Your roommate comes into the room and turns the channel, saying 'That's a dumb show, Let's watch the ballgame.' " The patient then responds, and the clinician extends the interaction through two or three subsequent interchanges. It is relatively easy to administer up to 15 or 20 brief role play scenarios, covering a diverse array of relevant interactions. Responses can be audiotaped or videotaped for subsequent analysis, or the clinician can assess performance on an ongoing basis.

Role play tests have been extensively analyzed and subjected to a variety of criticisms (see Bellack, 1979, 1983 for a review and analysis of this literature). Regardless of their limitations their utility is aptly summarized by Liberman (1982, p. 71). They provide,

> . . . a standardized, easily replicable assessment situation. The interpersonal tasks and challenges posed by the role-play test can be generated in quantity, with judges rating each task for degree of difficulty and type of skill, thereby enabling different task situations to be used for pre- and posttesting after a period of training. . . . Role-play tests also provide opportunities to assess both discrete component behaviors of social skill . . . as well as global features . . . Role plays are also convenient to administer and can be harnessed to a measurement approach that uses direct observation, videotapes, and 'blind raters'.

Training Procedures

Social skills training is a highly structured educational procedure (see Beidel, Bellack, Turner, Hersen, & Luber (1981) for a detailed description of the training). In many respects it is more similar to programs for teaching motor skills (such as tennis, playing a musical instrument, or speaking a foreign language), than to traditional psychotherapeutic interventions. The participants are better viewed as students than as patients in the traditional sense. A premium is placed on rehearsal of new responses, rather than on understanding, insight, or the therapeutic process. The procedure is analogous to teaching someone how to serve a tennis ball or play a new piece on the piano. Regardless of how much the student reads about how to do it or watches experts perform, initial efforts are clumsy and imperfect. Only by countless repetitions does the response gradually become smooth and effortless. Furthermore, performance of newly learned skills often suffers in the heat of competition or the tension stimulated by an audience. Hence, the student must practice in life like (i.e., stressful) situations as well as in artificial conditions.

The skills training model is especially suited to schizophrenic patients. It focuses on small units of behavior, proceeds in a very gradual fashion, and requires a minimum of complex abstraction abilities. Progress is tailored to the needs and limitations of the individual patient, even when training is conducted in groups. Thus, patients are assured of success experiences rather than the frustration that results from tasks that are too difficult. The extensive rehearsal helps make new responses relatively automatic, minimizing the need for extensive planning of decision making. This feature facilitates effective responding even under stressful conditions or when cognitive abilities are otherwise hampered. Finally, skills training does not force the patient to delve into highly threatening issues or engage in highly stressful activities. Rather, training teaches functional skills that are relevant to daily living and are likely to secure positive reinforcement for the patient.

Training Format

Social skills training can be administered individually or in small groups. Individual training permits greater intensity, and sessions can be precisely tailored to the needs of the patient. It is not highly cost effective, however, and few settings can afford to provide individual treatment. In addition to being much more economical, group training has several clinical advantages: patients can practice interacting with one another, they are exposed to diverse styles of interactions, and they can "relax" for brief periods during each session. The latter is an important factor for many patients, who find it difficult to tolerate the intensity of one hour individual sessions.

Groups should be limited to six to ten patients. While this might seem like a luxury in many settings, there are sharply diminshed returns with larger groups. First, it is essential that patients get ample opportunity to rehearse within sessions. With larger groups, it is not possible to provide all members sufficient rehearsal time. Second, the larger the group the greater the likelihood that members will be at different skill levels or have problems with different repertoires: hence, training becomes less tailored. Third, most patients will have some residual symptoms and attentional difficulties. Once the group gets larger than eight to ten patients, it becomes impossible to keep all patients attentive and involved.

Whenever possible, sessions should be conducted by two therapists. As will be discussed further, training involves an extensive amount of role playing and modeling (demonstration). It becomes very difficult for one therapist to play all roles, provide didactic information, and simultaneously control the behavior of all group members. In addition, the training procedures often are quite fatiguing because therapists play such an active role. Co-therapists can alternate control and responsibilities within sessions. While leading a group is demanding, the procedure is highly standardized and can be effectively employed by nurses, paraprofessionals, or bachelors' degree level staff. Hence, the cost of having two therapists is balanced, to some extent, by the use of sub-doctoral level clinicians.

The final format issue concerns scheduling and the duration of treatment. This is a most difficult issue to resolve given the depth and breadth of deficits typical of most chronic patients. We have typically employed a 12 week program consisting of 3 1-hour sessions per week. Often, this serves as a bare minimum, developing only rudimentary skills. Wallace and associates (1980) have recommended as much as 5-hours of training, 5-days per week for an extended period. This might well be more than most patients can tolerate, but it does reflect the fact that extensive, long term rehabilitation is required. Life long deficits accentuated by a long history of social avoidance are not easily corrected. Brief (i.e., less than 6 months), low intensity (i.e., 1–2 hours per week) interventions are not sufficient to produce meaningful or lasting changes.

Training Techniques

The first step in the training process is to identify a set of brief scenarios (analogous to those employed for the role play test) that are applicable to the skill repertoires to be taught during training. For example, initiating a conversation with another patient on the unit, with another patient in the cafeteria, with someone you recognize but do not know at a bus stop, and with someone you do not know at a social function. These scenarios provide the core around which training is organized. They should be typical of situations patients experience in their daily lives, and be graduated in terms of level of difficulty. In order to insure that training is relevant to the patients, they should be asked to volunteer situations that they have actually encountered. The therapist, however, will generally have to develop most scenarios himself. Treatment proceeds by training on each deficient response element (one at a time in order of increasing difficulty) in each situation (sequentially, in order of increasing difficulty). Specific responses are attached in an order and at a rate that maximizes patient's success throughout training.

Training consists of five elements: (1) Instructions, (2) Modeling, (3) Rolc play, (4) Feedback and positive reinforcement, and (5) Homework.

Instructions

The patient is first given specific instructions about the response at issue, including why and how it should be performed. For example, "If people are going to know you are serious, you must look at them when you speak. Try to look at my eyes or nose when you answer me." Instructions should be straight-forward and presented in simple language. They should always include a simple, practical rationale emphasizing why it is important for the patient to learn the particular response. As with all aspects of training, the emphasis should be on what the patient should do, rather than what they should not do.

Modeling

Some behaviors are relatively easy to learn (e.g., eye contact, response latency), and instructions, role play, and feedback will be sufficient. Similarly, higher functioning patients can master many of the responses with only these three techniques (e.g., McFall & Twentyman, 1973; Rimm, Snyder, Depue, Haanstad & Armstrong, 1976). More complex responses (e.g., most verbal content elements, intonation) and more regressed patients, however, almost invariably require modeling (Edelstein & Eisler, 1976; Hersen, Eisler, Miller, Johnson, & Pinkston, 1973; Rimm et al., 1976). Rather than simply instructing the patient how to respond, the therapist or role model actually performs (models) the appropriate response. The modeling display should focus on the particular response element at issue and should be prefaced and followed by a description of the relevant aspects of the display (e.g., "Watch the way I nod my head and look at his face while he speaks"). The targeted response is first illustrated and then performed in a role played scenario. If there are co-therapists, they would enact the scenario with one another; a single therapist would role play with one of the patients. The enactment should be kept brief, so as not to introduce extraneous material. Typically, it will have to be repeated in order for patients to grasp the critical elements.

Role Playing

After the therapist has demonstrated the response, the patients practice it by role playing. This is perhaps the most important component of training. The therapist selects one patient to role play first, reviews the instructions, and then portrays the partner in the role play scenario. Following feedback and reinforcement, the situation is enacted again, and possibly for a third time. A second patient is then selected and the procedure is repeated. This sequence continues until each patient has had two or three trials with the therapist. At that point, they begin role playing with one another (under the therapist's direction). Once most patients have shown improvement or reached a satisfactory plateau, a new scenario is introduced and the sequence is repeated. Alternatively, further instructions and modeling may be provided if needed.

Feedback and Social Reinforcement. Following *each* role play trial, the patient is given feedback about his or her performance. Feedback should be specific and should include positive social reinforcement for improved aspects of performance. Our clinical work suggests that social reinforcement, encouragement, and the frequent experience of some success plays a vital role in maintaining interest and effort on the part of the patient. An example of feedback is as follows: "You did much better that time. You told me that you wanted to go home in a clear manner and you looked at me while you spoke. Let's try it again, and this time try to emphasize the word 'no.' It will make your statement more convincing." This statement would be followed by further role play. Once again the emphasis is on what the patient should do, not what they should not do or what he or she did wrong.

Homework. Regardless of how effectively the patient performs the requisite response during training sessions, there is little likelihood that performance will generalize to the natural environment or be maintained in the absence of directed practice in vivo. The importance of practice is underscored by research in which success was achieved by practice alone (e.g., Christensen, Arkowitz, & Anderson, 1975; King, Liberman, Roberts, & Bryan, 1977). Practice is encouraged both by general instructions to "try things out," and by giving specific homework assignments at the conclusion of each session (beginning after at least one response element has been mastered).

Assignments should be relatively specific, and should be geared to a level of difficulty and a situation that will maximize the probability of success (and reinforcement by the environment). Appropriate assignments are of the form: "Say 'Good Morning' to at least one person each day until the next session," "Whenever you speak with someone, look at his eyes at least once during the conversation;" "When you go to the cafeteria for lunch tomorrow, ask for a larger portion of something you have ordered;" and "Tell your roommate that on your days to prepare dinner, you will eat at 6:00 P.M. whether she is home or not." Non-specific assignments such as "Try to strike up some conversations this week," are not likely to be carried out. Similarly, if the patient is not yet able to perform the assignment effectively, or if it precipitates conflict with the interpersonal partner (as with a long-standing marital disagreement), the patient will not be reinforced and future performance both in and out of sessions will be deleteriously affected. Review of homework and social reinforcement for effort should be the first activity in each session.

Training in Social Perception

As we have already indicated, social perception skills are vital for effective performance, but specific training techniques for developing these skills are only beginning to be empirically tested. We have integrated perception training with the response training procedures described above. Once the patient has attained some minimal level of competency, the therapist can begin to vary his or her role play prompts, adding nuances of inflection and increasing the complexity of the responses. The patient is given information about the different meanings of the variations and about the factors that determine the meanings. The patient's reactions to the variations can also be explored, and labels (e.g., "It makes you angry") can be provided when appropriate. For example, "Listen to two different responses to your question. First, 'That's a stupid question; find out yourself.' Second, 'I don't know; you'll have to ask someone else.' The first one makes you uncomfortable, doesn't it. That's because I insulted you by calling your question stupid and was nasty rather than helpful. The second response didn't answer your question either. How did it make you feel? . . . Right, I was not nasty and tried to give a helpful suggestion. So do you see how you could make people feel uncomfortable when you respond as in my first answer?" As training progresses, the therapist can portray a variety of different emotions: discordance between verbal and non-verbal response elements, double-bind messages, etc. Response variations of this type can also be presented on videotape (especially by the less "theatrical" clinician). Most patients functioning at a lower level of overall adjustment, however, will require the control and reinforcement provided by live training.

Generalization and Maintenance

There are four issues that must be addressed in planning and evaluating skills training programs: (1) Does the patient learn the targeted responses? (2) Does the patient perform the targeted responses in the natural environment? (3) Does the patient retain the new skills over time? and (4) Do the new skills play a meaningful role in improving the patient's life?

As we shall discuss, the literature documents that the answer to the first question is yes; social skills training is effective in developing new skills. However, the data are much less clear about the last three questions: the extent to which new skills generalize to the natural environment, the extent to which they are maintained over time, and the extent to which they impact on day to day social functioning. Perhaps the only definitive statement that can be made about generalization and maintenance is that they are not an automatic correlates of training. They only occur when they are carefully and systematically programmed. Our clinical experience and preliminary data suggest several factors that should be considered to optimize outcomes.

Relevance. Most patients referred for social skills training will have gross deficits in a wide variety of areas, and have a generally poor quality of life. It is easy to identify problem areas, deficits, and needs. Yet many of the potential targets are only relevant in the abstract. A realistic appraisal often suggests that the patient is not likely to achieve many ideally desirable goals, at least in the near future. For example, work, marrige, and independent living frequently are beyond the near term reach of many chronic patients. Consequently, teaching skills in these areas is counter-productive. Patients often will find such training threatening, and they will resist attending sessions or fail to pay attention when they do attend. Even if they do learn the rudiments of new skills, the responses are apt to quickly drop out as there is no opportunity to practice in vivo. It seems essential that training focus on skills that have current or near term relevance. For example, if work skills are currently applicable they should be taught. But, they should not be included simply because it would (ideally) be nice if the patient could work.

Similarly, for those skills that are taught, goals and expectations should be conservative. We typically focus on the minimum acceptable response: The simplest response needed to allow the patient to achieve his or her goals. Social niceties and subtle response variations are generally beyond the competence of severely deficient patients. It is neither reasonable nor practical to make demands or set standards that the patient cannot meet. Conversely, standards should not be unduly low; rather, they should be raised gradually and systematically as the patient becomes more competent.

In vivo experience. It is essential that the patient practice new skills in the natural environment. Homework insures that some such practice occurs, but the one assignment per session is really only a minimum. The new responses must be employed regularly if they are to become a meaningful and active part of the response repertoire. Admonishing patients to utilize new skills is rarely sufficient. If the patient has an active social network, significant others (e.g., parents, house mates) can sometimes be enlisted to stimulate and reinforce desired responses. In that regard, new forms of family therapy are becoming an increasingly common component of comprehensive programs (see chapter 10). Patients lacking such a network or a cooperative other present a much greater challenge. Social skills training itself probably cannot undo the effects of habitual social isolation or negative symptoms (e.g., Andreasen, 1982; Strauss, et al, 1974). It is best viewed as a necessary but not sufficient cog in the process of establishing regular, appropriate social activity. Consequently, the broader treatment system (e.g., partial hospital program) must provide a social environment for the patient where none exists. Where possible, outings and evening and weekend activities should be provided in addition to the typical coffee klatch, card games, and activity groups (see Chapter 8). Once the patient can function effectively and comfortably in this manufactured environment (with the help of social skills training), he or she can then be directed outward to the community at large.

Patient characteristics. A third issue, related to the first two, pertains to characteristics of appropriate patients. Because training procedures are graduated and tailored to the needs of individual patients, they are suitable for a large proportion of patients. Yet they are not universally applicable. Not all schizophrenic patients have social skill deficits, and others are too symptomatic or disruptive to sit in a therapy group and follow the instructions. Other factors may reduce the appropriateness of training for some patients at particular points in time. For example, there is some literature to suggest that schizophrenics respond negatively to intensive therapy programs during the acute stages of their illness (see Keith & Mathews [Chapter 11] in this volume). If this finding is supported by future research, it might be necessary to delay training until the patient is well into remission. These various possibilities underscore the need for care in prescribing social skills training.

It should also be remembered that few patients request social skills training. More often than not, it is imposed upon them as part of a comprehensive treatment program. Other things being equal, there is little reason for patients to be interested or cooperative, especially if they have a long history of social withdrawal. The training itself is hard work and tedious, and changing long standing (albeit maladaptive) habits is difficult and anxiety provoking. Without some incentive, patients either will not cooperate during sessions, or will meet the therapist's demands with minimal effort and no enthusiasm. There is no chance of generalization under such circumstances. Thus, it is incumbent upon the therapist to promote the program, make it enjoyable, and ensure early success experiences both within and between sessions.

EMPIRICAL EVALUATIONS OF SOCIAL SKILLS TRAINING WITH SCHIZOPHRENIC PATIENTS

We have discussed the conceptual framework and clinical procedures comprising social skills training. We will now review the empirical evidence regarding the outcome of skills training with schizophrenics, using as initial guidelines the four issues which we previously identified as critical to the evaluation of training.

Does the Patient Learn the Targeted Response?

As noted, the answer to this question is yes. Numerous studies have demonstrated that social skills training based on the skills deficit model is effective in ameliorating the social deficits of schizophrenic patients. Single case (Bellack, Hersen & Turner, 1976; Edelstein & Eisler, 1976; Hersen & Bellack, 1976b; Hersen, Turner, Edelstein, & Pinkston, 1975; Williams, Turner, Watts, Bellack, & Hersen, 1977) and group designs (Bloomfield, 1973; Doty, 1975; Field & Test, 1975; Goldsmith & McFall, 1975; Lomont, Gilner, Spector, & Skinner, 1969; Monti, Curran, Corriveau, DeLancey, & Hagerman, 1980; Monti, Fink, Norman, Curran, Hayes, & Caldwell, 1979; Percell, Berwick, & Beigel, 1974) have repeatedly demonstrated that social skills training leads to positive changes in targeted behaviors. The typical strategy in these investigations has been to apply the techniques discussed above, or some subset of the techniques, to specific targeted deficits in patients who were selected on the basis of pervasive interpersonal dysfunction. Assessments of training effects are typically conducted using pre-, post-, and follow-up role play assessments of social skill.

As an example of this particular methodology, Hersen and Bellack (1976b) reported the results of a single case design with two chronic schizophrenics. In one case, treatment consisted of instructions and feedback. In the second case, instructions, feedback, and modeling were used. Targeted behaviors included eye contact, speech duration, speech disruptions, smiles, requests for new behavior, and compliant statements. A multiple baseline design was used in which behaviors were treated sequentially and cumulatively. Role play scenes from the Behavioral Assertiveness Test-Revised (Eisler et al., 1975) were used in both assessment and training. Training was initiated only after each patient's phenothiazines were regulated. Drug dosages were maintained at a constant level during baseline, training, and follow-up. The results indicated that treatment was effective in that positive gains were noted in specific target behaviors when training was specifically directed towards them. Gradual gains in overall assertiveness were noted by independent observers. Treatment gains were maintained at 2-, 4-, 6-, and 8- week follow-ups.

Many other studies have been conducted, using similar experimental designs, with similar results. It should be noted, however, that there is variability among individuals' response to treatment. Not everyone improves, and among those who do, not everyone improves an equal amount or reaches the same level of skill. Of course, this is not particularly surprising as there is a range of responding to almost any clinical intervention. Further work is needed, however, to identify (and control) factors that may relate to an individual's likelihood of deriving benefit from training. These include: motivational factors, premorbid social competence, intelligence, drug regimens that may either impair or enhance attention on learning ability, intelligence, and the degree to which psychotic symptomatology is either in control or in remission. A further factor in this regard is the heterogeneity of schizophrenia itself. Far from being a homogeneous entity, schizophrenia is comprised of numerous subtypes, each differing in specific symptomatology (American Psychiatric Association, 1980). Even within specific subtypes there can be variability on such factors as positive vs. negative symptoms, affective symptoms, etc. The response to social skills training of each of the various subtypes of schizophrenia may differ. To date, it has not been possible to determine whether or not this is the case, as studies have typically failed to provide appropriate specification regarding diagnosis. Often mixed groups of patients are run through experimental procedures (e.g., Monti et al., 1979; Monti, 1980). In those cases in which studies have involved only schizophrenic patients, no consideration has been given to particular subtypes. Also, the use of group data obscures information regarding individual variability in responding. Consequently, it has often been impossible to empirically identify factors that might relate to either a poor or a good response to training. Despite the methodological complexity that is required to derive information of this sort, future research should attempt to identify and evaluate these factors.

Does the Patient Perform the Targeted Response in the Natural Environment?

Recently, there has been considerable discussion in the literature regarding the generalization of the effects obtained with social skills training. Earlier investigations typically did not include means by which to assess whether or not generalization had occurred. Indeed, as was the case in the single case study by Hersen and Bellack (1976b), most studies relied exclusively on responses to role play scenes as outcome measures. In many instances, the same scenes on which patients were trained were used to assess outcome. Only gradually did investigators begin to consider aspects of generalization. Initially, responses to novel role play scenes were used as a measure of generalization (e.g., Belleck et al., 1976; Monti et al., 1979). An alternative strategy, which was implemented later, was to conduct in vivo assessments of behavior (e.g., Bellack, Hersen, & Turner, 1979; Finch & Wallace, 1977; Liberman, Lillie, Falloon, et al., 1978).* Obviously, the use of in vivo assessments is preferable in that it permits the most accurate depiction of behavior in the natural environment.

The results of studies that have evaluated the generalization of social skills training have been previously characterized by Hersen and Bellack (1976a) as "mixed." This conclusion was based on a review of investigations that had included a variety of subject populations, although most had involved analogue populations. Two studies that they reviewed had been conducted with psychiatric patients (Goldsmith & McFall, 1975; Hersen, Eisler, & Miller, 1974). The results of these investigations were conflicting. Goldsmith and McFall (1975) found good evidence of generalization to an assessment in a "more real-life context" among a sample of 36 male psychiatric inpatients. Hersen et al. (1974) observed only minimal generalization to an independent in vivo test of generalization of assertiveness training among 50 male psychiatric patients. It should be noted that neither study involved the assignment of extra-session practice to subjects, or any other procedure specifically intended to facilitate transfer of training.

A more recent study that did include homework assignments as part of training was that by Liberman et al. (1978). In addition, these investigators obtained data regarding whether or not homework was actually completed, and reported these data as a measure of generalization. The effects of 30 hours per week of social skills training with

---

*Liberman, RP, Wallace, CJ, Falloon, IR, Vaughn, CE, Harper, E, Leff, J, Hutchinson, W, Ryan, P, & Stoute, M. Social skills training for schizophrenic patients and their families. Unpublished manuscript, 1978.

three schizophrenic patients were evaluated using a multiple baseline design across three areas of homework assignment. These three areas involved specified interactions with: (1) members of the nursing staff; (2) parents; and (3) social and vocational contacts in the community. Training was evaluated during a 10-week period. During weeks one and two, performance on all assigned tasks was assessed. Training was then introduced for interactions with nursing staff during weeks three to six. Training was shifted to interactions with parents as well as nursing staff during weeks seven to eight. Finally, during weeks nine and ten training was focused on interactions with community agents, family, and nursing staff. The results indicate that completion of homework assignments did not change until training was directed at that specific area. Thus, the results of the study suggest that generalization is not automatic, and even when specific homework assignments are made, which presumably will enhance generalization, they may not always be effective because subjects may not complete them. Additional techniques should be employed to insure that homework is completed by the patient. In order to increase homework completion, Finch and Wallace (1977) assigned homework to pairs of male schizophrenic inpatients, to be completed together. In comparison to a matched, non-treatment control group, patients in the skills training group showed improvements in social skills across both training and novel role play scenes, as well as spontaneously enacted situations occurring in the natural environment.

Although it remains appropriate to conclude that the results of studies that have assessed generalization to the natural environment are mixed, it is also true that generalization can be obtained if specific strategies are used to program its occurrence (Baer, Wolf, & Risley, 1968). One effective programming strategy appears to be the assignment of homework, along with techniques to insure, or at least increase the probability of, its completion. Other possibilities include the application of self-control techniques, and/or the use of more concrete sets of generalization instructions (Hersen, Eisler, & Miller, 1973).

Does the Patient Retain the New Skills over Time?

In general, the durability of the effects of social skills training on specific targeted behaviors appears to be relatively good, provided that efforts are made to program maintenance of responding. A number of researchers have found the effects of training to be maintained for at least an 8-week follow-up period (e.g., Bellack et al., 1976; Hersen & Bellack, 1976; Monti et al., 1980). Monti et al. (1979) found that a social skills training group maintained their significantly higher level of social functioning over a typical hospital-treatment group for up to ten months.

However, at issue is the manner in which maintenance has been assessed at follow-up. In most instances, self-report and/or laboratory role play assessments have been used. Performance on such measures is an important indicator of whether the targeted responses remain in the person's repertoire. These measures, however, do not reflect the clinical significance of training in terms of the patient's overall quality of life and the course of his or her schizophrenic disorder.

Do the New Skills Play a Meaningful Role in Improving the Patient's Life?

Perhaps the most critical issue with regard to the use of social skills training based on the skills deficit model with schizophrenic patients is the clinical impact of such training. The goal of social skills training is to permit better adjustment in the community and, thus, ultimately prevent or postpone relapse. At issue is whether there is evidence to indicate that it can do this. Some have argued that this has already been demonstrated. Brown (1982) has stated that,

> There are many studies in the literature that support the premise that intensive social skills training can lead to chronic schizophrenic patients acquiring a level of social competence that enables them to live in the community with lower relapse rates" (p. 108).

We believe, however, that judgments of this sort may be somewhat premature. Few, if any, studies have adequately addressed this issue. Most studies of social skills training with schizophrenic patients have been concerned with topographic outcome, and, in some cases, changes in internal states as a result of training (Wallace et al., 1980). Those studies that have considered outcome in terms of relapse/rehospitalization have suffered from methodological problems. In the study by Finch and Wallace (1977), data were reported regarding hospital discharges among the experimental and control groups during a 3-month follow-up. During this period only one of the eight control patients was discharged. Five of the eight patients in the experimental group, however, were discharged and resumed life in the community within 3-months after treatment. Unfortunately, no further follow-up was provided regarding these patients. It is not known how long they maintained their community tenure. While the findings thus suggest that social skills training may have resulted in significantly improved functioning in the hospital setting, it is not clear whether the effects of training were maintained in the community. Longer follow-ups are necessary in order to evaluate the impact of training on relapse in schizophrenic patients.

Field and Test (1975) reported the results of an innovative study in which assertion training was one component of a comprehensive, community-based treatment program. The program emphasized training in community living skills. Patients in the training program demonstrated changes on a role play test of assertiveness that were maintained at a 6-month follow-up. In addition, none of the patients who had participated in the training program had been rehospitalized during the follow-up. However, only ten patients had participated in treatment. They were selected from among voluntary referrals to an inpatient facility, and thus may not have been an entirely representative sample. Finally, assertion training represented but one component of a multifaceted, comprehensive intervention. Its effect, independent of other treatment components, cannot be determined. These methodological concerns notwithstanding, some further support for the effectiveness of the training program is provided by a later report by Test and Stein (1978). Their findings show that during the course of the 14-month community-based treatment program, patients who participated in it evidenced significantly less unemployment, higher competitive income, more independent living, and better social relationships than hospital-treated control patients. While patients in the experimental program were only rarely hospitalized during the treatment program, control patients experienced a 40 percent rate of rehospitalization during the corresponding 14-month period. However, these group differences disappeared by the end of the 14-month posttreatment follow-up period. Thus, the treatment was apparently effective in preventing relapse while patients were actively involved in it. However, treatment effects were not maintained upon discharge. The maintenance of treatment effects is of obvious importance in relationship to the clinical impact of any intervention. It is critical that research be conducted to develop ways to maintain the beneficial effects that patients may derive from skill-based interventions. Further research is also needed about relapse in schizophrenia. At this point it is not known what specific changes in skill/behavior may occur prior to, and thus perhaps be influential in the occurrence of, relapse. Longitudinal assessment of the social functioning of schizophrenics is necessary so that appropriate "booster" interventions might be developed.

In conclusion, although there have been numerous reports of the use of social skills training with schizophrenic patients, several critical issues remain to be resolved. Studies of comprehensive treatment programs, such as that by Test and her colleagues, suggest that multicomponent, skills-oriented training programs may hold the greatest promise. It is becoming increasingly apparent that neither the skills deficit model or social skills training as typically practiced is sufficient to account for the complexities of interpersonal behavior. Skills other than motoric response components must be considered. An adequate conceptualization of the social functioning of schizophrenics requires an integrated and divergent model of behavior that includes recognition of factors such as social perception, cognitive and problem-solving skills, and family and social networks. Indeed, as we discussed in the introduction to this chapter, it is not just the ability to assert himself or interact with a stranger that is likely to be disordered in the schizophrenic patient. Rather, the patient is likely to lack any significant social network, and is likely to have difficulty understanding both subtle and not-so-subtle aspects of communication. The schizophrenic patient may have only family to turn to, and, here too, he or she may be overwhelmed by socially stressful communications from family members. Assuredly, common sense would dictate that in order for an adequate psychosocial treatment to be derived, these factors must be considered.

Attentional Factors and Social Perception

Social skills training programs that fail to consider an individual's ability to accurately perceive and comprehend the behavior, feelings, and motives of other individuals and to generate response alternatives in the face of these factors are incomplete. Unfortunately, this social perceptual ability has been given very little empirical consideration in the social skills literature (Morrison & Bellack, 1981). Recent studies have demonstrated that schizophrenics have marked difficulties in identifying non-verbally displayed emotions (Cutting, 1981, Livesay, 1981). Platt and his colleagues (Platt & Siegel, 1976; Platt, Siegel, & Spivack, 1975; Platt & Spivack, 1972, 1974), have conducted a series of studies in which they have found that psychiatric patients generate fewer solutions to personal and interpersonal problems than do normals. Also, the solutions generated by psychiatric patients were generally less relevant than those generated by normals. (Unfortunately, these investigators have not provided any information regarding the diagnoses of patients in their studies).

The etiology of these difficulties is unclear. They may be the result of more basic cognitive and attentional deficits that have frequently been reported among schizophrenic patients. These include attentional deficits (Cromwell, 1978; Kornetsky & Orzack, 1978; Wohlberg & Kornetsky, 1973), distractibility (Oltmanns & Neale, 1975, Oltmanns, Ohayan, & Neale, 1978), and slowed information processing

(Davidson & Neale, 1974; Rochester, 1978). Regardless of their etiology, these deficits must be addressed for skills training to be effective. Wallace and his colleagues (Wallace, 1978, 1982; Wallace, Nelson, Lukoff, Webster, Rappe, & Ferris, 1978) have developed a comprehensive model of social skill that emphasizes perceptual and problem-solving skills. They have applied this model to the development of an assessment and training program to be used with schizophrenic patients. Training involves question and answer sessions based on videotaped social vignettes that are presented to the patient. After viewing a vignette, the patient is questioned relating to receiving of the situational parameters, and processing of response options to the situation. (e.g., Who are the people talking in the above scene? What did the first speaker say? What is the problem in this situation? What is the best solution to this problem?). If the patient answers a question incorrectly, the relevant portion of the situation is reshown and he or she is asked the question again. Patients are assisted by the therapist if they are unable to provide the correct response on their own. After the patient has demonstrated that he or she has accurately received the parameters of the situation and processed an appropriate response alternative, he or she is instructed to role play that alternative. From this point on, the training program resembles "traditional" social skills training. Wallace (1983) has evaluated the training package with schizophrenic patients in an inpatient setting. In addition to daily 2-hour training sessions, the program included generalization training to new persons and places, practice sessions in the community, sessions designed to increase problem-solving skills in non-interpersonal areas, and weekly meetings of patients and their families that were designed to increase family communication skills. The program was conducted throughout nine weeks of inpatient treatment after which patients were discharged to aftercare facilities. Patients in the skills training program were compared to patients in a control therapy designed on the basis of a holistic health rationale. The control therapy also lasted for nine weeks. Preliminary results indicate that significantly fewer patients in the skills training group relapsed or had been rehospitalized than in the holistic health group at a 9-month follow-up.

The results of Wallace's (1982) training program appear promising. Again it was intended to have a maximum impact on relapse and rehospitalization. The data are noteworthy in that patients in the experimental condition had only a 25 percent relapse rate during the 9-month follow-up period. It should be mentioned that an additional component of the experimental condition was to closely coordinate provision of aftercare services from community agencies. A program social worker assisted patients and their relatives to obtain maximum services from the various community aftercare agencies. This increased aftercare service may have served to enhance the effects of the experimental training program. Nonetheless, research is needed to further examine ways in which to ameliorate the social perceptual deficits of schizophrenic patients.

Family Network and Communication Deviance

A great deal of attention has recently been directed to the topic expressed emotion in families of schizophrenics. A number of studies have shown that schizophrenic patients living in households that are characterized by high levels of family stress have had poorer outcomes than those living in households without high stress levels (Brown et al., 1972; Brown, Monck, Carstairs, & Wing, 1962; Vaughn & Leff, 1976; Vaughn, Synder, Freeman, Jones, Falloon, & Liberman, 1982). Vaughn and Leff (1976) reported that although maintenance on neuroleptic medications significantly reduced relapse rates, patients residing in high-stress households still relapsed more often during the first nine months of aftercare than patients on neuroleptics residing in households with lower or normal levels of stress. Again, these findings emphasize the importance of psychosocial interventions, especially those designed to decrease stressors occurring in the family and/or increase patients' abilities to cope with stressors within the family. Relatively few controlled outcome studies have analyzed the effectiveness of family therapy in the aftercare of schizophrenic patients.

Goldstein, Rodnick, Evans, May, and Steinberg (1978) randomly assigned acute schizophrenic patients who had been stratified by personal adjustment to one of four aftercare conditions for a 6-week controlled trial. Conditions involved one of two dose levels of phenothiazines and presence or absence of crisis-oriented family therapy. Relapses during the 6-week study period and at a 6-month follow-up were fewest in patients who had received high-dose phenothiazines and family therapy, and most frequent among low-dose family therapy condition (n = 25) had been rehospitalized at the 6-month follow-up. The results thus support the combined use of phenothiazines and family therapy.

Perhaps the most comprehensive investigation of the application of a skills-oriented family therapy program to the treatment of schizophrenia was conducted by Falloon and his colleagues (Falloon, Boyd, McGill, Ragani, Moch & Gilderman, 1982). These investigators have developed a family management approach that they believe

> . . . recognizes that effective community aftercare of schizophrenia requires both optional drug therapy and a supportive milieu. The family-treatment approach was designed to train patients and their parents to reduce environmental stress effectively (p. 1438).

Families are taught structured behavioral problem-solving methods in order to derive solutions to family issues. The at-home family therapy was compared with clinic-based individual supportive care in the community management of 36 schizophrenic patients taking neuroleptic maintenance medications. Patients participated in either treatment for nine months. Results at posttreatment indicated that the family treatment approach had been superior in preventing exacerbations of major symptomatology. Only one patient in the family treatment group was judged to have relapsed, compared to eight who were treated individually. Family-treated patients had averaged 0.83 days in the hospital, compared with 8.39 days for patients who received individual treatment. Finally, patients in the family-treatment group obtained significantly lower scores on blind rating-scale assessments of schizophrenic symptomatology at post-treatment.

The results of these two investigations suggest that family therapy can have a significant effect in reducing, or at least postponing, relapse in schizophrenia. The findings highlight the critical role of the patient's environmental support system in the community adjustment of schizophrenics. Obviously, the family is but one source of support that is available to the patient. A second source is the individual's social network.

Social Networks and Schizophrenia

The relevance of social networks and social support to schizophrenia was emphasized by a recent NIMH Conference on "Stress, Social Support, and Schizophrenia," which was held at the University of Vermont in 1979. Although surprisingly few empirical evaluations of the social networks of schizophrenic patients have been conducted, it is a frequent clinical observation that the schizophrenic patient is likely to have few friends or associates.

Those persons with whom the patient does associate are frequently functioning poorly themselves, and as a result are incapble of fulfilling significant support functions. One of the few studies to examine the structure and function of the social networks of schizophrenics was reported by Lipton, Cohen, Fischer, and Katz (1981). The result of their investigation suggested that the schizophrenic patient's social network typically decreases dramatically following his or her first hospitalization. While numerous factors may contribute to this decrease, the authors suggest that active intervention at the time of the first psychotic episode may be helpful in preventing the patient's subsequent social isolation. One strategy that they suggest is to educate members of the network regarding the schizophrenic disorder.

The re-establishment of a patient's social network is a potentially monumental task. Also, it should be noted that in some patients with poor premorbid competence it may have been years since any such network existed. It would seem that rather than directing efforts towards potentially recalcitrant former members of a patient's social network, it may be more effective to focus on the patient and his or her possible responses to changes or losses in existing networks. Training programs must be developed to educate the patient about making and maintaining friends. In addition, it may be of value to teach patients how to utilize support networks. That is, patients could be taught to discriminate the sorts of issues appropriate to discuss with friends or significant others from those which are more appropriately discussed with mental health professionals.

SUMMARY AND CONCLUSIONS

Social skills training is one of the most widely used and valuable psychosocial treatments for schizophrenic patients. The past decade has seen the technique of social skills training evolve from a relatively simplistic intervention to a comprehensive treatment package comprising numerous parameters of interpersonal functioning and capable of modification to meet varied individual needs and clinical demands. This evolution has been primarily based on research evaluations of skills training, which have questioned the clinical utility of the earlier and simpler training protocols. While the clinical impact of some of the recent applications of social skills training has also been the subject of some debate, the more comprehensive skills training protocols have shown considerable promise vis-a-vis the treatment of schizophrenia. Evidence suggests that at least some versions of skills training can affect the course of the disorder and/or apparently prolong remission. To be sure, numerous issues remain to be resolved and a great deal of further research is needed in order to refine social skills training as an intervention in the treatment of schizophrenic patients. However, it seems apparent from the progress which has been made to date that careful evaluation of issues can lead to even further resolution of the technique, resulting in still greater impact on the lives of patients who participate in training.

REFERENCES

American Psychiatric Association, *Diagnostic and statistical manual of mental disorders (3rd Edition).* Washington, D.C. ATP, 1980

Andreasen NC. Negative symptoms in schizophrenia. *Archives of General Psychiatry,* 1982, *39,* 784–788

Andreasen NC, & Olsen S. Negative vs positive schizophrenia: Definition and validation. *Archives of General Psychiatry,* 1982, *39,* 789–794

Argyris C. Explorations in interpersonal competence: I. *Journal of Applied Behavioral Science,* 1965, *1,* 58–83

Arkowitz H. Measurement and modification of minimal dating behavior. In M Hersen, RM Eisler, & PM Miller (Eds.), *Progress in behavior modification, Vol. 5.* New York: Academic Press, 1977

Baer DM, Wolf MM, & Risley TR. Some current dimensions of applied behavior analysis. *Journal of Applied Behavior Analysis,* 1968, *1,* 91–97

Beidel DC, Bellack AS, Turner SM, Hersen M, & Luber RF. Social skills training for chronic psychiatric patients: A treatment manual. *JSAS Catalog of Selected Documents in Psychology,* 1981, *11,* 36 (MS. 2257)

Bellack AS. A critical appraisal of strategies for assessing social skill. *Behavioral Assessment,* 1979, *1,* 157–176

Bellack AS. Recurrent problems in the behavioral assessment of social skill. *Behaviour Research and Therapy,* 1983, *21,* 29–42

Bellack AS, & Hersen M (Eds.), *Research and practice in social skills training.* New York: Plenum, 1979

Bellack AS, Hersen M, & Turner SM. Generalization effects of social skills training in chronic schizophrenics: An experimental analysis. *Behaviour Research and Therapy,* 1976, *14,* 391–398

Bellack AS, Hersen M, & Turner SM. The relationship of role playing and knowledge of appropriate behavior to assertion in the natural environment. *Journal of Consulting and Clinical Psychology,* 1979, *47,* 670–678(b)

Bellack AS, & Morrison RL. Interpersonal dysfunction. In AS Bellack, M Hersen, & AE Kazdin (Eds.), *International handbook of behavior modification and therapy.* New York: Plenum, 1982

Bloomfield HH. Assertive training in an outpatient group of chronic schizophrenics: A preliminary report. *Behavior Therapy,* 1973, *4,* 277–281

Brown M. Maintenance and generalization issues in skills training with chronic schizophrenics. In JP Curran & PM Monti (Eds.), *Social skills training: A practical handbook for assessment and treatment.* New York: Guilford, 1982

Brown GW, Birley JLT, & Wing JK. Influence of family life on the course of schizophrenic disorders: A replication. *British Journal of Psychiatry,* 1972, *121,* 241–258

Brown AW, Monck EM, Carstairs GM, & Wing JK. Influence of family life on the course of schizophrenic illness. *British Journal of Preventive Social Medicine,* 1962, *16,* 55–68

Christensen A, Arkowitz H, & Anderson J. Practice dating as treatment for college dating inhibitions. *Behaviour Research and Therapy,* 1975, *13,* 321–331

Cromwell RL. Attention and information processing: A foundation for understanding schizophrenia? In LC Wynne, RL Cromwell, & S Matthysse (Eds.), *The nature of schizophrenia: New approaches to research and treatment.* New York: John Wiley & Sons, 1978

Cutting J. Judgement of emotional expression in schizophrenics. *British Journal of Psychiatry,* 1981, *139,* 1–6

Davidson GS, & Neale JM. The effects of signal-noise similiarity on visual information processing of schizophrenics. *Journal of Abnormal Psychology,* 1974, *83,* 683–686

Doty DW. Role playing and incentives in the modification of the social interaction of chronic psychiatric patients. *Journal of Consulting and Clinical Psychology,* 1975, *43,* 676–682

Edelstein BA, & Eisler RM. Effects of modeling and modeling with instructions and feedback on the behavioral components of social skills. *Behavior Therapy,* 1976, *7,* 382–389

Eisler RM, Hersen M Miller PM, & Blanchard EB. Situational determinants of assertive behaviors. *Journal of Consulting and Clinical Psychology,* 1975, *43,* 330–340

Falloon IRH, Boyd JL, McGill GW, Razani J, Moss HB, & Gilderman AM. Family management in the prevention of exaccerbations of schizophrenia: A controlled study. *New England Journal of Medicine,* 1982, *306,* 1437–1440

Field GD, & Test MA. Group assertiveness training for severely disturbed patients. *Journal of Behavior Therapy and Experimental Psychiatry,* 1975, *6,* 129–134

Finch BE, & Wallace CJ. Successful interpersonal skills training with schizophrenic inpatients. *Journal of Consulting and Clinical Psychology,* 1977, *45,* 885–890

Fischetti M, Curran JP, & Wessberg HW. Sense of timing: A skill deficit in heterosexual-socially anxious males. *Behavior Modification,* 1977, *1,* 179–195

Glazer W, Prusoff B, John K, & Williams D. Depression and social adjustment among chronic schizophrenic outpatients. *Journal of Nervous and Mental Disease,* 1981, *169,* 712–717

Gleser GC, & Gottschalk LA. Personality characteristics of chronic schizophrenics in relationship to sex and current functioning. *Journal of Clinical Psychology,* 1967, *23,* 349–354

Goldsmith JB, & McFall RM. Development and evaluation of an interpersonal skill training program for psychiatric patients. *Journal of Abnormal Psychology,* 1975, *84,* 51–58

Goldstein MJ, Rodnick EH, Evans JR, May PRA, & Steinberg MR. Drug and family therapy in the aftercare of acute schizophrenics. *Archives of General Psychiatry,* 1978, *35,* 1169–1177

Harper RG, Wiens AN, & Matarazzo JD. *Nonverbal communication: The state of the art.* New York: John Wiley & Sons, 1978

Hersen M, & Bellack AS. Social skills training for chronic psychiatric patients: Rationale, research findings, and future directions. *Comprehensive Psychiatry,* 1976, *17,* 559–580 (a)

Hersen M, & Bellack AS. A multiple-baseline analysis of social-skills training in chronic schizophrenics. *Journal of Applied Behavior Analysis,* 1976, *9,* 239–245 (b)

Hersen M, & Bellack AS. Assessment of social skills. In AR Ciminero, KS Calhoun, & HE Adams (Eds.), *Handbook for behavioral assessment.* New York: John Wiley & Sons, 1977

Hersen M, Bellack AS, & Turner SM. Assessment of assertiveness in female psychiatric patients: Morot and autonomic measures. *Journal of Behavior Therapy and Experimental Psychiatry,* 1978, *9,* 11–16

Hersen M, Eisler RM, & Miller PM. Development of assertive responses: Clinical, measurement and research considerations. *Behaviour Research and Therapy*, 1973, *11*, 505–521

Hersen M, Eisler RM, & Miller PM. An experiemtnal analysis of generalization in assertive training. *Behaviour Research and Therapy*, 1974, *12*, 295–310

Hersen M, Eisler RM, Miller PM, Johnson MB, & Pinkston SG. Effect of practice, instructions, and modeling on components of assertive behavior. *Behaviour Research and Therapy*, 1973, *11*, 443–451

Hersen M, Turner SM, Edelstein BA, & Pinkston SG. Effects of phenothiazines and social skills training in a withdrawn schizophrenic. *Journal of Clinical Psychology*, 1975, *34*, 588–594

King LW, Liberman RP, Roberts J, & Bryan E. Personal effectiveness: A structured therapy for improving social and emotional skills. *European Journal of Behavioural Analysis and Modification*, 1977, *2*, 82–91

Klein DN, & Williamson P. Premorbid adjustment and affective symptomatology in schizophrenia. *Journal of Nervous and Mental Disease*, 1981, *169*, 497–502

Kornetsky C, & Orzack MH. Physiologic and behavioral correlates of attention dysfunction in schizophrenic patients. In LC Wynne, RL Cromwell, & S Matthysse (Eds.), *The nature of schizophrenia: New approaches to research and treatment*. New York: John Wiley & Sons, 1978

Liberman RP. Assessment of social skills. *Schizophrenia Bulletin*, 1982, *8*, 62–83

Liberman RP, Wallace CJ, Falloon IR, & Vaughn CE. Interpersonal problem-solving therapy for schizophrenics and their families. *Comprehensive Psychiatry*, 1981, *22*, 627–630

Libet JM, & Lewinsohn PM. Concept of social skill with special reference to the behavior of depressed persons. *Journal of Consulting and Clinical Psychology*, 1973, *40*, 304–312

Lipton FR, Cohen CI, Fischer E, & Katz SE. Schizophrenia: A network crisis. *Schizophrenia Bulletin*, 1981, *7*, 144–151

Livesay JR. Inconsistent interpersonal judgement in thought-disordered schizophrenia. *Psychological Reports*, 1981, *49*, 179–182

Lomont JF, Gilner FH, Spector NJ, & Skinner BF. Group assertion training and group insight therapies. *Psychological Reports*, 1969, *23*, 463–470

McClelland DC, & Walt NF. Sex role alienation in schizophrenia. *Journal of Abnormal Psychology*, 1968, *12*, 217–220

McFall RM, & Twentyman CT. Four experiments on the relative contributions of rehearsal, modeling, and coaching to assertion training. *Journal of Abnormal Psychology*, 1973, *81*, 199–218

Monti PM, Curran JP, Corriveau DP, Delancey A, & Hagerman S. Effects of social skills training groups and sensitivity training groups with psychiatric patients. *Journal of Consulting and Clinical Psychology*, 1980, *48*, 241–248

Monti PM, Fink E, Norman W, Curran JP, Hayes S, & Caldwell A. The effects of social skills training groups and social skills bibliotherapy with psychiatric patients. *Journal of Consulting and Clinical Psychology*, 1979, *47*, 189–191

Morrison RL, & Bellack AS. The role of social perception in social skill. *Behavior Therapy*, 1981, *12*, 69–79

Oltmanns TF, & Neale JM. Schizophrenic performance when distractors are present: Attentional deficit or differential task difficulty? *Journal of Abnormal Psychology*, 1975, *84*, 205–209

Oltmanns TF, Ohayon J, & Neale JM. The effect of antipsychotic medication and diagnostic criteria on distractibility in schizophrenia. In LC Wynne, RL Cromwell,

& S Matthysse (Eds.), *The nature of schizophrenia: New approaches to research and treatment.* New York: John Wiley & Sons, 1978

Percell LP, Berwick PT, & Beigel A. The effects of assertive training on self-concept and anxiety. *Archives of General Psychiatry,* 1974, *31*, 502–504

Platt JJ, & Siegel J. MMPI characteristics of good and poor social problem-solvers among psychiatric patients. *Journal of Psychology,* 1976, *94,* 245–251

Platt JJ, Siegel JM, & Spivak G. Do psychiatric patients and normals see the same solutions as effective in solving interpersonal problems? *Journal of Consulting and Clinical Psychology,* 1975, *43,* 279

Platt, JJ, & Spivak G. Problem-solving thinking of psychiatric patients. *Journal of Consulting and Clinical Psychology,* 1972, *39,* 148–154

Platt JJ, & Spivak G. Means of solving real life problems: I. Psychiatric patients versus controls, and cross-cultural comparisons of normal females. *Journal of Community Psychology,* 1974, *2,* 45–48

Rimm DC, Snyder JJ, Depue RA, Haanstad MJE, Armstron DP. Assertive training versus rehearsal and the importance of making an assertive response. *Behaviour Research and Therapy,* 1976, *14,* 315–322

Rochester SR. Are language disorders in acute schizophrenia actually information-processing problems. In LC Wynne, RL Cromwell, & S Matthysse (Eds.), *The nature of schizophrenia: New approaches to research and treatment.* New York: John Wiley & Sons, 1978

Serban G. Functioning ability in schizophrenia and normal subjects. Short-term prediction for rehospitalization of schizophrenics. *Comprehensive Psychiatry,* 1975, *16,* 447–456

Strauss JS, Carpenter WT, Jr, & Bartko JJ. The diagnosis and understanding of schizophrenia. Part III. Speculation on the processes that underlie schizophrenic symptoms and signs. *Schizophrenia Bulletin,* 1974, *11,* 61–69

Test MA, & Stein LS. Training in community living: Research design and results. In LS Stein & MA Test (Eds.), *Alternatives to mental hospital treatment.* New York: Plenum, 1978

Trower P, Bryant B, & Argyle M. *Social skills and mental health.* Pittsburgh, University of Pittsburgh Press, 1978

Vaughn CE, & Leff JP. The influence of family and social factors on the course of psychiatric illness: A comparison of schizophrenic and depressed neurotic patients. *British Journal of Psychiatry,* 1976, *129,* 125–137

Vaughn CE, Synder KS, Freeman W, Jones S, Falloon IRH, & Liberman RP. Family factors in schizophrenic relapse: A replication. *Schizophrenia Bulletin,* 1982, *8,* 425–426

Wallace CJ. The assessment of interpersonal problem-solving skills with chronic schizophrenics. Paper presented at the Annual Meeting of the American Psychologic Association, New York, September, 1978

Wallace, CJ. The social skills training project of the Mental Health Clinical Research Center for the study of schizophrenia. In JP Curran & PM Monti, (Eds.), *Social skills training: A practical handbook for assessment and treatment.* New York: Guilford Press, 1982

Wallace CJ, Nelson CJ, Liberman RP, Aitchison, RA, Lukoff D, Elder JP, Ferris C. A review and critique of social skills training with schizophrenic patients. *Schizophrenia Bulletin.* 1980, *6,* 42–63

Wallace CJ, Nelson C, Lukoff D, Webster C, Rappe S, & Ferris C. Cognitive skills training. Paper presented at the Annual Meeting of the Association for Advancement of Behavior Therapy, Chicago, Ill., November,1978

Weiss RL. Operant-conditioning techniques in psychological assessment. In P McReynolds (Ed.), *Advances in psychological assessment.* Palo Alto, CA: Science & Behavior, 1968

Weissman MM, Paykel ES, Siegel R, & Klerman GL. The social role performance of depressed women: Comparisons with a normal group. *American Journal of Orthopsychiatry,* 1971, *41,* 390–405

Williams MT, Turner SM, Watts JG, Bellack AS, & Hersen M. Group social skills training for chronic psychiatric patients. *European Journal of Behavioural Analysis and Modification,* 1977, *1,* 223–229

Wohlberg G, & Kornetsky C. Sustained attention in remitted schizophrenics. *Archives of General Psychiatry,* 1973, *28,* 533

Zigler E, & Phillips L. Social competence and outcome in psychiatric disorders. *Journal of Abnormal and Social Psychology,* 1961, *63,* 264–271

Zigler E, & Phillips L. Social competence and the process-reactive distinction in psychopathology. *Journal of Abnormal and Social Psychology,* 1962, *65,* 215–222

Michael J. Goldstein

10
Family Intervention Programs

A group of people are seated together in a room. Recently, they have shared two important experiences—they have lived with a close relative who has been through an episode of a major mental disorder, most often of a schizophrenic type, and they have also particpated in an experimental program designed to assist them and their disturbed relative to modify family patterns in order to foster rehabilitation. The experimental program involves maintenance pharmacotherapy as well as a combination of family education and therapy. Since a number of the relatives experienced the problems of dealing with a mentally ill relative before such a program existed, they were asked to contrast their current experiences with earlier ones. An interviewer asked about previous experiences with mental health professionals when the relatives asked for information about their offspring or spouse's mental disorder. One mother answered, "Everything seemed to be kept such a dark secret from the parents, from the people that are involved— whether that's the thing to do, I don't know, but I think that the parents need a lot of support in whatever the program. The psychiatrist didn't give us that much. He was dealing with the patient but not with the family."

A father from another family echoed these feelings of isolation, "We had the same problems, they would deal with the patient but not with the family at all. Everyone that our son went to, I mean, we went but that was it. We were there, but we never saw anybody."

SCHIZOPHRENIA
ISBN 0-8089-1640-8

The interviewer asked, "Did you ask to see somebody?" The father replied, "Yeah, you could see them, but they never had time to talk with you."

Another mother from still another family stated, "I first got absolutely nowhere, they would tell me, 'You won't understand if I tried to explain it to you, you wouldn't understand,' and this went on and on in a big circle, nowhere,—no information at all!"

The feelings of these relatives are not unique. Until recently, many relatives of schizophrenic patients experienced some form of rebuff by mental health professionals while their relative was treated as an inpatient, and little or no involvement in the aftercare process when the relative returned home. These attitudes of mental health personnel reflected both the prevailing wisdom of the time that the family, because of its pernicious impact, needed to be isolated from the patient and his treatment, as well as a sense of helplessness concerning what information and advice could be provided that would be useful and helpful.

The tendency to isolate and distance the relatives of severely disordered mental patients conformed with the treatment pattern in the United States that existed from the end of World War II until the early 1960s. Patients, when symptomatic, were removed from their families for an extended inpatient stay. If and when released, they were unlikely to return to parental or spousal homes. Also, patients discharged during this period typically had attained reasonable levels of remission from their psychosis, so that when they did return home, relatives did not have to deal with active psychotic symptoms.

The patterns of care that have evolved since the mid 1960s have forced both mental health professionals and families of mental patients to rethink their respective roles. The pattern of community care for schizophrenic patients has evolved into a two-phase pattern in which a relatively brief inpatient stay is followed by extended aftercare in the community. Because adequate transitional living environments are rare, and even when they do exist patients resist staying in them, patients frequently return to a family environment in varying states of partial remission. Examination of these family environments and the problems of reentry of a disturbed and frequently disturbing relative has revealed that families often experience considerable difficulty fulfilling the newly assigned role of primary caretaker. Even when families appear to cope well, there is a notable impact on the mental health status of relatives. In one study by Hawks (1975), 50 percent of relatives stated that their own mental health had been adversely affected in the process of coping with the patient's mental disorder.

Research has indicated that attitudes expressed by the relatives towards the returning mental patient are highly predictive of the likelihood that the patient will remain in the community nine months after discharge from the hospital. The work of Brown and his associates (Brown, 1959; Brown, Birley, & Wing, 1972), followed up by Vaughn and Leff (1976a), has gone beyond informal clinical observation to provide empirical evidence that those deleterious aspects of the family environment associated with high risk for relapse could be specified and measured with standardized procedures. Their work on expressed emotion (EE) revealed that relatives' attitudes of criticism, hostility and/or emotional overinvolvement possess powerful prognostic information about the likelihood of relapse. These attitudes, assumed to reflect ongoing family transactions, suggest a particular sensitivity of the schizophrenic patient to discriminable attributes of the family environment.

The awareness that family members are increasingly responsible for the aftercare of schizophrenic relatives and that specific attributes of the family environment may be particularly pernicious has led to renewed interest in family intervention programs designed to support the family system, prevent relapse, and foster the social recovery of the patient. Many of these family intervention programs have utilized measures of EE to identify the relapse-prone family units in special need. Previous attempts at using traditional family therapy with families of schizophrenics were not successful or widely adopted. Further, these programs were, in the past, viewed as alternatives to maintenance pharmacological treatment. The newer models described in this chapter are not based on such an either/or conceptualization and all, in fact, acknowledge the importance of antipsychotic drugs as maintenance agents during the posthospitalization phase of treatment. These newer, experimental programs, which are frequently very pragmatic in orientation, attempt to provide an additional psychosocial dimension to aftercare beyond the protection against relapse provided by pharmacological agents.

In recent years, several models of family treatment have been developed that attempt to include an educational component as part of a larger program of intervention for schizophrenic patients and their families. These models have been classified as psychoeducational family therapies (Anderson, 1982). The key elements of these programs, which have been utilized in controlled clinical trials, are summarized in a monograph by Goldstein (1981). These programs are designed to help patients out of hospitals and return them to a productive life in the community. Working in tandem with medication programs, they teach patients and families about the disorder and its management. Treating the family as a resource rather than as a stress, the programs focus on concrete problem solving and specific helping behaviors for coping with stress. These models recognize the likelihood of a biological basis of the illness and the negative impact of stress on patient ability to function. The underlying assumption of all psychoeducational family programs developed to date is that giving families information about the nature of the disorder, along with specific suggestions for coping with it effectively, can decrease the intensity and conflict inherent in family life, and thus reduce the likelihood of relapse in the index patient, and the emergence of mental disorders in the previously non-affected relatives. Thus, these family-oriented programs combine two levels of preventive intervention—one at a secondary prevention level for the patient and one at a primary level for his or her relatives. In general, evaluation to date of controlled trials using these psychoeducational family programs has focused more attention on their impact on the secondary than the primary preventive objective.

Published reports of the controlled trials (Falloon, Boyd, McGill, Razani, Moss, & Gilderman, 1982; Goldstein, Rodnick, Evans, Phillip, & Steinberg, 1978; Leff, Kuipers, Berkowitz, Eherlein, Vries, & Sturgeon, 1982), contrasting patients who received some type of psychoeducational family program with those who did not, suggest that such programs are quite effective supplements to medication in maintaining patients in their communities, thus avoiding the need for psychiatric hospitalization. All of these programs appear to have certain common components: (1) The establishment of a collaborative relationship between therapist(s) and family members, (2) the provision of information and support, and (3) the creation of highly structured predictable environments in the treatment setting and in the home.

While a number of the family based programs have a great deal in common, there are substantial differences among them. For example, the programs of Goldstein et al., (1978), Anderson, Hogarty, and Reiss (1981), and Falloon et al. (1982), all involve the patient in the sessions, while the Leff et al., (1982) program focused primarily, but not exclusively, on group sessions with the relatives without the patient present. While family system theorists might object heartily to a family program carried out without the identified patient present, there is no empirical evidence for differential impact of two orientations to family intervention. Another difference among family programs tested in controlled clinical trials relates to the locus of the intervention. Some programs are carried out within the home while others are clinic based. Once again, there is no evidence for the relative efficacy of each strategy.

An interesting aspect of these newer programs is that the originators of their programs—with the exception of Carol Anderson—have not been strongly identified with the family therapy movement. Despite the fact that the origins of the family systems perspective grew out of experimental attempts to treat schizophrenia, little activity with schizophrenic patients was evident by representatives of the family systems orientation. To some extent, this has been due to a certain polarization in the family therapy field that set itself in opposition to pharmacotherapy, as well as negative reviews of the field (Beels, 1975) that considered studies in which family therapy alone was used to treat schizophrenia. The one exception to this is seen in the writings of Italian family therapy groups (Andolfi, Menghi, Nicolo, & Saccu, 1980, Selvini, Palazzoli, Boscolo, Cecchin & Prata, 1978) who describe, with fascinating case examples, the application of strategic therapies with families containing schizophrenic relatives. Neither the strategic nor the structural family therapies (Minuchin, 1974), however, have been subjected to controlled clinical trials involving schizophrenic patients and their families. Hopefully, future research will contrast their imaginative and unusual therapeutic approaches, with those described by Anderson et al. (1982) as psychoeducational. The latter term refers to direct and rather overt attempts to control and modify family interaction and stands in contrast to the more covert strategies evident in such techniques as paradoxical injunctions.

The psychoeducational family therapies typically contain two parts, a brief program of family education about schizophrenia, and a more extended program of family contact designed to reduce overt manifestations of conflict and to alter patterns of family communication and problem solving. Because the term *psychoeducational* was originally used by Anderson, Hogarty, and Reiss (1980) to describe this approach, workers in the field often assume that it refers only to the brief, family education phase of these programs. They tend to ignore the complexity of the more extended family therapy. The extended programs warrant the term psychoeducational only because they represent organized attempts to teach families new ways to relate. But they are not didactic in the same sense as the brief family education. Most of these therapists, however, do concur with a recent statement by Wynne (1982), "However, I now regard education as a fundamental component of all the family therapy that I do."

Since people find the concept of brief family education modules attractive and easy to organize, there is a strong temptation to develop and implement such programs outside of the context of an extended family intervention program. It should be pointed out that there is little evidence for the impact, either positive or negative, of such an isolated program. Systematic research that evaluates the impact of family education about schizophrenia as a free-standing program is sorely needed before mental health professionals implement them on a large scale.

Despite this caveat, we shall cover issues surrounding family education separately from those involved in the more extended programs. In this way, we hope to sharpen some of the issues that are still unresolved.

FAMILY EDUCATION ABOUT SCHIZOPHRENIA

"I don't think the lay person knows very much about what schizophrenia means. So it was a big education and a big learning experience just to learn what schizophrenia is." This comment by a respondent who has just gone through a brief family education program is very typical. There is a general sense of relief that comes from knowing that this disorganized pattern of behavior has a name. Other aspects of family education serve to further reduce confusion, guilt, and blaming. Most programs of family education have many common features, but they differ in detail and emphasis. Table 10-1 presents an overview of four family education programs that have been utilized as part of an extended family intervention program in controlled clinical trials. Note that the four programs vary in the number of sessions but average between four and six hours of family education. In two programs, the sessions are held without the patient present while in the others the patient is present. The program by Falloon et al. represents the initial phase of an extended family education program carried out entirely in the home. It combines some didactic material with encouragement for patient and relatives to share their experiences with psychosis. Whether or not the patient is present appears related to when in the course of the patient's treatment history the program is offered. When the patient is still actively symptomatic, the program generally does not include him. If a period of stabilization has transpired, as in the Falloon et al. (1982) program it seems more appropriate to include the schizophrenic relative.

Another difference among these programs relates to format. Some are carried out with the individual family unit while others involve group presentation. The relative advantages of each have not been evaluated. Obviously, one fosters group cohesion among families sharing a common problem while the other permits patient and relatives to relate highly personal material without strangers present. Educa-

Table 10-1
Overview of Family Education Programs

Research Group	Number of Sessions	Length of Sessions	Location	Number of Families Present	Patient Present	Timing of Education	Type of Presentation
Leff et al. (1982)	2	No set length	Hospital or home	1	no	ASAP after patient discharge	Brief text is read to participants and given to them to take home, questions are answered
(1981) Snyder & Liberman	2	2 hrs.	Storefront	3 patients & their families	yes	During hospitalization most after a few weeks	3 co-leaders jointly lead 1st hour & then separate into individual therapy groups, structured syllabus, classroom format—handouts & homework assignments
(1980) Anderson et al.	1	5 hrs	Hospital	3–4 families	no	Early in treatment most patients still in hospital	Seminar structure—lecture/ handouts
(1982) Falloon et al.	2 or 3	1½ hrs.	Home	1 family	yes	when patient is (re)stabilized on medication	At home discussion where family members are asked to share their experiences and the patient is encouraged to discuss personal and interpersonal experiences.

tion administered to the family by the clinician who subsequently implements the extended family intervention program obviously serves an important introduction to the longer-term treatment program. It is not clear whether the impact of such a family education module is sharply different when the presenter(s) are unlikely to have further clinical contact with the family.

The Content of Various Education Programs

The informational content of the family education component in the programs previously mentioned is quite similar. They all present definitions of a schizophrenic disorder, a description of key symptoms, theories concerning etiology, prognosis, and treatment recommendations concerning pharmacotherapy and family behavior. While the nature of the information across programs is similar, the manner of presentation and details vary considerably. The key information transmitted in the various family education sessions covers diagnosis, key symptoms, etiology and course and treatment.

Diagnosis.

All of the programs begin with a discussion of the diagnosis of schizophrenia including commom misconceptions about the disorder (e.g., "the term does not refer to a split personality; most schizophrenics are not violent" etc.), the statistical occurrence of schizophrenia, and personal accounts of patients who have experienced the disorder.

A major purpose is to emphasize the notion that the bizarre behavior manifested by the patient relative is actually part of a "known" psychiatric disorder and that the symptoms are similar world-wide. Another objective is to foster a reconceptualization of the patient's deviant behavior as reflections of his mental disorder rather than as "bad" or "willfull" behavior. While many clinicians with a family system orientation may object to this reidentification of the already identified patient as contrary to an effective family intervention strategy, Berkowitz et al. (1981) report that there is frequently a reduction in high EE attitudes when this shift in attribution is accepted by a relative.

The description of schizophrenia, designed to normalize the experience for relatives, typically is done in a fashion likely to build empathy and support among members of the family unit and an alliance with mental health professionals who will subsequently be working with them. Consider the following excerpts from the Leff et al. (1982) education lecture that is presented to relatives without the patient present:

> ... Schizophrenia is an illness. It affects people in many ways. The difficulty is that the sort of experiences it gives rise to seem completely real to the people suffering from it. For instance, someone who hears voices may talk back to them because he thinks they are voices of people who are actually there ... Because the patient cannot usually explain what is happening in his mind, it is not always easy for other people, even those who live with him like yourselves, to realize that many of the odd or upsetting things he does are caused by the illness ... Schizophrenia is not a rare illness ... it can affect anyone.

Or in another educational program designed to be presented to both relatives and patients together* it is stated:

> Schizophrenia means a disintegration of the personality where a person finds it difficult deciding what is real and what is not real. It is a little like having dreams when you are wide awake ... We describe schizophrenia as a major illness because it has a great effect on nearly every aspect of a person's life. Everything that is important in our lives may be affected by schizophrenia. The symptoms of schizophrenia are not identical for every person, but they nearly always produce a handicap in many aspects of everyday living.

Key Symptoms

A discussion of symptoms usually follows this general definition of a schizophrenic disorder. Descriptions of the prominent positive symptoms of schizophrenia (delusions, hallucinations, incoherent talk) are followed by a discussion of the negative or deficit symptoms, which are frequently more troubling to relatives after the patient returns home from the hospital. An example of a segment of the Leff et al. (1982) program indicates how one cluster of negative symptoms can be described in a compassionate way.

> Schizophrenia can also affect feelings ... You may have noticed that he doesn't seem to care for you as he did before, or show his love for you in the same way. There may be fewer times when you can really talk to each other, and you may sometimes wonder whether he still feels anything for you at all. He can't help this, because his usual feelings have been swamped by the illness and he has become very wrapped up in himself.

In the Anderson-Hogarty survival skills workshop, excerpts of first person reports of the inner experience of a psychotic break are read aloud and handouts of such accounts are also provided to relatives. A unique aspect of the Falloon et al. (1982) family education sessions,

*Liberman RP, Aitchison RA, & Falloon, I. Family therrapy in Schizophrenia: Syllabus for therapists. Unpublished manuscript, 1979

carried out in the home, is that patient and relatives are encouraged to share their experiences of these symptoms. For example, after describing a delusion of thought insertion, the clinician might, in an offhand manner, turn to the patient and say, "Did you ever experience anything like that and could you share with us what it was like?" The relatives would then be queried about their awareness of such symptoms.

Etiology and Course

Although the mental health field is far from agreement concerning the origins of schizophrenia, most family educational programs attempt to convey the current state of knowledge about etiology. This covers some description of genetic, biochemical, and life-stress theories. Since most programs are oriented around a stress-diathesis model, both sides of the equation are covered. The programs outlined in Table 10-1 vary greatly in the amount of detail presented about biological theories, ranging from detailed exposition of the dopamine theory in the Anderson et al. (1980) survival skills workshop, to a more general reference to deviations in brain chemistry as in the following from Liberman et al. (1979, unpublished manuscript):

> It is probably a better idea to think of the causes of schizophrenia rather than a *single* cause. And it is also important to think of factors which can make the symptoms and life functioning better or worse in a person who already has schizophrenia. Since medication can improve the symptoms of schizophrenia, it is likely that brain chemistry changes are part of the problem. On the other hand since psychotherapies and behavior therapies which focus on the patient's environment also produce therapeutic change, it is felt that the environment . . . especially other people's reactions to the person with schizophrenia—is crucial in the development and outcome of schizophrenia.

Almost all of these programs de-emphasize the role of family relationships as etiological agents and emphasize their role as potential environmental stressors that can affect the course of the disorder. This characterization of conflictual family interaction as a special case of environmental stressors sets the stage for emphasizing the central importance of reducing life stress for the patient and relatives during the aftercare period. The disassociation of the pre-illness family relationships from those operational during the aftercare period gives patients and relatives a sense that they can alter future events without having to feel undue guilt or blame about the part of their life that is unalterable—the past.

When genetic data are presented in great detail, such a presentation is likely to stimulate considerable discussion of risk factors for other offspring as well as revive old family arguments concerning whose side of the family passed on the "bad" genes. Thus, it is a topic covered in most family education programs that must be handled with great tact and sensitivity.

While discussions of the course of the illness emphasize hope and possibility, most programs attempt to present a realistic expectation about relapse. Preparation that another episode of the disorder is possible is seen as a good form of stress innoculation.

> Some people only have one attack of schizophrenia; they recover from this and never have another. Others, luckily, only a small number, do not respond to treatment at all. However, most patients, although they recover from the attack, are likely to have other attacks. These may occur within weeks of recovery, or may happen years later. During further attacks new kinds of odd behavior can appear, but often the same pattern will repeat itself, (Leff et al., 1982).

Treatment

All four of the educational programs emphasize the importance of both pharmacological and psychosocial interventions. Once again there is a wide variation in the amount of detail provided relatives about medication. The goal, however, is to reinforce medication compliance by the patient and support of this activity by the relatives. Both positive effects as well as disturbing side effects of antipsychotic drugs are emphasized. All programs, however, emphasize medication as the cornerstone of the aftercare program. Consider two quite different styles for describing the role of medication:

> These (drugs) play an important part in the treatment of schizophrenia. They help to stop the voices in the patient's head, they make him less anxious and restless and help him to think more clearly. They protect him against stresses coming from his own experiences and his everyday life cannot always be seen straight away. Some patients are not given tablets but are put on injections. These have the same effect as tablets but can be given less often (Leff et al., 1982).

> My guess is that everyone in this room has a family member that has been ill who is receiving some form of medication which we call antipsychotic medication or antischizophrenic medication. You may hear them referred to as tranquilizers. It turns out that they don't tranquilize people, they operate on this (dopamine transmission) process . . . They put back the chemical imbalance. Those molecules look like the dopamine and they take its place, they block the crevice . . . They'll compete and substitute with the dopamine and sneak in there. The effect is to tone down the strength of the message, not as much can get through. This whole process of being excited and distracted and too much coming

in at once. This is a chemical way of enhancing the . . . toning down process in the cell which is not working at the moment. It helps the body tone down and get equilibrium back. It's the tune up—we're playing a trick on the receptors with medication. That's all we're doing (G. Hogarty, from a transcript of a Survival Skills Workshop).

While the drugs operate on the anomalies in brain chemistry described in the etiology section of a family education program, the need to reduce family stress, particularly the high EE behaviors of criticism and/or emotional overinvolvement, are heavily emphasized. Whether carried out with relatives only or with the patient, relatives are given considerable variation in the specificity of recommendations. Some are fairly complete and linked to the EE research as in this excerpt from the Leff et al. (1982) syllabus:

The best thing you can do in this situation is firstly, not to spend so much time with him so that you don't get on each other's nerves. It is important that the patient leads as independent a life as possible . . . If you have to be together a lot of the time, the best thing to do is not to shout or criticize or get too involved.

The recommendations from the Anderson-Hogarty program are more elaborate and focus on two areas—suggestions for patient management and things that the relatives can do for their own mental health. These recommendations derived from Anderson's extensive clinical experience with schizophrenics as well as family system theory, emphasize the importance of realistic expectations for the patient, the virtue of benign indifference in responding to minor symptomatology, the normalization of family life, and the need to set limits on severely deviant behavior by the patient. In order to promote the mental health of relatives, they are advised that the patient's recovery will be a long-term process; one year at minimum. They are also advised of the need to pursue their own interests and needs and of the value of forming mutual support groups with other families facing similar problems.

The recommendations for stress management in the Falloon et al. program are not clearly discriminable from the extended family program that follows. Since all sessions are carried out in the home, the educational sessions merge into those oriented towards family intervention.

Impact of Family Education

A brief education module about schizophrenia can be evaluated by two criteria: (1) Do recipients of the program acquire and retain the information presented?; and (2) Do the session(s) alter the attitudes of family members vis a vis each other? Few systematic studies have been carried out on either question, and where some evaluation has been attempted, the family education module has been the initial stage of an extended family education program. One investigation, Berkowitz et al. (1981), reports equivocal results regarding information acquisition with repeat administrations of the "Knowledge Interview" before and after their four session education program. These authors suggest that the interview itself may have limited the possibility of demonstrating change as relatives initially had difficulties formulating answers to the open-ended questions. Snyder and Liberman (1981) report that both relatives' and patients' scores on a "facts about schizophrenia questionnaire" jumped from 40 percent to 80 percent correct after a family education program carried out in a group format. Data for the control group who did not receive this program are not presented. In the Falloon et al. (1981) report on family education sessions carried out in the home as the initial phase of their extended family intervention program, parents and relatives showed a 50 percent increase in scores on a multiple choice test about schizophrenia.

Despite these positive results, most authors who have carried out family education programs emphasize that the educational process does not cease after the brief exposure but is addressed repeatedly in the context of enduring family contacts. There is very little data concerning the retention of information over the longer term. In one pilot study by Cozolino and Nuechterlein (1982), ten relatives from six different families were interviewed six months after a family education program similar to the survival skills workshop of Anderson, Hogarty, and Reiss (1981). The interview covered their retention of information as well as their attitudes about different components of the educational package (diagnosis, etiology, etc.). A unique aspect of this study was that the family education program was not part of a longer term family education package so that the effects of the education could be evaluated in isolation. These investigators found that informants recalled the program as beneficial but recalled little of the specific information concerning etiological theories, particularly those describing biological mechanisms. Despite this limited retention, relatives enjoyed hearing the technical information about neurotransmitter processes and how they might relate to schizophrenia. "It's comforting to know that it's something electrical," one said. Another parent recalled this about the dopamine hypothesis, "Schizophrenia is like a tear in the brain—too much chemical was the brain," or "there is a spot here (points to the top of his head) she is missing this particular thing and the medication can kind of work on that area . . . I can see that the medication has not made the gap any better, so far."

Despite this limited recall, relatives expressed appreciation that mental health professionals took the trouble to inform them about the current state of knowledge about schizophrenia. Less satisfaction was reported by informants in the Cozolino and Nuechterlein (1982) study with the material about prognosis. This may have been due to the fact that the relatives in this study were mainly dealing with the first lifetime episode of schizophrenia in an offspring, a factor that will be amplified in more detail below.

Most valued by relatives in this study were suggestions about patient management, both the importance of maintenance drug therapy and the handling of intrafamilial relationships. While relatives appreciated guidelines concerning the latter, they reported considerable frustration because they were not given suggestions specific to the problems encountered with their patient-relative or mechanisms for implementation. As one relative stated it, "You think, 'that sounds easy . . . I can do that,' but when it comes right down to it lots of times you can't. We have the leaflet they gave us—don't be sarcastic and all that stuff and that's fine . . . it was useful . . . but it wasn't very effective. The things they said were the right things to do if you could do them." These reports suggest that recommendations about modifying family behavior presented without a follow-up family program, designed to support and assist relatives in modifying behavior may, in fact, engender effects opposite to those intended as family tension may be raised rather than lowered.

The impact of these programs on family attitudes has not been assessed systematically. There are numerous informal reports of positive attitude change following exposure to such a brief program. A frequent comment from respondents in the Cozolino and Nuechterlein study was that the program affected relatives' attitudes towards the mental health system because they finally felt that they had an ally after prior terrifying experiences with police, hospital staff, and doctors. As one mother stated it, "Everything was a feeling of relief because we felt so isolated—once you get talking with other people who deal with these problems and that there was some place to turn for help—that's what gave me relief—not so much the information . . . This program was a Godsend!"

Another report about attitude change came from the study by Leff et al. (1982). At a recent research planning workshop (Goldstein, 1982), Leff and Berkowitz indicated that prior to a family education program relatives classified as high EE perceived their patient-relative to be chronically-ill even between psychotic episodes, while low

EE relatives did not. High EE relatives also saw the patient as having control over his symptoms and could not emphasize with his or her perspective regarding various experiences. Low EE relatives could see the patient's point of view and saw the illness as a legitimate cause of symptom and social deficits.

After family education, high EE relatives seemed less pessimistic about the future course of the illness, seeing it as episodic rather than continuous. Also, they were able to explain proper home management techniques. High EE relatives who did not receive a family education program had not changed their pessimistic outlook regarding the patient and could not articulate proper home management techniques.

Limitations of Family Education

Most family education programs have been offered to relatives (and patients) where repeated episodes of schizophrenia have transpired. In these families of chronic patients, the diagnosis is reasonably clear and prognostic information is on solid ground. However, whether these programs, as currently construed, are appropriate for the relatives of patients undergoing their first lifetime episode of a major mental disorder is very questionable. Wynne (1982) argues cogently that family education programs should follow a quite different path for families of acute psychotics. He points out that diagnostic issues are ambiguous so that family education programs should provide information about a number of psychiatric syndromes that may be associated with an acute psychotic reaction such as schizophrenia, affective psychoses, borderline problems, and street drugs. Wynne suggests that by discussing a series of disorders rather than one disorder presumed diagnostic for their relative, clinicians can convey the complexity of diagnosis at a sensible, understandable level. He suggests that families value this sort of presentation and then do not demand a definite diagnosis prematurely. Wynne also suggests that coverage of developmental-life cycle issues as they may relate to the onset of these disorders can also provide relatives with a sense of coherence about what is transpiring with their patient relative. Wynne also notes that because families of acute, recent onset psychotics are in crisis, they are less likely to accept the notion that their relative is manifesting a defined mental disorder. "They will look for the source of 'the problem' in possible marijuana usage, bad companions or in some specific life event, and only rarely consider whether something within the family may be relevant" (Wynne, 1982). They are also less likely, possibly because of this attribution, to want to continue participation in a family intervention program, a fact noted previously in this chapter in a study that offered a short-term crisis-intervention program to patients undergoing their first lifetime episode of schizophrenia and their families (Goldstein et al., 1978). Thus, not only must family education be modified for families experiencing the first breakdown in a relative, but it is unlikely to be successful unless it is embedded in a program of crisis-intervention for that family.

Extended Intervention Programs

As indicated previously, family education typically serves as an introduction to a more extended program of family intervention. While a family education program is administered in a single day or over a few days, extended intervention programs occur over periods of months, or in some cases, for more than a year following discharge. In this section of the chapter we shall review those programs that have been evaluated in the course of controlled clinical trials during which maintenance medication models have been continuously provided. A number of different theoretical models have guided the formulation of these programs. Despite these varying origins the commonalities are more notable than the differences.

The first published controlled trial that attempted to provide patients and families with some understanding of the schizophrenic disorder and ways of coping with it, was carried out by Goldstein and associates (1978). This program, specifically targeted for patients undergoing their first lifetime admission for schizophrenia, involved a brief six week program of family therapy that was concrete and problem focused. The goals of the program were to identify the events that were stressful to the patient, and then to prevent the occurrence of these events or to mitigate their destructive impact. Family sessions began by exploring the psychotic experience, with the therapist helping the patient and the family to discuss the illness and its symptoms. Out of these discussions, the therapist attempted to assist the family to identify and agree upon specific stresses that were of particular concern. Following the identification of stressors, the therapist attempts to help families to develop strategies to avoid these stresses or methods of coping with them when they occur. A full description of this model of brief, crisis-oriented family therapy is contained in Kopeikin, Marshall, and Goldstein (1983).

In this study, which followed a 2 × 2 design, patients were assigned to family therapy or no family therapy and to a moderate (25 mg) or low (6.25 mg) dose of injectable fluphenazine for the six week period immediately following discharge. The results of this study revealed a notable effect of family therapy in reducing relapse rates during the six week trial, which was sustained at a six month follow-up point, particularly for those cases who had originally received the higher drug dose. In that group no relapses had been observed at six months, in contrast to a 48 percent relapse rate in the group originally treated on the low dose without family therapy.

King and Goldstein (1979) reported, in a detailed analysis of the family therapy group, that when therapists could achieve the higher level objectives of the program (anticipating future stresses and developing coping plans), patient adjustment at six months was notably enhanced. In contrast to those who did not achieve these objectives, the achiever family units showed a continued decline in schizoprehnic thinking as rated on the Brief Psychiatric Rating Scale (Overall & Gorham, 1962).

Subsequent family programs that have appeared in the literature have been more extensive than those developed by Goldstein et al. This seems at least partially due to the fact that they were developed for a different type of more chronic schizophrenic patient who may, in fact, have had a number of prior episodes. It remains to be seen whether families of patients undergoing their first lifetime episode of schizophrenia are readily engaged in such a long term commitment. The author's experience with families of first admission is very similar to those reported by Wynne (1982):

> My recent experience strongly indicates that the willingness of families during and after a first admission to be interested in extended programs of this kind, is quite different from that of families of chronic patients. Although the work with families of chronic patients may not be continuous, it often is useful simply in the form of a phone call or a visit from a family member, sometimes about some new problem, sometimes to make sure that the staff member was available. With the families of acute psychotics, the kinds of questions that are raised, the kind of anxiety and alarm is quite different. The families of chronic patients are often focused on themselves. They are inclined to blame themselves or, more usually, feel blamed and neglected by the psychiatrists, all too often with justification. In contrast, the families of first-admission patients are more inclined to look for "the problem" in possible marijuana usage, bad companions, or in some life event, and only rarely wonder whether something within the family may be relevant. Nevertheless, these families of acute psychotics are in a crisis; they are distressed, and they are responsive to those who will listen to them and who will respond with

information and guidance. A major task for the future in the field of prevention lies in developing early support and educational programs for the families of acute psychotics. These programs require careful design and are not so easily organized in a standard format as those developed for families of chronic schizophrenics.

Programs for the Chronic Patient and his Family

The four programs that have been through some form of evaluation trial are summaried in Table 10-2. This table describes the duration of the programs, the length of the sessions, the location, number of families present, whether or not the patient is present, and when in the course of events the therapy program begins. The programs do differ notably in some of these formal properties, varying from those in which the relatives are the primary target of the intervention (Leff et al., 1982), to those where the patient is continuously present from family education onwards (Falloon et al., 1982). Most programs last a minimum of nine months post-discharge and have provisions for a maintenance phase lasting up to two years. Thus, these programs, which involve continuous maintenance medication, represent a major commitment of the institution to the family and visa-versa. It is not clear from published reports how many families refuse to make such long term commitments. A number of authors (Anderson et al., 1980; Falloon et al., 1982), however, indicate that few families withdraw from such a program after the early sessions. The details of these extended programs are described in Goldstein (1981).

Regardless of the orientation of the program initiations, all extended family programs operate from the premise that there is a strong relationship between patient vulnerability and family anxiety or behaviors. Thus, these programs are designed to accomplish two goals: (1) to decrease the patient's vulnerability to stimuli through a program of maintenance chemotherapy; and (2) to decrease the intensity of the family environment through a program of support, information, structure, and specific coping mechanisms for dealing with a partially-remitted psychotic family member. Most programs involve family sessions that are structured to some degree and involve a directive therapeutic attitude designed to increase the predictability and stability of the family environment.

The therapeutic models guiding these activities vary from the behavioral approach of Falloon et al., which combines communica-

Table 10-2
Overview of Therapy Programs

Research Group	Number of Sessions	Length of Sessions	Location	Number of Families Present	Patient Present	Timing of Therapy	Format
(1982) Leff et al.							
Group Meetings	18	1½ hrs.	Hospital	Parents or spouses only	no	ASAP after discharge	2 therapists in group setting
Family Sessions	variable from 5 to 25	± 1 hr.	Home	1 family	yes	after discharge	2 therapists go to the home
(1981) Snyder & Liberman	7	2 hrs.	Hospital	3 patients & their families	yes	During hospitalization	3 co-leaders who jointly present 1st hr. and then work individually with a family for the next hour
(1980) Anderson et al.							
Connection	2 × week throughout hospitalization	no standard meeting format		1 family	no	ASAP after admission	Individual clinician contacting family
Reentry	every 2–3 weeks for 6 mos.–year		Hospital	1 family	yes	ASAP after acute stage of illness has passed	Individual clinician with one family
Maintenance	weekly 2–3 weeks gradually diminishing		Hospital	1 family	yes		
(1982) Falloon et al	weekly for 3 mos. bi-weekly for 6 mos. Monthly thereafter. 40 sessions over 2 yrs.		Home for 1st 9 mos.	1 family	yes	4–8 weeks after discharge	Therapist goes to the home

tion and problem-solving training in social skills carried out in a family context, to the Anderson, Hogarty, and Reiss model, which draws loosely from structural family therapy concepts to emphasize the importance of encouraging boundary and inter-generational differentiation. Despite these quite different orientations, most extended intervention programs emphasize highly structured, low-key family sessions initiated as soon as the acute phase of the illness has been controlled. Most therapies reinforce family boundaries and encourage the gradual (but not premature) resumption of responsibility by the patient. Both the Anderson and Falloon programs involve the use of some form of "homework" through which family members are encouraged to support the gradual assumption of social role functioning by the patient. Despite notable differences in specific theoretical orientation, both the Falloon and Anderson approaches operate broadly within what has been termed the family systems model, as they emphasize the need for reciprocal changes in behavior by all family members participating in the program.

One thing that characterizes all extended family programs for schizophrenia is the critical importance of the therapist controlling the affective intensity of the sessions. The expression of affect, particularly negative affect of the high EE type, which may be valued in some therapeutic contexts, is actively discouraged and/or interrupted by the therapist. The vulnerability of schizophrenic patients to affective and critical messages demands this stance. In addition, such incidents provide the therapist with an opportunity to model more appropriate ways of handling intrafamilial conflict.

Impact of Extended Family Education Programs

As indicated previously, the controlled trials involving extended family intervention programs have evaluated the combined impact of a brief family education module and the extended intervention. No evaluations of extended family intervention programs have been carried out with programs that begin directly to modify family behavior. Despite this caveat, the results of these controlled trials are very impressive in terms of relapse reduction.

Figure 10-1 presents the relapse rates from the three controlled trials, one with a six and the others at nine month follow-up. Although no final report has appeared as yet from the Anderson-Hogarty trial,

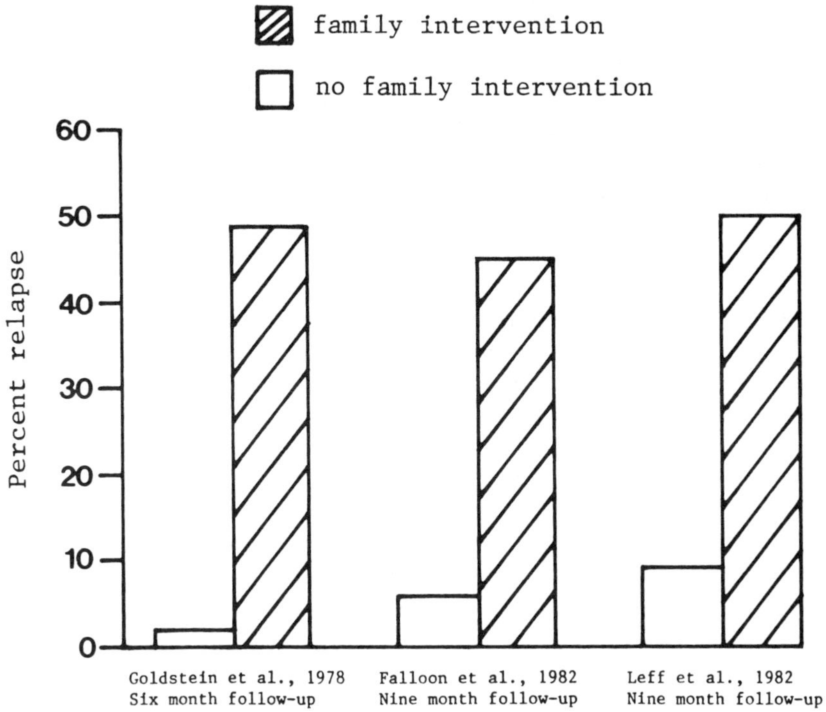

Fig. 10-1. Relapse rates from three studies contrasting a family intervention program with the absence of such a program (all schizophrenic patients on continuous medication)

preliminary reports (Anderson et al., 1981) indicate a similarly low rate of relapse (10 percent) in their family therapy condition, with this figure attenuated even further when family therapy and individual social skills training for the patient were combined. The relapse rate of 34 percent in their medication-only control, while significantly higher than when family therapy was combined with medication, is considerably lower than the figure reported in other studies for a comparable condition.

Overall, the pattern is very dramatic as four out of four studies report that some form of extended family intervention overlaid on a program of regular pharmacotherapy can make a substantial contribution to the reduction of relapse in recently discharged schizophrenic patients, even with those who have been chronically ill for a number of years. Longer term follow-ups are needed to establish the durability of these changes as well as whether such programs impact upon social role functioning as well.

SOME UNRESOLVED ISSUES

It seems quite clear that some form of family intervention is a very effective part of a comprehensive aftercare program. Given that the programs evaluated so far in controlled clinical trials very widely in their format, however, it is hard to know what aspects of the family intervention are significantly related to relapse prevention. The Leff et al. program did not involve the patient at all, and while some family sessions were held, they relied primarily on relatives' groups to reduce contact and the likelihood of high EE behaviors at home. The other programs discussed do involve the patient and operate within the traditional mode of individual family sessions. Yet, evidence to date suggests comparable rates of relapse for all studies. This raises the question of whether these diverse family intervention programs offer a highly organized program of family support or whether, in contrast, they offer specific interventions beyond family system support. Further research is needed concerning the impact of these diverse models of family intervention in order to evaluate the specificity of their mode of action. Only one study so far has addressed this issue, as the Leff et al. study repeated the Camberwell Family Interview (the instrument used to assess expressed emotion) before and after therapy for experimental and control subjects. Their family intervention program was found to reduce high EE attitudes in most cases as compared to controls; and, where attitude change had occurred, relapse was unlikely.

While there are no sharp differences to date in relapse rates, variations in family intervention programs may relate to the longer term criteria of improvements in social role functioning in the patient. Obviously, reducing the likelihood of relapse is a critical goal but given the notoriously poor results to date in the rehabilitation of schizophrenic patients, evidence that any particular type of family intervention leads to improvement in social role performance would be very significant. Both the Falloon et al. and Anderson-Hogarty programs have longer term (two years) follow-ups built into them and, hopefully, can provide data on these important issues.

Another issue that has not been addressed in recent controlled trials involving family and drug therapy has to do with possible interactions between drug dose level and family intervention. Only the earlier study by the author (Goldstein et al., 1978) investigated this issue and found superior results when family therapy cases were maintained on the higher drug dose for the six week controlled trial. This, however, is a very brief period of both drug and family therapy and more recent programs extend for a much longer period. Therefore, we still do not know whether an effective program of family intervention permits a reduction in drug dosage level, if not initially, at least at some point during the first year of aftercare treatment. Also, it would be valuable to investigate whether an effective program of family intervention can facilitate the use of a "targeted" medication program in which patients are maintained at minimal or no drug status until prodromal signs of the disorder are evident, at which time therapeutic drug levels are utilized. Given the noxious side effects of phenothiazine drugs and the risk of tardive dyskinesia, any evidence that a systematic and organized family intervention program can permit a reduction in drug dose levels would be very significant.

The emphasis of this chapter has been on family intervention programs organized and implemented by mental health workers. It is important to recognize that many programs for families are being developed by consumer groups that are designed to provide information and support to both relatives and patients. These programs represent very important efforts and there is some evidence (Anderson et al. 1980) that participation in a family therapy program can facilitate the formation of and participation of relatives in these groups.

REFERENCES

Anderson CM. Psychoeducational family therapy. In Goldstein, M (Ed.), *Preventive intervention programs for family units with a mentally ill relative: Proceedings of a research planning workshop,* Manuscript submitted for publication, 1982

Anderson C, Hogarty G, & Reiss D. Family treatment of adult schizophrenic patients: A psychoeducational approach. *Schizophrenia Bulletin.* 1980, *6,* 490–505

Anderson CM, Hogarty G, & Reiss DJ. The psychoeducational family treatment of schizophrenia. In Goldstein, MJ (Ed.), *New developments in interventions with families of schizophrenics.* San Francisco: Jossey-Bass, 1981

Andolfi M, Menghi P, Nicolo AM, & Saccu C. Interaction in rigid systems: A model of intervention in families with a schizophrenic member. In Andolf, M & Zwerling, I (Eds.), *Dimensions of family therapy.* New York: Guilford Press, 1980

Beels C. Family and social management of schizophrenia. Schizophrenia Bulletin, 1975 *13,* 97–118

Berkowitz R, Kuipers L, Eberlin-Fries R, & Leff J. Lowering expressed emotion in relatives of schizophrenic patients. In MJ Goldstein (Ed.), *New developments in interventions with families of schizophrenics.* San Francisco: Jossey-Bass, 1981.

Brown GW. Experiences of discharged chronic schizophrenic mental hospital patients in various types of living groups. *Millbank Memorial Fund Quarterly,* 1959, *37,* 105–131

Brown GW, Birley JLT, & Wing JF. Influences of family life on the course of schizophrenic disorders: A replication. *British Journal of Psychiatry,* 1972, *121,* 241–258

Cozolino LJ, & Nuechterlein, K. Family education as a component of extended family-oriented treatment programs for schizophrenia. In Goldstein, MJ (Ed.), *Preventive intervention programs for family units with a mentally ill relative: Proceedings of a research planning workshop.* Manuscript submitted for publication, 1982

Falloon IRH, Boyd JL, McGill CW, Razani J, Moss HB, Gilderman, AM. Family management in the prevention of exacerbations of schizophrenia: A controlled study. *New England Journal of Medicine,* 1982, *306,* 1437–1440

Falloon IRH, Boyd JL, McGill CW, Strang JS, & Moss HB. Family management training in the community care of schizophrenia. In Goldstein, MJ (Ed.), *New developments in interventions with families of schizophrenics.* San Francisco: Jossey-Bass, 1981

Goldstein MJ (Ed.), *New developments in interventions with families of schizophrenics.* San Francisco: Jossey-Bass, 1981

Goldstein MJ (Ed.), *Prevention intervention programs for family units with a mentally ill relative: Proceedings of a research planning workshop.* Manuscript submitted for publication, 1982

Goldstein MJ, Rodnick EH, Evans JR, Phillip RAM, & Steinberg M. Drug and family therapy in the aftercare of acute schizophrenics. *Archives of General Psychiatry,* 1978, *35,* 1169–1177

Hawk D. Community care: An analysis of assumptions. *British Journal of Psychiatry,* 1975, *127,* 276–283

King CE, & Goldstein MJ. Therapist ratings of achievement of objectives in psychotherapy with acute schizophrenics. *Schizophrenia Bulletin,* 1979, *5,* 118–129

Kopeikin HS, Marshall V, & Goldstein MJ. Stages and impact of crisis-oriented family therapy in the aftercare of acute schizophrenia. In McFarlane, WR (Ed.), *Family therapy in schizophrenia.* New York: Guilford Press, 1983

Leff J, Kuipers L, Berkowitz R, Eberlein-Vries R, & Sturgeon D. A controlled trial of social intervention in the families of schizophrenia patients. *British Journal of Psychiatry,* 1982, *141,* 121–134

Minuchin S. *Families and Family Therapy.* Cambridge: Harvard University Press, 1974

Overall JE, & Gorham DR. The Brief Psychiatric Rating Scale. *Psychological Reports,* 1962, *10,* 799–812

Selvini Palazzoli M, Boscolo L, Cecchin G, & Prata G. *Paradox and counter-paradox.* New York: Janson Aronson, 1978

Snyder KS, & Liberman RP. Family assessment and intervention with schizophrenics at risk for relapse. In MJ Goldstein (Ed.), *New developments in interventions with families of schizophrenics.* San Francisco: Jossey-Bass, 1981

Vaughn CE, & Leff JP. The influences of family and social factors on the course of psychiatric illness: A comparison of schizophrenic and depressed neurotic patients. *British Journal of Psychiatry,* 1976, *129,* 125–137(a)

Vaughn C, & Leff JP. The measurement of expressed emotion in the families of psychiatricpatients. *British Journal of Social Clinical Psychology, 1976, 15,* 157–165(b)
Wynne LC. Working with families of acute psychotics: Problems for research and reconsideration. In MJ Goldstein (Ed.), *Preventive intervention programs for family units with a mentally ill relative: Proceedings of a research planning workshop.* Manuscript submitted for publication, 1982

Beverly Gomes-Schwartz

11

Individual Psychotherapy of Schizophrenia

Freud (1914) originally proposed that the schizophrenic's withdrawal from the external world and inability to sustain intimate relationships prohibited effective engagement in psychoanalysis. Nonetheless, therapists from a number of analytically-oriented perspectives, including Adlerian (Adler, 1971), Jungian (Perry, 1961), and Sullivanian (Sullivan, 1962), attempted to formulate techniques for individual psychotherapy with schizophrenic patients. Theoretical issues related to etiology and technique, and efficacy of approaches to treatment based upon several psychoanalytic theories will be reviewed in this chapter.

The primary etiological concepts can be categorized as: (1) deficit theories, which posit a basic flaw in the development of the patient's psychological processes; (2) defense or conflict theories, which conceive of schizophrenic symptoms as a defense against intolerable affects; and (3) interactional theories, which emphasize the complex interactions between possible biological predisposition and experiences with the environment (e.g. Gunderson, 1979). These theories play an important role in determining the stance that a therapist is expected to assume, the technical operations of treatment, and the implicit and explicit goals of therapy.

Deficit theories suggest that the schizophrenic does not possess the capacity to make use of early nurturing relationships to develop a stable sense of self (Arieti, 1971). This failure may be due to some organic or genetic predisposition that interfers with perception, learn-

SCHIZOPHRENIA
ISBN 0-8089-1640-8

ing, or cognitive processing (Wexler, 1971), or may arise from massive trauma in the child's early relationships with parenting figures (Grotstein, 1975). Whatever the cause, the child does not develop the capacity to adequately distinguish fantasy (internal experience) from reality (the external world). He or she is unable to make use of repressive mechanisms to protect himself or herself from the intrustion of primitive, chaotic thought processes (Hartmann, 1953).

Some theorists conclude that the magnitude of the impairment in the schizophrenic's capacity for rational thought precludes conventional interpretive treatment (Wexler, 1971; Freeman, 1959). The type of regression encouraged in neurotic patients (i.e., developing conscious awareness of primitive thoughts and impulses) is seen as potentially destructive (Federn, 1952).

Defense theorists, in contrast, suggest that schizophrenia differs from neurosis in quantity rather than in quality (Arlow & Brenner, 1964; Boyer, 1971; Giovacchini, 1969). Psychotic symptoms develop as a defense against intolerable affects. The psychic distress may arise because of maternal rejection or infantile emotional deprivation (Fromm-Reichmann, 1959; Sechehaye, 1951). Interpersonal demands during the adolescent passage into adulthood may evoke decompensation in patients with such a history of relationship problems (Sullivan, 1962).

Some theorists postulate that the primary affect, which is intolerable for the schizophrenic, is anger (Arlow & Brenner, 1964) or, more specifically, anger directed toward the mother (Rosenfeld, 1966, Segal, 1950). Sullivan (1962) suggests that the adolescent schizophrenic is defending against sexual impulses. Others suggest that the schizophrenic is defending against the anxiety evoked by the prospect of loss of a significant person from his life (Searles, 1965).

Some defense theorists (e.g., Boyer, 1971) suggest that schizophrenic patients who are able to function on an outpatient basis can be treated with classical analytic techniques (e.g., use of the couch, free association). However, most of those who subscribe to the theory that schizophrenic symptoms are on a continuum with neurotic conflicts believe that analytic techniques must be adapted to be responsive to the fragility of the schizophrenic's psychic structure (e.g., Fromm-Reichmann, 1959; Searles, 1965).

Attempts to reconcile deficit and defense theories of schizophrenia have yielded explanations for the schizophrenic conditions that are applicable whether the primary problem is seen as an organic defect or as a failure in psychological development. A number of theorists believe that the principal issue for schizophrenics is achieving individuation (Jacobson, 1967; Schulz, 1975; Stierlin, 1975). Either because of the inability of the mother to foster the process of separation or because of some defect in the child's psychic apparatus, he or she is not able to negotiate this process of developing a stable sense of self as separate from the mother. Wynne (1970) sees the core issue in schizophrenia as failure in the interaction between mother and child, which interferes with the child's capacity to use language. This failure may occur because of some genetically determined inability in the child to focus attention or because of the mother's inability to teach. Other interaction theories see the schizophrenic condition as an outgrowth of a complex interaction of hereditary predisposition, early nurturing experiences, and later interpersonal difficulties (Grinker, 1973; Holzman, 1975).

Notions of the ideal therapeutic stance are related to controversies about the nature of schizophrenia. Deficit theorists are most likely to suggest that the therapist function as an auxiliary "ego," firmly and reliably providing the schizophrenic with external structuring to take the place of the internal cognitive structure he or she lacks (Wexler, 1952). This is in direct contrast to the thinking of some therapists who see early emotional deprivation as the cause of schizophrenia. They suggest that the schizophrenic patient, who has retreated from contact with reality because of the traumas of early existence, can be retrieved by entering into his or her psychotic world and offering him or her the love that he never received as an infant.

For example, Sechehaye (1951) treated a severely regressed young woman be determining the infantile needs symbolized in her psychotic thoughts and behaviors and participating in the symbolic gratification of those needs. By meeting primitive desires that the patient was incapable of coherently articulating, the therapist suggested she offered the maternal love necessary for emotional development. In contrast to Sechehaye's prolonged remothering process, Rosen (1953, 1947) attempted to rapidly draw acutely disturbed schizophrenics from their autistic worlds by assuming the role of an omnipotent protector, then unrelentingly interpreting their psychotic communications. Other approaches, emphasizing restitution for maternal failings, entailed symbolic gratifications of primitive wishes (e.g., spoon feeding, Eissler [1952]; providing patients with food and "toys," Azima, Wittkower, & LaTendresse [1958]).

Sullivan (1956, 1962) and those therapists who drew inspiration from his theoretical formulations (Arieti, 1955, 1959; Fromm-Reichmann, 1952, 1959; Searles, 1965), essentially disagreed with the concept of supplying motherly love and treating the patient as a child. They asserted that excessive sympathy or parental over-solicitousness evoked anxiety and resentment in schizophrenic patients because these patients suffer from intense conflicts between their desires for closeness and emotional dependence and their fears of rejection. Although the patient may respond to the therapist as if he were the fearsome parent, the therapist does not attempt to gratify the patient's emotional needs through benevolent parent support (Searles, 1961). Instead the therapist is expected to function as a dependable, trustworthy collaborator in the therapy (Will, 1968).

Other major controversies among schools of therapy focus on the goals of treatment and the approaches that are necessary to achieve those goals. Some therapists emphasize the importance of insight. This insight might involve patients' awareness of the genesis of their psychosis (Fromm-Reichmann, 1959; Schulz, 1975; Semrad, 1969; Whitehorn, 1944) or it might focus upon realization of undesirable patterns of behavior (Spotnitz, 1969; Stanton, 1978). The primary route to self-awareness involves interpretation. There is considerable dispute, however, about the appropriate focus of that interpretation. Rosen (1947, 1953) advocated interpretation of the infantile sexual impulses implicit in the patient's psychotic communications. In contrast, Fromm-Reichmann (1952) emphasized interpretation of the patient's interpersonal behavior rather than the content of his or her communications. Some therapists emphasize the need to bring aggressive wishes into consciousness (Boyer, 1971) while others focus upon the importance of gaining awareness of the pain evoked by loss of a significant relationship (Searles, 1965).

Some therapists suggest that a primary goal of therapy is to provide the patient with a new, restitutive relationship that will permit him or her to identify with the healthy aspects of the therapist's personality and to learn to accept intimacy and mutual dependency without overwhelming anxiety (Greenson & Wexler, 1969). Grotstein (1975), however, argues that the schizophrenic does not necessarily lack any positive figures in his life; rather, it is that he is unable to make use of these relationships. Thus, it is unlikely that a therapist who is simply being trustworthy and reliable will produce change.

There seems to be general agreement among therapists on one point. Psychotherapy with schizophrenic patients is seen as a long-term endeavor that requires from a therapist exquisite patience and freedom from the need to prove oneself by effecting change (Benedetti, 1955). Spotnitz (1969) suggests that a schizophrenic must be in treatment a minimum of two years before changes are likely to occur. Rubins (1976) has demonstrated that maximal changes in schizophrenic patients occur 2.5 years into treatment. Other case studies report treatment durations of many years before patients regain some degree of independent functioning (e.g., Burnham, 1961; Schulz & Kilgalen, 1969; Will, 1961).

THE EFFICACY OF TREATMENT

Case Reports

Despite the extensive theoretical and clinical literature on psychodynamic therapy with schizophrenics, there have been few attempts to systematically demonstrate the extent of changes in patients treated with these techniques. Some therapists have attempted to collect summary data on groups of patients they have treated. The case histories they present richly describe nuances of the psychotherapeutic interaction. However, such material also contains striking deficiencies. Therapists' subjective evaluations of their own patients are seriously prone to bias. Furthermore, it is impossible to determine what portion of the observed change was due to the therapeutic intervention as opposed to a host of unmeasured factors (e.g., the passage of time or environmental changes), or indeed whether any appreciable changes really occurred. The results reported by highly experienced therapists of schizophrenics are applicable to clinical practice only insofar as the skills and motivation of the "gifted" therapist can be duplicated.

Given these limitations it is nonetheless instructive to examine the results reported by experts in the treatment of schizophrenia. It is noteworthy that even the most illustrious therapists report modest success rates. For example, Sullivan (1962) reported that of the 100 schizophrenic patients he treated at Sheppard and Enoch Pratt Hospital, 32 percent of those with insidious onset and 61 percent of those with acute onset evidenced improvement. During 14 years on the staff of Chestnut Lodge, a private psychiatric hospital at which both Sullivan and Fromm-Reichmann had practiced, Searles (1965) treated 18 chronic schizophrenic patients with intensive psychotherapy. After treatment periods varying from 3 months to 14 years, 13 patients showed "remarkable" improvement. Only six were able to function outside the hospital, however.

In a report of the results of outpatient treatment for acute-onset schizophrenics, Rubins (1976) described the outcomes of 42 patients who had received therapy based on Karen Horney's theories (Rubins, 1972) for 6 months to 4½ years. Evaluations by clinicians involved in the treatment indicated that between 58 and 88 percent of the patients showed at least moderate improvement on the criteria for change. It is important to note, however, that the sample was a rather select group of the best prognosis patients (e.g., high motivation for treatment, no evidence of chronicity) and the individual psychotherapy took place in the context of a comprehensive day hospital program.

The shortcomings of case reports as evidence for the efficacy of psychotherapy are highlighted by the controversy surrounding the treatment successes Rosen (1947, 1953) reported. Remarkable "cures" in 37 of approximately 100 patients were described. Patients who had spent as long as 11 years in psychiatric hospitals recovered after less than 1 year of intensive treatment. In a follow-up evaluation of 19 of the 37 patients deemed "cured," however, Horowitz, Polatin, Kolb, and Hoch (1958) determined that Rosen's achievements may have been less dramatic than he originally suggested. They indicated that seven patients who had been most successfully reintegrated into the community had originally been incorrectly diagnosed as schizophrenic. Of the 12 genuinely schizophrenic patients, 9 had been readmitted to the hospital 2–5 times in a 10 year period. Although two of the patients had made fairly adequate adjustments, they had not met Rosen's (1947) own stringent criteria for recovery—sufficient emotional stability "to withstand at least as much environmental assault as is expected of a normal person (p. 5)."

Controlled Research

Systematic comparisons of the effects of individual therapy with those of other treatment modalities (e.g., psychotropic medication, milieu treatment) have seldom been attempted. Certainly there are numerous difficulties inherent in the study of individual psychotherapy. A full course of treatment in a private psychiatric hospital often requires several years of intensive therapy with a highly skilled therapist (Schulz & Kilgalen, 1969). Thus, conducting even a small scale study calls for enormous investments of time and money. Even when researchers are prepared to make the necessary commitments, methodological considerations pose almost insurmountable obstacles to the conduct of controlled outcome studies. Investigators should insure that subjects in each treatment group are comparable, that treatments are not contaminated by uncontrolled variables—differences in drug usage or in treatment settings—and that the processes labeled *psychotherapy* are not practitioner-specific. The longer the treatment takes the more impractical it becomes to insure that extraneous factors have not confounded treatment. Thus, most of the controlled studies of psychotherapy with schizophrenics do not test the efficacy of ideal treatment. Instead the principles of treatment have been adapted to meet the exigencies of a managable research design.

Brief or Limited Contact Therapy Approaches

Several groups of investigators have attempted to assess the efficacy of therapy approaches that include short treatment durations, infrequent or very brief sessions (i.e., less than four hours per month), or both factors. Since these treatment techniques are so different from the usual psychodynamic psychotherapy described in the clinical literature, questions about the applicability of the findings are raised. Nonetheless the findings may have some relevance for determining the value of a very limited dyadic relationship in the context of treatment programs for schizophrenia.

Inpatient Treatment

Three studies have assessed the effects of very brief treatment on hospitalized schizophrenic patients. Walker and Kelley (1960) determined that 44 recently hospitalized schizophrenic patients treated with short-term (5–43 hours) psychotherapy either individually or in groups did not significantly differ from 38 control patients, who had not received therapy, as measured by nurses', ward administrators', and psychiatrists' ratings of symptomatology and overall community adjustment 90 days after discharge. No differences were observed between patients who received individual versus group treatment or between those who received relatively more versus relatively fewer hours of therapy. Indeed, psychotherapy patients were less likely to be discharged from the hospital during the study than were controls. This finding is particularly striking since therapy patients were initially more cooperative and less withdrawn than controls. In a follow-up three years after therapy, Walker and Kelley (1963) found no differences between experimental and control patients in discharge or readmission rates, time spent in the community, freedom from symptoms, or frequency of employment. The validity of the findings is qualified, however, by other deficiencies in the study in addition to the brevity of treatment. Biases in therapists' personal selection of patients for treatment and differing criteria for discharge for therapy and control patients may have influenced results.

Zirkle (1961) designed an examination of short-term psychotherapy in which 30 chronic schizophrenic patients (average hospitalization = 18 years) were assigned to 1 of 3 groups—2 months of individual therapy for 5 minutes a day, 5 times a week; one 25 minute session of weekly therapy for 2 months; or no therapy. Ratings made by the ward doctor, nursing supervisor, and head attendant of an 11-factor rating scale tended to favor the two therapy groups, particularly the brief, daily contact group, over the control group, but the differences were not significant. Given that the average treatment lasted four hours, the failure to observe emotional changes among such long term patients is completely understandable.

In a study of the effects of psychotherapy and drugs upon young adults (17–35 years old) newly admitted for acute schizophrenic reactions (Grinspoon, Ewalt, & Shader 1972; Shader, Grinspoon, & Ewalt, 1969), 41 patients were randomly assigned to one of three groups: psychotherapy with either halperidol, thioridazine, or placebo medication. After eight weeks of psychotherapy (conducted by supervised first-year psychiatric residents) and medication, patients who received thioridazine with their psychotherapy showed consistently greater improvements than those who had received halperidol or placebo capsules, according to ratings of hospital adjustment, behavioral disturbance, quantified mental status, and overall manifest psychopathology. Examination of the specific patterns of change associated with each treatment program revealed that psychotherapy without concurrent medication produced greater change in anxious intropunitiveness than therapy with either drug and greater improvements in overtly disturbed behavior than therapy plus halperidol. Nonetheless, the thioridazine plus therapy group showed the greatest behavioral change on several dimensions.

Although the investigators have demonstrated the value of combining psychotherapy and drugs in treating schizophrenia, the study is not an adequate exploration of the unique effects of psychotherapy. No attempt was made to compare psychotherapy in the absence of medication with medication per se. More importantly, the expectation that novice psychotherapists employing psychoanalytic principles could produce observable changes in only eight weeks is inconsistent with the clinical literature on the minimal conditions for effective psychotherapy of schizophrenics.

The findings from these studies suggest that a little bit of psychotherapy with a hospitalized schizophrenic may not be much better than none at all. The Grinspoon et al. (1972) findings suggest that specific psychoactive drugs may enhance the effects of such brief therapy; however, their design leaves unanswered the question of whether the observed treatment effects were due to medication or psychological intervention.

Therapy as Aftercare

A number of investigators have examined the utility of individual therapeutic contacts as an aspect of aftercare for schizophrenic patients who have been discharged from hospitals. For the most part, the therapy they are examining is not geared toward insight or substantial character change. Instead the thrust of treatment is providing sufficient support, encouragement, and concrete instruction to assist the patient in negotiating some of the demands of daily life outside the hospital.

Four studies compared the relative merits of individual versus group sessions in aftercare programs. Levene, Patterson, Murphey, Overbeck, and Veach (1970) defined individual treatment as a 15–30 minute monthly session to review the patient's status, and they defined group treatment as a 1 hour monthly meeting. After one year in these aftercare programs there were no differences between individual and group patients in social adjustment or rehospitalization rates. Forty-two percent of the patients required rehospitalization. Herz, Spitzer, Gibbon, Greenspan, and Reibel (1974) obtained very similar results in a study of after care services provided by first year psychiatric residents to a group of patients, 66 percent of whom were schizophrenic. In a contrast of the effects of a weekly 1½ hour group treatment with those of individual supportive sessions averaging 15–60 minutes per month, they found no differences between the treatments after 11 months. Although relatively few of their patients were rehospitalized (15 percent), the investigators indicated that improvements on measures on psychopathology were minimal. Despite the observation that more patients dropped out of group treatment (37 versus 24 percent), they concluded that group aftercare was more desirable.

Two other studies demonstrated a superior effect from group as opposed to individual aftercare. Donlon, Rada, and Knight (1973) found that 12 chronic schizophrenics treated with supportive group therapy for 30 minutes bi-weekly for 18 weeks were more likely to show increases in social interaction and to comply with the treatment program than a similar group of 12 patients who received 10–20 minute, bi-weekly individual interviews with a warm supportive therapist. Interpretation of the data on treatment compliance is complicated by the fact that patients in individual treatment were assigned to a standard clinic appointment block and had to wait as long as 1½ hours before their brief sessions. O'Brien, Hamm, Ray, Pierce, Luborsky, and Mintz (1972) randomly assigned 100 newly discharged schizophrenics to either individual or group therapy. Evaluations at 12 and 24 months showed that patients in group therapy were more likely to show marked improvements in overall psychopathology and social effectiveness. Since more individual therapy patients dropped out of treatment prematurely, it is not possible to determine whether the superiority of group treatment was due to the fact that the average patient received more therapeutic contact or that group techniques are more effective.

As a group, these studies indicate that when treatment resources are limited, group management of discharged schizophrenics may be preferable to brief individual contacts. Perhaps the skills in social interaction that group treatments may reinforce are more important than a single personal relationship in preparing schizophrenics to get along outside the hospital. An important factor in deciding between group and individual treatment may be which treatment is more acceptable to patients. Although the data on which type of treatment resulted in more dropouts are conflicting, it is clear that treatment compliance has an effect upon how successful recently discharged patients will be in staying out of the hospital.

A group of investigators have conducted two studies of the interaction between psychoactive drugs and a type of supportive, social casework. In the first study (Hogarty & Goldberg, 1973; Hogarty, Goldberg, & Schooler, 1974; Hogarty, Goldberg, Schooler, & Ulrigh, 1974), they employed a factorial design crossing chlorpromazine and placebo conditions with therapy and minimal contact to study treatment effects in 374 schizophrenics. After both 1 and 2 years of treatment, which averaged 2.04 sessions per month for the therapy groups and 1.04 sessions per month for the non-therapy groups, the drug but not the therapy condition significantly contributed to a reduction in relapse rates. If patients receiving therapy managed to stay out of the hospital during the first 6 months of aftercare, however, they were less likely than non-therapy patients to relapse at a later point (i.e., 44 percent versus 58 percent relapse rates). Analysis of the degree of psychopathology in nonrelapsed patients indicated a complex interaction of drugs and therapy at the 18 and 24 month evaluation points. Patients who received both medication and social therapy exhibited least pathology, while those receiving therapy in the absence of drugs were even more incapacitated than patients who had received no active treatment.

In a second study comparing longacting intramuscular versus oral fluphenazine and social therapy versus minimal contact, the investigators obtained somewhat similar results (Hogarty, Schooler, Ulrich, Mussare, Ferro, & Herron, 1979). After two years of treatment no main effects of either type of medication or social therapy were found. There was a trend approaching significance, however, which suggested that the combination of long-acting medication and social therapy reduced relapse rates if the patient could be maintained at least eight months without decompensation.

The results of these studies suggest that individual psychosocial interventions with relatively limited objectives and amounts of patient contact may nonetheless enhance the effects of drug treatment in outpatient schizophrenics. An important aspect of the findings is that the effects of this social therapy on relapse rates may not be detectable until patients have been in treatment for more than 7–8 months, and unique effects of therapy on psychopathology in nonrelapsed patients may not be apparent until 18–24 months. This is completely consistent with clinical wisdom and serves to reinforce the impression that small doses of psychotherapy with schizophrenic patients accomplish little.

Client-Centered Therapy

Client-centered psychotherapy was initially designed as a treatment modality for relatively well-functioning neurotic patients. Some Rogerian therapists (e.g., Gendlin, 1962), however, suggested that the principles of treatment could be generalized to work with schizophrenics. It was hypothesized that the conditions necessary for therapeutic movement—therapists' warmth, empathy, and genuineness and clients' willingness to fully experience feelings—were also applicable to schizophrenics with only minor modification. In their study on the relative effectiveness of such client-centered therapy, Rogers, Gendlin, Kiesler, and Truax (1967) compared 14 patients treated for up to 2 years, with 14 control patients who had been matched for sex, age, socioeconomic status, chronicity, and degree of disturbance, and who received standard hospital treatment. No differences between experimental and control patients were observed on a variety of measures of change in psychopathology. Only in a separate analysis of the TAT responses of 12 experimental and 11 control patients did those who had received therapy show greater decreases in emotional distancing, less discussion of authority figures in TAT stories, and greater overall sociability.

Data on the effects of therapists' warmth, empathy, and genuineness and patients' experiencing of affect were generally incompatible with the hypotheses formulated from Rogerian theory. Patients did not increase their levels of self-awareness or "experiencing" during the course of therapy, nor did they exhibit greater awareness than controls, regardless of the quality of the therapist's interactions. Patients' perceptions of the level of therapist-offered "conditions" were sharply divergent, often even the inverse, of therapists' observations of their own behavior. Although there were some suggestions that patients who received high levels of empathy or congruence were likely to improve, while those who received low levels were not, the evidence was not constant across outcome variables.

Several methodological problems make interpretation of the findings rather difficult. Initially the investigators planned to test each patient at three month intervals. When this was not feasible, they resorted to comparisons between "early" and "late" testings, which often could not legitimately be considered as pre- and post- therapy measures. Because of large discrepancies between patients in the number of testings and the amount of time between the pre- and post-measures, individual matches between patients and controls were disrupted. The alternatives for statistical analysis—pairing subjects according to the length of time between evaluations or totally disregarding matching (e.g., on the TAT analysis)—produced results contaminated by individual differences.

Differential administration of psychoactive drugs across treatment conditions introduced an additional confound. Although the researchers attempted to prevent the prescription of medication for therapy patients, some experimental and all control subjects received indeterminate amounts of medication during the study. Thus, it was not possible to evaluate how much of the variation in patients' thinking or behaviors could be attributed to psychotherapy, as opposed to drug effects.

The results of this study suggest that client-centered approaches that focus upon unequivocal acceptance of the patients and development of greater self-awareness in the context of a supportive relationship (Rogers et al., 1967) may not be appropriate for schizophrenics. Patients' frequent refusals to interact with therapists, and the discrepancy between their perceptions of the therapists' warmth, empathy, and genuineness, and his self-evaluations suggest that schizophrenic patients may often be suspicious and resentful of unconditional "niceness." Excerpts from one of Rogers' (1967) own cases indicated the stiltedness that the technique of reflecting feelings could assume. As Rollo May (Rogers et al., 1967) has commented, the client-centered therapist appeared to be reflecting the patient's words rather than his or her feelings and dealing with a limited range of affects excluding strong, negative emotions (e.g., anger, aggression and, hostility).

Psychoanalytically-Oriented Therapy

Only four studies have been completed that have evaluated the merits of psychotherapeutic practices that were reasonably congruent with the principal theories of psychotherapy with schizophrenics. In one study the effects of intensive therapy with chronic schizophrenics was examined. In the remaining three studies, nearly all of the patients were experiencing first psychotic breaks.

Grinspoon, Ewalt, and Shader (1967, 1968, 1972) examined the impact of 20 months of intensive (twice weekly) psychoanalytic therapy by experienced therapists on chronic schizophrenic patients. Two groups of ten male schizophrenics with at least three years of prior hospitalization were transferred to a specially staffed research ward for two years. After 13 weeks, during which all patients received placebo capsules, half were randomly assigned to active drug treatment (thioridazine) for the remainder of the study period, except for a 3 month interval of placebo treatment midway through the second year. The remaining patients received placebo medication throughout the entire experimental period. By rating hospital adjustment and behavioral disturbance on a bi-weekly basis, the investigators hoped to determine whether behavioral changes could be related to alterations in medications (i.e., placebo to drug shifts) and to events in the environment (e.g., therapist's vacation, a family death). Material from each patient's daily diary was used to gauge feelings toward the therapist and responses to external events.

Results from both the first group of patients (Grinspoon et al., 1967) and the total sample (Grinspoon et al., 1968) were similar. Examination of the rating profiles for each patient revealed fairly consistent responses to changes in drug treatment. Patients generally deteriorated during the initial placebo period, improved with the introduction of thioridazine, and became worse during the drug withdrawal interval. Most of the patients who had received psychotherapy without active drug treatment throughout the study showed minimal fluctuations in ward adjustments or disturbed behavior. Analysis of the differences between ratings made in two six-week periods—during a drug phase and during a non-drug phase—indicated that while receiving active medication patients were significantly better adjusted and exhibited less disturbed behavior than while receiving placebos. Patients' diary notations and observations of changes in behavior concurrent with the therapist's vacation indicated that patients did not noticeably react to their therapists' absence or return, which the investigators interpreted as a lack of emotional investment in therapy.

Although the initial research project did not include a control group of patients who received drug treatment without psychotherapy, Messier, Finnerty, Botuin, and Grinspoon (1969) completed a follow-up comparison of the 20 research subjects with 21 patients who had met the criteria for inclusion but had remained in a nearby state hospital, usually because they or their families opposed transfer to the research facility. Analyses of general psychotic characteristics, of employment, recreational and living adjustment, and of readiness for discharge (for those patients who remained hospitalized at the time of follow-up) yielded no significant differences between experimental and control subjects or between drug and placebo groups. Interestingly, the first group of ten research patients, who had completed therapy three years before the follow-up, displayed consistently poorer social adjustment than the second group, who were measured one year after treatment. These results suggest a deterioration of any ameliorative effects of treatment over time.

Several criticisms of the Grinspoon et al. research with chronic patients have been raised. The absence of control patients in the original study really could not be rectified by comparing patients in a specially staffed research unit with those in an essentially custodial institution, particularly when there was an initial bias in assignment of patients to the special facility. Other methodological criticisms have been directed toward the small number of subjects (Hollister, 1967) and the confusion in statistical analyses of intra-patient changes over time with intergroup differences (May, 1967). Cole (1967) has indicated that the ratings of adjustment and disturbance were ambiguous as to the actual level of patient functioning. He asserts that it was not possible to determine from the ratings whether patients were sufficiently adjusted to warrant discharge at the conclusion of the study, or whether they had shown significant improvements from pre- to post-therapy.

Bookhammer, Meyer, Schober, and Piotrowski (1966) sought to determine whether patients treated with Rosen's (1953) technique of "direct analysis" would show more enduring improvements in personality functioning than patients who had been selected for control treatments by sequential assignment or than randomly selected patients who had not been participants in the original study but met the criteria for inclusion—15–35 years old, first admission, and acute onset of psychosis. Five years after the initiation of treatment, direct analysis patients did not differ from either the designated or random control according to the investigators' subjective ratings of improvements in feelings, reasoning, or overt behavior. The alternative treatments that the control patients received, however, were not specified and could have included some psychotherapy. Furthermore, the subjectivity and the susceptibility to bias of ratings made by the researchers themselves from undefined data sources raises serious doubts about the credibility of the findings.

Another study that tested the effects of psychotherapy based upon Rosen's techniques was conducted by Karon and his associates (Karon

& O'Grady, 1969; Karon & VandenBos, 1970, 1972). Although the investigators attempted to limit the patient sample to first admissions with acute onset of symptoms, 12 of the 36 patients had concealed information about previous hospitalizations. Patients were randomly assigned from matched sets to either active psychoanalytic therapy, which included "direct" interpretations, ego-analytic therapy with adjunct phenothiazine treatment, or standard hospital routine including phenothiazines and minimal supportive therapy. Two psychiatrists with at least ten years experience in analytical therapy with schizophrenic patients each treated four patients with their preferred mode of therapy, and supervised five trainees in clinical psychology and psychiatry who treated the remaining eight patients in each group. Therapy was offerred for 20 months, regardless of whether the patient remained in the hospital or was discharged. Control patients who did not show improvement after two weeks of drug treatment were transferred from the research unit to a state hospital.

Evaluation of all patients after 6, 12, and 20 months revealed significantly greater improvements in patients who had received psychotherapy than in controls. At six months (Karon & O'Grady, 1969), patients treated by experienced therapists already showed greater changes, relative to control patients and to patients treated by inexperienced therapists, on measures of intellectual performance and concept formation. By 12 months (Karon & VandenBos, 1970), differential rates of discharge were also apparent. Patients treated by both supervisors exhibited better overall functioning, less thought disorder, and shorter hospitalization than controls. Student therapists were less successful in effecting comprehensive changes. Their patients who received medication and psychotherapy were hospitalized for shorter periods than controls, but did not manifest changes in thought disorder. In addition, only the patients treated with active ("direct" analysis) psychotherapy (either by the supervisor or by students) exhibited better overall functioning than controls according to blind ratings of interview behavior by independent clinicians.

Two years after the program was terminated, patients of both experienced therapists had spent significantly fewer days in the hospital than controls (0–10.8 as opposed to 99.8 days). Although novice therapists using drugs and psychotherapy had been able to reduce initial hospitalization, their patients spent slightly longer periods in the hospital during the follow-up phase than did controls. In contrast, patients treated solely with psychotherapy by inexperienced therapists originally spent more time in the hospital, but were less likely to be readmitted.

Certain critical flaws in the design and implementation of this study influence the validity of the results. Since style of psychotherapy was confounded with use of medication, it is impossible to determine whether differences between patients treated with "direct" analytic therapy and those treated with egoanalytic therapy and drugs were due to drug effects or to the variations in therapy technique. May and Tuma (1970) have argued that the transfer to a state hospital of control patients who did not respond to drug treatment introduced a distinct bias. The message implicit in transfer (that the patient was not improving) may have had a negative impact. In addition, comparisons between experimental and control patients were confounded by differences in staffing and treatment milieu in the two settings.

The most elaborately designed study of psychotherapy with acute schizophrenics contrasts five treatment alternatives (May, 1968; May & Tuma, 1964, 1965). A total of 228 first admission patients, judged by a team of psychiatrists to be in the middle third of the prognostic range (i.e., likely to be discharged after 2 or less years of treatment, but not evidencing rapid spontaneous readmission), were randomly assigned to: (1) milieu treatment, (2) ECT, (3) stelazine alone, (4) "ego-supportive, reality defining" psychotherapy alone, or (5) a combination of stelazine and psychotherapy. All treatments were administered by relatively inexperienced psychiatric residents under the supervisions of senior therapists. Improvement after six months to one year of treatment was measured by discharge data, ratings from nurses, therapists and psychoanalysts uninvolved in treatment, and psychometric data. On a substantial number of these measures patients who had received drugs alone or drugs and psychotherapy manifested the greatest improvements. They had higher release rates than all other patients and displayed less symptomatic behavior than patients in the other treatment groups. In three-way analyses of variance measuring the relative contributions of drugs and psychotherapy, beneficial changes were consistently attributable to drugs rather than to psychotherapy or to interaction effects. On a majority of indices both psychotherapy alone and milieu treatment produced the least beneficial effects.

During a five year follow-up period, the group of patients who received psychotherapy alone showed consistently poorer outcomes than those in other treatment conditions (May, Tuma, & Dixon, 1981; May, Tuma, Yale, Potepan, & Dixon, 1976). They spent more time in the hospital than all the other groups except those who received milieu alone. Even among the patients who had improved sufficiently to be released from the hospital within the first year ("treatment successes"), those who received psychotherapy alone spent the most time in the hospital during the combined treatment and follow-up period and during the follow-up period alone. Comparisons of the five groups on a series of other outcome criteria tapping symptomatology and social functioning yielded essentially consistent findings. Three years after the start of treatment patients receiving only psychotherapy functioned the worst on nearly every criterion, regardless of whether they had initially been positive treatment successes. The positive effects attributable to drug treatment gradually diminished during the follow-up and failed to reach statistical significance after three years.

Although May's (1968) study was quite rigorously designed, a number of criticisms have been raised that challenge the validity of the findings. The strongest criticisms have been leveled against the quality of the psychotherapy offered by the novice psychiatrists (Hamilton, 1969; Michels, 1969; Rosen, 1969). Although their supervisors may have been experts, many of the therapists who actually administered treatment had almost no training in psychotherapy. Moreover, there was no evidence that most of the therapists were particularly motivated to engage in psychotherapy with schizophrenic patients. Since the importance of the therapist's interpersonal skills is a recurrent theme in the theoretical literature, the absence of positive change could be attributed to therapists' inadequacies.

In addition, it is unlikely tht there was marked consistency among the 41 therapists in their choice of therapeutic techniques. As Dyrud and Holzman (1973) have suggested, psychotherapy cannot be reduced to a set of quantifiable operations; procedures are largely subject to personal preferences and biases. Thus, the process that May (1968) terms "psychotherapy" very probably included a wide variety of differing human interactions—some with positive, others with negative effects (Ostow, 1969).

The differences between the May findings and those of Karon have generated considerable debate with each investigator resoundingly criticizing the other's work (Karon & VandenBos, 1975; May & Tuma, 1970). It may be possible to partially reconcile the results, however. When the inexperienced therapists from the Karon study are compared with those from the May study it is clear that neither group was successful in effecting substantial improvements in 6–12 months. It was only with continued effort and increased treatment that Karon's student therapists were able to achieve positive results. The suggestions that positive effects from psychotherapy do not appear in a few months is consistent with the Hoagarty et al. findings (1974, 1979) and clinical judgment.

An additional study contrasting the effects of intensive psychoanalytic therapy with supportive patients-management is currently being conducted at McLean Hospital and Boston University Medical Center (NIMH Grant #25246, J Gunderson, A Stanton, and P Knapp, Principal Investigators). This study was designed to meet some of the criticisms of the prior research. All therapists were highly experienced, treatment duration was designed to be two or more years, and all patients received psychoactive drugs. Although major results from the study are not yet available, preliminary data describing a new outcome measure suggest that some effects of intensive psychotherapy may be measurable. Gunderson and Gomes-Schwartz (1980) found that differences between intensive and non-intensive treatment groups could be discerned on interview measures of awareness of the genesis of one's psychosis and affective flexibility, and that the magnitude of the differences increased with longer treatment. Although the study is limited by a small sample and non-random assignment of patients in the longest-term treatment, the findings are provocative.

In summary, the results of the major studies of psychoanalytically-oriented therapy are sobering. There is very little to indicate that the average schizophrenic accomplishes a great deal in much of the psychotherapy that is currently practiced. Gunderson (1979) has observed that when the Grinspoon (1968) study was initiated it was considered unethical not to include psychotherapy in a treatment program. Since that time the tide of opinion has changed. It is currently considered unethical to offer psychotherapy without drug treatment. Before dismissing psychotherapy with schizophrenics as generally useless, however, it is important to attempt to determine whether there are specific characteristics in some patients and in some therapists that dramatically increase the chances of success. As May (1968) has indicated, it may be financially wasteful to routinely offer psychotherapy, as it is practiced by the average psychiatric resident, to schizophrenic patients. Conversely, settling for the marginal level of functioning outside the hospital that can be produced with routine drug treatment may be depriving some patients of the potential for deeper personality changes.

PREDICTING SUCCESS IN PSYCHOTHERAPY

The primary conclusion from the major controlled studies of psychotherapy with schizophrenics has been that on average individual treatment does not play an important role in reducing symptoms, decreasing hospitalization, or enhancing community adjustment. How are these results to be reconciled with numerous case reports detailing major psychological and social rehabilitation in schizophrenic patients? Some have suggested that some patients who demonstrate such remarkable recovery actually may not have been schizophrenics (Horowitz et al., 1958; North & Cadoret, 1981). Indeed, there is considerable controversy over whether the majority of "good prognosis" schizophrenics are more appropriately diagnosed as affective disorders (Pope & Lipinski, 1978).

A less negative interpretation of the successes reported by renowned therapists is that some unique interaction of qualities in the particular therapist and the particular patients optimized the prospects of positive outcome (Fromm-Reichmann, 1952; Strupp & Bergin, 1969). If this is the case, clinical and research attention should be directed toward measurement of the personal qualities in the therapist and the schizophrenic patient that may predict therapy outcome. Thus far, only a few theoreticians and researchers have considered these issues.

Therapist Characteristics

There is considerable diversity of opinion about the therapist qualities that are most likely to lead to positive outcome with schizophrenics. Debate wages over how much tolerance of regressed behavior is therapeutic (Foster, 1975; Meltzer, 1975) or over how much the therapist should gratify the patient's primitive wishes (Fromm-Reichmann, 1959; Rosen, 1953). There are, however, certain themes that reappear in numerous theoretical discussions. The good therapist emerges as an ideally sensitive, tolerant individual who possesses a zeal for working with schizophrenics that is not extinguished by the inevitable feelings of frustration, despair, and helplessness that arise during the course of treatment (Brody, 1952; Friedman, Gunderson, & Feinsilver, 1973). This therapist possesses a unique capacity to empathize or identify with the overwhelming feelings the schizophrenic patient experiences (Searles, 1965; Stone, 1971; Will, 1980). Therapist qualities that have been identified as undesirable include anxiety in the face of the patient's tumultuous affects (Benedetti, 1955; Brody, 1952; Fromm-Reichmann, 1952; Semrad, Menzer, Mann, & Standish, 1952). Also, therapists who tend to seek power in relationships or experience a reformer's zeal are unlikely to be successful with schizophrenics (Benedetti, 1955; Sullivan, 1962).

Unfortunately, few empirical investigations of therapist characteristics have specifically addressed the dimensions mentioned in the clinical literature. One major line of inquiry grew from the Whitehorn and Betz (1954) efforts to retrospectively identify the personal qualities in a group of 14 psychiatric residents, which discriminated those who were especially successful in therapy with schizophrenics (i.e., improvement rates in their patients averaged 75 percent) from those who were consistently less helpful (an average of 27 percent of their patients improved). They indicated that the more successful *A* therapist's were characterized by the ability to gain the confidence of their patients, by their understanding of the motivations and meanings of patients' behavior, and by active personal involvement with their cases. In treatment, they focused upon developing a trusting relationship and demonstrating to the patient his own capabilities for conflict resolution. The less successful *B* therapists differed in their treatment goals and styles of interaction. They emphasized developing conscious awareness of psychopathology through interpretation and modifying symptomatic behavior through direct instruction.

In an attempt to retrospectively identify *A* and *B* therapists, Whitehorn and Betz (1960) discovered that the groups differed in their responses to the Strong Vocational Interest Blank (SVIB). Thus, the groundwork was laid for an extensive research literature in which therapists were dichotomized into *A*'s and *B*'s on the basis of several scales derived from the SVIB, and their therapy outcomes were compared (see reviews by Heaton, Carr, & Hampson, 1975; May, 1974; Razin, 1971).

Perhaps because of the major conceptual differences between the personal qualities Whitehorn and Betz (1954) initially described and the variables measured by the SVIB (Carson, 1967), the literature on *A-B* distinctions has yielded conflicting results. The disparity among the findings is illustrated by analysis of the *A-B* dimension in two of the major controlled outcome studies. Shader, Grinspoon, Harmatz, and Ewalt (1971) found some evidence of an interaction between therapist type and use of psychoactive medication. *A* therapists were more successful than *B*'s only with patients who received medication. In contrast, Tuma, May, Yale, and Forsythe (1978) found no effects of *A-B* status in patients treated with either psychotherapy alone, medication alone, or the combination of both. They did find, however, that differences in outcome among patients in the drug and psychotherapy with drug groups were related to variability among therapists, suggesting that some as yet unmeasured therapist characteristic does influence outcome.

Given the ambiguity about what qualities the *A-B* dimension is tapping and the failure to find consistent effects of *A-B* status upon process of outcome of psychotherapy, it appears that further research on the *A-B* dimension is contraindicated. As Chartier (1971) has observed, a very interesting clinical phenomenon has been befuddled by premature translation into laboratory research.

Similarly, research on the relationship between treatment outcome and therapist variables from client-centered theory has yielded inconsistent results. Truax's (1963) findings that patients who received high levels of warmth, empathy, and genuineness from their therapists manifested greater improvements than those who received low levels of these "therapeutic conditions," is complicated by interactions with characteristics of the patients such as intelligence and by lack of reliability in the ratings. Current evaluation of the research on Rogerian facilitative conditions suggests that the measures of these variables are so fraught with conceptual and methodological problems, that their validity is highly questionable (Gomes-Schwartz, Hadley, & Strupp, 1978).

One intriguing finding that merits further investigation appeared in the Karon and VandenBos (1972) outcome study. They found that therapists who tended to unconsciously use a dependent person to meet their own needs were less successful in psychotherapy with schizophrenics. Findings about this quality, which they labeled pathogenesis, are congruent with clinical thinking about the dangers of a therapist's seeking gratification of wishes for power or esteem from his work with schizophrenics (Sullivan, 1962).

Patient Qualities

A synthesis of the opinions of experienced psychotherapists has yielded a composite description of the characteristics of the schizophrenic patient who is likely to be successful in psychotherapy (Friedman et al., 1973; Gunderson & Hirschfeld, 1975). The variables accorded the most importance by these therapists were suddeness of onset, acute as opposed to chronic course of illness, and clear precipitating stresses prior to the psychotic decompensation. These factors are consistent with the general research literature on prognosis in schizophrenia (see Vaillant, 1962). The therapists' conclusions that history of prior psychotic episodes, failures in prior therapy, and lack of motivation for therapy were largely unimportant, however, deviates from conventional wisdom. The therapists who were surveyed also suggested that a number of psychological strengths—the capacity to reality test, to integrate experiences, to observe oneself, and to express psychic pain—were important in determining therapy outcome.

The validity of some of these dimensions as predictors of outcome has been tested in empirical studies. Several investigtors have assessed the role of patient's psychological strengths. Kiesler (1971) demonstrated that the greater the schizophrenic's capacity to accept his feelings and understand their meaning, the greater the chances of his profiting from therapy. Similarly, McKeever, May, and Tuma (1965) found that among patients who received both psychotherapy and medication, males with greater conceptual ability, clearer thinking, and fewer psychotic symptoms remained in the hospital less time. Interestingly, these findings were not replicated with female patients. Goldberg, Schooler, Hogarty, and Roper, (1977) found that patients with greater disorganization and poorer prior work functioning were unlikely to benefit from supportive therapy. In fact, such patients did more poorly if they received therapy than if they did not. Although these findings were not precisely replicated in a second study (Hogarty et al., 1979), the investigators did find that patients with greater conceptual disorganization were more likely to relapse.

In contrast, Shader et al. (1969) found that acute schizophrenic patients who improved with brief psychotherapy (with or without phenothiazines) showed greater pathology on measures of paranoia, over-activity, and lack of restraint. If one considers the latter symptoms as indicators that these patients might have been included misdiagnosed affective disorders, the disparity between these results and those of other investigators are more understandable.

Not only are psychologically healthier schizophrenic patients more likely to benefit from treatment, they are also more likely to stick with intensive psychotherapy rather than drop out (Gunderson, in press). Given the Hogarty et al. (1974) findings that patients do not begin to show positive effects of psychosocial treatment for at least six months, it is possible that factors that facilitate a patient's engagement in therapy may also increase the likelihood of successful outcome.

From these studies, which employed different therapy approaches and different measures of prognostic variables, convergent results emerge. Although the criteria for greater emotional strengths or lesser gross psychopathology differed in each study, the repeated finding was that "healthier" patients did better in therapy. The presence of interactions with sex of the patients and presence or absence of medication suggests that other dimensions may modify the role of psychological strengths as predictors of outcome. Research that permits a further refinement in description of the patient characteristics that are associated with success in varying types of psychotherapy is now needed.

Patient-Therapist Matching

Data from several studies of schizophrenic patients have indicated some association between patient and therapist variables and improvement in treatment. The effects, however, are neither robust nor consistent. Rather than continuing to search for variables that identify universally successful therapists or inherently responsive schizophrenic patients, perhaps researchers also should consider investigation of the qualities that lead to a good match between patient and therapist. Although the concept that the quality of the therapeutic interaction is determined by a fit between patient and therapist qualities has been emphasized throughout the literature on psychotherapy research (e.g., Parloff, Waskow, & Wolfe, 1978), studies of patient-therapist interaction with schizophrenic patients have been exceedingly rare.

In examining ten cases of schizophrenic patients who had made striking gains in therapy, often after years of unsuccessful treatment with several other therapists, Stone (1971) observed that the successful therapists often felt some personal sense of identification with their patients. Gunderson (1979) has noted that such similarities between the therapist's and the patient's personality may either enhance or undermine treatment, depending upon the therapist's self-knowledge.

Some preliminary empirical work on patient-therapist matching was undertaken by Gunderson and colleagues (Gunderson, 1978; Gunderson, Feinsilver, & Schulz, 1975). They developed a set of hypotheses about productive matches between patient and therapist, which were tested by having therapists and supervisors rate patient and therapist characteristics and therapeutic progress. They found support for a number of their hypotheses: (1) anxious schizophrenic patients work well with stable, composed therapists and poorly with disorganized therapists; (2) aggressive patients work well with therapists who are comfortable passively tolerating aggression or meeting aggression with dominant control; (3) sexualized patients do well with benign "grandfatherly" therapists who can accept their behavior without judgment or titillation; (4) depressed patients do well with therapists who have experienced depression; (5) schizophrenics who manifest a chronic deteriorative course do poorly with optimistic, expansive therapists. The conclusions support the notion that a subtle mix of similarity between patient and therapist and the therapist's capacity to avoid falling into a conventional complementary role (e.g., "cheering" the pessimistic patient) is important. It would be valuable to attempt to replicate these findings with patient-therapist dyads from controlled outcome studies.

CONCLUSIONS

The role of individual psychotherapy in the treatment of schizophrenic is more controversial now then it has ever been. The efficacy of psychoactive drugs in ameliorating schizophrenic symptoms has been repeatedly demonstrated (Appleton & Davis, 1973; Cole & Davis, 1969). In contrast, several investigators have found little measurable benefit from psychotherapy alone or in combination with drugs. At a time of increasing concerns about the cost effectiveness of treatment intervention, indications that the addition of psychotherapy to inpatient treatment may double the costs of care while yielding little tangible benefit (May, 1968) have probably contributed to a decline in routine psychotherapy.

Yet even those investigators whose findings about the effects of psychotherapy with schizophrenics have been the most pessimistic still suggest that psychotherapy may play a role in outpatient treatment of schizophrenics (May, Tuma, & Dixon, 1981). Perhaps this reluctance to completely dismiss psychotherapy grows from a recognition that patients whose symptoms have been reduced through medications often remain seriously impaired. These patients frequently relapse (Hogarty et al., 1979) or function at minimal levels in the community. Gunderson and Mosher (1975) have suggested that the costs incurred by loss of productivity in schizophrenic patients who are unable to maintain wage earner roles far outweigh costs of providing treatment. Thus, there is a pressing need to find some combination of intervention that maximizes psychological and social functioning in schizophrenic patients. The reports of a number of dedicated psychotherapists indicate that the intensive dyadic relationship achieved in effective psychotherapy sometimes can significantly enhance functioning. The task of future research is to establish the special conditions under which psychotherapy has a major impact.

REFERENCES

Adler A. Present-day Alderian psychiatric practice. *Journal of Individual Psychology*, 1971, *27*, 153–159

Appleton WS, & Davis JM. *Practical clinical psychopharmacology*. New York: Medcom Press, 1973

Arieti S. *Interpretation of schizophrenia*. New York: Robert Brunner, 1955

Arieti S. Schizophrenia. *American Journal of Psychiatry*, 1971, *128*, 348–350

Arlow J, & Brenner C. *Psychoanalytic concepts and the structural theory*. New York: International Universities Press, 1964

Azima H, Wittkower ED, & LaTendresse J. Object relations therapy in schizophrenic states. *American Journal of Psychiatry*, 1958, *115*, 60–62

Benedetti G. Possibilities and limitations of psychotherapy in schizophrenia. *Schweizerischen Akademie der Medizinischen Wissenschaften Bulletin*, 1955, *11*, 142–159

Bookhammer RS, Meyer RW, Schober CC, & Piotrowski AZ. A five year follow-up study of schizophrenics treated by Rosen's "direct analysis" compared with controls. *American Journal of Psychiatry*, 1966, *123*, 602–604

Boyer LB. Psychoanalytic technique in the treatment of certain characterological and schizophrenic disorders. *International Journal of Psychoanalysis,* 1971, *52,* 67–85

Brody E. The treatment of schizophrenia: A review. In EB Brody & FC Redlich (Eds.), *Psychotherapy with schizophrenics.* New York: International University Press, 1952

Burnham DL. Autonomy and activity-passivity in the psychotherapy of a schizophrenic man. In A Burton (Ed.), *Psychotherapy of the psychoses.* New York: Basic Books, 1961

Carson RC. *A* and *B* therapist "types:" A possible critical variable in psychotherapy. *Journal of Nervous and Mental Disease,* 1967, *144,* 47–54

Chartier GH. *A-B* therapist variable: Real of imagined. *Psychological Bulletin,* 1971, *75,* 22–33

Cole JO. A lack of controls. *International Journal of Psychiatry,* 1967, *4,* 129–131

Cole, JO, & Davis JM. Antipsychotic drugs. In L Bellack & L Loeb (Eds.), *The schizophrenic syndrome.* New York: Grune & Stratton, 1969

Donlon PT, Rada RT, & Knight SW. A therapeutic aftercare setting for refractory chronic schizophrenic patients. *American Journal of Psychiatry,* 1973, *130,* 682–684

Dyrud JE, & Holzman PS. The psychotherapy of schizophrenia: Does it work? *American Journal of Psychiatry,* 1973, *130,* 670–673

Eissler, KR. Remarks on the psychoanalysis of schizophrenia. In EB Brody & FC Redlich (Eds.), *Psychotherapy with schizophrenics.* New York: International University Press, 1952

Federn P. *Ego psychology and the psychoses.* New York: Basic Books, 1952

Foster B. The recapitulation of development during regression: A case report. In JG Gunderson & LR Mosher (Eds.), *Psychotherapy of schizophrenia.* New York: Jason Aronson, 1975

Freeman T. *Psychopathology of the psychoses.* New York: International Universities Press, 1969

Freud S. On narcissism: An introduction. Jarbuch, VI, 1914. Reprinted in *Collected Papers,* IV:30–59, 1925

Friedman RJ, Gunderson JG, & Feinsilver DB. The psychotherapy of schizophrenia: An NIMH program. *American Journal of Psychiatry,* 1973, *130,* 674–677

Fromm-Reichmann F. Some aspects of psychoanalytic psychotherapy with schizophrenics. In EB Brody & FC Redlich (Eds.), *Psychotherapy with schizophrenics.* New York: International University Press, 1952

Fromm-Reichmann F. *Psychoanalysis and psychotherapy.* Chicago: University of Chicago Press, 1959

Gendlin ET. Client-centered developments and work with schizophrenics. *Journal of Counseling Psychology,* 1962, *9,* 205–212

Giovacchini PL. The influence of interpretation upon schizophrenic patients. *International Journal of Psychoanalysis,* 1969, *50,* 179–187

Goldberg, SC, Schooler, NR, Hogarty GE, & Roper M. Prediction of relapse in schizophrenic outpatients treated by drug and sociotherapy. *Archives of General Psychiatry,* 1977, *34,* 171–184

Gomes-Schwartz B, Hadley SW, & Strupp HH. Individual psychotherapy and behavior therapy. *Annual Review of Psychology,* 1978, *29,* 435–471

Greenson RR, & Wexler M. The non-transference relationship in the psychoanalytic situation. *International Journal of Psychiatry,* 1969, *50,* 27–39

Grinker R. Changing styles in psychoses and borderline states. *American Journal of Psychiatry,* 1973, *130,* 151–152

Grinspoon L, Ewalt JR, & Shader R. Long term treatment of chronic schizophrenia. *International Journal of Psychiatry,* 1967, *4,* 116–128

O'Brien GP, Hamm KB, Ray BA, Pierce JF, Luborsky L, & Mintz J. Group versus individual psychotherapy with schizophrenics: A controlled outcome study. *Archives of General Psychiatry*, 1972, *27*, 474–478

Ostow M. Economy in treatment and economy in research. *International Journal of Psychiatry*, 1969, *8*, 744–747

Parloff MB, Waskow IF, & Wolfe BE. Research on therapist variables in relation to process and outcome. In SL Garfield & AE Bergin (Eds.), *Handbook of psychotherapy and behavior change: An empirical analysis*. New York: Wiley & Sons, 1978

Perry JW. Image, complex and transference in schizophrenia. In A Burton (Ed.), *Psychotherapy of the psychoses*. New York: Basic Books, 1961

Pope HG, & Lipinski JF. Diagnosis in schizophrenia and manic-depressive illness. *Archives of General Psychiatry*, 1978, *35*, 811–828

Razin AM. *A–B* variable in psychotherapy: A critical review. *Psychological Bulletin*, 1971, *75*, 1–21

Rogers CR, Gendlin EG, Kiesler DJ, & Truax CB. *The therapeutic relationship and its impact*. Madison, Wisconsin: University of Wisconsin Press, 1967

Rosen JN. The treatment of schizophrenic psychosis by direct analytic therapy. *Psychiatric Quarterly*, 1947, *21*, 3–25

Rosen JN. *Direct analysis: Selected papers*. New York: Grune & Stratton, 1953

Rosen JN. Psychotherapy and schizophrenia. *International Journal of Psychiatry*, 1969, *8*, 748–752

Rosenfeld H. *Psychotic states: A psychoanalytic approach*. New York: International Universities Press, 1966

Rubins J. A holistic approach to the schizophrenias: The therapeutic process. *American Journal of Psychoanalysis*, 1972, *32*, 16–44

Rubins JL. Five-year results of psychoanalytic therapy and day care for acute schizophrenic patients. *American Journal of Psychoanalysis*, 1976, *36*, 3–26

Schulz CG. An individual psychotherapeutic aproach with the schizophrenic patient. *Schizophrenia Bulletin*, 1975, *13*, 46–49

Schulz CG, & Kilgalen RK. *Case studies in schizophrenia*. New York: Basic Books, 1969

Searles HF. The evolution of the mother transference in psychotherapy with the schizophrenic patients. In A Burton (Ed.), *Psychotherapy of the psychoses*. New York: Basic Books, 1961

Searles HF. *Collected papers on schizophrenia and related subjects*. New York: International Universities Press, 1965

Sechehaye MA. *Symbolic realization*. New York: International Universities Press, 1951

Segal H. Some aspects of the analysis of a schizophrenic. *International Journal of Psycho-Analysis*, 1950, *31*, 268–278

Semrad EV. A clinical formulation of the psychoses. In D Van Buskirk (Ed.), *Teaching psychotherapy of psychotic patients*. New York: Grune & Stratton, 1969

Semrad EV, Menzer D, Mann J, & Standish CT. A study of the doctor-patient relationship in psychotherapy of psychotic patients. *Psychiatry*, 1952, *15*, 377–385

Shader RI, Grinspoon L, & Ewalt JR. Drug responses in acute schizophrenia. In DVS Sankar (Ed.), *Schizophrenia: Current concepts and research*. Hicksville, New York: PJD Publications, 1969

Shader RI, Grinspoon L, Harmatz J, & Ewalt JR. The therapist variable. *American Journal of Psychiatry*, 1971, *127*, 1009–1012

Spotnitz H. *Modern psychoanalysis of the schizophrenic patient*. New York: Grune & Stratton, 1969

Stanton AH. The significance of ego interpretive states in insight-directed psychotherapy. *Psychiatry* 1978, *41*, 129–140

Stierlin H. *Schizophrenic core disturbances.* In JG Gunderson & LR Mosher (Eds.), *Psychotherapy of schizophrenia.* New York: Jason Aronson, 1975

Stone MH. Therapists' personalities and unexpected success with schizophrenic patients. *American Journal of Psychotherapy,* 1971, *25,* 543–552

Strupp HH, & Bergin AE. Some empirical and conceptual bases for coordinated research in psychotherapy: A critical review of issues, trends and evidence. *International Journal of Psychiatry,* 1969, *7,* 18–90

Sullivan HS. *Clinical studies in psychiatry.* New York: WW Norton, 1956

Sullivan HS. *Schizophrenia as a human process.* New York: Norton & Co., 1962

Truax CB. Effective ingredients in psychotherapy: An approach to unraveling the patient-therapist interaction. *Journal of Counseling Psychology,* 1963, *10,* 256–263

Tuma AH, May PRA, Yale C, & Forsythe AB. Therapist characteristics and the outcome of treatment in schizophrenia. *Archives of General Psychiatry,* 1978, *35,* 81–85

Vaillant GE. The prediction of recovery in schizophrenia. *Journal of Nervous and Mental Disease,* 1962, *135,* 534–543

Walker RG, & Kelley FE. Short-term psychotherapy with hospitalized schizophrenic patients. *Acta Psychiatrica Scandinavica,* 1960, *35,* 34–56

Walker RG, & Kelley FE. Short-term psychotherapy with schizophrenic patients evaluated over a 3-year follow-up period. *Journal of Nervous and Mental Disease,* 1963, *137,* 349–352

Wexler M. The structural problem in schizophrenia. In EB Brody & FC Redlich (Eds.), *Psychotherapy with schizophrenics.* New York: International Universities Press, 1952

Wexler M. Schizophrenia as conflict and deficiency. *Psychoanalytic Quarterly,* 1971, *40,* 83–100

Whitehorn JC. Guide to interviewing and clinical personality study. *Archives of Neurology and Psychiatry,* 1944, *52,* 197–216

Whitehorn JC, & Betz BJ. A study of psychotherapeutic relationships between physicians and schizophrenic patients. *American Journal of Psychiatry,* 1954, *111,* 321–333

Whitehorn JC, & Betz BJ. Further studies of the doctor as a crucial variable in the outcome of treatment with schizophrenic patients. *American Journal of Psychiatry,* 1960, *117,* 214–223

Will OA. Process, psychotherapy and schizophrenia. In A Burton (Ed.), *Psychotherapy of the psychoses.* New York: Basic Books, 1961

Will OA. Schizophrenia and psychotherapy. In J Marmor (Ed.), *Modern psychoanalysis.* New York: Basic Books, 1968

Will OA Jr. Comments on the "elements" of schizophrenia, psychotherapy and the schizophrenic person. In JS Strauss, M Bowers, TW Downey, S Fleck, S Jackson, & I Levine (Eds.), *The psychotherapy of schizophrenia.* New York: Plenum, 1980

Wynne LC. Communication disorders and the quest for relatedness in families of schizophrenics. *American Journal of Psychoanalysis,* 1970, *30,* 100–114

Zirkle GA. Five minute psychotherapy. *American Journal of Psychiatry,* 1961, *118,* 544–546

Samuel J. Keith
Susan Matthews

12

Group Psychotherapy

In discussing any therapeutic approach to the person suffering from schizophrenia, it is important to establish a conceptual framework for the disorder that has relevance toward our clinical armamentarium. To do otherwise is to invite inappropriate treatment assignments or the withhoding of potentially useful approaches. From the time of Kraepelin and Bleuler, many have struggled with various components of schizophrenia in an attempt to unify the clinical description, etiologic discrimination, and treatment implication. No completely satisfactory system has been developed. The past decade has seen remarkable progress in establishing the reliability of the diagnosis of schizophrenia through the clinical application of DSM III (APA, 1980), but even the very best reliability has failed to bring validity to the diagnosis. To date, no single, multiple, or cluster of biologic, psychophysiologic, psychologic, or social variables can be found in all schizophrenics. Additionally, the deterioration in course and the six-month chronicity requirement of DSM III have the unfortunate tendency to create a therapeutic pessimism that may not be entirely warranted.

There are available to us, however, a number of ways of reorganizing our descriptive understanding of schizophrenia, which present possible interfaces with our current treatment armamentarium. The approach that we found most useful was first presented by Strauss, Carpenter, and Bartko (1974). Drawing from the work of Hughlings Jackson on the evolution/dissolution theory, they have presented a

SCHIZOPHRENIA
ISBN 0-8089-1640-8

rather compelling argument based on precursors and prognosis for there being three groupings of problems associated with schizophrenic symptoms: positive symptoms, negative symptoms, and disorders of personal relationships. By positive symptoms they refer to symptoms of schizophrenia that characterize it by their presence—hallucinations, delusions, etc.; by negative symptoms they refer to those symptoms that characterize it by their absence—lack of goal directed behavior, blunting of affect, verbal paucity, etc.; by disordered personal relationships they refer to patterns of asociality, withdrawal, and lack of close personal ties. Their data supported the following conclusions:

1. Positive Symptoms
   a. Develop over a short period of time.
   b. Are a reaction to biologic or socioenvironmental causes.
   c. Are of minimal prognostic importance.
2. Negative Symptoms
   a. Develop over an extended period of time.
   b. Are conceptualized as either the source of chronicity or the result of it.
   c. Are prognostically important
3. Disordered Personal Relationships
   a. Develop over long term.
   b. Are conceptualized as interactive process of uncertain etiology.
   c. Are prognostically important for productive functioning in its own area as well as in negative symptomatology and positive symptomatology.

Applying our current treatment modalities to this nosologic conceptual framework offers us the possibility of achieving realistic treatment expectations from both pharmacologic and psychosocial approaches. Although advances in psychopharmacology and psychosocial treatments combined to produce a major revolution in the treatment of schizophrenia in the 1950s, the ensuing two decades have seen a parallel, but, until recently, separate development of knowledge about these two elements of treatment.

The well-designed, rigorous clinical trails of neuroleptics have produced an imposing body of data pointing to their efficacy in the control of the positive symptoms of schizophrenia. Almost no one would question that positive symptomatology is profoundly affected by pharmacologic treatments. Further, controlled studies of maintenance chemotherapy demonstrate a decided advantage to those assigned to receive drugs as compared with those assigned to placebo (Davis, Janicak, Chang, & Klerman, 1982). The distinct advantage of neuroleptic treatment is in controlling the flagrant, psychotic symptoms of schizophrenia. For those patients for whom neuroleptic medication is effective (and there is, unfortunately, a small but significant group who are non-responders) this approach establishes a psychosis-free state. At this point in our understanding of schizophrenia and its effective treatment, this freedom from positive symptoms approaches a sine-qua-non status for psychosocial treatments. We say this even though we fully acknowledge the point made earlier: positive symptoms are the least enduring and least prognostic aspect of schizophrenia. They are schizophrenia's most characteristic, dramatic, and, most significantly, its most frightening aspect. While, indeed, there are a few dedicated and talented clinicians working in settings where regressed behavior and florid symptomatology are accepted as relevant to therapeutic recovery (e.g., Mosher, 1972), most clinicians find it difficult to address issues of the negative symptoms and social competence in the presence of florid psychosis.

What must be equally borne in mind, however, is that recovery from schizophrenia is not synonymous with recovery from positive symptomatology. Unless new drugs that have a more direct impact on negative symptoms and disordered interpersonal relationships, and not just creating the possibility for improvement in these areas, are found we shall apparently have to rely on other interventions to bring improvement in these areas.

PSYCHOSOCIAL TREATMENT

Given the long and rich history of psychosocial treatment (including individual, group, and family therapies) for schizophrenia, going back well before the advent of neuroleptics, the availability of reported studies evaluating its utility is seriously lacking. Searching for explanations for this, we have come up with two thoughts. The first was eloquently expressed by Carpenter and Heinrichs (1980):

> Psychotherapy was the most prestigious form of psychiatric treatment, and the need for testing the therapeutic efficacy was not readily appreciated by those who presumed a treatment effect. We looked to the philosopher, the essayist, the metapsychologist, and the indoctrinated clinicians for new knowledge. Many leading psychiatrists came from the ranks of those who had a prolonged educational experience which stressed inculcation of beliefs, with neglect of scientific principles of hypothesis testing and theory disproof. Arrogance is no friend of science and we now face the consequences of having failed to establish a data

> base suitable for testing therapeutic efficacy of social treatments in general, and psychotherapy of schizophrenia in particular (p. 242).

The second reason that we must consider is that perhaps we have not defined our expectations from psychotherapy adequately. If we try to define psychotherapy as a panacea for schizophrenia, we are almost certain to be profoundly disappointed. The impact of psychotherapy in the absence of neuroleptic medication has been repeatedly shown to be minimal (Klein, 1980). There is an expanding literature that suggests the possibility of a "toxic" effect of psychosocial treatments when these are given to patients not taking medication or if the treatment itself is too intrusive or over stimulating. In one of the most elegantly designed, large scale studies of schizophrenics, Hogarty, Goldberg, and Schooler (1974a) found that among non-relapsed patients in the community, adjustment not only favored those patients who received both drug and sociotherapy, but also that among those receiving placebo alone, those not receiving sociotherapy did better. In addition, this group (Goldberg, Schooler, Hogarty, & Roper, 1977) found that among symptomatic patients, sociotherapy hastened relapse. Lest an assumption be made that the sociotherapy was not a useful treatment, this group has also reported that sociotherapy has a significant effect in reducing future relapse on those patients who do not relapse in the first six months (Hogarty, et al., 1974b) and, perhaps more importantly, in those patients who remained in the study significantly better social adjustment was achieved by those treated with sociotherapy plus drugs than drugs alone. It is significant to note that this effect did not appear until 18 months, and was even stronger at 24 months. It would appear, therefore, that, at least in this study, a balance between gains made in negative symptomatology and losses suffered in positive symptomatology (relapse) can be dramatically shifted in an advantageous manner by the use of medication in conjunction with sociotherapy.

The other aspect of psychosocial toxicity—the too intrusive, too intensive treatment—has been suggested by Wing (1978) in his study of remitted schizophrenics in a "total push" rehabilitation program, which, in addition to not fostering improvement, led to an alarming number of relapses. This interpretation of the Wing study has been bolstered by studies that have emphasized the impact of intrusive, overinvolved, critical environments (Vaughn & Leff, 1976) in the families of schizophrenic patients, which leads to high levels of relapse. This environmental impact is reduced but not eliminated by medication, and only by altering the patient-family interaction patterns can it be virtually eliminated (Falloon, Boyd, McGill, Razini, Moss, & Gilderman, 1982).

It becomes rather obvious that the panacea rationale for psychosocial treatments is not one that can be substantiated by research evidence. What we would like to suggest, however, is that if the more modest target of improving negative symptoms and interpersonal relationships is set, there can be a reasonable expectation of success. What should also be borne in mind is that unlike the neuroleptic sensitive positive symptoms, the negative symptoms and disordered interpersonal relationships are all pervasive, frequently developmental in origin, and do not spontaneously remit. It becomes less likely, therefore, that a treatment that is time limited (treatment for X weeks) or circumscribed (Y therapy for 1 hour/week) can be expected to contribute to reversing this process except in a rather ancillary manner. Further, any psychosocial intervention that does not take into account the environment in which the patient is attempting to recover, is inviting treatment failure—just as a noxious environment can overwhelm a biological treatment that is present 24 hours a day, so it can most certainly overwhelm the impact of a treatment that is present for an hour and a half each week. We feel it is imperative in evaluating the usefulness of any psychosocial treatment to consider (1) What is the research evidence for its effectiveness; (2) What are the potential toxicities of the treatment; and (3) What is the environment in which the treatment is trying to have an impact.

Group Therapy

There is no shortage of review articles on the efficacy of group therapy in the treatment of schizophrenia (Keith & Matthews, 1982; Luborsky, Singer, & Luborsky, 1976; Meltzoff & Korneich, 1970; Mosher & Keith, 1980; Parloff & Dies, 1977). Each of these reviewers has identified a positive rationale for the use of group therapy and each has reported rather meager positive results. As we have pointed out in our earlier review, the ubiquitous nature of group therapy programs in both inpatient and outpatient settings does not seem to be dependent on its demonstrated efficacy. Indeed, from what we have discussed under the general principles of psychosocial treatment, group therapy for schizophrenics in an inpatient setting may not be the optional treatment modality.

Inpatient treatment in most settings occurs at a time when positive symptomatology or social disorganization is at its highest point. As we have learned from studies examining inpatient milieus (Mosher & Keith, 1980), a stimulus decreaing environment is most useful in the early stages of acute symptomatology. Because group therapy is, in fact, a multiple stimuli situation frequently high in intensity, it may be counter-productive early in treatment. Pattison, Brissenden, and Wohl (1967) suggest, in fact, that psychoanalytically-oriented group psychotherapy showed no advantage and at least one disadvantageous measure of self-acceptance when used in an inpatient setting. Kanas, Rogers, Kreth, Patterson, and Campbell (1980) found that psychotic patients treated in insight-oriented group therapy scored worse on both an objective rating scale and on a behavioral measure when compared to a group of psychotic patients who did not receive this form of treatment. They suggest that insight-oriented group therapy is not effectually used during the first three weeks of inpatient treatment with psychotic patients. We feel that to be effective in an inpatient setting, group therapy should begin after the resolution of the most flagrant psychotic symptoms, be focused on current problems in a structured fashion, and follow the patient into the community as an available and ongoing treatment.

From a practical standpoint in those settings where short-term hospitalization is the rule, it may be difficult if not impossible to begin group therapy with only inpatients. Thus, it may be best to introduce an inpatient into an ongoing outpatient therapy group after the florid symptoms have remitted but prior to discharge from the hospital.

Outpatient Group Therapy

We feel that group therapy in an inpatient setting for psychotic individuals presents some clear problems. The clinical state of the patient in the inpatient setting argues strongly for a treatment approach that addresses the disruptive positive symptoms that have necessitated admission to the hospital. To draw upon an analogy from medicine, at the time of fracture of the head of the femur, proper setting of the bone is what is required and not physical therapy. As the fracture becomes stabilized, however, rehabilitation steps become necessary and will predominate for longer than the immobilization. The issue is not relative utility of the two treatments but the relative timing of their introduction. Because we feel that the major impact of group therapy is in the area of negative symptoms and socialization, it would seem to be appropriate to introduce this therapeutic modality at a time when these are the central problems. As we have stated earlier, negative symptoms and problems in interpersonal relationships are, over the long-term course, far more important prognostic factors than the positive symptoms. Our caveat, however, must also be borne in mind: an intrusive, multiple-stimuli approach to a vulnerable patient may lead to reappearance of psychotic symptoms. The approach a therapist must take, therefore, requires a balance between intensity and vulnerability. In terms of treatment approach, this translates into a careful monitoring of the intensity of the psychosocial treatment and the availability of neuroleptic medication to reduce the vulnerability of the patient. These points were nicely demonstrated in a recent study from Sweden (Malm, 1982). In this study, the effect of one year of communication-oriented group therapy, when added to the standard treatment program of depot neuroleptics and social skills training, was examined in newly admitted schizophrenic patients. As expected, for all measures of acute psychopathological manifestations of schizophrenia, there was dramatic improvement over the first 30 days of neuroleptic treatment for all subjects. Patients who had completely recovered over this intial month were excluded from the study. The remainder were randomly assigned to receive either treatment as usual, social skills training and depot neuroleptics (N=40), or the standard treatment plus group therapy (N=40). Six patients in each group, however, either did not start or did not complete the study, leaving a final N of 34 patients in each group. Outcome measures included signs and symptoms, social function, life events, course of illness variables such as relapse rate, and global measures of recovery.

Results of the study indicated that overall, few differences in change scores for symptoms and signs were found for either the therapy or control groups from the start of therapy through two years. Individual items on the Comprehensive Psychopathological Rating Scale (CPRS) showing significant differences favored the therapy group, however. Measures of social functioning and life events significantly favored the therapy group in several areas: more free-time activities, entries and re-entries into social field, and increase in new personal habits. Variables related to the course of illness revealed a 15 percent relapse rate in both groups.

The author noted potential sources of error in the study—the inclusion of 11 subjects (32 percent) in the therapy group despite the fact that they did not complete the therapy that may have had the impact of reducing differences between the therapy and control groups. Also, the author had multiple roles in the study, including ratings upon which conclusions were based. Interrater reliability checks between the author and independent raters, however, showed no significant score differences.

The results of this study support those reported by Hogarty et al. (1974a) in that several differences were not detected until one or two years after treatment, indicating that treatment is a long-term process. In addition, the results substantiate the findings of Klein (1979) in that the initiation of the communication-oriented group therapy did not begin until about one month after the patient had been hospitalized and stabilized with neuroleptic medication, thereby allowing the opportunity for a treatment effect to be demonstrated.

We feel that the design and results from the Malm study provide evidence for the efficacy of psychosocial treatment in the alleviation of the negative symptoms inherent in schizophrenia. By introducing the treatment (group therapy) at a time when the patient was less vulnerable to the toxic effects resultant from an over-stimulating treatment approach, the combined treatment efficacy of drugs and psychosocial treatment in the areas of negative symptoms and socialization was demonstrated.

CONCLUSION

In a previous review (Keith & Matthews, 1982), we concluded that the results of research examining the efficacy of group therapy with persons diagnosed as schizophrenic could only be described as disappointing. Indeed, our current state of knowledge regarding this therapeutic approach provides little additional support. This lack of positive evidence, however, may be an artifact of the limited number of recent controlled investigations examining the effectiveness of group therapy rather than a failure of the treatment itself. The Malm study (1982) is one of the few recent reports providing support for the utility of group therapy within the therapeutic context previously described as being conducive for demonstrating positive results (i.e., a balance of stimulus intensity and patient vulnerability) with appropriate outcome measures. It remains clear that additional studies are required to adequately assess the impact of group therapy in the areas of negative symptoms and socialization.

REFERENCES

American Psychiatric Association. *DSM III: Diagnostic and Statistical Manual of Mental Disorders.* (Third Edition). Washington, D.C.: American Psychiatric Press, 1980

Carpenter WT Jr, & Heinrichs DW. The role of psychodynamic psychiatry in the treatment of schizophrenic patients. In JS Strauss, M Bowers, TW Downey (Eds.), *The psychotherapy of schizophrenia.* New York: Plenum Publishing, 1980

Davis JM, Janicak P, Chang S, & Klerman K. Recent advances in the pharmacologic treatment of the schizophrenic disorders. In L Grinspoon (Ed.), *Psychiatry 1982: Annual review.* Washington, D.C.: American Psychiatric Press, 1982

Falloon I, Boyd J, McGill CW, Razini J, Moss HB, & Gilderman AM. Family management in the prevention of exacerbations of schizophrenia: A controlled study. *New England Journal of Medicine,* 1982, *306,* 1437–1440

Goldberg SC, Schooler NR, Hogarty GE, & Roper MT. Predictions of relapse in schizophrenic outpatients treated by drug and sociotherapy. *Archives of General Psychiatry,* 1977, *34,* 171–184

Hogarty GE, Goldberg SC, & Schooler NR. Drug and sociotherapy in the aftercare of schizophrenic patients. VII. Adjustment of nonrelapsed patients. *Archives of General Psychiatry,* 1974, *31,* 609–618

Hogarty GE, Goldberg SC, Schooler NR, Ulrich RF, & the Collaborative Study Group. Drug and sociotherapy in the aftercare of schizophrenic patients. II. Two-year relapse rates. *Archives of General Psychiatry,* 1974, *31,* 603–608(a)

Kanas N, Rogers M, Kreth E, Patterson L, & Campbell R. The effectiveness of group psychotherapy during the first three weeks of hospitalization. A controlled study. *Journal of Nervous and Mental Disease,* 1980, *168,* 487–492

Keith SJ, & Matthews SM. Group, family, and milieu therapies and psychosocial rehabilitation in the treatment of the schizophrenic disorders. In L Grinspoon (Ed.), *Psychiatry 1982: Annual review.* Washington, D.C.: American Psychiatric Press, 1982

Klein DF. Psychosocial treatment of schizophrenia, or psychosocial help for people with schizophrenia? *Schizophrenia Bulletin,* 1980, *6,* 122–130

Luborsky L, Singer B, & Luborsky L. Comparative studies of psychotherapies: Is it true that 'everybody has won and all must have prizes'? *Proceedings of the American Psychopathological Association,* 1976, *64,* 3–22

Malm U. The influence of group therapy on schizophrenia. *Acta Psychiatrica Scandinavica,* 1982, Supplement 297

Meltzoff J, & Korneich M. *Research in psychotherapy.* New York: Atherton Press, 1970

Mosher LR. Research design to evaluate psychosocial treatments of schizophrenia. In D Rubinstein & YO Alanen (Eds.), *Psychotherapy of schizophrenia.* Amsterdam: Excerpta Medica Foundation, 1972

Mosher LR, & Keith SJ. Psychosocial treatment: Individual, group, family, and community support approaches. *Schizophrenia Bulletin,* 1980, *6,* 10–41

Parloff MB, & Dies RR. Group psychotherapy outcome research 1966–1975. *International Journal of Group Psychotherapy,* 1977, *27,* 281–319

Pattison EM, Brissenden A, & Wohl T. Assessing specific effects of inpatient group psychotherapy. *International Journal of Group Psychotherapy,* 1967, *17,* 283–297

Strauss JC, Carpenter WT Jr, & Bartko J. Part III. Speculations on the processes that underlie schizophrenic signs and symptoms. *Schizophrenia Bulletin,* 1974, *2,* 61–69

Vaughn CE, & Leff JP. The influence of family and social factors in the course of psychiatric illness. *British Journal of Psychiatry,* 1976, *129,* 125–137

Wing JK (Ed.), *Schizophrenia: Towards a new synthesis.* London: Academic Press, 1978

Mary Ann Test

13
Community Support Programs

The framework of *community support system* (CSS) has emerged recently as a conceptual model that is potentially useful in the treatment and care of adults with long-term seriously disabling mental health problems. The phrase *community support program* (CSP) has been used to denote specific service elements that are consistent with the CSS philosophy and contribute to its implementation. This chapter will begin with an introduction to the CSS framework.

COMMUNITY SUPPORT SYSTEM AS A CONCEPTUAL FRAMEWORK

The concept of community support system was formalized as a planning framework for the treatment and care of persons with chronically disabling mental disorders in 1976 and 1977 by the National Institute of Mental Health (NIMH). Since a number of programs consistent with this framework had already been developed, and since many community support programs have subsequently been initiated apart from federal auspices, coverage in this chapter will go far beyond NIMH related efforts. The background to and formal NIMH definitions and guidelines of CSS will be presented here, however, because they summarize succinctly the reasons for the emergence of the CSS philosophy, and the spirit and intent of this framework.

SCHIZOPHRENIA
ISBN 0-8089-1640-8

The formal CSS framework was a product of a series of initiatives by NIMH that attempted to respond to the serious and well publicized plight of many persons with chronically disabling mental disorders in the wake of the deinstitutionalization movement. Following the reliance in the United States for over 100 years on a system of care that involved a clearly centralized organizational component—the mental hospital—it became apparent that neither an adequate treatment system, nor even the conceptual framework for such a system, existed when national policies shifted in the late 1950s and early 1960s to those of decentralized community care. These shortcomings were documented in 1977 in a report from the Comptroller General to the Congress (General Accounting Office, 1977). Meanwhile, in 1974 the NIMH formed an ad hoc work group and shortly thereafter began an extensive participatory planning process to deal with the difficulties in community-based care (Turner & Ten Hoor, 1978). Two outcomes resulted (Turner & Shifren, 1979). First community support sytem emerged as a new conceptual framework to describe the network of services required by mentally disabled adults living in the community. Second, in 1977, the NIMH launched the Community Support Program, a pilot program to try out the CSS planning framework through the provision of contracts to a number of states.

At the NIMH participatory planning conferences (Turner & Ten Hoor, 1978), considerable effort was directed at defining the population group of concern and delineating their functional characteristics. This followed from concensus that services must be developed to meet the unique needs of the specific target population. The client group of concern was designated as follows:

> Adults 18 and over, with a severe and/or persistent mental disorder that seriously impairs their functioning relative to such primary aspects of daily living as personal relations, living arrangements, or employment, but for whom long-term 24-hour care in a hospital, nursing home or protective facility is unnecessary or inappropriate (NIMH, 1982, p. 209).

Consideration of the functional characteristics of these individuals (see NIMH, 1982) led to the realization that adequate care and treatment in the communty would need to involve far more than that usually provided to better functioning "neurotic" outpatients. In particular, persons with long-term disabling mental health problems require assistance in meeting basic life support needs as well as mental health needs. They need assistance in gaining access to and maintaining and sustaining rewarding personal relationships or "social supports." They require help in increasing independent coping skills. They also must receive aid in negotiating and staying involved with what is often a dispersed and fragmented service delivery system. Additionally, the community often requires help in coping with those with severe mental disorders.

To meet these divergent needs, it became apparent that a system of care was necessary. Hence emerged the CSS planning concept:

> A community support system (CSS) is an organized network of caring and responsible people committed to assisting a vulnerable population meet their needs and develop their potentials without being unnecessarily isolated or excluded from the community (NIMH, 1982, p. 208).

To further delineate what is needed for an adequate system of care, the following functions of a CSS were specified. It was recognized that each community would need to make different arrangements for meeting these provisions:*

1. Locate CSS clients, reach out to inform them of available services . . .
2. Help CSS clients meet basic needs . . .
3. Provide adequate mental health care . . .
4. Provide 24-hour, quick response crisis assistance . . .
5. Provide comprehensive psychosocial services . . .
6. Provide a range of rehabilitative and support housing options . . .
7. Offer backup support, assistance, consultation, and education to family and community . . .
8. Recognize natural support systems . . .
9. Establish grievance procedures and mechanisms to protect client rights . . .
10. Facilitate effective use by clients of formal and informal helping systems . . .

(see NIMH, 1982, pp. 210–211 for a fuller explication of all functions).

Additionally, it was recognized that the various services developed or utilized to meet the above functions needed to be integrated into a system. Hence, requirements to fix responsibility at various levels of government, as well as to provide a fixed point of responsibility for each client, were specified.

---

*The NIMH recognizes that the CSS concept is in its formative stages and is subject to refinement based on new information and experience. Thus, the original definition and parameters of CSS (Turner, 1977) were recently revised (NIMH, 1982). The newer material is presented here.

The reader should be aware that since the original NIMH concepts, considerable confusion in terminology has existed. For instance, many use the phrases "community support system" (CSS) and "community support program" (CSP) interchangeably. Also, while CSS is sometimes used to refer to a conceptual framework, it is also used to refer to a local system of care. This author believes it important to make distinctions between these concepts. In this chapter, CSS will be used most often to refer to a *conceptual framework* or *planning tool*. More specifically, CSS is viewed as a *hypothesized* set of functions that must be met if chronic patients are to live adequate and optimal lives in the community. Meanwhile, the term CSP will be used to denote actual service *programs* that meet a *cluster* of CSS functions. (It will be seen that some of these programs [e.g., partial hospitalization] have been discussed at length in other chapters of this volume). Finally, this author will take the position that, if a group of service programs exist and are coordinated to the extent that they meet *all* CSS functions, then this system can be called a CSS or "community support system"—i.e., the "conceptual framework" has become a reality. This terminology appears to be consistent with a recent informal communication by the NIMH that attempts to clarify the definitional confusion between local community support *systems* and community support *programs*. It says,

> A community support *system* (CSS) assumes responsibility for the target population and arranges for, develops and/or provides all of the necessary CSS components within a defined CSS planning area. Community support *programs* provide a cluster of CSS components; that is, they provide specific program elements, but do not necessarily assume overall systems planning, organizing and management responsibility for the client population in a given area (Community Support Program[†]).

Since evaluations of total systems of care for defined planning areas are lacking to date, the research reviewed below will be concerned primarily with assessments of community support programs (CSPs)—i.e., the more specific service elements developed to carry out CSS functions. The review will concurrently examine the validity of the CSS conceptual framework, however, by inquiring as to whether chronic patients fare better if they are involved in a system in which a number of the CSS functions are met.

---

†Community Support Program, National Institute of Mental Health, 1982 Research Initiative. *Draft:* Description of Research and Evaluation Projects. Sept., 1982, p. 3.

COMMUNITY SUPPORT SYSTEMS AND SCHIZOPHRENIA

The CSS concept was developed as a planning tool to provide better services for adults with chronically disabling mental disorders. In a chapter on the treatment of schizophrenia through community support programs, two points regarding client populations require clarification. First, not all persons with chronic mental disorders carry diagnoses of schizophrenia. Second, not all persons with schizophrenic diagnoses suffer the severe chronic disability that constitutes the focus of CSS type interventions.

The functionally defined population termed the *chronically mentally ill* include persons with diagnoses of schizophrenia, affective disorder, paranoid and other psychoses, personality disorders, and other disorders (Goldman, Gattozzi, & Taube, 1981; Toward a National Plan, 1980). It is generally agreed, however, that schizophrenia makes up the largest single diagnostic category, with many estimating that one half to two thirds of the chronically mentally ill are schizophrenic. Of interest is a recent study (Tessler, Bernstein, Rosen, & Goldman, 1982) describing the clients being served during 1980 in community support systems sponsored by the NIMH Community Support Program. Sixty-nine percent of a random sample (n = 1471) of these clients in 18 different community support systems were diagnosed as schizophrenic.

It also must be pointed out that not all persons with schizophrenic diagnoses would be considered appropriate candidates for CSS interventions, as these are intended to meet the widespread and long-term needs of persons with serious chronic disability. Depending on one's definition of schizophrenia, some persons so diagnosed would not appear to require an intervention as comprehensive or enduring. Indeed, clear specification of the proportion of kinds of persons with schizophrenic disorders who require or can benefit from community support programs is one of the many empirical questions facing this field.

RESEARCH ON THE EFFECTIVENESS OF COMMUNITY SUPPORT PROGRAMS

The question of the usefulness and effectiveness of CSPs in the care and treatment of schizophrenia will now be addressed. In turning to the research literature to study this issue, the reviewer encounters immediate difficulties in deciding which interventions qualify as "community support programs." This is in part because the CSS and

CSP terminology is new to the field. Thus, many programs that appear to meet the spirit and intent of community support programs were not originally conceptualized or described as such. A more serious obstacle is that the formal NIMH definitions are vague. They lack the specificity of an operational definition. Hence it is difficult to "know one (CSP) when we see one" (see Bachrach, 1982, for extensive discussion of this issue).

Without making pretense of solving these definitional dilemmas, the current author searched the literature for evaluations of programs that seemed to meet the intent of CSS and CSP as discussed in the previous pages. Accordingly, interventions were considered to be "community support programs," whether or not they were so described, if they served to meet a cluster of the ten functions of CSS outlined in the NIMH conceptualization. Based on this approach, three bodies of literature emerged that have bearing on the questions of the effectiveness of CSPs and the usefulness of the CSS framework. They are: (1) alternative to mental hospital studies; (2) alternative to continued hospitalization studies; and (3) community care studies. Within each area, only studies are reviewed that involved prospective experiments and that systematically compared outcomes for a group of patients treated by one particular method with outcomes of a comparable (usually randomly assigned) group treated in some other way. Further, since relatively few of these studies have included only persons with schizophrenic disorders, studies on diagnostically mixed groups of "chronic psychiatric patients" are covered as well.

Alternative to Mental Hospital Studies

In the past two decades there have been a number of controlled studies of programs that have been developed to serve as alternatives to the mental hospital. Instead of being admitted to an institution, persons who would traditionally be viewed as "in need of hospital care" are treated in the community. The community alternatives, while not originally conceptualized as CSPs, can be considered as such because all meet a cluster of CSS functions. The studies evaluating these programs bring evidence to bear on the validity of CSS concepts because all hypothesize that the active provision of support and treatment in the community can prevent and/or reduce the incidence and length of hospitalization, and may have other positive benefits (when compared with hospitalization) as well.

The controlled studies of alternatives to mental hospital programs are listed in Table 13-1 (see also reviews by Braun, Kochansky, Shapiro, Greenberg, Gudeman, Johnson, & Shore, 1981; Test & Stein,

Table 13-1
Alternative to Mental Hospital Studies

Family Plus Intervention	
	Pasamanick et al., 1967
	Langsley & Kaplan, 1968
	Rittenhouse, 1970
	Fenton et al., 1979
Residental Milieu	
	Rutman, 1971
	Mosher & Menn,* 1978
	Polak, 1978
Day Hospital Treatment	
	Wilder et al., 1966
	Herz et al, 1971
	Michaux et al.,* 1972
"In Community" Treatment	
	Stein & Test, 1978

*Indicates studies which involved only persons with schizophrenic diagnoses.

1978a). It can immediately be seen that a variety of different types of models of CSPs have been utilized as alternatives to the mental hospital. These various programmatic approaches will be described briefly along with evidence regarding their feasibility. Then the effectiveness of these programs relative to hospital treatment will be considered.

Four studies (Fenton, Tessier, & Struening, 1979; Langsley & Kaplan, 1968; Pasamanick, Scarpitti, & Dinitz, 1967; Rittenhouse, 1970) evaluated the feasibility and effectiveness of a model of community treatment that involved clients living with their family combined with some kind of assistance from visiting mental health staff. In these programs the family itself met many of the CSS functions, supplemented by the mental health team. In all four studies the home treatment involved a relatively minimal therapeutic input. Home treatment in the Pasamanick project consisted of visits by public health nurses to patients' homes weekly or less often to provide drugs and supportive therapy. In the Langsley study the home treatment was Family Crisis Therapy aimed at teaching the patient and family ways of handling crises without hospitalization. In the Rittenhouse project the home treatment consisted of Family Unit Therapy as developed by Satir. In the Fenton study a member of an interdisciplinary team visited the home weekly or twice weekly to provide support and monitor medications. All four studies involved randomly assigning patients about to be admitted to a hospital to the home treatment or to an in-hospital condition. All found that a large proportion of the experimental patients (at least 77 percent) could be kept continuously out of the hospital, or out for all but a day or two per year, as long as the home visitation component was in effect.

Three studies utilized a non-family *residential setting/milieu* as an alternative to the mental hospital. In each case many of the CSS functions were met through programs offered within the living environment. Rutman (1971) successfully diverted a random sample of non-assaultive or suicidal new state hospital admissions to a half-way house type setting where patients were treated in a token economy milieu. Mosher (Mosher & Menn, 1978; Mosher, Menn, & Matthews, 1975) treated young first-break schizophrenics in need of hospital admissions in Soteria House, a residential setting with a permissive, unstructured milieu staffed primarily by paraprofessionals who attempted to guide clients through their psychoses, usually without the use of medication. Only 2 of 30 patients had to be transferred to in-patient care because Soteria was not able to deal with them effectively. Polak (Polak, 1978; Polak & Kirby, 1976) admitted patients in the Southwest Denver area to "crisis homes" rather than to the hospital. Those homes were run by private families who provided support and shelter for patients for relatively short periods of time (i.e., several days to several weeks) with the assistance of mental health workers who provided outreach and consultation. While 10 of the first 40 patients could not be treated in this alternative and had to be admitted to a hospital, this percentage declined over time and should be considered in light of the fact that Polak dealt with a totally unselected sample.

A non-residential type of CSP, which has been used in lieu of hospitalization, is *day hospital treatment,* sometimes called partial hospitalization. Two recent reviews (Mason, Louks, Burmer, & Scher, 1982; Moscowitz, 1980) describe the variations of this model. Three controlled studies (Herz, Endicott, Spitzer, & Mesnikoff, 1971; Michaux, Chelst, Foster, & Pruin, 1972; Wilder, Levin, & Zwerling, 1966) compared day treatment with 24-hour in-hospital care for patients seeking admission to an in hospital setting. Of note is the fact that one study (Wilder et al., 1966) rejected a third of the patients randomly assigned to the day hospital condition, whereas the other two studies only sampled from those patients "for whom both treatments were judged equally feasible" (Herz et al., 1971). The day treatment studies thus exclude a rather large and undefined group who are judged a priori "too ill" to be treated in a day setting. Among those patients involved in day treatment, however, all but approximately 20 percent were able to be kept out of the hospital completely.

Finally, *in community treatment* has been used as an alternative to the mental hospital through a model called Training in Community Living (TCL) (Stein & Test, 1978; 1980; Test & Stein, 1978b). In this approach patients live primarily in "normative" community settings (e.g., rooms and apartments) and are provided intensive treatment and support by a mobile interdisciplinary team of staff who work with patients "on the scene" in their homes and neighborhoods to teach and assist them in daily living, social, and employment activities. Patients are also assertively maintained on medications where appropriate. This model was evaluated in a controlled study in which an unselected group of patients (excluding persons with organic brain syndrome or primary alcoholism) seeking in-hospital admission to a state hospital were randomly assigned to a community (TCL) or hospital condition. With this very comprehensive CSP model, hospitalization was totally eliminated for all but 18 percent of the sample while treatment was in effect.

What is clear from the above studies is that, if the hospital alternatives programs are viewed as CSPs, CSPs can be a highly effective way of avoiding or reducing hospitalization for a large proportion of those patients who are often admitted. That is, the provision of a number of the CSS functions in the community—such as assistance in meeting basic needs, and provision of mental health care, crisis assistance, and supportive housing options—can obviate or greatly reduce the need for hospitalization. Given that CSPs can effectively "replace" the hospital for many patients who are in some kind of a crisis, are there any other advantages (or disadvantages) of CSPs relative to hospital treatment? To answer this question, the relative performance of the CSPs (hospital alternatives) and the hospitalization conditions in the previously mentioned studies on a variety of outcome variables will now be summarized. (The reader may wish to consult the reviews of Braun et al., 1981, and Test & Stein, 1978a, for more detail regarding the methodology of these studies).

On the variable *time in hospitals*, patients in the CSP conditions spent less time in the hospital than those in the hospitalization conditions. This finding is certainly not surprising since in the alternative conditions patients were usually not initially admitted to hospitals and there were subsequent concentrated efforts to keep them out. It is noteworthy, however, that in some studies even after the CSP was no longer available to experimental patients, these patients spent less time in the hospital than the controls during the first 6–12 months of the follow-up period. This was due to the fact that community treatment patients were readmitted less often than the in-hospital controls (e.g., Herz et al., 1971; Langsley, Flomenhaft, & Machotka, 1969; Test & Stein, 1978b). Very important to note, however, is that over time, in every study that contained a post-treatment follow-up period in which the CSP was no longer available, the difference between CSP and hospitalization groups on time spent in the hospital disappears, often by one year (e.g., Davis, Dinitz, & Pasamanick, 1974; Langsley, Machotka, & Flomenhaft, 1971; Mosher & Menn, 1978; Stein & Test, 1980). Hence, without the continued availability of special supports, a number of patients in the CSP condition cannot survive in the community.

Regarding *psychiatric symptomatology*, the most consistent finding was that during treatment, symptomatology decreased significantly for patients in both community and in-hospital conditions, but that there were no differences in the amount of reduction between the two treatment conditions (e.g., Fenton et al., 1979; Langsley & Kaplan, 1968; Mosher & Menn, 1978; Pasamanick et al., 1967; Rittenhouse, 1970). Exceptions to this finding were the Michaux et al. (1972) study, in which symptomatology decreased more in the in-hospital group, and the Herz et al. (1971) and Stein and Test (1980) studies, in which the decrease was greater in the community alternatives groups. A number of investigators hypothesize that reduction in symptomatology is most closely tied with pharmacological intervention. Therefore, it is possible that in the above studies, whichever treatment kept drug intervention more available resulted in more consistent symptom reduction. This interpretation cannot be made for all treatment environments; Mosher and Menn (1978) reported impressive results in achieving and maintaining symptom reduction in their CSP condition with minimal use of neuroleptics.

Not all of the studies contained measures of *psychosocial functioning*. Of those that did, however, the majority revealed no differences between the in-hospital and CSP groups on amount of change in psychosocial functioning, with the level of psychosocial functioning often being quite low (e.g., Fenton et al., 1979; Langsley & Kaplan, 1968; Pasamanick, et al., 1967; Polak, 1978; Rittenhouse, 1970; Rutman, 1971; Wilder et al., 1966). Two exceptions to this finding are the Mosher and Menn (1978) and Stein and Test (1980) studies. Mosher and Menn found that significantly more Soteria treated patients were living alone or with peers than controls at two years post-admission. They also found less decline in the overall occupational level of experimental patients from baseline to two year post admission, although there were no significant intergoup differences in percentage of subjects working full or part-time. Stein and test, meanwhile, found that during treatment, community subjects showed significantly less unemployment, higher competitive income, more independent living, and better social relationships than the controls. During a 14 month follow-up period these differences generally diminished, and by 28 months from baseline the experimental group remained superior to the controls only on the variables of income earned from competitive employment and social relationships.

Only three studies (Polak, 1978; Test & Stein, 1978b; Wilder et al., 1966) measured *client satisfaction,* but all three found that patients in the community treatment conditions were more satisfied with their treatment and/or their lives than patients in the in-hospital control groups.

A potential disadvantage of CSPs if used as hospital alternatives, is that they may lead to greater burden on family and community members relative to hospitalization. While this area may not have direct clinical relevance for the patient, it is an important aspect to consider in assessing the feasibility and costs of implementing CSPs for patients who are in acute phases of their disorders. While methodology needs to be improved in this area, it is of interest that the two hospital alternative studies that assessed relative burden (Fenton et al., 1979; Test & Stein, 1980) found that the CSP alternative results in no more burden on family or community than the hospital condition. Perhaps not insignificant is that both of these CSP models actively provide an important CSS function, that of "backup support, assistance, consultation and education to family and community" (see p. 368).

In summary, of this group of studies, it appears that CSPs can be a useful and effective alternative to the mental hospital for patients on the brink of admission. They reduce time spent in hospitals and lower symptomatology as much as hospitalization. A few CSP models show advantages in the psychosocial area. Also, when assessed, patients indicated greater satisfaction when treated in this option relative to hospitalization.

Alternatives to Continued Hospitalization

A second body of research that provides information about the effectiveness of CSP type interventions are studies of community alternatives to continued hospitalization. These studies, summarized in Table 13-2, all involve samples of patients who are being treated in hospitals and who are deemed in need of further hospital care. In each case, however, some community alternative to continued hospitalization is developed, and the feasibility and effectiveness of this alter-

Table 13-2
Alternative to Continued Hospitalization Studies

Residential Milieu
Linn et al., 1977
(Weinman & Kleiner, 1978—see below)
Day Hospital Treatment
Washburn et al., 1976
"In Community" Treatment
Marx et al., 1973
Weinman & Kleiner, 1978

native is evaluated by randomly discharging a part of the hospitalized sample to the community program and comparing their outcome to another group that receives continued hospitalization until deemed ready for discharge. As in the alternative to mental hospital programs, the community models meet a cluster of CSS functions and hence meet the spirit of CSPs. Again, several different models of community care have been studied.

Linn, Caffey, Klett, and Hogarty (1977) utilized a *residential model*, foster care, as an alternative to continued hospitalization for VA patients whose current hospitalization averaged 45 months. Patients whom social workers judged "suitable candidates" were ramdomly assigned to preparation for foster care (and eventual discharge to foster care) or continued hospitalization. Seventy three percent of the foster care patients were placed. Evaluation four months after placement revealed that two thirds of those placed were still in the community and showing less social dysfunction and better global adjustment than their matched in-hospital controls. Linn, Klett, and Caffey (1980) then examined the characteristics of foster homes that were associated with this improvement in social functioning. They found that favorable outcome was related to more children in the homes, fewer borders, and smaller size. Noteworthy, however, is that for schizophrenic patients, too much stimulation in the environment, more supervision by foster care sponsors, and more intensive follow-up by social work staff was related to negative outcome.

Washburn, Vannicelli, Longabaugh, and Schoff (1976) evaluated *day treatment* as an alternative to continued hospitalization. Patients who had been in McLean Hospital for two to six weeks were randomly assigned to a continued hospitalization or day treatment condition. Like the day treatment studies previously described, the sample was limited to those patients for whom day treatment appeared a feasible option. Results showed that patients in both groups generally improved over time, with day patients showing less subjective distress than controls. During the first year, day patients also revealed significantly better community adjustment than controls, but there was no difference on this variable after one and one half years. Informants of the day patients were more satisfied with the treatment modality than informants of the in-hospital group.

Weinman (Weinman & Kleiner, 1978; Weinman, Sanders, Kleiner, & Wilson, 1970) conducted a study that compared continued hospitalization with both a residential alternative and a kind of *"in community" treatment* alternative. Patients were chronic psychotics (averaging 13 years of continuous hospitalization) who were judged to have the potential for developing community living coping skills. These patients were randomly assigned to an 8–12 month in-hospital socioenvironmental therapy condition, to a community residential alternative that consisted of patients living in the homes of paid indigenous community members ("live-in enablers"), or to a condition in which patients lived in independent apartments but were visited daily by the enablers ("visiting enablers"). Results revealed that more community than control patients were successfully separated from the hospital. There were no differences between the groups in psychiatric symptomatology. There were several differences favoring the community groups in instrumental and social performance, and self-esteem was higher for the community alternatives patients. Comparing the two community alternatives, Weinman and colleagues found recidivism lower and self-esteem higher for patients in the residential model, but instrumental performance better for patients in the visiting enabler "in community" model. The investigators hypothesized that these findings stemmed from the different expectations of the two conditions—i.e., low expectations (live-in condition) led to less stress and less recidivism, whereas higher expectations (visiting enabler) resulted in higher recidivism but better functioning.

Finally, Marx, Test, and Stein (1973) randomly assigned an unselected group of patients who were in the hospital for 3–18 months to an "in community" alternative or to a continued hospitalization control group. The experimental (community) group received an early version of the Training in Community Living model (Stein & Test, 1980) for five months. Results demonstrated that it was feasible to release the experimental patients early, and that at the end of the five months treatment period these patients revealed more autonomous living and employment situations than did controls. There was no difference between groups on amount of symptom reduction. After the active treatment period ceased, differences between experimental and control groups disappeared.

The findings of the alternatives to continued hospitalization studies are quite consistent with the alternative to hospitalization studies and provide further support and generalizability to the utility of the CSS concepts. Specifically, if these alternatives are considered CSPs, it is clear that the presence of CSPs can make possible earlier discharge of already hospitalized patients. Indeed, even very chronic patients (Linn et al., 1977; Weinman et al., 1978) can enter and survive in the community if programs meeting a number of CSS functions are provided. Further, in those programs that involved intensive psychosocial input, the community groups showed better social or instrumental functioning, although differences here typically diminished after the CSP was no longer available. In those studies that measured subjective satisfaction or self-esteem, the community alternatives showed an advantage.

Community Care Studies

While the above two groups of studies involve comparisons of community programs with hospital care, the research designated as "community care studies" here (see Table 13-3) all contain comparisons of two or more programs of treatment in the community, which differ from one another in their degree of comprehensiveness. The programs or interventions involved are a diverse group and vary in the extent to which they might be considered CSPs according to the NIMH definition. These investigations contribute information about the validity of the CSS framework in that they yield information about the relative effectiveness of programs that meet more CSS functions with programs that meet fewer such functions. Seemingly the CSS framework is supported if the more comprehensive programs show greater benefits relative to the less comprehensive ones.

The sub-group of studies identified as *Out-Patient Contacts* in Table 13-3 will be discussed only briefly because all of these studies involved community treatment interventions that were quite limited in their comprehensiveness and therefore they probably would not qualify as CSPs. These studies are of relevance, however, because they examine whether the provision of some aftercare programming in the community is better than none, and whether a low intensity social therapy plus drugs is more effective than drugs alone.

The results of the Out-Patient Contacts studies taken as a whole strongly support the hypothesis that the provision of even low intensity programming in the community for discharged patients reduces

Table 13-3
Community Care Studies

Out-Patient Contacts
Sheldon, 1964
Caffey et al., 1971
Claghorn & Kenross-Wright, 1971
Hogarty et al.,* 1973
Claghorn et al.,* 1974
Hogarty et al.,* 1979
Family Plus Intervention
Goldstein et al.,* 1978
Falloon et al.,* 1982
Day Treatment
Meltzoff & Blumenthal, 1966
Guy et al., 1969
Linn et al.,* 1979
Residential Milieu
Velasquez & McCubbin, 1980
Residential and Work Milieu
Fairweather et al., 1969
Lamb & Goertzel, 1972
Psychosocial Rehabilitation Programs
Beard et al., 1963
Dincin & Witheridge, 1982

*Indicates studies which involved only persons with schizophrenic diagnoses.

hospital recidivism relative to conditions in which no aftercare is provided. The only two of these studies that attempted to examine the relative contribution of drugs and social therapies to outcome found complex relationships, however. In the first such study Hogarty and colleagues (Hogarty & Goldberg, 1973; Hogarty, Goldberg, & Schooler, 1974; Hogarty, Goldberg, Schooler, & Ulrich, 1974) found that drugs had a powerful effect in reducing readmissions, whereas "Major Role Therapy" (twice per month social casework and vocational counseling) had only a small effect (appearing only after six months and being additive rather than interactional with the drug effect). Additional findings from this study (Goldberg, Schooler, Hogarty, & Roper, 1977) suggested that asymptomatic patients benefited from Major Role Therapy, while therapy appeared to hasten relapse in patients with greater symptom severity. Further, there was no main effect of either drugs or therapy on psychosocial functioning. After 18 months, however, a significant interaction indicated that among patients on drugs, those with therapy did better, whereas among patients on placebo, those without therapy did better. Finally, a more recent study (Hogarty, Schooler, Ulrich, Mussare, Ferro, & Herron, 1979) also suggested that social therapy makes a contribution in addition to drugs in reducing relapse, but again, its benefits did not appear right away.

Subjects in the two *"Family Plus Intervention"* studies were young schizophrenic patients who were either living at home or were in close contact with their families. Goldstein, Rodnick, Evans, May, and Steinberg (1978) randomly assigned such patients following a brief hospitalization to one of four aftercare conditions consisting of combinations of low and high dose phenothiazines and brief (six week) crisis-oriented family therapy or no therapy. The high drug, family therapy condition might be viewed as a low-intensity CSP intervention in that a number of CSS functions were met. Interestingly, even this very minimal, short-term "community support" treatment revealed a significant effect in reducing relapse relative to the condition in which patients received low-dose medication and no therapy.

Falloon, Boyd, McGill, Razani, Moss, and Gilderman (1982) compared at-home family therapy with clinic-based individual supportive care in the community management of schizophrenic patients taking neuroleptic maintenance medication. Both therapies occurred weekly for the first three months and less frequently thereafter. Although not intensive in terms of frequency, the family management condition appeared to be quite comprehensive in meeting CSS functions as it provided education and support to family and patient and taught them problem-solving skills to deal with various areas of community living. While the individual approach had a similar focus, it was client-oriented and did not have as much potential for impacting on the patient's environment. The results at the end of nine months revealed the family approach to be more successful in preventing major symptomatic exacerbations. These findings support the validity of the CSS framework because the community program that met more CSS functions was more effective than the one that met fewer.

The effectiveness of day treatment has also been studied relative to less comprehensive community approaches. Meltzoff and Blumenthal (1966) compared day treatment to a conventional outpatient approach for discharged patients and, after 18 months, found that patients assigned to day treatment had fewer readmissions, were less symptomatic, and were more often employed. Medications were not controlled in this study. Later, Guy, Gross, Hogarty, and Dennis (1969) investigated the use of drugs alone versus day treatment plus drugs.

Results revealed several findings favorable to the day treatment condition. Finally, in a well designed, multi-site collaborative study involving only schizophrenic patients, Linn, Caffey, Klett, Hogarty, and Lamb (1979) also studied the effectiveness of drugs along versus day treatment plus drugs. Findings revealed that while all ten of the day centers studied were effective in improving patients' social functioning, only six of the centers significantly delayed relapse and reduced symptoms relative to the drug only condition. The data suggested that less stimulating, less threatening environments were more characteristic of the successful centers, while more professional staff hours, group therapy, and a high patient turnover treatment philosophy were associated with poor-results centers. The Linn et al. study is a critical addition to the community support literature, for like the Hogarty and Goldberg (1973) study it suggests that more comprehensive environments are not necessarily better than less comprehensive ones for all schizophrenic patients. Rather, the characteristics of the environments must also be considered.

Residential settings can be regarded as CSPs if they provide a cluster of CSS functions rather than simply a place to live. While numerous such "special living arrangements" exist, there have been surprisingly few controlled studies evaluating their effectiveness. One recent study (Velasquez & McCubbin, 1980) found support for the utility of a 40-bed residential setting that contained an intensive therapeutic milieu that helped patients to learn problem-solving skills. Patients (mostly young; 76 percent with psychotic disorders) were referred to the residential program from either in-hospital or community settings. Referred patients were randomly assigned to the residential setting or to a control condition that apparently received the existing treatments that the community had to offer. At the end of six months, experimental patients scored higher than controls on ratings of self-responsibility, social participation, continuation in employment, and decreased hospitalization. The study does not report where patients were living at this point, or whether the positive findings held up if patients moved out of the residential milieu.

The only other controlled studies of residential settings that could be found contained an intensive employment component in addition to a special living arrangement. Fairweather, Sanders, Cressler, and Maynard (1969) randomly assigned patients ready to be discharged from a VA hospital to a "community lodge" or to a traditional community aftercare control group. In the lodge condition the patients with staff supervision formed a kind of "sub-society" in which they lived and worked together in a janitorial business. A 36-month follow-up revealed that experimental patients spent significantly fewer days in the hospital than controls. They also demonstrated greater employment, though this was due to the lodge related jobs that they held. There were no differences between groups on symptomatology, other measures of psychosocial adjustment, or satisfaction with life.

A final study involving residential settings looked more generally at the variable of environmental expectations on outcome among chronically disabled patients. Lamb and Goertzel (1972) randomly assigned patients ready for hospital discharge to a "high expectancy" condition, which consisted of day treatment, halfway house, and sheltered workshop or a "low expectancy" condition in which patients were placed in boarding and family care homes. Findings revealed that patients in the high expectancy group were released from the hospital earlier and were readmitted more often in the first six months, but showed no overall difference in community stay across a two year follow-up period relative to the low expectancy patients. High expectancy patients were more integrated socially and were involved in more structured activity than the low, although this was related to sheltered employment since the number of patients in competitive employment was approximately the same for each group. This pattern of findings is consistent with the results of Weinman and Kleiner (1978) and appear to indicate that while high expectancy environments do not reduce hospitalization rates (and may even increase them), they do have positive effects on psychosocial functioning.

The final two community care studies involve evaluations of *psychosocial rehabilitation centers* and their related programs. Although a number of such centers were developed over a decade ago (Glasscote, Cumming, Rutman, Sussex, & Glassman, 1971) and are now abundant, controlled studies of their impact are rare. In an early study of Fountain House, a center in New York City, Beard, Pitt, Fisher, and Goertzel (1963) followed relatively long-stay patients discharged to either Fountain House or to a no aftercare control group. Two years after admission significantly fewer of the Fountain House patients had been rehospitalized relative to the controls. There were no differences in employment rates. At a nine year follow-up (Beard, Malamud, & Rossman, 1978) the differences between the two groups on rehospitalization had diminished. In a recent study, Dincin and Witheridge (1982) evaluated Thresholds, a psychiatric rehabilitation center in Chicago. Patients referred to Thresholds (many were young schizophrenics) were randomly assigned to the comprehensive Thresholds program or to a part-time supportive treatment at a separate location. Thresholds patients received individual casework, and vocational and social rehabilitation, and were eligible to live in special transitional residential facilities. After nine months, there were significant differences in the number of patients who had been rehospitalized (14 percent of Thresholds; 44 percent of controls). There were no differences between groups on employment outcomes.

It is difficult to summarize findings from a group of studies as diverse as these "community care studies." However, in regards to the question of, "Are community programs that provide more CSS functions more effective than those that provide fewer?" some tentative conclusions can be drawn. First, all of the studies that compared some kind of organized community treatment—whether it be individual outpatient contacts (Claghorn & Kenross-Wright, 1971; Sheldon, 1964), residential care (Velasquez & McCubbin, 1980), the "lodge" society (Fairweather et al., 1969), or a psychosocial rehabilitation center (Beard et al., 1963)—with no organized system of community care (often called "traditional" after care) found that relapse was significantly reduced in the community care condition, and that with some programs, social functioning was improved. Second, in all but one study (Lamb & Goertzel, 1972) that compared a more comprehensive community treatment with a less comprehensive one—i.e., family management versus individual (Falloon et al., 1982); day treatment versus outpatient contacts (Meltzoff & Blumenthal, 1966); a psychosocial center with supportive treatment (Dincin & Witheridge, 1982)—the more comprehensive programs resulted in fewer relapses and, in some cases, better social adjustment. In all of the studies in these two groups, however, medications were confounded with psychosocial treatments, and it is possible that the patients in the more comprehensive community care condition were maintained more consistently on medication, possibly accounting for or contributing to the reductions in relapse. A third group of studies (Claghorn, Johnston, Cook, & Itschner, 1974; Goldstein et al., 1978; Guy et al., 1969; Hogarty et al., 1973; Hogarty et al., 1979; Linn et al., 1979), therefore, is useful in attempting to sort out the relative contributions of medications and psychosocial interventions in the positive effects of community care programs. Even though the majority of these studies involved a rather low intensity psychosocial intervention, the findings in general suggest that a psychosocial component may add something to the often powerful effect of medications in reducing relapse. For symptomatic patients not on medications, however, psychosocial interventions may be lethal (Goldberg et al., 1977). Indeed, the studies of Lamb and Goertzel (1972) and Linn et al. (1979) also suggest that characteristics of the psychosocial intervention/environment may be a critical influence on whether the psychosocial component is helpful or harmful.

Thus, while in general "something" appears to be better than "nothing" in community care, and while "more" usually reveals greater benefits than "less," an important caveat in developing CSPs is that one must be attentive to what the "something" is, and how it may interact with the patient's clinical status. This point will now be further elaborated.

ISSUES IN THE PLANNING AND IMPLEMENTATION OF COMMUNITY SUPPORT SYSTEMS AND PROGRAMS

Although research that evaluates the outcomes of total community support systems has not yet been completed, a body of literature bearing on the CSS concepts has been reviewed above. This research appears to lend strong support to the validity of the CSS framework, and also suggests the effectiveness of a variety of CSP models. This section will highlight several critical issues in the planning and implementation of community support systems and programs (see also Test, 1981).

Populations for Whom CSS and CSP Are Appropriate

While the CSS framework evolved most immediately to meet the needs of formerly hospitalized, long-stay patients who had been or were being "deinstitutionalized," it can be seen that CSPs have been implemented and evaluated with a variety of other client populations as well. For instance, CSPs have served as alternatives to the mental hospital and as aftercare programs for "revolving door" type patients; they have been utilized as interventions for quite young first admission patients following very brief hospitalization; and they have been employed as sources of extra support for patients currently living in the community who appear to be suffering acute exaberrations of their illnesses. Indeed, this general expansion of CSPs from programs that focused on older, long-stay, deinstitutionalized patients to programs involving revolving door, single admission, or even never admitted patients reflects the growing concern of the field with the prevention of institutionalization for the "next generation" of individuals facing chronic disability (e.g., Pepper & Ryglewicz, 1982).

The literature indicates that CSPs have been demonstrated to be effective with all of these groups. Specifically, it appears that regardless of whether an individual is leaving an institution or is living in the community at the time of referral, the provision of comprehensive support in the community is likely to enhance the person's ability to remain in the community. Thus, planners of mental health services need to develop CSPs that can serve patients who vary in terms of their institutional histories and sources of referral. Seemingly, the distinctions between "aftercare," "hospital alternatives," and "community care" programs can be eliminated. This is not to say that all patients should receive the same programs, but the individual needs of the patient, rather than the individual's place in the service delivery system at time of entry into a community program, should dictate what services he or she receives.

Choosing and Implementing CSPs and CSSs

In the three groups of studies previously reviewed, it was seen that a variety of models of CSPs were utilized to meet clusters of CSS functions. These included patients living with families aided by staff interventions of a variety of types, residential milieus of differing characteristics, day treatment programs, psychosocial rehabilitation centers, and "in community" treatment interventions involving mobile staff. An obvious question facing planners of community support systems is, thus, what kinds of services or programs to develop to meet the CSS functions.

The research reviewed previously does not address this issue directly because most studies involved comparisons of a CSP with hospitalization, or a CSP with the provision of very limited "traditional" community care. With few exceptions (e.g., Weinman & Kleiner, 1978), comparisons of two or more different kinds or models of comprehensive CSPs have not been made. By way of coming to some suggestions about how to program for schizophrenic patients in the community, however, the following series of summative observations from the literature can be considered:

(1) Community programs that provide medications alone to schizophrenic patients are helpful in reducing relapse (e.g., Hogarty & Goldberg, 1973). Even when receipt of medications is guaranteed, however, relapse continues to be high (Hogarty et al., 1979). Meanwhile, it appears that the provision of even low intensity psychosocial treatments in addition to medications can have a beneficial effect. Thus, programs that involve medication management and some psychosocial programming are recommended.

(2) While it is extremely difficult to make comparisons across studies, it appears that the more comprehensive CSPs that provide

support and assistance to clients in many areas of their lives (e.g., Dincin & Witheridge, 1982; Mosher & Menn, 1978; Polak, 1978; Stein & Test, 1980) reduced recidivism more than the less comprehensive ones (e.g., Hogarty & Goldberg, 1973; Hogarty et al., 1979). Programs in which patients live with their families and in which family and patient receive assistance in dealing with a range of problem areas also revealed very low rates of relapse (e.g., Falloon et al., 1982). Thus, more comprehensive programs seem to have greater benefits than less comprehensive ones.

(3) If an outcome of better social and instrumental functioning is of major concern in addition to the goal of prevention of relapse, CSP models that contain direct assistance and teaching in various areas of psychosocial functioning may be needed. Most of the CSPs evaluated above, while reducing relapse, did not show advantages in the psychosocial areas. The few that did lead to clinically significant changes in social adjustment (e.g., Fairweather et al., 1969; Meltzhoff & Blumenthal, 1966; Stein & Test, 1978; Weinman & Kleiner, 1978) involved very intensive interventions targeted specifically towards the psychosocial areas.

(4) While comprehensive intensive CSPs that include direct assistance with and teaching of community living skills appear to offer the most potential for favorable outcomes, some important caveats, already mentioned, need to be fed into programming decisions. Specifically, while programs with a high degree of expectancy and "push" for better social functioning may lead to improved instrumental functioning for some patients, others may show a higher likelihood of relapse under these conditions (Lamb & Goertzel, 1972; Weinman & Kleiner, 1978). Environments high in their degree of stimulation may result in worse outcomes for some schizophrenic patients (Linn et al., 1977; Linn et al., 1979). Such intense and/or stimulating environments may be especially lethal for those schizophrenics who are "unprotected" by medications (Goldberg et al., 1977).

The sum of these observations do not yield an easy job for the mental health planner who is trying to decide what kinds of CSPs to develop. They imply, for instance, that there may be a fine line between programs or environments that are "stimulating enough" and those that are "too stimulating." Also, it is likely that different patients require different kinds of environments and programs at different times in the course of their disorders. Given the apparent complexity of the situation, it is hoped that guidance for the planner and clinician will eventually come from future research that addresses the important "specificity" issues of *what kinds of programs are most beneficial to what kinds of patients under what conditions.*

Meanwhile, it is recommended here that a client-focused rather than a program-focused approach be taken to the care of schizophrenic patients in the community. This means that each patient needs to be carefully assessed in all areas of functioning and need by skilled clinicians. Based on this assessment, a highly individualized treatment plan, or community support plan, needs to be developed. This plan may involve placing the patient in some exisiting CSPs in the community and/or developing some new resources for the patient if existing ones do not meet his or her needs. Decisions about specific programs, then, need to be based on the assessment of the client, knowledge of the research literature, and continued monitoring and assessment of the patient's status and progress. The goal is to see that for each patient, all of the CSS functions are met. The clinician (or team of clinicians) thus serve as a kind of "case manager" to see that this is accomplished (Test, 1979).

The practice of client-focused, individualized treatment planning serves as a critical bridge between the concepts of "community support *program*" and "community support *system.*" That is, from the literature reviewed above it is apparent that a variety of CSPs are potentially helpful to chronically disable psychiatric patients. Therefore, it would be useful for each community to develop a range of such options to have available as resources. It will not suffice, however, simply to "plug" patients into these CSPs. Rather, only careful assessment, individual programming, and continued monitoring of each patient's progress in all areas of community living will assure that all of the CSS functions are met. The results will be the implementation of a true community support system.

SUMMARY

The framework of CSS was developed in the 1970s to fill a conceptual vacuum created by the deinstitutionalization movement regarding the care of persons with long-term disabling mental disorders. Many of these persons carry diagnoses of schizophrenia. The CSS concept provides a way to begin to think about what services are needed if chronic psychiatric patients are to be treated primarily in community rather than institutional settings. It emphasized the fact that patients who suffer serious, widespread, and long-term disabilities require fare more than traditional mental health services to survive and live at an optimal level in the community. While this need may appear to be obvious, in the 1960s and 1970s and even currently in numerous settings, many chronic patients received, and now receive, only traditional out-patient therapy, if that. Thus CSS is a potentially useful planning tool in that it specifies the range of functions that must be met if community programming is to be adequate.

While there is strong support for a framework that suggests that effective treatment and care must address the total needs of schizophrenic and other chronic psychiatric patients, research is still in its infancy regarding the specification of what kinds of programs are most useful for whom. Thus, it was emphasized that the implementation of community programming needs to be done in a client-focused, highly individualized fashion. Only through consideration of the unique and changing needs of each patient can all of the CSS functions be met and can outcomes be optimized.

REFERENCES

Bachrach LL. Assessment of outcomes in community support systems: Results, problems, and limitations. *Schizophrenia Bulletin,* 1982, *8,* 39–60

Beard JH, Malamud TJ, & Rossman E. Psychiatric rehabilitation and long-term rehospitalization rates: The findings of two research studies. *Schizophrenia Bulletin,* 1978, *4,* 622–635

Beard JH, Pitt RB, Fisher SH, & Goertzel V. Evaluating the effectiveness of a psychiatric rehabilitation program. *American Journal of Orthopsychiatry,* 1963, *33,* 701–712

Braun P, Kochansky G, Shapiro R, Greenberg S, Gudeman JE, Johnson S, & Shore MF. Overview: Deinstitutionalization of psychiatric patients, a critical review of outcome studies. *American Journal of Psychiatry,* 1981, *138,* 736–749

Caffey EM, Galbrecht CR, & Klett CJ. Brief hospitalization and aftercare in the treatment of schizophrenia. *Archives of General Psychiatry,* 1971, *24,* 81–86

Claghorn JL, Johnstone EE, Cook TH, & Itschner L. Group therapy and maintenance treatment of schizophrenics. *Archives of General Psychiatry,* 1974, *31,* 361–365

Claghorn JL, & Kenross-Wright J. Reduction in hospitalization of schizophrenics. *American Journal of Psychiatry,* 1971, *28,* 344–347

Davis AE, Dinitz S, & Pasamanick B. *Schizophrenics in the new custodial community.* Columbus, Ohio: Ohio State University Press, 1974

Dincin J, & Witheridge TF. Psychiatric rehabilitation as a deterrent to recidivism. *Hospital and Community Psychiatry,* 1982, *33,* 645–650

Fairweather GW, Sanders DH, Cressler DL, & Maynard H. *Community life for the mentally ill.* Chicago: Aldine, 1969

Falloon IRH, Boyd JL, McGill CW, Razani J, Moss HB, & Gilderman AM. Family management in the prevention of exacerbations of schizophrenia. *New England Journal of Medicine,* 1982, *306,* 1437–1440

Fenton FR, Tessier L, & Struening EL. A comparative trial of home and hospital psychiatric care. *Archives of General Psychiatry,* 1979, *36,* 1073–1079

General Accounting Office. *Returning the Mentally Disabled to the Community: Government Needs to Do More.* (HRD-76-152). Washington, D.C.: The Office, 1977

Glasscote RM, Cumming E, Rutman IP, Sussex JN, & Glassman SM. *Rehabilitating the mentally ill in the community*. Washington, D.C.: Joint Info. Serv. of APA and Nat'l Assoc. for Mental Health, 1971

Goldberg SC, Schooler NR, Hogarty GE, & Roper M. Prediction of relapse in schizophrenic outpatients treated by drug and sociotherapy. *Archives of General Psychiatry*, 1977, *34*, 171–184

Goldman HH, Gattozzi AA, & Taube CA. Defining and counting the chronically mentally ill. *Hospital & Community Psychiatry*, 1981, *32*, 21–27

Goldstein MJ, Rodnick EH, Evans JR, May PRA, & Steinberg MR. Drug and family therapy in the aftercare of acute schizophrenics *Archives of General Psychiatry*, 1978, *35*, 1169–1177

Guy W, Gross M, Hogarty GE, & Dennis H. A controlled evaluation of day hospital effectiveness. *Archives of General Psychiatry*, 1969, *20*, 329–338

Herz MI, Endicott J, Spitzer RL, & Mesnikoff A. Day versus inpatient hospitalization—A controlled study. *American Journal of Psychiatry*, 1971, *127*, 1371–1382

Hogarty GE, Goldberg SC, & the Collaborative Study Group. Drug and sociotherapy in the aftercare of schizophrenic patients: One year relapse rates. *Archives of General Psychiatry*, 1973, *28*, 54–64

Hogarty GE, Goldberg SC, & Schooler NR. Drug and sociotherapy in the aftercare of schizophrenic patients. III. Adjustment of non-relapsed patients. *Archives of General Psychiatry*, 1974, *31*, 609–618

Hogarty GE, Goldberg SC, Schooler AR, & Ulrich RF. Drug and sociotherapy in the aftercare of schizophrenic patients. II. Two year relapse rates. *Archives of General Psychiatry*, 1974, *31*, 603–618

Hogarty GE, Schooler NR, Ulrich R, Mussare F, Ferro P, & Herron E. Fluphenazine and social therapy in the aftercare of schizophrenic patients. *Archives of General Psychiatry*, 1979, *36*, 1283–1294

Lamb RH, & Goertzel V. High expectations of long-term ex-state hospital patients. *American Journal of Psychiatry*, 1972, *129*, 471–475

Langsley DG, Flomenhaft K, & Mochotka P. Follow-up evaluation of family crisis therapy. *American Journal of Orthopsychiatry*, 1969, *39*, 753–759

Langsley DG, & Kaplan, DM. *The treatment of families in crisis*. New York: Grune & Stratton, 1968

Langsley DG, Machotka P, & Flomenhaft K. Avoiding mental hospital admission: A follow-up study. *American Journal of Psychiatry*, 1971, *127*, 1391–1394

Linn MW, Caffey EM, Klett CJ, & Hogarty G. Hospital vs. community (foster) care for psychiatric patients. *Archives of General Psychiatry*, 1977, *34*, 78–83

Linn MW, Caffey EM, Klett J, Hogarty GE, & Lamb HR. Day treatment and psychotropic drugs in the aftercare of schizophrenic patients. *Archives of General Psychiatry*, 1979, *36*, 1055–1066

Linn MW, Klett CJ, & Caffey EM. Foster home characteristics and psychiatric patient outcome. *Archives of General Psychiatry*, 1980, *37*, 129–132

Marx AJ, Test MA, & Stein LI. Extra-hospital management of severe mental illness. *Archives of General Psychiatry*, 1973, *29*, 505–511

Mason JC, Louks JL, Burmer GC, & Scher M. The efficacy of partial hospitalization: A review of recent literature. *International Journal of Partial Hospitalization*, 1982, *1*, 251–269

Meltzoff J, & Blumenthal R. *The day treatment center*. Springfield, Ill.: Charles C. Thomas, 1966

Michaux MH, Chelst MR, Foster SA, & Pruin RJ. Day and full-time psychiatric treatment: A controlled comparison. *Current Therapy Research*, 1972, *14*, 279–292

Moscowitz IS. The effectiveness of day hospital treatment: A review. *Journal of Community Psychology*, 1980, *8*, 155–164

Mosher LR, & Menn AZ. Lowered barriers in the community: The Soteria model. In LI Stein, & MA Test (Eds.), *Alternatives to mental hospital treatment*. New York: Plenum Press, 1978, pp. 75–113

Mosher LR, Menn AZ, & Matthews S. Soteria: Evaluation of a home-based treatment for schizophrenia. *American Journal of Orthopsychiatry*, 1975, *45*, 455–469

National Institute of Mental Health. *A Network for Caring: The Community Support Program of the National Institute of Mental Health*. (ADM-81-1063). Washington, D.C.: The Office, 1982

Pasamanick B, Scarpitti F, & Dinitz S. *Schizophrenics in the community*. New York: Appleton-Century-Crofts, 1967

Pepper B, & Ryglewicz H. (Eds.), *The young adult chronic patient: New direction for mental health services series*. San Francisco: Jossey Bass, No. 14, June, 1982

Polak PR. A comprehensive system of alternatives to psychiatric hospitalization. In LI Stein & MA Test (Eds.), *Alternatives to mental hospital treatment*, New York: Plenum Press, 1978. 115–137

Polak PR, & Kirby MW. A model to replace psychiatric hospitals. *Journal of Nervous and Mental Disease*, 1976, *162*, 13–22

Rittenhouse JD. *Without hospitalization: An experimental study of psychiatric care in the home*. Denver, Co.: Swallow Press, 1970

Rutman ID. *Preventing chronicity: A study of three alternatives*. Unpublished report: Philadelphia: Horizon House, October, 1971

Sheldon A. An evaluation of psychiatric after-care. *British Journal of Psychiatry*, 1964, *11*, 622–667

Stein LI, & Test MA. An alternative to mental hospital treatment. In LI Stein, & MA Test (Eds.), *Alternatives to mental hospital treatment*, New York: Plenum Press, 1978, pp. 43–55

Stein LI, & Test MA. Alternative to mental hospital treatment, I. Conceptual model, treatment program, and clinical evaluation. *Archives of General Psychiatry*, 1980, *37*, 392–397

Tessler RC, Bernstein AG, Rosen BM, & Goldman HH. The chronically mentally ill in community support systems. *Hospital and Community Psychiatry*, 1982, *33*, 208–211

Test MA. Continuity of care in community treatment. *New Directions for Mental Health Services*, 1979, *2*, 15–23

Test MA. Effective community treatment of the chronically mentally ill: What is necessary? *Journal of Social Issues*, 1981, *37*, 71–86

Test MA, & Stein LI. Community treatment of the chronic patient: Research overview. *Schizophrenia Bulletin*, 1978 *4*, 360–364 (a)

Test MA, & Stein LI. Training in community living: Research design and results. In LI Stein & MA Test (Eds.), *Alternatives to mental hospital treatment*, New York: Plenum Press, 1978 pp. 57–74 (b)

Test MA, & Stein LI. An alternative to mental hospital treatment: III. Social cost. *Archives of General Psychiatry*, 1980, *37*, 409–412

Toward a National Plan for the Chronically Mentally Ill. Report to the Secretary by the Dept. of HHS Steering Committee on the Chronically Mentally Ill. Washington, D.C.: Public Health Service, 1980

Turner JC. Comprehensive community support systems for severely mentally disabled adults. *Psychosocial Rehabilitation Journal*, 1977, *1*, 39–47

Turner JC, & Shifren I. Community support systems: How comprehensive? *New Directions for Mental Health Services,* 1979, *2,* 1–23

Turner JC, & TenHoor WJ. The NIMH Community Support Program: Pilot approach to a needed social reform. *Schizophrenia Bulletin,* 1978, *4,* 319–349

Velasquez JS, & McCubbin HI. Towards establishing the effectiveness of community-based residential treatment: Program evaluation by experimental research. *Journal of Social Service Research,* 1980, *3,* 337–359

Washburn S, Vannicelli M, Longabaugh R, & Schoff BJ. A controlled comparison evaluation of psychiatric day treatment and inpatient hospitalization. *Journal of Consulting and Clinical Psychology,* 1976, *44,* 665–675

Weinman B, & Kleiner RJ. The impact of community living and community member intervention on the adjustment of the chronic psychotic patient. In LI Stein and MA Test (Eds.), *Alternatives to mental hospital treatment.* New York: Plenum Press, 1978, pp. 139–159

Weinman B, Sanders R, Kleiner R, & Wilson S. Community based treatment of the chronic psychotic. *Community Mental Health Journal, 1970, 6,* 13–21

Wilder JF, Levin G, & Zwerling J. A two-year follow-up evaluation of acute psychotic patients treated in a day hospital. *American Journal of Psychiatry,* 1966, *122,* 1095–1101

William A. Anthony
Patricia B. Nemec

14

Psychiatric Rehabilitation

Historically the treatment of persons with severe psychiatric disabilities has focused on causes and cures. The traditional intervention approaches have attended primarily to the client's symptoms or intrapsychic pains and conflicts. At times these approaches have mistakenly been guided by the assumption that rehabilitation is unnecessary if a client's symptoms can be prevented or reduced or if the client can achieve therapeutic insights into the reasons for his or her difficulties. While many of these approaches have resulted in a reduction of symptomatology, this has not led automatically to improved rehabilitation outcomes (Anthony, Buell, Sharratt, & Althoff, 1972; Anthony, Cohen, & Vitalo, 1978). For example, a review of the literature on drug therapy concluded that evidence for a direct effect of pharmacotherapy on the work performance of schizophrenic patients is not yet available (Engelhardt & Rosen, 1976).

Rehabilitation programs have many possible outcome criteria for measuring client improvement, many of which are not impacted by traditional treatment. These include, among others, client skill gain and improvements in the client's vocational functioning and level of independent living. A treatment program that makes use of group therapy and psychotropic medications may result in a client experiencing severe hallucinations less frequently and allow the client to

SCHIZOPHRENIA
ISBN 0-8089-1640-8

achieve greater insight into what types of situations cause him or her stress, but will not necessarily teach the client to ride the bus to work, to control his or her temper with co-workers, or to follow directions.

Medical and psychiatric thinking tends to conceptualize health in terms of the absence of pathology (Offer & Sabshin, 1974). In the "medical model," a decrease in symptomatology (such as may be achieved through drug therapy) equals an improvement in health. Both physical and psychiatric rehabilitation view health in positive terms, such as competence and coping. In the rehabilitation model, an increase in skills and abilities enabling a person to better cope with his or her environment equals an improvement in health. Traditional psychiatric treatment aims for symptom reduction; psychiatric rehabilitation has health induction as its goal.

Many mental health professionals now recognize the need for a rehabilitation intervention to complement existing treatment approaches. The term *rehabilitation* is used increasingly in professional jargon and program descriptions, and is used as if it were a clear and unambiguous term. In-patient as well as community programs are described as having a rehabilitation orientation (Allen & Vasco, 1980; Fairweather, 1978; Furman & Lund, 1979). The increased acceptance and use of this, however, term does not mean that a psychiatric rehabilitation approach is actually being implemented in the settings in which it is advertised. While the setting may differ from those of more traditional programs, this may be the extent of the difference. The approach may remain a duplicate of more traditional approaches, and the traditionally trained staff may interact with patients as they always have.

> In essence, the present state of psychological rehabilitation can be summarized by means of a somewhat facetious yet nevertheless accurate description: the development of nontraditional psychiatric settings for the purpose of using traditional psychiatric techniques by traditionally trained personnel (Anthony, 1977, p. 660).

The method of psychiatric rehabilitation needs to be understood as well as the concept. The ideas, principles, and theories are implemented by persons with unique practitioner skills, special programs, and system supports. Practitioners require skills over and above traditional therapy skills. Certain program elements, such as skill teaching, may need to be added; the system in which the program operates may need to change, for example, to allow more time for a thorough rehabilitation assessment or to include a new referral process that makes greater use of the specification of client goals.

PSYCHIATRIC REHABILITATION DEFINED

The overall mission of psychiatric rehabilitation is to assist in the reintegration of the psychiatrically disabled into the community and/ or to maintain the ability of the formerly psychiatrically disabled to continue functioning in the community. In other words, rehabilitation practitioners work towards reducing their clients' dependence on the mental health system or towards maintaining their clients' current level of independence (Anthony et al., 1978).

The goal of psychiatric rehabilitation is to insure that the disabled person posseses the physical, emotional, and intellectual skills needed to live, learn, and work in his or her own particular environment. Rehabilitation goals are always tied to an environment, and treatment focuses on the client's skills and the environmental resources needed by a client to function in a specified environment.

THE NEED FOR A PSYCHIATRIC REHABILITATION APPROACH

The need for a comprehensive rehabilitation approach can be seen in the wake of the admitted failure of traditional treatment to successfully rehabilitate the psychiatrically disabled. The mental health system's rehabilitation efforts have been characterized elsewhere as "plagued by poor outcome figures, saddled with inefficient treatment approaches, distracted by an irrelevant diagnostic system, and burdened by a fragmented and unresponsive community based treatment system" (Anthony, Cohen, & Cohen, in press). Taken individually, each of these inadequacies can be supported with empirical as well as anecdotal evidence.

Plagued by Poor Outcome

Anecdotal evidence abounds pointing to poor rehabilitation outcome of mental health treatment. The lack of success in treating "chronics" is reflected in the low priority and lack of interest in serving the severely psychiatrically disabled (Stern & Minkoff, 1979), the high degree of staff "burn-out", and the label itself: "chronic" mental patient. Descriptions of the deinstitutionalization movement provide both anecdotal and empirical evidence of poor rehabilitation outcome (Bachrach, 1976a, 1978; Bassuk & Gerson, 1978; Davis, Dinitz, & Pasamanick, 1974; Erickson & Hyerstay, 1980; Klerman, 1977; Ozarin, Redlich, & Taube, 1976; Smith, 1979; Zax, 1980).

Critics of deinstitutionalization have suggested that the movement of patients from the hospital to the community is often neither effective nor humane, citing as evidence the development of community "back wards" (Bassuk & Gerson, 1978; Lamb & Goertzel, 1972) and the "revolving-door syndrome" (Redlich & Kellert, 1973). One critic writes, "the ideals of 'community treatment' have become a matter of empty words rather than practice" (Erikson & Hyerstay, 1980, p. 35).

Copious empirical evidence also attests to the poor rehabilitation outcome, but its interpretation often proves difficult due to the variety of outcome criteria and follow-up periods used, as well as some methodological problems and differences across studies. Base rates for two outcome criteria have, however, been calculated through literature surveys. The first criterion, recidivism, is defined as the percentage of discharged psychiatric patients who are competitively employed at follow-up, or are employed full-time during the entire follow-up period. These are essentially two different criteria. Rehabilitation programs that attempt to have an effect on post-hospital employment cannot assume that they will also have an effect on recidivism (Fairweather, 1964; Freeman & Simmons, 1963; Paul, 1969). In fact, change on any single outcome measure does not indicate that apparently related measures have also affected (Anthony & Farkas, 1982; Bolton, 1974).

A large number of studies provide estimates of the recidivism base rate for hospitalized psychiatric patients who receive the traditional hospital regimen of drug therapy and individual or group therapy. Though the studies differ in years sampled, geographic location, and type of institution, their results are remarkably similar and suggest a recidivism rate for a one-year period of 35–50 percent. Estimates of recidivism at 3 to 5 years reach 65–75 percent. The employment data suggest that during the year following discharge; approximately 20–30 percent of the ex-patients worked either full-time throughout the year or were employed at the one year follow-up date (see Anthony, et al., 1972, 1978 for more detail).

These two measures of outcome have been used almost exclusively in early psychiatric rehabilitation outcome studies and have clear advantages. They are easily objectified, have meaning to lay persons, translate readily to economic benefits, and make it possible to compare studies using similar outcome measures. In spite of the advantages, though, a broader range of outcome measures must be used in future studies (Anthony et al., 1972; Anthony et al., 1978; Anthony & Farkas, 1982; Bachrach, 1976b; Erickson, 1975; Mosher & Keith, 1979).

Distracted by an Irrelevant Diagnostic System

The current psychiatric diagnostic system is not relevant to psychiatric rehabilitation. This is not surprising, as the present diagnostic system was developed primarily to categorize symptom patterns, rather than to present information relevant to a client's rehabilitation potential. In fact, controversy still exists concerning the ability of the present diagnostic system to do what it was developed to do, and questions have been raised regarding it reliability and validity (Beck, Ward, Mendelson, Mock, & Erbaugh, 1962; Rosenhan, 1973; Schmidt & Fonda,1956; Thaler, 1973; Ward, Beck, Mendelson, Mock, & Erbaugh, 1962; Zubin, 1967). In relation to rehabilitation, the present diagnostic system is neither predictive, descriptive, nor prescriptive. Knowing a client's psychiatric diagnosis does not tell a practitioner the likelihood, for example, of the client living more independently or obtaining employment. The diagnostic categories do not objectively describe a person's skills nor do they provide much assistance in helping a practitioner develop a rehabilitation treatment plan. The focus on symptoms rather than skills encourages the practitioner to think in terms of what the client is, rather than what he or she is able to do, and may encourage a belief that the client cannot change.

With respect to the concerns of psychiatric rehabilitation, the third edition of the *Diagnostic and Statistical Manual of Mental Disorders* (DSM-III, 1980) is a small improvement over its predecessors. The inclusion of a global assessment scale (Highest Level of Adaptive Functioning Past Year, Axis V) and of a global assessment of the client's environment (Severity of Psychosocial Stressors, Axis IV) is to be commended, but their inclusion as optional categories "for use in special clinical and research settings" is unfortunate. No information on client skills is included, nor is any method of specifying the environment in which the client needs or wants to function. As described in the manual's introduction, this edition attempts to be more descriptive and can be used in the initial steps of treatment planning; however, it focuses on collecting information that has limited predictive value for psychiatric rehabilitation practitioners. As a useful document in the area of rehabilitating the psychiatrically disabled, the DSM-III leaves much to be desired.

Saddled by Inefficient Treatment Approaches

Evidence is also available pointing to the inefficiency of the treatment approaches historically available to the severely psychiatrically disabled. Following any client through the maze of inpatient and outpatient services is a testimony to their ineffectiveness and inefficiency (e.g., Sheehan, 1982).

The traditional inpatient treatment methods do not differentially affect rehabilitation outcome (Anthony et al., 1972). These methods were originally designed solely to reduce symptoms or provide therapeutic insight, and little evidence exists suggesting they can do more than this. The recidivism rates and employment percentages for different inpatient treatment modalities are similar to the base-rate figures for hospitalized patients. Although some new treatment techniques have shown dramatic improvements in patients' in-hospital behavior, they have not yet demonstrated a similar effect on community functioning. In-hospital behavior does not correlate with community behavior (Erickson, 1975; Erickson & Hyerstay, 1980). The behavior of the psychiatrically disabled is determined to a large extent by the situation in which the behavior occurs, and the behaviors demanded by the hospital environment do not necessarily resemble those needed to function in the community. However, several inpatient programs—all extremely comprehensive in nature—have demonstrated an effect on community functioning (Becker & Bayer, 1975; Carkhuff, 1974; Heap, Boblitt, Moore, & Hord, 1970; Jacobs & Trick, 1974; Paul & Lentz, 1977; Waldeck, Emerson, & Edelstein, 1979). These approaches are characterized by a primary focus on developing patient skills in a well-organized, active, and comprehensive treatment milieu, often including skills training programs, and by an atmosphere in which the treatment staff believe themselves to be an important component of the treatment program.

Outpatient treatment techniques only improve client functioning during the time the psychiatrically disabled person is being treated by the outpatient program (Anthony et al., 1972; Dellario & Anthony, 1981). If the client stays involved with a person or facility providing services in the community, his or her chances of remaining out of the hospital are increased. Recidivism is also likely to be reduced through contact with non-professionals (Carkhuff & Truax, 1965; Katkin, Zimmerman, Rosenthal, & Ginsburg 1975; Poser, 1966).

In comparing the effectiveness of institutional and alternative placements for the psychiatrically disabled, one review (Stein & Test, 1978) concluded that community treatment initially results in less time spent in the hospital, but after one year there is no longer a difference. The amount of symptom reduction does not differ between a community alternative and in-hospital treatment. There is also no difference between the in-hospital and community treatment groups in the amount of change in psychosocial functioning, though the patients in the community were found to be more satisfied with their treatment. Another review (Dellario & Anthony, 1981) concluded that once treatment is withdrawn, there is no significant difference between the community and hospital treatment settings in the areas of symptom reduction, psychosocial functioning, instrumental functioning, and personal adjustment. Any initial differences reported regarding rehospitalization, time spent in the hospital, and employment tend to disappear by 18 months following treatment termination. Thus, the available evidence suggests there is no long-lasting superiority of time-limited community-based alternative treatment over time-limited in-hospital treatment, regardless of the type of community-based alternative.

The goals achieved by drug therapy are reduction of symptoms, reduction in the use of physical restraint, an increase in the time spent by clients in various forms of psychiatric therapy, and an increase in psychiatric hospital discharges. The psychiatric rehabilitation goal of health induction has been neither a goal nor a by-product of the introduction of psychotropic medications. Now, three decades after the discovery of the first anti-psychotic drug, there is little evidence that drug therapy increases a client's strengths and assets. While drug therapy does allow more inpatients to receive more types of therapy, the research suggests that the typical in-hospital therapy and treatment offered does not affect community behavior (Anthony, et al., 1971; 1978). Effective comprehensive rehabilitation treatment programs that could capitalize on the symptom-reducing ability of psychiatric drugs have been long in coming. Instead a simultaneous increase in discharges and admissions to psychiatric hospitals has accompanied the popularity of drug therapy (Anthony, 1979). This "revolving door syndrome" (Redlich & Kellert, 1978) has provided some of the impetus for developing a psychiatric rehabilitation approach.

Burdened by a Disorganized Community Support System

The community-based treatment system has been described as "fragmented and unresponsive" (Anthony, et al., 1983), and has not been fully accepted by either the clients it serves or the community in which it is located. The mental health care delivery system does not consider the goals of all of the parties involved in the treatment arrangement, and provides no place for negotiating conflicting goals (Erickson & Hyerstay, 1980). Of the patients referred to community facilities, one- to two-thirds do not show up (Wolkon, 1970); of those who do, 40–50 percent do not come back after one session (Sue, McKinney, & Allen, 1976).

In summary, the need for a new approach can be seen in this wealth of evidence that the currently popular treatment methods are neither systematically organized, efficient, effective, nor responsive to the needs of the client. Psychiatric rehabilitation is a comprehensive approach, developed in direct response to the needs of the psychiatrically disabled and to the shortcomings of existing techniques.

PSYCHIATRIC REHABILITATION APPROACH

The psychiatric rehabilitation approach integrates the philosophy and principles of physical rehabilitation with various techniques of the psychotherapeutic approach. The "rehabilitation model," as practiced with severely physically disabled persons (e.g., people with quadraplegia, blindness, etc.), serves as a conceptual model for the basic goals and treatment process of psychiatric rehabilitation.

The basic philosophy of rehabilitation provides direction to the psychiatric rehabilitation process: i.e., disabled people need skills and support to function in the living, learning, and working environments of their choice. There are obviously vast differences between a severe psychiatric disability and a severe physical disability, but there is also enough similarity for the physical rehabilitation approach to be used as a conceptual model for psychiatric rehabilitation. For example, both groups of service recipients need a wide range of service, exhibit impairment of role performance, may be receiving these services for a long period of time, and often do not experience complete recovery from their disabilities. Physically disabled clients are less stigmatized than the psychiatrically disabled. A physical disability seems more understandable than "mental illness," and the treatment of physical disorders appears more credible and recognizable to the layperson than the treatment of psychiatric disorders. By showing how the psychiatric approach is modeled on the philosophy and practice of physical rehabilitation, the concept of psychiatric rehabilitation can be made more clear, legitimate, and acceptable.

Client rehabilitation goals are achieved by two fundamental interventions: (1) developing in clients the particular skills they need to function in their environments, and (2) developing the environmental resources needed to support or strengthen the clients' present level of functioning. In other words, rehabilitation practitioners attempt to increase the client's and/or the environment's resources.

The fundamental goal and treatment interventions of psychiatric rehabilitation are modeled on the physical rehabilitation approach .

In physical rehabilitation the treatment focus in on developing the physically disabled person's skills or developing resources within the environment to maximize the client's present skill level so that the client can function more independently. For example, a physical rehabilitation team focuses on helping a person with paraplegia use existing skills, learn new skills, or obtain environmental resources (like a wheelchair or wheelchair ramp) so as to better accommodate his or her skill level.

Like the approach used in physical rehabilitation, the rehabilitation approach with the psychiatrically disabled client focuses on diagnosing and building client skills and environmental resources. The psychiatric rehabilitation approach is based on the research literature, which indicates that it is the psychiatrically disabled client's skills, not symptoms, that relate most strongly to rehabilitation outcome (research summarized in Anthony, 1979; Anthony et al, 1978). In addition, rehabilitation research has shown repeatedly that psychiatric clients can learn a variety of physical, emotional, and intellectual skills regardless of their present symptomatology. Furthermore, these skills, when properly integrated into a comprehensive rehabilitation program that provides reinforcement and support for the use of these skills in the community, can have significant impact on the clients' rehabilitation outcome (Anthony & Margules, 1974). In summary, the means of achieving the goal of rehabilitation are client skill and environmental resource development.

The psychiatric rehabilitation approach is also based on many of the techniques and principles of psychotherapy (Berenson & Carkhuff, 1967). For example, several principles of psychiatric rehabilitation are rooted in the practice of effective psychotherapy: i.e., the emphasis of the psychiatric rehabilitation approach on client involvement in the rehabilitation process (Carkhuff, 1969), and the necessity of an empathic, trusting relationship between psychiatric rehabilitation practitioners and their clients (Carkhuff, 1972; Rogers, 1951).

In essence, then, the psychiatric rehabilitation approach is grounded in the fields of physical rehabilitation and psychotherapy. Much of what has been learned from these two fields can be used to facilitate the understanding of the philosophy, treatment process, and principles of psychiatric rehabilitation.

PSYCHIATRIC REHABILITATION TREATMENT PROCESS

The rehabilitation philosophy and its assumptions with respect to treatment goals, intervention strategies, and desired client outcomes are reflected in the psychiatric rehabilitation treatment process. This treatment process consists of three phases: the diagnostic phase, the planning phase, and the intervention phase (DPI process).

Psychiatric Rehabilitation Diagnosis

In order to begin rehabilitation treatment, the practitioner must first make a rehabilitation diagnosis of the client. Individual rehabilitation treatment plans cannot be developed and implemented effectively unless this diagnosis is made.

Since rehabilitation outcome is a function of the client's skills and community supports, the rehabilitation diagnosis is strikingly different from the typical psychiatric diagnosis. The rehabilitation diagnostic process yields behavioral and descriptive information about the disabled client's current skills and the skill level demanded by the community in which he or she wishes to function. Such information enables the rehabilitation practitioner to work with the client to develop a treatment plan designed to increase the client's skills and/or to identify and develop an environment more supportive to the client's functioning (Anthony, Pierce, Cohen, & Cannon, 1980(b)). Client and environmentally focused interventions based on this plan lead to an improved ability on the part of the client to reach his or her rehabilitation goal.

Table 14-1 is an example of a rehabilitation diagnosis for a client who is attempting to move from an inpatient setting to a halfway house and from non-working status to work in a sheltered workshop. The diagnosis indicates that the client has two distinct but interrelated rehabilitation goals. Both of these goals involve moving from a present to a future environment. In both instances, the diagnosis indicates the client's present level of skills in relation to the level of skills that will be needed to function in each of the new environments. Note that some of the clients' skills are strengths (+) while some are deficits (−).

A similar assessment is carried out with respect to the strengths and weaknesses of the client's environment. Table 14-2 shows a sample of environmental strengths and deficits that might be critical to a client's rehabilitation outcome. While such an extensive list would not occur for every client, the list in Table 14-2 provides some common examples of environmental strengths and deficits.

The development of a rehabilitation diagnosis (rather than simple reliance on information derived from the traditional psychiatric diagnostic assessment) is necessary because of two fundamental facts. First, the present psychiatric diagnostic categories simply do not provide much input relevant to rehabilitation outcome (as discussed

Table 14-1
Sample Skill Assessment Chart for Client with Two Rehabilitation Goals

Rehabilitation Problem I: No Housing Upon Hospital Discharge
Rehabilitation Goal I: To Live Successfully In a Halfway House

Relevant Environment	Skill Type (PEI)	+/−	Defined Skill Behavior	Level of Functioning Present	Level of Functioning Needed
Halfway House					
Hygeine	P	−	% of time client washes self once a day	60	100
	p	+	% of time client brushes teeth at least once a day	100	100
Nutrition	I	+	# of foods in each basic food group client can list	8	5
	I	−	% of trials client can develop a menu representing a balanced meal	60	80
Responsibility	P/E	+	% of time client does chores when asked	90	80
		−	without being asked	60	80
Relationships	E	+	# of times per day client can appropriately initiate social conversation with house members	5	3
	E	+	% of time client makes supportive statements to others when sadness or discomfort is expressed.	80	70
CMHC					
Support Seeking	E	+	% of time client requests tional assistance when anxiety level is high	100	100
Assistance Awareness	I	−	# of names and phone numbers client can list for potential support people	0	3
Halfway House					
Responsibility	I	+	% of trials client can set alarm clock for given time	90	80
	P	−	# of days per week client has clean clothes ready to wear in a.m.	3	5
	P	−	# of day/week client gets out of bed at specified time on own initiative	2	5

(continued)

Table 14-1 (continued)

Sheltered Workshop					
Dependability	I	+	% of trials client can accurately repeat, from memory, the absence report phone number at workshop	90	80
	P	−	# of days/week client can arrive at job site on time	0	5
	P	−	# of days per year client misses work due to illness	>30	<12
Getting Along	E	−	% of time client can accept correction from supervisor without swearing	75	100
Task Performance	E	−	Consecutive amount of time client can stay on task without talking or reacting to voices	50 min	90 min
	P	−	# of minutes client can go between smoking breaks	50	90

previously). Secondly, it is the presence or absence of specific skill behaviors and environmental supports, not symptom patterns, that relates to rehabilitation outcome (research summarized in Anthony, 1979).

Psychiatric Rehabilitation Plan

The psychiatrically disabled client often has an overwhelming number of skill and resource goals that have been identified during the diagnosis. Assigning priorities to the goals specifies what rehabilitation interventions are needed immediately and why. Some criteria for assigning priorities are urgency, client motivation, and likelihood of achieving the goal. After the high priority goals have been selected, a plan can be developed that identifies the appropriate and necessary rehabilitation interventions.

The plan specifies how the client and/or the resources in the client's goal environment must change in order to reach the rehabilitation goals identified during the diagnostic phase. With respect to client changes, steps of the rehabilitation plan identify what the client needs to do in order to move from the present to the required level of functioning. The rehabilitation diagnosis, which is the basis for the rehabilitation plan, has identified and defined the relevant skills needed to achieve the client's rehabilitation goals as well as identified which of these skills are strengths and which are deficits. The rehabilitation plan specifies how the client will learn new skills and utilize existing skills to achieve his or her rehabilitation. In addition, the plan iden-

Table 14-2
Sample Environmental Assessment Chart

Rehabilitation Problem: No Employment
Rehabilitation Goal: Sheltered Workshop Employment

Relevant Environment	Person	+/−	Defined Environmental Factors	Level of Functioning: Present	Level of Functioning: Needed
Sheltered Workshop					
	Director	+	# of work slots director will make available by needed date	1	1
	Supervisor	+	% of times supervisor will give praise to client when job performance meets or exceeds expectations	100	100
	Workers	−	# of workers available to orient client to worksite social routine	0	2
	Bus Driver	−	# of minutes bus driver waits for client to come from house to bus after sounding horn	2	3
Halfway House					
	Manager	−	# of times per week manager will check to see if client is out of bed by needed time (during first month)	0	5
	Housemate(s)	−	Average # of times per day housemates give positive support in relation to client working in sheltered workshop	0	2
CMHC					
	Counselor	+	Level of programming skills counselor has to plan, monitor, and support client progress	high	high
	Day Treatment Staff	−	% of skill teaching programs staff has for remediating essential client skill deficits	75	100

tifies which practitioners are responsible for implementing what parts of the plant.

With respect to planning for the changes needed in the client's environment, the rehabilitation diagnosis has previously identified the strengths and deficits of the client's environmental resources. Similar to the client planning process, a sequential plan is designed that describes how the necessary modifications can be made in the client's environment, including who is responsible for insuring that these changes get made (Cohen, Vitalo, Anthony, & Pierce, 1980).

Psychiatric Rehabilitation Interventions

The primary rehabilitation interventions are client skill development and environmental resource development. Similar to recent developments in the practice of psychotherapy (Carkhuff & Berenson, 1976; Hersen & Bellack, 1976), the practice of psychiatric rehabilitation frequently involves directly teaching clients the specific skills they need in order to function successfully in their own particular environment (Curran & Monti, 1982; Goldstein, 1981; Liberman, Eckman, Kuehnel, Rosenstein, & Kuehnel, 1982). Some of the skill deficits of the more severely disabled psychiatric clients are the result of the clients never having learned these skills or of an extended lack of practice of the skill. In these cases, the client usually requires a more formalized direct teaching experience. Direct teaching is more than modeling the skill for the client, and more than simply reinforcing approximate skill behaviors. Direct teaching involves developing an outline of the critical knowledge needed to perform the skill (i.e., skill definition, skill purpose, skill steps, skill applications, and skill evaluation), and the use of comprehensive teaching methods such as explanation, demonstration, and practice opportunities to facilitate skill acquisition and application. There are existing skill curricula (e.g., budgeting skills) that can be useful to the practitioner as a source of additional knowledge about many of the skills psychiatrically disabled clients need, as well as how to teach these skills (Danley, Ridley, & Cohen, 1982). These curricula do need to be adapted to reflect the specific skill deficits of the client as well as the client's unique learning needs. Psychiatric rehabilitation requires a skilled teacher capable of sequencing the skills that need to be taught as well as individualizing the way in which the skills are taught.

Client skill development can also occur without a complete teaching intervention. On many occasions clients have the skills in their repertoire but are unable to use them in the needed environment. In this particular instance a rehabilitation program is developed that specifies how the client will utilize existing skills to achieve his or her goals. The rehabilitation program states what the client needs to do in a step-by-step fashion, in a way that builds on the client's strenghts and leads to a reduction of the client's deficits. The program includes the timelines and reinforcement that may be needed to facilitate the client actually doing the steps in the program. The level of detail of the program is individualized to the client's level of functioning. Often, the more severely disabled psychiatric client needs a very detailed program to ensure achievement of rehabilitation goals (Anthony, Pierce, Cohen, & Cannon, 1980(b)).

The environmental resource development intervention may involve teaching skills to the client's significant others (e.g., how to reward the client for following the plan). More typically, however, the resource development intervention in the client's environment involves helping the client choose an environment that is more supportive of his or her present level of functioning. Examples of this type of resource development program might be implementing the steps to choosing a different job, school, or residential program. If there are no environmental resources commensurate with the client's present level of functioning, then the resource development intervention might involve the creation of new resources. Examples of this type of intervention might involve developing a new foster home placement, a new tutoring arrangement, or a new transitional employment slot.

The recognition that many client skill and environmental resource deficits are common to many clients has led to the development of a variety of treatment settings that teach skills and provide needed environmental resources to the client. Rehabilitation treatment settings in which both types of interventions might occur include workshops, halfway houses, alternative schools, and day hospitals.

Psychiatric Rehabilitation Principles

Basic to the philosophy of rehabilitation, and integrated within the rehabilitation treatment process itself, are a number of rehabilitation principles. These principles guide rehabilitation treatment and are reflected in the organizational structure and values of the settings that provide rehabilitation services. Seven rehabilitation principles, which have emerged from the rehabilitation philosophy, practice, and research, are articulated here (Anthony, Cohen, & Cohen, 1982; Anthony, 1980a).

Principle 1. Client involvement is necessary in all phases of the rehabilitation treatment process.

Involving the client in the psychiatric rehabilitation approach means the active participation by the client throughout all the phases of rehabilitation—for example, communication of values, experiences, feelings, ideas, and goals. The psychotherapy research literature suggests that the rehabilitation goals of clients and practitioners frequently differ (Makas, 1980). The literature also confirms that the impact of psychotherapy (Carkhuff, 1969) and teaching (Aspy & Roebuck, 1977) is partially a function of client involvement. An exploration of the client's perspective is necessary to insure that the diagnosis, rehabilitation plan, and intervention strategies each reflect an understanding of both the client's and the practitioner's perspectives. Involvement of the more severely disabled psychiatric client is often difficult, and requires practitioner interviewing skills and creative methods of involvement. The practitioner may need to initially spend time just "being with" the client or to initiate an experience of activity that stimulates the client to react with an expression of ideas or preferences.

When the diagnostic, planning, and intervention phases can be explained to and understood by the client, client involvement is increased, in contrast to the more typical psychiatric diagnostic, planning, and intervention procedures. A psychiatric diagnostic label may be arrived at without client understanding of the treatment, its effects, and side effects (Geller, 1982). In contrast, the rehabilitation intervention cannot seem mysterious to the client. The practitioner is constantly trying to orient the client and demystify the rehabilitation process. Most critical to client involvement is the practitioner's commitment to the goal of client involvement and the belief that rehabilitation is done *with* clients and not *to* clients.

Principle 2. Newly learned skill behaviors are usually situation specific.

Practitioners of psychiatric rehabilitation who have attempted to teach clients the skills needed to function in specific environments have often failed to get the client to accurately use those skills in the environment of need (Hersen & Bellack, 1976). For example, occupational skills learned in a hospital-based workshop setting are not readily transferred to the community (Anthony, 1979).

Practitioners of physical rehabilitation have long understood this principle of situational specificity. The ability to learn to transfer oneself from a wheelchair to a hospital bed does not guarantee a successful wheelchair to bed transfer in one's own bed at home. The practitioner, in teaching, must work toward the application goal and understand the specific skill demands of the home environment. Training also might take place in the home.

In order to insure skill generalization, psychiatric rehabilitation teaching programs must become less contrived and simulated. Efforts need to be made to arrange for training to take place in the environment of need, or at least in more natural settings. Psychiatric rehabilitation, like physical rehabilitation, must operate on the principle that generalization does not just occur, but must be planned.

Principle 3. Each client must have individualized skill goals.

There seems to be a tendency in mental health and rehabilitation settings to teach all clients certain skills because those are the skills that practitioners can best teach, rather than because they are the skills needed by the clients. All schizophrenics in a day treatment center might be taught assertiveness skills, apparently independently of whether or not assertiveness is their most critical skill need. A similar practice in physical rehabilitation might be to teach all physically disabled clients how to use a guide dog, whether they be spinal cord injured, deaf, or blind.

Skill training must be tailored to the diagnosed skill needs of the client. Without a diagnosis, which identifies the individual skill needs of the client, the benefits to the client of any skill training cannot be measured.

Principle 4. The reduction of a client's personal and environmental discomfort does not automatically result in improved client skills.

Reducing the client's symptomatology or "sickness" does not lead directly to increased client health or competence. Similarly, reducing the "sickness" in a person's environment does not automatically lead to increased client health or competence. Health and competence are more likely to be achieved through effective teaching of skills, not simply by means of symptom removal or by improving the physical qualities of one's environment.

Principle 5. The "restrictiveness" of an environment is a function of the characteristics of both the environment and the client.

The concept of "least restrictive environment" as used in mental health treatment is totally different from this concept as used in rehabilitation practice. Bachrach (1980) correctly argues that the restrictiveness of an environment is not just a function of the environment, but a function of the unique needs of the patient within that environment. An environment that is unduly restrictive for one patient may be ideal for another patient. The quality of restrictiveness does not reside exclusively in the environment outside of the patient.

Bachrach's argument reflects the physical rehabilitation concept of least restrictive environment. physical rehabilitation practitioners realize that environments cannot be graded in terms of their restrictiveness without taking into account the needs and abilities of the client who functions in that environment. A quadriplegic might find his pre-morbid home setting (theoretically the "least restrictive") much more limiting than an architecturally modified Center for Independent Living. A blind person lacking mobility skills will find a busy street corner much more restrictive than the hospital corridor.

A physical rehabilitation philosophy replaces the least restrictive environment concept with the principle of most facilitative environment. A facilitative environment is an environmental setting that places no unnecessary restrictions on the client's functioning, while at the same time accommodating the client's present abilities. At certain points in time, some psychiatric clients may find a humane and responsively run inpatient setting to be the most facilitative environment.

Principle 6. Increased client dependency can produce improved client functioning.

In some mental health treatment programs client independence has become so valued that "dependence" has become "a dirty word." Yet from a rehabilitation perspective client dependence is not always seen as negative. Rehabilitation interventions with the physically disabled often encourage dependence on persons or things in one environment so that the client can function more effectively in another environment. For example, a person with quadriplegia may depend on a personal care attendant to help dress her for work, but this allows her to hold a full-time job. Dependence in one area of functioning can set a client free in another area of functioning. In other words, dependence can be functional.

Psychiatric rehabilitation interventions must also recognize the value of client dependence. The technology of rehabilitation is limited in its ability to achieve maximal client independence. Furthermore, dependence on people, places, or things is a normal state of affairs. Interventions that allow for a certain degree of dependence at certain times, such as the use of "enablers" or aides, may in fact be maximizing the client's functioning in other environments at other times (Weinman & Kleiner, 1978).

Principle 7. Hope is an essential ingredient of the practice of psychiatric rehabilitation.

The practitioners of both physical rehabilitation (Wright, 1960) and psychotherapy (Frank, 1973) have recognized the importance of "hope" or positive expectations for improvement as a critical factor in the treatment and rehabilitation process. The hope for client improvement, regardless of the statistical probabilities of improvement, is an important component of any rehabilitation intervention. In contrast, the absence of hope for improvement makes the practice of psychiatric rehabilitation problematic (Stern & Minkhoff, 1979). When hopelessness permeates a setting and contaminates the practitioners, the interminable and difficult demands of psychiatric rehabilitation practice seem overwhelming, and the potential for client gain is diminished.

At the present state of our knowledge, the abandonment of hope for any one psychiatrically disabled person is unrealistic. In fact, our inability to correctly predict who will and who will not benefit from a psychiatric rehabilitation intervention (Anthony, 1979) prevents us from ruling out the possibility of improvement for any one client. In essence, there exists both a clinical and an empirical basis for the value of hope in the practice of psychiatric rehabilitation.

PSYCHIATRIC REHABILITATION OUTCOME

The outcome of those psychiatrically disabled clients receiving services from the mental health/rehabilitation system is a function of three main sources of effect:

(1) the skills and knowledge of the various *people* who interact with the client (e.g., counselors, psychiatrists, family members, other clients)
(2) the *programs* used by these people (e.g., day treatment programs, independent living skills programs)
(3) the service delivery *system*, which supports thee people and programs (e.g., VR agencies, state departments of mental health).

These three areas of people, programs, and systems provide a conceptual framework for selecting and organizing critical research and training projects in psychiatric rehabilitation. In essence, the rehabilitation outcome of clients with severe psychiatric disabilities is a function of the effectiveness of the people, program, and system variables with which the client interacts. People, program, and systems are the potential units of analysis by means of which the rehabilitation process can be investigated and further refined.

Psychiatric Rehabilitation Personnel

Psychiatrically disabled clients interact with a number of people who can have either a positive or negative impact on the client's rehabilitation outcome. Typically, these personnel include professionals, other patients and ex-patients, family members, paraprofessionals, and community members.

Professionals.

Due to the current emphasis on rehabilitating severely psychiatrically disabled persons, treatment professionals are required to perform tasks for which traditional professional training programs have not adequately prepared them (Anthony, 1979) and for which they may have little interest (Stern & Minkhoff, 1979). This is particularly true when professionals must perform a functional assessment of the skills and resources needed by the clients to function in the community, then teach and coordinate the use of many different supportive services.

Curricula need to be developed for university training programs so that professionals currently being trained for work in community and hospital rehabilitation settings will be better able to perform the necessary rehabilitation treatment tasks. Training programs need to equip rehabilitation practitioners with the skills and knowledge needed to develop and coordinate client support systems (Anthony, 1977, 1979).

A rehabilitation-oriented skill training package has been developed (Anthony, 1980b). The training content was developed, field-tested, and revised, using as trainees undergraduate and graduate students and Masters level professionals working in mental health and rehabilitation settings. Six training manuals and an instructors' guide constitute the package. Skill areas addressed are diagnostic planning (Anthony et al., 1980a), rehabilitation programming (Anthony et al., 1980b), professional evaluation (Cohen et al., 1980), career counseling (Pierce, Cohen, Anthony, Cohen, & Friel 1980(a)), career placement (Pierce, Cohen, Anthony, Cohen, & Friel 1980) and community service coordination (Cohen et al., 1980).

The results of the project that developed this training included measurements of trainee knowledge and skills (pre/post-tests), trainee self-ratings of the value of the skills taught, and a follow-up of a number of the clients of the trainees. The skills were successfully learned and are capable of being observed and measured. The trainees rated themselves as improved and considered these skills important in performance of their jobs. A positive relationship existed between trainee/counselor score on a skill assessment measure and client ratings of feeling involved, understood, and of having been taught new skills. The clients who were more involved in the rehabilitation process reported increased satisfaction with their living situation as well as increased employment and satisfaction with their work (Anthony, 1980b).

A new practitioner skill training package is currently being developed. The three phases of the rehabilitation treatment process (diagnosis, planning, intervention) are addressed through a series of modules. The diagnostic package, for example, includes modules designed to teach practitioners how to set an overall rehabilitation goal and to conduct a functional assessment and a resource assessment. Each training module has been developed, piloted, evaluated, and revised, with the goal of developing a training unit that can then be provided to trainers in the field. So, for example, a treatment program administrator interested in developing a psychiatric rehabilitation program will be able to have a group of trainers from the program learn to use these modules to develop and improve the rehabilitation skills of the program staff.

Recently, a psychiatric rehabilitation videotape series was developed to demonstrate some of the major principles of psychiatric rehabilitation (Cohen & Farkas, 1982). Actual practitioners in the field are shown interviewing and teaching their clients. Each demonstration is preceded by introductory teaching points and followed by a brief summary. A *User's Guide* (Unger, Cohen, & Cohen, 1982) provides suggestions and teaching plans for using the videotape series. The introduction and conclusion sections of each tape and the *User's Guide* were developed through a series of pilot presentations with various audiences, and the audience feedback and informal satisfaction reports were built into the series in an effort to respond to audience concerns.

A client skills training model is also in the developmental stage (Center for Rehabilitation Research & Training in Mental Health, 1982). This training package will teach practitioners how to teach skills directly to clients.

Functional Professionals

In addition to those disciplines commonly referred to as "professionals" are the ranks of the "functional professionals" (Carkhuff, 1971)—more often labeled non-professionals, para-professionals, companions, volunteers, lay professionals, and sub-professionals. The functional professional may be defined as a person who, lacking formal credentials, performs those functions usually reserved for credentialed professionals.

Research indicates that functional professionals can be effective in the mental health field. Carkhuff (1968) reviewed over 80 articles concerned with the use and effectiveness of functional professionals and concluded that functional professionals can effect significant constructive changes in their clients, can be trained to function at facilitative levels over relatively short periods of time, and can be seen, in directly comparable studies, to have patients who demonstrate change as much or more than the clients of credentialed professionals. A recent review confirmed these same conclusions (Anthony & Carkhuff, 1978). More recent studies support the earlier conclusions of Carkhuff (e.g., Katkin, Ginsborg, Rifkin, & Scott 1971; Katkin et al., 1975; Verinis, 1970; Weinman, Sanders, Kleiner, & Wilson, 1970), as do some anecdotal reports (Gelineau & Evans, 1970; Goldberg, Evans, & Cole, 1973; Koumans, 1969; Lewington, 1975).

To make the best use of functional professionals, the following points need to be considered (Anthony, 1979):

(1) The mental health worker (or "aide") can have a beneficial effect on psychiatric patients only when he or she is given additional training and responsibility—proper training and utilization are necessary.
(2) Unselected and untrained lay personnel have not consistently demonstrated their therapeutic effectiveness.
(3) The functional professional housewife volunteer has consistently shown herself to have a constructive impact on both psychiatric inpatients and outpatients by increasing the patient's changes of discharge or remaining out of the hospital.
(4) The treatment approaches in which functional professionals are most adept would appear to be the ability to develop a friendly, supportive relationship with the client and the ability to train the client in the skills necessary to function productively in the community. These abilities are not, of course, mutually exclusive.

Families

Families are perceived as a central resource impacting on client rehabilitation outcome. An estimated 50–60 percent of all hospital discharges return home (Lamb & Oliphant, 1978; Minkhoff, 1979). Due to the importance of the family and home environment in the rehabilitation of the psychiatrically disabled person, means of maximizing its positive influences need attention from the treatment team. Proponents of community mental health have called for the expansion of services to the family as an essential priority (Davis, Dinitz, & Pasamanick, 1974; Weiner, Becker, & Friedman, 1967). Specifically, families need to acquire the knowledge and skills necessary to cope with their psychiatrically disabled member as they go through the stages of adjustment with him or her (Vaughn & Leff, 1981). Moreover, in order to insure that families receive adequate knowledge and training, service providers need training in techniques and approaches to assist the family in working effectively with the discharged family member.

The problems that families encounter may be addressed from the psychiatric rehabilitation perspective. In such a framework, family members are viewed as varying in the repertoire of skills and knowledge that the need to cope with the identified client and his or her impact on their own lives. This implies that a family may also develop needed competencies and knowledge through a learning process (Anderson, Hogarty, & Keiss, 1980; Miller, 1981).

Approaches to families that are consistent with the psychiatric rehabilitation approach are aimed at developing the information and competencies needed to deal with the problematic situation. Type of family intervention is consistent with the approach to families used in physical rehabilitation. Psychiatric rehabilitation attempts to translate human problems into observable, measurable events that can be changed. For example, a family member is unable to deal with a certain stressful situation in relation to a disabled relative. Instead of concentrating on the childhood patterns that contribute to their present attitudes toward life, or prescribing medication to either the relative or family member, the rehabilitation approach focuses on how the family member can acquire knowledge or skills to learn to deal more effectively with the stressful situation. Families have indicated needs for a number of services to address their problems in dealing with their disabled members. First and foremost is the recurring theme of insufficient knowledge and information regarding mental illness, its treatment, availability of services, and practical management techniques (Creer & Wing, 1974; Doll, 1976; Evans, Solomon, 1961; Hatfield, 1979; Hibler, 1978). The need for assistance with management of behavior and tasks of daily living is stressed (Creer & Wing, 1974; Hatfield, 1979), as is a need for emotional support (Creer & Wing, 1974; Doll, 1976; Hatfield, 1979; Lamb & Oliphant, 1978).

Related to the need for assistance and support to family members is the need to teach service providers how to be most helpful to the family (Starr, 1982). Families have noted that service providers are not always helpful and are sometimes detrimental in encouraging family members to be a part of the process (Appleton, 1974; Creer & Wing, 1974; Doll, 1976; Hatfield, 1978). Providers need to offer supportive services to families to enable them to function optimally in relation to the situation of a returning psychiatrically disabled family member. Such services may involve the provision of pratical knowledge of mental illness, the teaching of practical behavior management strategies, and a knowledge of resource development and utilization.

Clients

The influence of ex-patient groups or clubs or rehabilitation outcome is gradually being recognized. Clients can obviously influence one another, and some evidence exists that this influence can be positive in terms of rehabilitation outcome. Ex-patients have indicated that these types of groups are helpful (Chamberlin, 1978; Peterson, 1978; Zinman, 1982). Practitioners provide anecdotal evidence of rehabilitation success (Dincin, 1975; Glasscote, 1971; Grob, 1970; Wechsler, 1960). Some research indicates that persons who become involved in social rehabilitation "clubhouse" programs emphasizing peer support are hospitalized less often than those not involved (Beard, Malamud, & Rossman, 1978; Webb, 1976; Wolkon, Karmen, & Tanaka, 1971; Wolkon & Tanaka, 1966). Alternative residences and support/drop-in groups, which are exclusively patient-run, provide an opportunity for self-determination, allowing each resident or member to control his or her own life. These patient-controlled alternatives allow the helping relationship to be one of equals (Zinman, 1982).

Psychiatric Rehabilitation Programs

In addition to the people who interact with the client, a major source of rehabilitation outcome variance is the variety of psychiatric rehabilitation programs that are used by these people. Psychiatric rehabilitation practitioners use a number of techniques and procedures that have become charcterized as rehabilitation oriented.

A number of currently operating community mental health settings, community residential alternatives, community-based workshops, and other sheltered work sites publicize that they are or have rehabilitation programs. These programs are often considered variations and modifications of the originators of psychiatric rehabilitation programming, i.e., the large, well-publicized psychosocial rehabilitation centers such as Fountain House, Horizon House, Center Club, Thresholds, etc. Yet, it is often not clear whether the programs that these new settings provide are actually psychiatric rehabilitation programs, or simply variations of traditional inpatient treatment programs now offered in a community-based setting. Many of these programs resemble the same traditional treatment programs that have been unable to demonstrate a significant impact on client rehabilitation outcome (Anthony et al., 1978).

The critical question thus becomes: Are programs that are labeled as rehabilitation programs actually providing rehabilitation services or are many so-called rehabilitation programs simply modern labels for more traditional techniques? For example, one might ask whether group therapy on the inpatient ward is being called a community group meeting when it occurs in the community residential setting, or if prodding persons to cooperate with outpatient drug treatment is being called a medication complicance group when conducted in a workshop setting. Misimpressions of what constitutes a psychiatric rehabilitation program abound. For example, the development of less costly treatment settings and less expensive tratment techniques are not necessarily rehabilitation strategies. They are simply good management practices.

This confusion surrounding what constitutes a rehabilitation program is of increasing concern to persons involved in the practice of psychiatric rehabilitation. These misimpressions can lead administrators and policy makers to believe that rehabilitation programs are actually in place, when in fact what often exists is only the rehabilitation setting and rehabilitation name, and not the rehabilitation program. Thus, when these "rehabilitation-name-only" programs are found to be ineffective in improving client rehabilitation outcome, the concept of rehabilitation as well as the ineffective program may be discarded. Mental health policy makers will be heard to say: "We tried rehabilitating persons with psychiatric disabilities, but it didn't work." Just as in the field of corrections, the rehabilitation concept will be abandoned before the practice of rehabilitation has been truly tried.

In order to guard against the premature demise of the field of psychiatric rehabilitation, the essential and observable components of a rehabilitation orientation must be identified. By identifying the essential components of a rehabilitation program the evaluation of existing rehabilitation programs will be facilitated. The evaluation results can also assist the dissemination of those rehabilitation programming techniques that have been found to be effective.

Based on the present state of our knowledge about what programmatic variables impact client rehabilitation outcome, Anthony, Cohen, and Farkas (1982) have identified ten essential ingredients of a rehabilitation program. These programmatic components are capable of being observed and monitored, and do not exist simply as theoretical concepts. The assumption is that the greater the number of these components in a rehabilitation treatment program, the more closely it approximates an ideal rehabilitation intervention. Table 14-3 lists these ten essential ingredients that cumulatively indicate whether the

Table 14-3
The Essential Ingredients of a Psychiatric Rehabilitation Program

Ingredient	Examples of How Observed
1. Functional assessment of client skills in relation to environmental demands.	1. Client records show a listing of client skill strengths and deficits in relation to environmental demands; strengths and deficits are behaviorally defined and indicate client's present and needed level of functioning.
2. Client involvement in the rehabilitation assessment and intervention phases.	2. Record forms have places for client signoff and comments; percentage of clients who actually sign off; sample of audiotapes of client interviews indicate client understanding of *what* program is doing and *why*.
3. Systematic individual client rehabilitation plans.	3. Written or taped examples of objective, behavioral, step-by-step client plans; a central "bank" of available rehabilitation curricula; client records specify on which plans client is working.
4. Direct teaching of skills to clients.	4. Practitioners can identify the skills they are capable of teaching, describe the teaching process, and demonstrate their teaching techniques. Program's daily calendar reflects blocks of time devoted to skill training.
5. Environmental assessment and modification.	5. Practitioners can describe characteristics of client's environment to which client is being rehabilitated and how the environment may be modified to support the client's skills level. Functional assessment should have assessed unique environmental demands.

6. Follow-up of clients in their real-life environments.	6. Client records indicate a monitoring plan and descriptions of monitoring results; audiotapes of practitioner and client feedback sessions; record-keeping forms provide spaces for changes in the intervention plan. Percentage of clients whose plans have changed; number of appointments for "follow-along" services.
7. A rehabilitation team approach.	7. Team members can verbally describe each client's observable goals and the responsibilities of each team member in relation to those goals (may refer to client's records for this information).
8. A rehabilitation referral procedure.	8. Client records indicate referral letters requesting specific outcomes by specific dates; telephone referrals demonstrate these same rehabilitation referral ingredients.
9. Evaluation of observable outcomes and utilization of evaluation results.	9. Agency records show the pooled outcome data for all clients; agency directors can verbally describe their setting's most significant client outcomes.
10. Consumer involvement in policy and planning.	10. Administrators can list the number of joint meetings with consumers; consumer ratings of satisfaction with the rehabilitation program.

Reprinted from Anthony WA, Cohen M, & Farkas M. A psychiatric rehabilitation program: Can I recognize one if I see one? *Community Health Journal*, 1982, *18*, p. 95. With permission.

psychiatric rehabilitation process of diagnosis, planning, and intervention (DPI) is in fact occurring programmatically. Ingredients 1 through 6 reflect the DPI process and have been discussed previously.

Ingredient 7, a rehabilitation team approach, is necessary because the skill needs of the clients are varied and extensive, requiring more than one practitioner to be involved in the rehabilitation intervention. These practitioners usually have different specialty areas (e.g., vocational, residential, educational). In the psychiatric rehabilitation approach, the client has clearly stated skill goals, systematic program steps, defined teaching roles, and expected behavioral outcomes. It is this level of specificity that facilitates the ability of different practitioners to work together as a team.

A psychiatric rehabilitation referral (Ingredient 8) specifies the particular client benefits expected and the timelines for achievement of the results. The most important aspect of the referral is that the goal is stated in a way that makes it possible to know whether it has been achieved. This type of behavioral referral allows the referring practitioner to monitor and evalaute how well the referral goal has been attained. A rehabilitation referral is goal-directed, not activity-oriented.

The evaluation of observable outcomes and utilization of evaluation results are essential. The functional client assessment provides the foundation for an evaluation of practitioner and agency accomplishments through follow-up clients in their real-life environments. The evaluation is based on the diagnosed needs of the clients receiving the service. Records for the entire agency can indicate the pooled outcome for all clients, and the practitioners can each monitor and report their individual client outcome results.

Ingredient 10 indicates the importance of client involvement not only in the client's individual plan, but also in the functioning of the agency. Consumers can readily contribute to the development of rehabilitation policy by bringing a perspective and experiential base that cannot be duplicated by professionals (Chamberlin, 1978). This perspective adds to the professional's perspective and is useful in planning to address unmet needs, correcting problems in existing programs, and sharing positive outcomes. By involving consumers in planning meetings and soliciting consumer satisfaction ratings of services, practitioners and administrators increase their learning opportunities and further incorporate client involvement in the rehabilitation process.

In conclusion, the concept of psychiatric rehabilitation programming is not synonymous with community-based programming. Rehabilitation is not defined by where a service is provided, but rather by what service is provided. The list of essential rehabilitation ingredients reflects the present knowledge about what program components facilitate improved client rehabilitation outcome. A setting that contains these program components can rightly be called a psychiatric rehabilitation program. Such a program can be recognized—if one sees it. The current problem is that one won't see very many settings that even approximate comprehensive psychiatric rehabilitation programming. The articulation of these ten psychiatric rehabilitation ingredients can serve as a guide for the continued development of more thorough and replicable programs.

Psychiatric Rehabilitation System

In addition to psychiatric rehabilitation programs and personnel, the system in which these people and programs operate also influences client rehabilitation outcome. A system is "a set of elements standing in interrelations" (von Bertalanffy, 1968). The phrase "psychiatric rehabilitation system" refers to the "interrelations," or the manner in which the people and programs that comprise the service delivery setting(s) are organized. The unit of analysis is an investigation of psychiatric rehabilitation systems can be a single type of service delivery setting (e.g., residential services or community mental health center) or a system comprised of many settings (e.g., a particular geographic area with a range of mental health/rehabilitation settings).

The conditions necessary for constituting a psychiatric rehabilitation service delivery system are:

(1) A range of environments in which rehabilitation programs operate (e.g., several different types of residences; or a setting that operates both residential and vocational components).
(2) Environments that have a rehabilitation mission and philosophy;
(3) Environments that attempt to employ practitioners with rehabilitation skills, knowledge, and attitudes.
(4) Environments that attempt to provide rehabilitation program components (i.e., techniques and procedures) that comprise the rehabilitation diagnostic, planning, and intervention (DPI) process.

Systems that attempt to rehabilitate the psychiatrically disabled client have a number of problems. In a study of community-based treatment for the mentally disabled, the United States General Accounting Office (1977) noted the lack of a planned, coordinated, and systematic approach to meeting the needs of this population. In the areas of accessing, planning, implementing, and evaluating services, the GAO found fragmentation and confusion of responsiblity among federal, state, and local agencies whose programs have an impact on mental health service delivery. The funding of these services has also lacked a systematic approach. The literature describing the Community Support Program (CSP) of the National Institute of Mental Health (Stroul, 1982; Turner, 1982; Turner & Shifren, 1979; Turner & TenHoor, 1978) repeats these criticisms. CSP attempts to remedy many of these problems through such activities as coordinating funding efforts, developing programs to fill identified service gaps (e.g., mental health services to minorities), describing and developing a system of service components necessary to fully meet the needs of the chronically mentally ill, and promoting the establishment of case management services and interagency agreements.

Case management (or what some would call resource management or community service coordination) is considered an essential component of the community support system. Case management is necessary to ensure that appropriate forms of assistant and support are available on a continuing basis to the severely psychiatrically disabled population (Turner & TenHoor, 1978). Many states receiving CSP funding have developed and implemented case management approaches (Benjamin & Ben-Dashan, 1979). A number of problems in the organization and delivery of mental health services are addressed specifically by case management. Beatrice (1979)* outlines a number of these difficulties, including fragmentation of services, service gaps, a lack of comprehensive service arrangement and delivery, and the multiple needs of the severely mentally disabled tht require a coordinated service approach. Case management attempts to integrate and individualize services, to help clients gain access to a continuum of services while following the clients to insure continued appropriateness of the services and to coordinate services so as to maximally meet the multiple and diverse client needs.

The success or failure of these solutions to existing system problems is largely due to the skills of the practitioner. Community service coordination skills are needed for identifying, selecting, and providing access to community resources. These skills are described in detail elsewhere (Cohen et al., 1980).

Another response to psychiatric systems development has been to focus on the area of interagency collaboration. Because the needs of the severely psychiatrically disabled are so numerous, a number of different agencies are usually involved in the delivery of services.

---

*Beatrice DF. *Case management: A policy option for long-term care.* Unpublished manuscript, June, 1979

Interagency collaboration has been especially necessary between mental health and vocational rehabilitation services. Current problems include unspecified agency responsibility for clients served by both mental health and vocational rehabilitation agencies, varying eligibility requirements for service recipients in the two agencies, and lack of sufficient funding and appropriate technology to provide adequate vocational rehabilitation services to the chronically mentally ill (Cohen, 1981). Current recommendations for remedying these problems include providing joint training and technical assistance to mental health professionals and vocational rehabilitation counselors, and appointing liaison persons within each agency to identify problems and opportunities for collaboration (Cohen, 1981; Stroul, 1982).

The Cohen (1981) report on interagency collaboration attempted to clarify the roles of the mental health and vocational rehabilitation systems in the following manner:

> The mental health system has historically accepted responsibility for severely psychiatrically disabled individuals (i.e., in the hospital) and still has the primary responsibility for meeting their needs, including work-related needs, in the community. The total continuum of work-related mental health services needs to be defined. The mental health system is responsible for providing work-related services that: (1) prepare the client for the world of work, (2) deliver and/or facilitate the delivery of work-related services to these clients (e.g., prevocational skills training, job placement, job development), and (3) follows-up the clients receiving VR services (p. 18).

All approaches to remedy systems problems must be viewed in the context of the elements of the system. Any effort to coordinate the system elements in an attempt to improve the systems must first be sure the elements are in place. For example, mental health-vocational rehabilitation interagency agreements are unsuccessful if budget cuts prevent the provision of vocational rehabilitation services to the mentally ill (Stroul, 1982). This is not to negate the importance of systems interventions, but to underscore the necessity for first establishing the elements of the system.

Surprisingly, a focus on the needs and goals of the client is sometimes missing in the construction or refinement of service delivery systems. Ideally, a psychiatric rehabilitation system is organized by first assessing the needs and goals of the clients to be served, followed by deciding which programs need to be operational in order to meet those needs, specifying the tasks that need to be performed in order to implement these programs, and identifying the skills, knowledge, and attitudes needed by the people who will carry out these tasks. The training and technical assistance needed to build this rehabilitation system is then based on this analysis. The actual implementation phase (program development and operation) will take place only after the careful and thorough assessment and planning are completed.

In order for a psychiatric rehabilitation system to operate successfully, all elements of the system must be committed to rehabilitation-type outcomes for clients and must be philosophically attuned to the psychiatric rehabilitation approach. Ryan, Bell, and Metcalf (1982) traced the installation of a psychiatric rehabilitation approach on an inpatient unit. Over a period of four years a psychiatric rehabilitation program was added to a traditional inpatient program; eventually the rehabilitation program replaced the traditional program. The treatment environment, as measured by the Community Oriented Programs Environment Scale (Moos, 1974) changed in a desirable direction only when the rehabilitation approach became the central treatment philosophy. It is this shared rehabilitation philosophy that facilitates organization and cooperation of the various people and programmatic elements of the system.

FUTURE DEVELOPMENTS IN PSYCHIATRIC REHABILITATION

The content of the psychiatric rehabilitation field has emerged in response to the unmet needs of the psychiatrically disabled, and has been based on the empirical and conceptual literature in the areas of physical rehabilitation and psychotherapy. The foundation for the development of this field of practice was laid by clinicians like Beard, Grob, Rutman, Dincin, and others who developed the prototypic psychosocial rehabilitation settings (e.g., Beard, Probst, & Malamud, 1982). As these types of settings have been replicated around the country, opportunities for developing new programs, personnel, and systems have increased dramatically. Psychiatric rehabilitation practitioners and researchers are building a credible field, anchored in practice and guided by research.

The authors of this chapter trace the conceptual beginning of the sicence of psychiatric rehabilitation to the writings of Carkhuff (1969, 1971), in which he first formulated and researched the idea of "training as a preferred mode of treatment." At that time Carkhuff suggested that training clients directly in the skills they needed in order to function in society could be a potent treatment methods. Initial studies with severely psychiatrically disabled patients attested to its promise (Pierce & Drasgow, 1969; Vitalo, 1971). These two studies found that severely disabled patients could be trained to function at higher levels of complex interpersonal skills, independent of symptomatology and diagnostic labels.

The future growth of psychiatric rehabilitation will be based on new research that will add significantly to what is already known, and on new training and technical assistance to make better use of this knowledge. The reserach focus must be on discovering the people, program, and system ingredients that contribute to client rehabilitation outcome (Anthony & Farkas, 1982).

The technical assistance and training focus must be on developing procedures to enable what is already known to be utilized. Various personnel skills and program and system components, which show some relationship to client rehabilitation outcome, have been noted in this chapter. Yet to get this knowledge and skill utilized in existing service delivery settings in a university-based practitioner training programs is a problem of amazing proportions. The Center for Rehabilitation Research and Training in Mental Health (1982) is currently engaged in a three-year project designed to pilot a utilization strategy for psychiatric rehabilitation technology. This project involves training trainers from a number of mental health sites. These training efforts are being extensively evaluated to determine the impact of the training on the trainer, the professional staff whom they train, and on the setting in which they function. In addition, the project is refining and demonstrating a method of teaching the skills of psychiatric rehabilitation, and developing and field testing a replicable strategy for implementing the training technology.

Concurrent with the implementation of this training project has been the development of an assessment package capable of measuring the present capacity of a treatment setting to successfully implement a psychiatric rehabilitation approach (Center for Rehabilitation Research & Training in Mental Health, 1982). This assessment package provides information about the ability of the personnel, program, and system to delivery psychiatric rehabilitation services to psychiatrically disabled clients. The ten essential ingredients discussed earlier (Anthony et al., 1982) have been further refined to specify approximately 80 components necessary for a psychiatric rehabilitation approach. The "diagnosis" of a treatment setting will be followed by planning for and implementation of the training and technical assistance activities needed for program change.

An overview of the psychiatric rehabilitation approach has been presented. The need for such an approach was outlined, the approach itself described, and present and future applications of the psychiatric rehabilitation approach were discussed. The psychiatric rehabilitation approach has progressed to the stage where its implementation can be observed, monitored, researched, and replicated. The approach can be described in sufficient detail to permit measurement of both the main components of the treatment process and the expertise of the practitioners implementing the process. The foundation is now in place for tremendous growth in psychiatric rehabilitation research, directed toward determining the effects of psychiatric rehabilitation on the client, both positive and negative, intended and unintended (Anthony & Farkas, 1982). Hopefully, the future growth of psychiatric rehabilitation approaches will be based on data relevant to the most basic of questions—What's in it for the client?

REFERENCES

Allen RE, & Velasco Fe. An inpatient setting: The contributions of a rehabilitation approach. *Rehabilitation Counseling Bulletin,* 1980, *23,* 108–117

Anderson CM, Hogarty, GE, & Reiss DJ. Family treatment of adult schizophrenic patients: A psycho-educational approach. *Schizophrenia Bulletin,* 1980, *6,* 490–505

Anthony WA. Psychological rehabilitation: A concept in need of a method. *American Psychologist,* 1977, *32,* 658–662

Anthony, WA. *The principles of psychiatric rehabilitation.* Baltimore, MD: University Park Press, 1979

Anthony WA. A rehabilitation model for rehabilitating the psychiatrically disabled. *Rehabilitation Counseling Bulletin,* 1980, *24,* 7–21 (a)

Anthony WA. *A skills training approach in psychiatric rehabilitation.* Final report prepared for National Institute of Mental Health Grant MH 14502, September 1980 (b)

Anthony WA, Buell GJ, Sharratt S, & Althoff, MF. The efficacy of psychiatric rehabilitation. *Psychological Bulletin,* 1972, *78,* 447–456

Anthony WA, & Carkhuff RR. The functional professional therapeutic change agent. In AS Gurman & AM Razin (Eds.), *Effective psychotherapy: A handbook of research.* Oxford: Pergamon Press, 1978

Anthony WA, Cohen M, & Cohen B. The philosophy, treatment process and principles of the psychiatric rehabilitation approach. *New Directions in Mental Health,* 1983, *17,* 67–69

Anthony WA, Cohen M, & Farkas M. A psychiatric rehabilitation treatment program: Can I recognize one if I see one? *Community Mental Health Journal,* 1982, *18,* 83–96

Anthony WA, Cohen MP, & Vitalo R. The measurement of rehabilitation outcome. *Schizophrenia Bulletin,* 1978, *4,* 365 383

Anthony WA, & Farkas M. A client outcome planning model for assessing psychiatric rehabilitation interventions. *Schizophrenia Bulletin,* 1982, *8,* 13–38

Anthony WA, & Margules A. Toward improving the efficacy of psychiatric rehabilitation: A skills training approach. *Rehabilitation Psychology,* 1974, *21,* 101–105

Anthony WA, Pierce RM, Cohen MR, & Cannon JR. *The skills of diagnostic planning: The psychiatric rehabilitation practice series* (Book 1). Baltimore, MD: University Park Press, 1980 (a)

Anthony WA, Pierce RM. Cohen MR, & Cannon JR. The skills of rehabilitation programming: The psychiatric rehabilitation practice series (Book 2). Baltimore, MD: University Park Press, 1980 (b)

Appleton W. Mistreatment of patients' families by psychiatrists. *American Journal of Psychiatry*, 1974, *131*, 655–657

Aspy DN, & Roebuck FN. *Kids don't learn from people they don't like.* Amherst, MA: Human Resource Development press, 1977

Bachrach L. *Deinstitutionalization: An analytical review and sociological perspective.* Washignton, DC: National Institute of Mental Health, Division of Biometry and Epidemiology, 1976 (a)

Bachrach L. A note on some recent studies of mental hospital patients released into the community. *American Journal of Psychiatry*, 1976, *133*, 73–75 (b)

Bachrach L. A conceptual approach to deinstitutionalization. *Hospital and Community Psychiatry*, 1978,*29*, 573–578

Bachrach L. Is the least restrictive environment always the best? Sociological and semantic implications. *Hospital and Community Psychiatry* 1980, *31*, 97–103

Bassuk E, & Gerson S. Deinstitutionalization and mental health services. *Scientific American*, 1978, *238*, 48–53

Beard JH, Malamud TJ, & Rossman E. Psychiatric rehabilitation and long-term rehospitalization rates: The findings of two research studies. *Schizophrenia Bulletin*, 1978, *4*, 622–635

Beard JH, Probst RN, & Malamud, TJ. The fountain house model of psychiatric rehabilitation. *Psychosocial Rehabilitation Journal* 1982, *5*, 47–53

Beck, AJ, Ward CH, Mendelson M, Mock JE, & Erbaugh JK. Reliability of psychiatric diagnosis. 2: A study of consistency of clinical judgements and ratings. *American Journal of Psychiatry*, 1962, *119*, 351–357

Becker P, & Bayer C. Preparing chronic patients for community placement: A four-stage treatment program. *Hospital and Community Psychiatry*, 1975, *26*, 448–450

Benjamin ML, & Ben-Dashan T. *Case management: Implications and issues.* Presented at the New Hampshire Case Management Conference, September 19, 1979

Berenson BG, & Carkhuff RR. *Sources of gain in counseling and psychotherapy.* New York: Holt, 1967

Bolton B. A factor analysis of personal adjustment and vocational measures of client change. *Rehabilitation Counseling Bulletin*, 1974, *18*, 99–103

Carkhuff RR. Training in counseling and psychotherapy. *Journal of Counseling Psychology*, 1966, *13*, 360–367

Carkhuff RR. The differential functioning of lay and professional helpers. *Journal of Counseling Psychology*, 1968, *15*, 117–126

Carkhuff RR. *Helping and human relations* (Vols. 1 & 2). New York: Holt, 1969

Carkhuff RR. *The development of human resources.* New York: Holt, Rinehart & Winston, 1971

Carkhuff RR. The development of systematic human resource development models. *The Counseling Psychologist*, 1972, *3*, 4–11

Carkhuff RR. *Cry twice! From custody to treatment: The story of institutional change.* Amherst, MA: Human Resource Development Press, 1974

Carkhuff RR, & Berenson BG. *Teaching as treatment: An introduction to counseling and psychotherapy.* Amherst, MA: Human Resource Development Press, 1976

Carkhuff RR, & Truax CB. Lay mental health counseling. The effects of lay group counseling. *Journal of Consulting Psychology*, 1965, *29*, 426–432

Center for Rehabilitation Research and Training in Mental Health at Boston University Annual Progress Report (No. 3). Boston: 1982

Chamberlin J. *On our own.* New York: McGraw-Hill, 1978

Cohen M. Improving interagency collaboration between mental health and vocational rehabilitation services. *Conference Summary Report.* Arlington, VA: 1981

Cohen MC, & Farkas M. *The skills of psychiatric rehabilitation.* Boston: Center for Rehabilitation Research and Training in Mental Health at Boston University, 1982 (Videotape Series)

Cohen MR, Anthony WA, Pierce RM, Spaniol LA, & Cannon JR *The skills of professional evaluation: The psychiatric rehabilitation practice series* (Book 3). Baltimore, MD: University Park Press, 1980.

Cohen MR, Vitalo RL, Anthony WA, & Pierce RM. *The skills of community service coordination: The psychiatric rehabilitation practice series* (Book 6). Baltimore, MD: University Park Press, 1980

Creer C, & Wing JK. *Schizophrenia at home.* London: Institute of Psychiatry, 1974

Curran JP, & Monti PM (Eds.) *Social skills training.* New York: Guilford Press, 1982

Danley KS, Ridley DE, & Cohen MR. *Review of skill teaching guides.* Boston: Center for Rehabilitation Research and Training in Mental Health at Boston University, 1982.

Davis AE, Dinitz S, & Pasamanick B. *Schizophrenics in the new custodial community: Five years after the experiment.* Columbus, OH: Ohio State University Press, 1974

Dellario DJ, & Anthony WA. On the relative effectiveness of institutional and alternative placement for the psychiatrically disabled. *Journal of Social Issues,* 1981, *37,* 21–33

Diagnostic and statistical manual of mental disorders (3rd ed.). Washington, DC: American Psychiatric Association, 1980

Dincin J. Psychiatric rehabilitation. *Schizophrenia Bulletin,* 1975, *13,* 131–147

Doll W. Family coping with the mentally ill: An unanticipated problem of deinstitutionalization. *Hospital and Community Psychiatry,* 1976, *27,* 183–185

Engelhardt DM, & Rosen B. Implications of drug treatment for the social rehabilitation of schizophrenia patients. *Schizophrenia Bulletin,* 1976, *2,* 454–462

Erickson RC. Outcome studies in mental hospitals: A review. *Psychological Bulletin,* 1975, *82,* 519–540

Erickson RC, & Hyerstay BJ. Historical perspectives on treatment of the mentally ill. In MS Gibbs, JR Lachermeyer, & J Sigal (Eds.), *Community psychology: Theoretical and empirical approaches.* New York: Gardner Press, 1980

Evans AS, Bullard DM, & Solomon MH. The family as a potential resource in the rehabilitation of the chronic schizophrenic patient: A study of 60 patients and their families. *American Journal of Psychiatry,* 1961, *117,* 1075–1082

Fairweather, GW (Ed.), *Social psychology in treating mental illness.* New York: Wiley, 1965

Fairweather G. The development, evaluation and diffusion of rehabilitation programs: A social change process. In L Stein & M Test (Eds.), *Alternatives to mental hospital treatment.* New York: Plenum Press, 1978

Frank JD. *Persuasion and healing: A comparative study of psychotherapy.* New York: Schocken Books, 1973

Freeman HE, & Simmons OG. *The mental patient comes home.* New York: Wiley, 1963

Furman WM, & Lund DA. The assessment of patient needs: Description of the level of care survey. *Journal of Psychiatric Treatment and Evaluation,* 1979, *1,* 29–37

Gelineau UA, & Evans AS. Volunteer case aides rehabilitate chronic patients. *Hospital and Community Psychiatry,* 1970, *21,* 34–37

Geller JL. State hospital patients and their medication—Do they know what they take? *American Journal of Psychiatry,* 1982, *139,* 611–615

General Accounting Office. *Returning the mentally disabled to the community: Government needs to do more.* Washington, DC: Comptroller General of the United States, 1977

Glasscote RM, Cumming E, Rutman ID, Sussex JN, & Glassman SM. *Rehabilitating the mentally ill in the community.* Washington, DC: The Joint Information Service of the American Psychiatric Association and the National Association for Mental Health, 1971

Goldberg MF, Evans AS, & Cole KH. The utilization and training of volunteers in a psychiatric setting. *British Journal of Social Work,* 1973, *3,* 55–63

Goldstein AP. *Psychological skills training: The structured learning technique.* New York: Pergamon, General Psychology Series, 1981

Grob S. Psychiatric social clubs come of age. *Mental Hygiene,* January 1970, *54,* 129–136

Hatfield AB. Help-seeking behavior in families of schizophrenics. *American Journal of Community Psychology,* 1979, *7,* 563–569

Heap FR, Boblitt EW, Moore H, & Hord EJ. Behavior milieu therapy with chronic neuropsychiatric patients. *Journal of Abnormal Psychology,* 1970, *76,* 349–354

Hersen M, & Bellack A. Social skills training for chronic psychiatric patients: Rationale, research findings, and future directions. *Comprehensive Psychiatry,* 1976, *17,* 559–580

Hibler M. The problems as seen by the patient's family. *Hospital and Community Psychiatry,* 1978, *29,* 32–33

Jacobs MK, & Trick OL. Successful psychiatric rehabilitation using an in-patient teaching laboratory. *American Journal of Psychiatry,* 1974, *131,* 145–148

Katkin S, Ginsburg M, Rifkin JJ, & Scot JT. Effectiveness of female volunteers in the treatment of out-patients. *Journal of Counseling Psychology,* 1971, *18,* 97–100

Katkin S, Zimmerman U, Rosenthal T, & Ginsburg M. Using volunteer therapists to reduce hospital readmissions. *Hospital and Community Psychiatry,* 1975, *26,* 151–153

Klerman F. Better but not well: Social and ethical issues in the deinstitutionalization of the mentally ill. *Schizophrenia Bulletin,* 1977, *3,* 617–631

Koumans AJ. Reaching the unmotivated patient. *Mental Hygiene,* 1969, *53,* 298–300

Lamb H, & Goertzel V. High expectations of long-term ex-state psychiatric hospital patients. *American Journal of Psychiatry,* 1972, *129,* 471–475

Lamb UR, & Oliphant E. Schizophrenia through the eyes of families. *Hospital and Community Psychiatry,* 1978, *9,* 803–806

Lewington J. Volunteer case aides in the U.S.A. *International Journal of Social Psychiatry,* 1975, *21,* 205–213

Liberman RP, Eckman T, Kuehnel R, Rosenstein J, & Kuehnel J. Dissemination of new behavior therapy programs to community mental health centers. *American Journal of Psychiatry,* 1982, *139,* 224–226

Makas E. Increasing counselor-client communication. *Rehabilitation Literature,* September-October 1980, 235–238

Miller TW. A model for training schizophrenics and families to communicate more effectively. *Hospital and Community Psychiatry,* 1981, *32,* 870–871

Minkoff K. A map of chronic patients. In J Talbott (Ed.), *The chronic mental patient.* Washington, DC: American Psychiatric Association, 1979

Moos RH. *Community oriented programs environment scales manual.* Palo Alto, CA: Consulting Psychologists Press, 1974

Mosher LR, & Keith SJ. Research on the psychosocial treatment of schizophrenia: A summary report. *American Journal of Psychiatry,* 1979, *136,* 623–631

Offer D, & Sabshin M. *Normality: Theoretical and clinical concepts of mental health.* New York: Basic Books, 1974

Ozarin L, Redlich R, & Taube C. A quarter century of psychiatric care: 1950–1974: A statistical review. *Hospital and Community Psychiatry*, 1976, *27*, 515–520

Paul L. Chronic mental patient: Current status—future directions. *Psychological Bulletin*, 1969, *71*, 81–94

Paul GL, & Lentz RJ. *Psychosocial treatment of chronic mental patients: Milieu versus social learning programs.* Cambridge, MA: Harvard University Press, 1977

Peterson R. What are the needs of chronic mental patients? In J Talbott (Ed.) *The chronic mental patient.* Washington, DC: American Psychiatric Association, 1978

Pierce RM, Cohen MR, Anthony WA, Cohen BF, & Friel TW. *The skills of career counseling: The psychiatric rehabilitation practice series* (Book 4). Baltimore, MD: University Park Press, 1980 (a)

Pierce RM, Cohen MR, Anthony WA, Cohen BF, & Friel TW. *The skills of career placement: The psychiatric rehabilitation practice series* (Book 5). Baltimore, MD: University Park Press, 1980 (b)

Pierce RM, & Drasgow J. Teaching facilitative interpersonal functioning to psychiatric in-patients. *Journal of Counseling Psychology*, 1969, *16*, 295–298

Poser EG. The effects of therapists' training on group therapeutic outcome. *Journal of Consulting Psychology*, 1966, *30*, 283–289

Redlich F, & Kellert S. Trends in American mental health. *American Journal of Psychiatry*, 1978, *135*, 22–30

Rogers CR. *Client-centered therapy.* Boston: Houghton Mifflin, 1951

Rosenhan DL. On being sane in insane places. *Science*, 1973, *179*, 250–258

Rayan ER, Bell MD, & Metcalf JC. The development of rehabilitation psychology program for persons with schizophrenia: Changes in treatment environment. *Rehabilitation Psychology*, 1982, *27*, 67–85

Scherl D, & Macht L. Deinstitutionalization in the absence of consensus. *Hospital and Community Psychiatry*, 1979, *30*, 599–604

Schmidt HO, & Fonda CP. The reliability of psychiatric diagnosis: A new look. *Journal of Abnormal and Social Psychology*, 1956, *52*, 262–267

Sheehan S. *Is there no place on earth for me?* Boston: Houghton Mifflin, 1982

Smith C. From hospital to community. *Canadian Journal of Psychiatry*, 1979, *24*, 113–120

Starr SR. Commentary: mental health education: The family's view. *Hospital and Community Psychiatry*, November 1981, *32*, 751

Starr SR. National alliance for the mentally ill: The first two years. *Psychosocial Rehabilitation Journal*, 1982, *5*, 3–4

Stein L, & Test M (Eds.). *Alternatives to mental hospital treatment.* New York: Plenum Press, 1978

Stern R, & Minkhoff K. Paradoxes in programming for chronic patients in a community clinic. *Hospital and Community Psychiatry*, 1979, *30*, 613–617

Stroul BA. *Community support program: Analysis of state strategies.* Boston: Center for Rehabilitation Research and Training in Mental Health at Boston University, September 1982

Sue S, McKinney H, & Allen DB. Predictors of the duration of therapy for clients in the community mental health center system. *Community Mental Health Journal*, 1976, *12*, 365–375

Talbott H. Deinstitutionalization: Avoiding the disasters of the past. *Hospital and Community Psychiatry*, 1979, *30*, 621–624

Thaler OF. Pseudo-research? *Saturday Review of the Sciences*, 1973, *55*,

Turner JC. Community support program update–1980. *Innovations*, 1980, *7*, 5–6

Turner JC, & TenHoor WJ. The NIMH community support program: Pilot approach to a needed social reform. *Schizophrenia Bulletin*, 1978, *4*, 319–348

Turner JE, & Shifren I. Community support system: How comprehensive? *New Directions for Mental Health Services*, 1979, *2*, 1–13

Unger KV, Cohen MR, & Cohen BF. *The skills of psychiatric rehabilitation videotape series user's guide. Boston: Center for Rehabilitation Research and Training in Mental Health at Boston University, 1982*

Vaughn CE, & Leff JP. *The influence of family and social factors on the course of psychiatric illness: A comparison of schizophrenic and depressed neurotic patients. British Journal of Psychiatry*, 1976, *129*, 125–137

Vaugh CE, & Leff JP. Patterns of emotional response in relatives of schizophrenia. *Schizophrenia Bulletin*, 1981, *7*, 43–44

Verinis JS. Therapeutic effectiveness of untrained volunteers with chronic patients. *Journal of Consulting and Clinical Psychology*, 1970, *34*,) 152–155

Vitalo RL. Teaching improved interpersonal functioning as a preferred mode of treatment. *Journal of Clinical Psychology*, 1971, *27*, 166–171

von Bertalanffy L. *General system theory* (Revised Edition). New York: George Braziller, 1968

Waldeck JP, Emerson S, & Edelstein B. COPE: A systematic approach to moving chronic patients into the community. *Hospital and Community Psychiatry*, 1979, *30*, 551–554

Ward CH, Beck AT, Mendelson M, Mock JE, & Erbaugh JK. The psychiatric nomenclature. *Archives of General Psychiatry*, 1962, *7*, 198–205

Webb LJ. Social rehabilitation: A theory program and evaluation. *Rehabilitation Literature*, June 1976, *37*, 172–175

Wechsler H. The ex-patient organization: A survey. *Journal of Social Issues, 1960, 16*, 47–53

Weiner L, Becker A, & Friedman TT. *Home treatment: Spearhead of community psychiatry*. Pittsburgh, PA: University of Pittsburgh Press, 1967

Weinman B, & Kleiner RJ. The impact of community living and community member intervention on the adjustment of the chronic psychotic patient. In L Stein & M Test (Eds.), *Alternatives to mental hospital treatment*. New York: Plenum Press, 1978

Weinman B, Sanders R, Kleiner R, & Wilson S. Community based treatment of chronic psychotic, *Community Mental Health Journal*, 1970, *6*, 12–21

Wolkon GW. Characteristics of clients and continuity of care into the community. *Community Mental Health Journal*, 1970, *6*, 215–221

Wolkon GH, Karmen M, & Tanaka HT. Evaluation of a social rehabilitation program for recently released psychotic patients. *Community Mental Health Journal*, 1971, *7*, 312–322

Wolkon GH, & Tanaka H. Outcome of social rehabilitation services for released psychiatric patients: A descriptive study. *Social Work*, 1966, *11*, 53–61

Wright BA. *Physical disability—a psychological approach*. New York: Harper and Row, 1960

Zax M. History and background of the community mental health movement. In MS Gibbs, JR Lachenmeyer, & J Sigal (Eds.), *Community psychology: Theoretical and empirical approaches*. New York: Gardner Press, 1980

Zinman S. A patient run residence. *Psychosocial Rehabilitation Journal*, 1982, *6*, 3–11

Zubin J. Classification of the behavior disorders. *Annual Review of Psychology*, 1967, *18*, 373–406

Index